The SPIRIT *and the* FORMS *of* LOVE

THE
SPIRIT
AND THE
FORMS OF
LOVE

Daniel Day Williams

UNIVERSITY
PRESS OF
AMERICA

ISBN: 0-8191-1692-0(Perfect)
0-8191-1691-2(Case)
Library of Congress Number: 81-40368

PREFACE

There are so many books on love because love is at the core of human existence. There are many loves, and innumerable angles of vision from which they can be seen. This book interprets love in a theological perspective. It seeks to answer the question, 'What is the meaning and truth of the Christian assertions that God is love, that love to God and the neighbour are the two great commandments, that the fulfilment of human love depends upon God's action of reconciliation, and that the love of God is the ground of all hope?'

We cannot escape the aura of implausibility which surrounds the claims that love is real, that love transforms human life, that it is the key to the foundation of all things. Yet along with the implausibility there is a blunt, solid truth. We live largely by our loves. Even our hates are twisted and frustrated loves. Men fight one another, slaughter in war, and kill in cold blood. Yet often they fight to defend something they love, their land, their families, their view of life. Indeed men fight to protect themselves, their securities, their sense of importance. Rather than find this a reason for cynicism I have come more and more to regard it as one ground of hope. For the power of love is great, and those who love can find more adequate objects. Achievement of a way of life beyond combat requires a transformation of our loves and their embodiment in new ways of life. This is why the analysis of the forms of love is relevant to human action. Far from being self-defining, love needs the discipline of knowledge and rational criticism. And it needs the clarification as well as the empowerment which faith can bring.

What I try to present in this book is a perspective on the meaning of the love of God and the loves of men derived from that mode of Christian thought which has come to be called 'process theology'. A revolution has taken place in our view of the world. The concepts of evolution, development, growth, and becoming have become indispensable terms for conceiving what things are. Process theologians believe that this revolution in our world view must be incorporated in Christian doctrine and that it brings us closer to the biblical view of the creative and redemptive working of God than theology has been since the first century. Among the recent books in process theology there are W. Norman Pittenger's *The Word Incarnate*, Bernard Meland's *The Realities of Faith*, John Cobb, Jr.'s *Toward a Christian Natural Theology* and Schubert Ogden's *The*

Reality of God. There are strong resemblances between these Protestant expressions and the concern of Roman Catholic thought with the evolutionary mysticism of Teilhard de Chardin, the work of Peter Schoonenberg, and Leslie Dewart's *The Future of Belief.* Most of the process themes are found in Nicolas Berdyaev's philosophical and religious writings. A special indebtedness must be expressed to my teacher and sometime colleague, Charles Hartshorne, whose interpretation of Whitehead's philosophy and whose constructive metaphysical reflection has been one of the authentically creative movements of religious and philosophical thought in our century. It is time process theologians turned to the analysis of particular Christian doctrines in the light of the new metaphysical outlook. This book hopefully is one small contribution to that end as it seeks to interpret the doctrine of love on the basis of the conviction that the eternal God is involved in the world's becoming, and that his love takes new forms in history.

In these days of complex academic pressures even a modest book becomes a project depending upon the support and co-operation of many institutions and persons. This book had its origin in lectures at the General Council of the Congregational Christian Churches in Claremont, California, in 1952 and the Nathaniel W. Taylor lectures at the Yale Divinity School in 1953. Some Christological themes were first worked out in the Oren E. Scott lectures in Christian Theological Seminary in Indianapolis. None of these lectures appears here in its original form but I am grateful for the opportunity to work out the ideas which the lectureships provided.

Time to write was made possible by the Faculty Fellowship of the American Association of Theological Schools, and by sabbatical leave and research aid from Union Theological Seminary in New York City where I am privileged to teach.

I remember with gratitude and affection students in Seminars on the doctrine of love over a period of twenty-five years. The completion of the manuscript was made possible by the critical work of Marvin Shaw, and expert and painstaking editorial criticism by Mrs. Margot Biersdorff. My wife, Eulalia, prepared the entire manuscript. More than this, her patience and understanding has been for me a demonstration of love deeper than any words can express.

'Brotherly love' has a broad meaning and a more special sense. I have dedicated the book to my brothers and to one who has become a brother to us.

D.D.W.

May 1967.

CONTENTS

Page

CHAPTER I

LOVE IN OUR HISTORY

That love is a mystery all lovers know, all human lovers and all who know the love of God. To discuss the mystery is not to dispel its wonder, but to try to distinguish reality from illusion and truth from sentimentality. Love in all its forms thrives on critical judgment and is starved by evasion. Since all understanding is partial there will always be more to say, and more books on love. The symposium goes on. Since the discussion is so complex this first chapter will be a prospect of the ground to be covered and an outline of the principal ideas to be encountered.

This book has three main contentions. The first is that to understand love in Western culture we have to know its roots in the tradition of Israel and Christianity. The biblical faith has given shape to our culture. Therefore our essay is theological in intention and perspective. We are inquiring after the meaning of the love of God and the loves of men as these have been seen within the faith of the Christian community. Every view of love in our tradition has been shaped by this tradition. This does not mean that we all agree on what love is. One of the dominant marks of present-day discussion is the revolt against traditional conceptions of all the human loves. There are those who with Sartre believe that man cannot really love in spite of his craving to belong with others in a society. There are also the humanists who believe that man can love but needs no God to fulfil his love. It is notable that the 'Death of God' theologians have clung to the tradition of love of neighbour, holding that the second commandment is the rule of life even though there is no meaning for the first, the love of God. This humanism is often expressed in psychological terms as by Erich Fromm and Herbert Marcuse. Freedom to learn the art of loving is man's high destiny. A completely eroticized civilization is possible. Work and play, life and death, are transformed by human love and the meaning of life is fulfilled.[1]

Here is a critical issue for our culture and for Christian faith: is there a love other than man's and if so, what difference does it

1. Erich Fromm, *The Art of Loving* (London: George Allen & Unwin Ltd., 1957).
Herbert Marcuse, *Eros and Civilization* (Boston: Beacon Press, 1956).

make? In this book therefore we move again over some familiar ground. How does the Bible understand the love of God and the human loves?

Before we go further we must look at one of the perplexities in all discussions of love, the problem of language. English has one word for love. Greek has at least four. In the vocabulary of love we can distinguish between *epithemia*, desire, often with the connotation of impurity or lust; *eros*, which is love of the beautiful, the true, and the good, the aspiration for fulfilment of the soul's yearning; *philia*, brotherly love, which can mean either the comradely and affectionate love of brother and friends, or the ethical love of neighbour; and *agape*, which in Greek can be used for most of the loves, but in the New Testament is the redeeming love of God shown in his action of forgiveness and redemption in Jesus Christ.[2]

Even if we use these terms with the strictest definitions we still find that the mystery of love creates its own difficulties, for the truth is that since the loves are not wholly separate the meanings shade into one another. Is love for the brother absolutely other than love for God? The Bible links them closely together. The ecstatic and loyal union in the love of man and woman suggests the bond of God with his people, and the Old Testament often uses this analogy for the love of God for Israel. Is the *agape* of the New Testament, the love of God for sinners, utterly different from *eros*, man's love of the good and the beautiful as Anders Nygren's great book, *Agape and Eros*, holds? Or is Paul Tillich right that: 'If *eros* and *agape* cannot be united, *agape* toward God is impossible.'[3] Evidently our language problem is more than a question of dictionary definitions. It is the problem of love itself. We need not belittle the difficulties here but we can be thankful that love never allows itself to be precisely catalogued in a linguistic scheme. Language, however, is our means of communication and we should be as clear as we can. I have adopted a simple device which may contribute some clarity in usage. Whenever the context requires especial precision I distinguish between the 'human loves' meaning man's love for man, other creatures, the world, beauty, all the things which call forth our natural capacities for love, and 'the love of God', meaning the gracious love which God gives to man and which takes on the special character of forgiveness and reconciliation. I use the word *agape* for

2. James Moffatt, *Love in the New Testament* (London: Hodder & Stoughton, 1929), is the classic analysis.
3. Paul Tillich, *Systematic Theology I* (Chicago: University of Chicago Press, 1951, p. 281, and London: James Nisbet & Co.).

God's love which the Bible sees taking form in God's election of Israel, and which is finally manifest in the story of Jesus.

This leaves ambiguities to be sure. What shall we say about man's love of God? Surely this is one of the human loves. We accept the intention of St. Thomas's doctrine that man naturally loves God. Man's love of God belongs to the human loves which express essential humanity. When we speak of the human loves we mean those which belong to our humanity, and distinguish these from God's love as *agape*, that is the new love which God puts into the world through his dealing with man's sin and unlove. Man's love of God can be renewed and transformed by *agape*.

We have to use as best we can the tool of an incomplete language. The question of the relation of God's love, the *agape* of the New Testament, to the human loves is the central theme of our inquiry. Before we explore our fundamental question more precisely let us state our second main contention.

The guiding conception which informs our understanding of all love is that love is spirit taking form in history. Love is an expression of spirit. It is spirit seeking the enjoyment of freedom in communion with the other. Spirit is the best word we have to indicate the concrete personal expression of living creative beings. God is spirit. Man, created in God's image, has spiritual existence, not as something added to his bodily substance, but as the expression of that concrete body-mind unity which he is as a person. The freedom of spirit is the freedom of God as the ultimate form-giving and life-giving reality. The freedom of man is also the freedom of spirit, but within the conditions of finite existence.

Here a complication appears, for while God's spirit always remains *one* in the integrity of Holy Love, man's spirit is subject to the distortions, estrangement and perversity of his finite freedom. Thus we use the term spirit for many kinds of human expression. We speak of a mean spirit, a prideful spirit, an artistic spirit, a courageous spirit, a perverse spirit. Man's spirit can express love or the opposite of love.

Love is that expression of spirit which has communion in freedom as its goal. The word goal here covers innumerable forms. The Spirit of God at work in the world creates a multitude of forms for its expression. It creates realms of conflict and of reconciliation. So also the human spirit lives within many forms. The presence of love in the spirit's work may be difficult to locate. There is a classic theological doctrine that every human act has love at work within it, even though it be a misguided or perverse love. This may be so. We may hold the view that man *is* his loves, or we may regard this as too simple. In any case we need to identify within the working of the human spirit that intention which leads toward the fulfilment of freedom in communion. Where that intention is present in any form we will speak of the presence of love.[4] In the divine life, that intention is always present, for God is spirit. Since his being is love itself he is always the Holy Spirit, the spirit of unqualified love.

While therefore the forms of love are in one sense innumerable there are certain archetypal forms which love takes in history which can be distinguished and analysed. They are the forms in which the human loves create communities and which embody man's response to the creative spirit of God.

When we search for the unity of love amidst those forms we discover that love has a history. The spirit is not a static ideal but a creative power which participates in the life it informs. Here is the key to everything we shall be saying in the discussion of love. We understand love when we see that it creates its own history. It changes form and brings new forms into being. This is true of the human loves and of God's love, and all the loves are interwoven in history.

There should be nothing strange in this doctrine that love has a history. Test it in the familiar experiences of life. Consider a workman's love for his tools. This love can only be known in the experience of long usage, the community of skill, the touch of familiarity, the pride of workmanship, the remembered accomplishments, the satisfaction in what the tools do. We learn to love. That is true of us as individuals, and it is true of the human adventure. In the learning we know love in many forms. We crave indeed the vision of love as one. Love drives toward unity, but we cannot grasp its unity by force. We have to explore its depth and mystery in the variety of modes encountered in experience.

We know that forms may hide the spirit and obstruct it. Nicolai Berdyaev felt profoundly the break between the personal reality of love in human life and the demands of finite historical existence. He saw form as the tragedy of spirit.[5] We need not take this as a universal principle, but we can recognize its element of validity. All human loves are marked by the estrangement and perversity which invades human existence. That is why we continually seek the meaning of love within our present experience but also in the intention and hope which lives hidden in the human spirit. If we take an historical view of love's work in the world we know that

4. In human living intentions are not always consciously defined of course.
5. N. Berdyaev, *Freedom and the Spirit* (New York: Charles Scribner's Sons, 1935), pp. 31–3.

work is manifested in the brokenness of existence. This leads us to consider three implications of our thesis that love has a history.

Three requirements follow from the doctrine that love has a history. The first is that we retrace the biblical outlook to see it as a history of the love of God moving amidst the human loves. This gives us a way of interpreting the biblical faith which has been too much neglected. The love of God and the response of man create a new history in which the forms of love's expression cannot be identified with only one pattern or motif. God reveals his love by reconstructing the relationship between himself and man and between man and man. He opens up new forms of community. God in his creativity and freedom reforms the modes of love's expression.

This interpretation owes much to the modern achievement of the historical interpretation of the Bible which is one of the outstanding results of historical scholarship. We are applying the radically historical view of the Bible and its faith to the understanding of love. The forms of love known in the Bible are derived from those events in which men come to knowledge of the meaning of life through what happens in history. The discovery of the love of God is the discovery of his creative power and redemptive action in historical experience.

Thus interpreted the Bible shows God's love as involving his participation in the history of his creatures. Love is known through the divine action and the divine suffering. Mercy, forgiveness, and reconciliation are not simply formal ideas of what love ideally is. They are the rendering in human terms of what the love of God is doing in human life. This analysis of the biblical doctrine of love and of the Christian claim that we know love decisively through the history which has Jesus of Nazareth at its centre, is dependent upon the view that time, freedom, and historical existence are the central realities of our self-understanding.

The Bible speaks of the love of God and of all the human loves and their involvements: sex, comradeship, love of neighbour, love of self, love of mammon, love of enemies. The Bible affirms the goodness of man's created life. Man bears the image of God in his responsible existence. Every human love shapes man's life before God. The Bible never leaves the human loves independent of their origin in God and their service to him. Hence the great ethical question is how the human loves serve God. It is a question of the true ordering of life in the light of the Kingdom of God. Nothing which belongs to man's need and vitality as man is rejected or disparaged. 'Our heavenly Father knoweth that you have need of these things,' Jesus says concerning the goods of this world. Here then the meaning of God's love in relation to human vitalities becomes a central issue for Christian theology. We have to review carefully the biblical faith about human needs for much in the contemporary search for a new Christian style of life and much of the estrangement between Christian faith and secular man lies just here. As we retrace the development of the biblical view of love we are in search of a point of view from which the concrete relationship of God's love and the human loves can be understood.

Our second obligation is to say how we see the history of love in the Christian tradition. There have been many theologies of love and many doctrines. A full history of the doctrine of love is still to be written, although there have been notable contributions to it. Anders Nygren's *Agape and Eros* and Denis De Rougemont's *Love in the Western World* are indispensable to an historical understanding. Along with them should be put C. S. Lewis's *The Allegory of Love in the Middle Ages*. We are much indebted to these works.

A full historical study of love in the Christian tradition would be a life task in itself. I adopt the alternative of offering a typology of the major forms in which love has been viewed in the tradition. My typology differs from Nygren's and De Rougemont's at some decisive points. I see three main types: the first is the Augustinian which is a synthesis of the New Testament faith with the neoplatonic vision of God and the world. This type is the root of all Western philosophical theologies, and of all doctrines of love which seek to bring *agape* and the human loves into an ordered structure in which the being of God is reflected in all the loves while his redemptive love transforms the whole.

The second type is the Franciscan. It is the free, radical expression of love in a sacrificial way of life. It is the nearest love comes to finding expression as pure spirit, breaking through the normal forms of life and society, and enacting the soul's joyful self-giving in the world.

The third type is the evangelical. It is clear that something radical happened in the Protestant reformation to the understanding of the freedom of the Gospel and the Christian style of life. What did happen is a complex story. We can approach it through the new way in which the love of God and the loves of men come to be understood within the affirmation of salvation by grace alone. Luther and Calvin united their radical doctrine of sin and of love as grace with a new freedom for the service of God in the secular order. Hence all the human loves and activities: marriage, production, politics—take on a new sense of vocation as they are held within the restraints of God's law and the ultimate reliance on God's love as forgiveness.

So far we can go in distinguishing the main doctrines in the history. But obviously these are insufficient, for when we come to the modern period and begin to look for examples of these types we make a discovery. All the types remain, but they undergo a transformation. Put briefly, what we trace in the chapter on the types of love is the way that the existentialist view of life has entered each of the classic types to transform it. Augustinians have come to terms with freedom, diversity and secularity in the world. Here the book which has meant the most to the present writer is Father M. C. D'Arcy's *The Mind and Heart of Love*. I interpret D'Arcy as a contemporary Augustinian seeking to incorporate an existentialist doctrine of man. He seeks the relation of the Christian *agape* to the two root loves in man, the love which seeks to grasp and master, and the love which gives itself away. With the spirit of D'Arcy's argument I am in fullest sympathy. The structure of my doctrine is different from his because I do not separate the mastering and the self-giving dimensions of love in quite the way he does. But I should be glad to think that my view is akin to Father D'Arcy's in its spirit and intent, and my indebtedness to him cannot be adequately expressed.

The Franciscan type reappears again and again in the history of the Church and beyond the Church. It thrusts its way into the complexity and tragedy of every culture with a spontaneous goodness and a renewing spirit. In our day it has reappeared in many great lives. The one I select for interpretation is Albert Schweitzer. This is not only because of Schweitzer's ethical stature but also because in his philosophical reflections he shows the perplexity of the Franciscan way as he attempts to meet some of its ultimate dilemmas in facing human necessities.

The evangelical way has given rise to the broad stream of the modern protestant ethic in all its forms—conservative, liberal and radical, idealistic and pragmatic, individualistic and collectivistic. Reinhold Niebuhr's ethical thought with its profound analysis of love in relation to political justice, and its insight into pride and idolatry, shows how the evangelical view of love undergoes the existentialist transformation in the contemporary scene.

Our typology leaves some blurred edges and unanswered questions as every honest typology should, for the 'ideal types' do not exactly fit the reality, and history outruns every classification. Yet the discovery of this inner transformation of the historic types helps to confirm our thesis about the development of the forms of love.

The third obligation which the interpretation of the history of love lays upon us is to interpret what happened to the concept of love in the first centuries when the Christian Gospel met the mind of the hellenistic world. The Church Fathers worked out the synthesis of biblical faith and Greek metaphysics which has been the foundation of most Christian theology to the present day. Whatever view we take of that synthesis there is no question that it made a difference in the way God's love and the human loves were understood.

We are led straight to St. Augustine's doctrine of love, for it was he who worked out a theological way of speaking of God as being itself. He united the absolute of neo-platonic metaphysics with the Creator-Redeemer of the New Testament who seeks and saves lost men with mercy and forgiveness. God infuses his spirit into the human soul to draw it back toward its true home. For Augustine all the human loves reflect the love of God. It is constitutive of all being. Love flows into all things from God who is being itself. Yet the human loves are distorted and frustrated except as they are redeemed by the love exhibited in Christ. This is Augustine's great synthesis of the classical doctrines. What we do with it will be decisive for our view of love.

It is here that Anders Nygren's *Agape and Eros* helps define our problem for Nygren sees the Augustinian doctrine, which he calls the 'caritas synthesis', as a distortion of the *agape* of the Gospel. Nygren is a profound critic of St. Augustine. He shows clearly how the motif of an *eros* love which seeks its own fulfilment enters into Augustine's description of the pilgrimage of the soul toward God. Nygren believes it is only in the Reformers, and especially Luther, that the New Testament theme of love as God's freely outpoured mercy for the unworthy is set free again. For Nygren the *agape* of the Gospel is the spontaneous unmotivated grace of God and it is contrasted with all *eros* love, which seeks its own fulfilment in goodness, truth, and beauty.

Whether Nygren has described fully and accurately the biblical account of love may be questioned. Many critical discussions have been given and I have offered one such criticism.[6] In relation to the Augustinian synthesis we must concentrate on one point. Nygren rightly sees that something happens to the conception of God as freely giving his grace to man when this is joined with the metaphysical doctrine of God as absolute being. But Nygren fails, it seems to me, to give sufficient attention to the central point, which is that not only did St. Augustine work out a rational doctrine of God's being but also he *accepted the Greek presuppositions about God's absolute and timeless being in doing so.* Nygren thinks the difficulty lies in trying to achieve any rational synthesis between

6. Daniel Day Williams, *God's Grace and Man's Hope* (New York: Harper & Row, 1965), pp. 67–73.

agape and the human *eros*, but I hold that the difficulty lies in the particular metaphysical outlook which St. Augustine took over from the neo-platonists. *Agape* and *eros* are not necessarily opposed.

This point is central to our discussion. What would it mean to relate the Christian doctrine of God to a metaphysical outlook in which God's being is conceived in dynamic temporal terms? Suppose God is joined with his world in the adventure of a real history where both God and the creatures have freedom to act and to respond, God supremely, and the creatures within the limitations of their creaturely status?

It is such a reconstruction of a metaphysical theology which is offered here. After a detailed criticism of St. Augustine's doctrine we go on to show what this metaphysical reconstruction means for the understanding of all the loves. The meaning of love is understood in a doctrine of God's being and the nature of the world which can be called 'process metaphysics'.

The background and meaning of 'process metaphysics', whose primary modern source is Alfred North Whitehead, is sketched briefly in Chapter V. It is necessary to say something here about the place of metaphysical analysis in the discussion of love because the very possibility of metaphysical knowledge is a matter of considerable debate at the present time. Why not just describe love in its biblical roots and human expressions? Why this concern with 'being'?

Our answer can be put quite simply—it is *beings* who love. If we do not develop our notion of what it means *to be* we leave the meaning of love more obscure than it needs to be. We must keep clear the nature and limits of our metaphysics, that is, our ideas about what it means to be. I mean by metaphysics the search for a coherent scheme of those general ideas which are necessary for the description of every aspect of experience. Familiar terms appear: time and space, structure and process, form and matter, freedom and law, individuality and community, body and spirit. The precise statement of our scheme of 'categories' and the analysis of how they go together in the make-up of the world is metaphysical inquiry. It is my view that all serious thought has an implicit metaphysical dimension. The question is whether or not we are going to get our categories into the open and criticize them.

Metaphysics then is not a search for being beyond all existence and experience. It is not a speculation about remote causes. It is as Whitehead has said, 'a description of the generalities which apply to all the details of practise'.[7] This statement, I hope, takes away

7. Alfred North Whitehead, *Process and Reality* (New York: Macmillan, 1929), p. 19.

from the term 'metaphysics' some of the fog of esoteric suggestion which often surrounds it. The inquiry is difficult enough, and it does lead us into the ultimate mysteries. But what we are doing is to inquire about what it means to grow, to love, to create, to remember, to become, to hope, to die, and in short, to be.

We shall not attempt here to establish the case for metaphysics against the critical attack which has been directed against it. Our possible contribution to that philosophical discussion would be to show the consequences of metaphysical analysis for the understanding of love. In this way we can demonstrate that metaphysical analysis has its relevance to a crucial area of human experience. There is this further point, one suspects much of the contemporary criticism of metaphysics ought to be directed, not at the inquiry into being, but against aspects of our inheritance from the Greek way of conceiving that inquiry. Much contemporary thought is trying to get rid of 'metaphysics', meaning by that trying to get rid of timeless, static, being. It is especially common in contemporary theology to find metaphysics identified with such a doctrine. But why not get rid of 'timeless metaphysics' by exploring a temporalistic doctrine of being? This is what process philosophy proposes to do. We explore its radical consequences for the doctrine of love. Contemporary thought is in process of making some discoveries here about love which are hopeful and exciting. We discover that love presupposes beings who can both give and receive in relation to one another, and that therefore God must have ways of receiving and responding to what happens in the world. We discover that suffering in its ontological sense of 'being acted upon' is a requirement of all love, and thus a new way is opened to reflection on the suffering of God. We discover that love implies communication so that the language of love is a constituent of love itself, and this opens the way to a reconception of the human loves and of sexuality.

A metaphysical system is an instrument of vision, not a dogmatic statement of final truth. We elaborate our temporalistic doctrine of being knowing that it is an abstraction from the full concreteness of experience. God is 'more than we can think'.[8] We reject the very respectable classic view of God which makes love all but unintelligible. If love has a history, then the categories through which we understand the structure of love have their history. Process philosophy wants to show that our categories must reflect the creative becoming which is exhibited in the world. God as the ground and source of the world's life really participates in that life and history.

Our metaphysical analysis is not a detour around theology. It is

8. The phrase is Henry Nelson Wieman's.

an indispensable element in theological analysis; but metaphysics is not the interpretation of the faith of the Christian community. That is the work of theology which interprets the faith which appears in the history which produced the Hebrew Bible and the Christian New Testament. In the Christian faith love is disclosed as the centre and spirit of that history. To say what love is in the Christian way means to say what we believe about God and man as known in Jesus Christ. Love is not an idea which we add to our beliefs about God and his self-revelation. Love is what God's spirit is in his action in history, as he deals with human loves and lovelessness, and opens the way to a new community of life whose spirit is informed by love.

If we fulfil our three obligations, to interpret the biblical witness, to analyse the historical development of Christian doctrine, and to show the relation of the new metaphysics to the classical synthesis, we are ready for the theological task of trying to see the meaning of the way of God with man as the disclosure of what love is and what it does in history. This discussion leads us to the themes of God and man, the Incarnation, and the Atonement. We restate theological doctrine from the standpoint of our interpretation of the meaning of love.

Our theological perspective stands in a close relation to the movement of modern theology which was initiated by Karl Barth and Emil Brunner, and which has had a broad influence upon all contemporary theological thought. What Karl Barth has shown is that Christian thought moves from within the action of God in Christ outward toward the understanding of life. In Christian thought we do not first get an idea of love which is then illustrated by the history of Jesus. We come to the Christian understanding of love through the history of Jesus. This insistence of Barth's on the centrality of Christology, an insistence which continues the insight of Schleiermacher, is of especial importance in relation to our thesis that love has a history. Christian faith sees in the story of Jesus the spirit of God reshaping human existence and opening the way to new forms of understanding of what that existence is. We understand Christianity in the light of our conception of love; but we derive that new conception from the history which has Jesus Christ as its centre. I accept this situation fully, and what is offered here is a theological reflection on the meaning of the Incarnation and the Atonement. What I shall argue against Karl Barth is that we should not eliminate metaphysics from theology, but that traditional doctrines of the Incarnation and Atonement have failed precisely because they have never fully incorporated the historical, temporal-istic aspect of the Christian revelation. The new metaphysics of social relationship can help to set free the theological insight which the Bible sustains. If this seems a large claim, it is offered in no spirit of Hegelian imperiousness, but as a proposal for critical discussion. Where the meaning of love, and therefore of human life is at stake, we need a radical attack on the fundamental problems.

This point of view is relevant to the recent 'Death of God' theologies.[9] It is possible that the new humanism and the declaration of the absence of God reflects a deep dissatisfaction with the traditional conceptions of God. None of the prominent 'Death of God' theologians seems to have considered a temporalistic doctrine of God as a possible alternative to traditional doctrine. The theological position of process thought does offer such an alternative. It preserves the freedom, creativity, and concern with the secular realms which the 'Death of God' theologians rightly hold. It is noteworthy that the 'Death of God' theologians want to hold to the Christian community with Jesus as its centre as the context of ultimate loyalty. They see more clearly than the liberal humanists that human devotion is shaped in communities of faith and life. Our doctrine of love asserts that all the freedom, creativity and risk which the new humanism asks for really obtains in God's life with man. When the history of Jesus is set free from the traditional kind of metaphysics, theology can recognize man's life with God and his neighbour in the authentic forms of freedom.

Theological interpretations have their ultimate validation in their power to illustrate human experience. A doctrine of love cannot be proved as a theorem, it must show that it can give intelligibility to the human loves. Therefore the final part of our book is concerned with the relation of Christian faith to four areas of human living: the nature of self-sacrifice; sexuality and love; social justice; and the intellectual life. Here are four realms of ethical decision, creative experience, and moral perplexity. The Christian Gospel declares that the love of God judges, fulfils and redeems these human realms from their futilities, confusion and despair. We require a point of view from which we can see how divine love and the human loves move against, toward and through one another. This is the most difficult part of our task, and it brings us into the concrete struggles of life today.

Among the many issues we follow one clue to the relation of the

9. I have given a brief account of this theological development in the 3rd edition of *What Present Day Theologians are Thinking* (New York: Harper & Row, 1967). An admirably balanced and critical estimate of the 'Death of God' theme is W. Richard Comstock's, 'Theology After the Death of God,' *Cross Currents*, Summer, 1966.

divine and the human loves. This is that all the loves work within the history of the self's becoming. No love, whether it be the ethical love of neighbour, or the love in the sexual life, or the love of God for man, is a 'thing', a static pattern or form. It is a spirit at work in life and taking form in the process of becoming. Therefore we have to understand love as history, and we are concerned with its origins, development and fruition.

In this point of view some new perspectives emerge. There is the question of the multiplicity of human loves and whether they are in any sense one. From one point of view the human loves are many and diverse; but from the dynamic point of view they may grow together and inform one another. When we look at them in process we ask how they inform, obstruct, and fulfil each other. There is the theological question of the relation of the *agape* of the Gospel to the human love of neighbour and all the forms of human *eros*. Looked at from one point of view these are utterly different loves. The human loves may be present without any reference whatever to the love of God. This is what humanists keep saying. Theologians agree that divine love breaks in upon the human loves with a radically new judgment and demand.

But when we look at *agape* and *eros* in the self's becoming we see that the important question is how and where the human loves discover that they cannot fulfil themselves, and how they are transformed by *agape* so that they remain human and yet are fulfilled from beyond themselves.

It is at this point, I believe, that the traditional Christian doctrine of love is in the deepest trouble with sensitive and critical minds in modern culture. The humanists suspect, and rightly, that the Christian view of love has become repressive, negates the full valuation of sexuality, sentimentalizes charity and neglects justice. I accept these criticisms; but I do not believe the way out is through the kind of humanism proposed by such thinkers as Erich Fromm, or the completely eroticized civilization envisioned by Herbert Marcuse, or through man's assertion of his autonomy without God as in the 'Death of God' theologies. The answer lies in an examination of where the traditional Christian doctrine has failed to grasp the real life of the human loves in their creativity and their power, and in their tendency to reach their own limits. We shall try to discover the point at which *agape* becomes the one viable answer to the blocking of the human *eros*.

Our doctrine of love then looks toward a Christian humanism which accepts the worth and creative power of all the human loves in both sacred and secular contexts. The self-destructive restlessness in modern culture will not be cured by the Nietzschean Superman. It will be healed when man discovers that his loves in sex, family, nation, work and art participate in the working of a reality which lends final significance to his broken efforts and which in forgiveness and mercy can restore his shattered spirit.

Arguments about love are often unseemly, yet love needs the purging and redirection which critical analysis can give. The present essay is aimed at getting our bearings about love in a world where the voices are strident and the noise of conflict shattering. The problems of war and survival are so pressing that it requires an act of inner redirection to give attention to the life of the spirit. But such an inner re-orientation is necessary if we are to speak about the truths which ultimately matter. Every writer is grateful for the qualities of patience and charity on the part of the reader. We finally depend upon the miracle of personal communication. Only love can do the work of reflection about love.

It is difficult to speak about this deeper level of communication, and often it is better to remain silent about it. It may help the reader, however, to sense the general direction of what is here written if I indicate one aspect of what has happened in my reflections about love through several years. I have come to believe that there is a kind of double vision necessary in the effort to see love clearly. On one hand we see it as the consummation of life. The goal of love is communion. The experiences of love are experiences of joyful ecstasy, delightful companionship and reconciliation. The power of love is the security which it gives in our relations to one another, a security which in the New Testament is marvellously affirmed by Paul's word, 'nothing can separate us from the love of God'. Without this consummatory experience we would not be able to speak about love at all. It is the reality to which we cling in a broken, confused and threatening existence. It is the root of life, and its binding power.

But if we look only at love's consummation we do not see it whole. Love has another mode, of faithful, courageous waiting for a consummation not yet realized. Love lives not only from the ecstasy of fulfilment, but from a loyalty not yet fulfilled. Love realizes itself, not only in the enjoyment of completion but in the suffering of the Not-yet.

Our culture is grasping for immediate possession. We need to learn that God waits and bears with his world. In no previous culture have the forms of love been so unresolved, so difficult to exhibit with clarity and precision. Therefore that form of love which is sustained loyalty to a humanity yet-to-be is most important for us. It is the love which Josiah Royce described in his philosophy of loyalty, a love which remains faithful to the on-going community of interpretation in spite of its brokenness. It is the love which sustains those who bear the heavy burdens of political decisions with all their ambiguity. It is the love which refuses to give up faith in reconciliation in spite of the abysses of prejudice and hatred which divide men. It is the mode of love which does not look for salvation through overriding power, but which allows itself to be 'edged out of the world' on a cross, as Dietrich Bonhoeffer saw.

Our search for the forms of love begins now with a look at the Bible with its witness that God has disclosed who he is and what love is through what he has done in history.

CHAPTER II

LOVE IN THE BIBLICAL TRADITION:
THE HEBREW FAITH

The biblical faith has given rise to more than one understanding of God's love and its relationship to our human loves. The meaning of love in the scripture is nothing other than the meaning of the history of God's dealing with man. It is the mystery of the divine being. In the Bible the relation of God's love to human loves is made explicit only in part and is never given a systematic statement. All interpretations of the biblical faith, therefore, are attempts to grasp the meaning of a love which is inexhaustible. It is not the case then that we have one normative concept in the scripture for which everything in later Christian thought represents either a variation or a misunderstanding. We shall see that there have been at least three major interpretations of the love of God in the history of Christian thought. Each has its integrity, its specific human expressions, and its grounding in the scriptural witness to God's actions which disclose his love. In a later chapter we shall be describing these three types. But our first task is to look at the biblical sources and at the result of the meeting of Christianity with Greek religion and philosophy in order to understand the formative conceptions of love we have inherited.

The encounter of Christian faith with classical culture is the crux of the development of the main structure of Christian theology. The attitude we take toward that encounter will depend both upon our view of the biblical faith and our understanding of the Greek metaphysical outlook.

In the New Testament the Christian message found expression in language and thought forms taken in part from the hellenistic world. The Fourth Gospel uses the *Logos* concept to speak of God and of Christ. Whatever the writer intended by it, that word would be heard by a Greek as involving the philosopher's conception of the intelligible structure of the world. The apostle Paul used religious symbols familiar in the world of Greek religion. This continued in the theology of the Church Fathers as they sought to appropriate for Christian faith the ways of speaking about God they found in Greek philosophy. Thus the main structure of Christian theology as it became formulated in the creeds of the Church reflects this process in which the biblical faith in God became fused with the neo-platonic doctrine of God as absolute being. We are today still trying to assess what really happened in the first centuries of Christian thought. It is a complex history, but broadly speaking two main attitudes are taken toward it.[1]

One position is that the main lines of Christian doctrine were laid down in the ecumenical creeds and the patristic theologies. They are the established foundation of all Christian thought. The other view, increasingly emphasized, as theology has become critical of the tradition, is that the fusing of Christian faith with Greek metaphysics was, if not a disaster, a wrong turn from which theology has yet to recover. There must be either a purging of Christian theology of all metaphysics, or we need a new metaphysical vision which embodies the conception of God as living, creative and responsive to his world.

The view we take will have important consequences for the understanding of love. For the classical tradition St. Augustine is the supreme doctor of love. It was he who worked out the synthesis of the platonic doctrine of being with the redemptive action of God in Christ. He brought ethics, metaphysics, and theology into a dynamic unity, and showed how the Christian understanding of God both completes and transcends the Greek doctrines. Christian faith satisfies the Greek craving for intelligibility and the mystical craving for communion with the divine. The critics of St. Augustine hold that the distinctive love of the Gospel is obscured in his theology. Bishop Nygren has stated the case in his *Agape and Eros*. According to Nygren, Augustine knows the distinctive theme of *agape* as disclosed in Christ, but corrupts it by synthesizing it with the Greek *Eros*. It was necessary for the reformers, especially Luther, to recover the biblical understanding. They had to find an alternative to meta-

1. The literature here is extensive. Supporting the view taken in the text is C. H. Dodd, *The Interpretation of the Fourth Gospel* (Cambridge University Press, 1953).

Rudolph Bultmann, *Theology of the New Testament*, English translation by Kendrick Grobel (London: S.C.M. Press, 1952, 1955; New York: Charles Scribner's Sons, 1957).

Robert H. Grant, *Gnosticism and Early Christianity* (New York: Columbia University Press, 1959).

On the development of dogma in the early period in relation to philosophical issues see Paul Tillich, *Systematic Theology*, Vol. II (Chicago: University of Chicago Press, 1957, pp. 140–5; London: James Nisbet & Co., 1957). Daniel D. Williams, 'Deity, Monarchy and Metaphysics, Whitehead's Critique of the Theological Tradition,' in Ivor Leclerc, ed., *The Relevance of Whitehead* (New York: Macmillan, 1961; London: Allen & Unwin, 1961).

physical structure to relate the *agape* of God to the human loves and their requirements.[2]

I shall try to show that the wise move for theology today is not to try to prove one of these views right and the other wrong, but to ask whether we can get a clearer perspective on the historical development of the doctrine of love. We can be helped in such a task if we adopt the presupposition that the understanding of the meaning of love in the Christian faith has a history. Love is spirit and the spirit shapes the forms in which it is conceived. It can plough up old forms and create new ones. We shall look at the biblical tradition and what happened to it in the first centuries as a disclosure of new facets of the meaning of love in concrete historical development. We may then be in a position to reconceive the meaning of love in the light of this development.

The view taken in this book is that the biblical witness to the meaning of the love of God must be reassessed in our time as it has been in other times. Christian theology has too often tried to grasp the meaning of love through one set of concepts, taken to be the only valid ones, whereas it may be that the truth lies in the history of developing concepts. The spirit takes form in history, and because love is spirit its capacity to take a variety of forms should be the first consideration in our attempt to understand it. We certainly know that human loves have a development, and have taken many forms in their self-expression. I propose that this is true of the divine love. We cannot grasp God's love under a single form. History exhibits the creativity of God's freedom and of man's freedom. If it is the very nature of love to seek expression in relation to the need of the other, then the unity of love must be found in the spirit's intention, not in any one form of its expression. Because this aspect of our knowledge of God has not been given its due place, the significance of love in relation to creativity, to suffering, to forgiveness, and to fulfilment in communion has been obscured.

To justify such an understanding we must first re-examine the main themes of love in the Bible.

(1)

GOD AND ISRAEL: THE COVENANT AND ITS HISTORY

The Hebrew people knew the love of God as the constitutive character of his relation to his people, his faithfulness to them in

2. Anders Nygren, *Agape and Eros*, revised English translation by Philip S. Watson (London: S.P.C.K., 1953).

the midst of their wandering and suffering. While the Hebrew scripture uses various words for love, as we do in English, for attraction or desire or caring for any object or person, the central meaning of God's love is that he has chosen to make this one people his own, and this choice is an act of his love. Once the covenant is established, God's care for and faithfulness to his erring people is his *chesed*, his lovingkindness (A.V.), his steadfast love (R.S.V.), or his mercy, as the Septuagint translates *chesed* into the Greek *eleos*.[3]

The terms 'election-love' and 'covenant-love' are used by Norman Snaith to distinguish the two aspects of God's relationship to Israel. Snaith finds the first expressed in the verb *'ahebh*, and the second in *chesed*. It is *'ahebh* which is used for many kinds of love, love for things, and for other persons, and it can be used for man's love of God as well as God's love of man. *Chesed* in contrast always implies a covenant. It can be used for the faithfulness which is required between man and man as in the making of the blood-brotherhood between David and Jonathan (I Samuel 20: 14–16). They pledge to each other the *chesed* of Jehovah, and David is not to withhold his *chesed* from Jonathan's house for ever.[4]

Before analysing the special aspects of the meaning of God's love with the help of this distinction, we see already that we have the fundamental example of the way in which for the Hebrews the love of God is disclosed through his actions. What love does, its concrete mode of expression, is always related to the actual history of God's relationships to men. Love as election is the act of choosing, of singling out and establishing a new relationship. Love shows its obligation and its character by the way the lover acts toward the other in the covenant. Thus, caring for the other becomes patience with his infirmities, and protection of the other may become resistance to his wrongdoing. These themes are expressed in three aspects of the Hebraic conception of the love of God.

First, the relationship between God and his people is described in concrete personal terms and is expressed in the language of love between father and son, and between husband and bride. Just here appears one of the most remarkable aspects of the entire treatment of love in the Bible. It is this: the metaphors and expressions of human love between father and son and between husband and bride

3. G. Quell and E. Stauffer, *Love*, English translation from the G. Kittel, *Theologisches Wörterbuch zum Neuen Testament* (London: Adam and Charles Black, 1949). Cf. critical comments on the influence of theological perspectives in the Wörterbuch in James Barr, *The Semantics of Biblical Language* (Oxford University Press, 1961).

4. Norman H. Snaith, *The Distinctive Ideas of the Old Testament* (London: Epworth Press, 1944), p. 103.

are fundamental in the speech about the love of God, and yet never are the erotic aspects and the emotional satisfactions of human love asserted to be the key to the relationship of man and God. The Bible does not reject the language of human emotion or even of passion for the divine love, yet it never makes the ecstatic or emotional fulfilment of familial or sexual experience the key to the experience of God. It is as if from the beginnings of the Hebraic faith human passion was always taken up into a fully personalized relationship where feeling, emotional desire and fulfilment were not rejected, but where their meaning was found in a personal order which absorbed them into a larger pattern of devotion and loyalty.

The love between God and his people is given and received on both sides. It is commanded to be returned, as in the commandment, 'thou shalt love the Lord thy God', and it has been returned in Israel's history. This is the view of the prophets.

Jeremiah, like other prophets, regarded the time in the wilderness as a time of purity and loyalty in the life of Israel:

> Thus says the Lord:
>
> I remember the devotion of your youth
>   Your love as a bride,
> How you followed me in the wilderness,
>   In a land not sown. (Jeremiah 2:2)

Here the image and metaphor of husband and bride is applied to the relationship of God and the people, not individuals. But Jeremiah also speaks of God's call to him and his 'wooing' him to become a prophet in the concrete images of personal love. God has over-powered him:

> O Lord, Thou hast seduced me,
> And I am seduced;
> Thou hast raped me
> And I am overcome. (Jeremiah 20:7)

Dr. Abraham Heschel helps us to enter into the concreteness of this language.[5] He says, 'Jeremiah also knew the bliss of being engaged to God, "the joy and delight" of being, as it were, a bride'.

> Thy words were found and I ate them,
> Thy words became to me a joy,
> The delight of my heart,
> For I am called by thy name,
> O Lord, God of hosts. (Jeremiah 15:16)

---

5. Abraham Heschel, *The Prophets* (New York: Jewish Publication Society of America, 1962), pp. 113–14.

The question comes as to what love can do with failures and unfaithfulness. Isaiah puts his description of what has happened in the history of Israel in the form of a love song to Yahweh's beloved:

> Let me sing for my beloved
>   a love song concerning his vineyard:
> My beloved had a vineyard
>   on a very fertile hill.
> He digged it and cleared it of stones,
>   and planted it with choice vines:
> He built a watchtower in the midst of it,
>   and hewed out a wine vat in it
> And he looked for it to yield grapes,
>   but it yielded wild grapes. (Isaiah 5:1–2)

This prophetic wrestling with the problem of Israel's sin is concerned with the question, what can God in his love do with an unloving and wandering people? The language of human faithfulness and unfaithfulness is constantly used to describe the personal history in which God and his people are involved. Hosea uses the metaphor of harlotry to describe Israel's defection from Yahweh's love.

> In the house of Israel I have seen a horrible thing.
> Ephraim's harlotry is there, Israel is defiled. (Hosea 6:10)

It is love, *chesed*, faithfulness and not sacrifice which Yahweh requires, but Israel's love is like the morning cloud, like the dew that goes early away (Hosea 6: 4). The classic eleventh chapter of Hosea penetrates to the ultimate problem of love as it is known in the Hebraic faith. It describes God's tender love for his people as he took them up in his arms and led them with the bands of love, easing their yoke. But the yoke will be restored because they have turned away, and Assyria will be their king. Now the crucial passage occurs in which God agonizes within himself. 'How can I give you up, O Ephraim, and how can I hand you over, O Judah. . . . My heart recoils within me, my compassion grows warm and tender. I will not execute my fierce anger, I will not again destroy Ephraim' (Hosea 11: 8).

No more concrete description of an inner conflict between love for another and the righteous indignation which judges the other could be given than this. Does it mean that God has two sides to his being? Some theology, notably Luther's, has come close to asserting that there is a conflict within God and love must contend with and overcome wrath. This question of the relation of love to judgment and punishment is one of the profoundest in all the discussion of love, and it will occupy us many times. Here we need to consider how the matter stands in the Hebraic faith.

It is not uncommon to find those who stand outside the Hebrew faith characterizing the God of the Old Testament as one whose nature is essentially that of the righteous law-giver who demands conformity to his law. The possibility of mercy is therefore a problem for God. Judgment is fundamental, mercy only a new and disturbing possibility. But this surely is a wrongheaded view of the Hebrew faith. God's love and mercy, his care and compassion, are the very foundation of his covenant with Israel. His wrath is the reaction of the righteous God to the unfaithfulness of his people. Much has been made of the 'unmotivated' character of God's love in the election of Israel. Whether that is the correct word is debatable; but what is clear is that his wrath and punishment are never unmotivated. They are occasioned by the people's violation of their obligations to God. The language does become vindictive and exaggerated, it is true; but it is the exaggeration of a righteous indignation. What calls forth God's wrath is the violation of the covenant of love which he has established. That is the fundamental connection between love and judgment.

It should also be remembered that God's judgment falls upon those outside the covenant, as in the prophecies of Amos, where many nations are punished for violations of the moral requirements of human decencies. For example, the charge against Edom is precisely that he 'pursued his brother with the sword, and cast off all pity, and his anger tore perpetually and he kept his wrath forever' (Amos 1: 11). Here in the words of the prophet who is usually associated with the message of divine wrath, the charge against the nations is that they have not honoured the basic requirements of ethical brotherhood and community. This is a clear case where the Hebraic faith strains against the bonds of a narrow interpretation of election.

Love and wrath then are woven together in the divine character as constituents of God's righteousness, that is the order which God wills and which he works out in history. That righteous order includes the divine care for the weak. The place to look for the meaning of love is in the history of a people who have been called into an intimate, personal relationship with God, and who have begun to learn the meaning of responsibility and the consequences of irresponsibility in that relationship.

So far, then, the love of God is known as his concern, his devoted care, his willingness to share in the life of a particular people to set them free and to deal with them graciously in their desires and passions, health and sickness, worship and pleasure, warfare and peace, life and death.[6]

(2)

HUMAN LOVES IN THE OLD TESTAMENT

We have seen how the language of human loves in friendship, in marriage, and in the forms of human passion has entered into the Hebraic speech about God. The relation of God's love to the human loves requires interpretation. It is not obvious, for God is God and not man. There is, for example, no simple and clear relationship between Yahweh's claim to complete worship from Israel and the Hebrew view of marriage. There is no strict monogamy in Israel until very late in the pre-Christian period, as David R. Mace has shown in his *Hebrew Marriage*.[7] This makes it all the more remarkable that the faithfulness of husband and bride becomes such a compelling image for the covenant between God and his people. It is as if the theological sense of the meaning of married love ran ahead of the social practice.

The great poem of sexual love, *the Song of Songs*, is a celebration of love in profoundly emotional and ecstatic terms, but it is not a religious poem, and makes no claim to throw light upon the relation of man's love and God's love. It is now clearly agreed that any esoteric theological significance read into the poem by allegorizing theologians and mystics has no basis in the book itself. Its inclusion in the canon, whatever the original motive, shows that sexual love is accepted as natural and good. There is no asceticism in the Hebrew mind with respect to natural human loves. What God requires is love to him, that is faithfulness within the covenant, and obedience to the moral requirements which God has established as the laws of the covenant.

These moral requirements include love to the neighbour. This love is commanded as obedience to the will of God, and is supported by the memory of God's love for Israel. The decisive statements come, curiously, in the book of Leviticus with its conglomeration of primitive and sophisticated morality, its elements of vengeance and its crudities. But it rises to this height:

6. Nygren's attempt to restrict the faith of Israel to the *nomos* motif seems to me to do less than justice to the place of love in Judaism. On the relation of love and righteousness see Snaith, *op. cit.* and Paul Ramsey, *Basic Christian Ethics* (New York: Charles Scribner's Sons, 1950; London: S.C.M. Press, 1953).

7. David R. Mace, *Hebrew Marriage* (London: Epworth Press, 1953).

> You shall not hate your brother in your heart,
> but you shall reason with your neighbour,
> lest you bear sin because of him.
> You shall not take vengeance or bear any grudge
> against the sins of your own people,
> but you shall love your neighbour as yourself;
> I am the Lord. (Leviticus 19:17–18)

This love is not restricted to one's people. 'The stranger who sojourns with you shall be to you as the native among you, and you shall love him as yourself; for you were strangers in the land of Egypt' (Leviticus 19: 34).

We have not reached here the prophetic conception of a universal requirement of love to men, and the question, 'Who is my neighbour?' will still be asked at a crucial juncture in the history of the ethics of love. But throughout the development of the Hebrew faith love as a concerned generous spirit toward the other was understood as a fundamental element in God's requirement of faithfulness to the covenant.

The prophetic and priestly interpreters avoid the systematizing of a doctrine of love. It is as if they assume the meaning of love for the neighbour and the source of this assumption is God's care and faithfulness to his people. To love is to seek the other's good, to give another the consideration and understanding one gives to one's self. It is avoidance of hate and destructive anger. It is personal expression of concern. Every human love belongs to the wholeness of life which God wills, and man's achievement or failure is judged in the light of the divine righteousness. But the various forms and expressions of human love are appropriate within specific conditions of life, its needs, its passions, and its values and limitations. Thus the Hebraic religion never commands particular forms of emotional experience either in worship or in sexual love. Neither does it become ascetic. We can see beginning here what might be called the 'secularizing' of life, not in the sense of separating the spheres of human action from the divine command, but of asserting the unity of all life within the order which God intends for it with no separation of 'sacred' from 'secular' experience. Perhaps here the secret of Israel's ethic lies, in the capacity to accept the natural requirements of human existence in man's creaturely state, and thus to keep every part of life ordered within man's single responsibility to the Lord and giver of life. Certainly this is the direction in which the prophetic ethic moves. Martin Buber puts the point powerfully:

> The world is not something which must be overcome. It is created reality, but reality created to be hallowed. Everything created has

a need to be hallowed and is capable of receiving it: all created corporeality, all created urges and elemental forces of the body. Hallowing enables the body to fulfil the meaning for which it was created.[8]

In consequence, human love is understood in its goodness within the intent of creation, but no human expression of love is to be deified. It is the Hebraic insight which embodies the truth later found in Plutarch's aphorism, 'The passions are not gods and the gods are not passions'.

(3)

LOVE AND THE SUFFERING OF GOD

We have now to observe that the Hebrew scripture leaves us with two major perplexities about the love of God. The first stems from the meaning of election and what this implies for the conception of God as the loving father of all. The second has to do with redemption. It is the question of how the loving God can and will deal with the sins of his people, and the meaning of God's suffering in redemption. We need to formulate these questions as sharply as possible, for they underlie the situation in which the New Testament faith speaks of the decisive disclosure of God's love in Jesus Christ.

The knowledge of the love of God which Israel professes is bound up with election. 'You only have I known of all the nations of the earth.' (Amos 3: 2a.) The verb 'know' here is the intimate verb which is used for sexual love. Israel knows the love of God only through the covenant. This is the clear implication of most of the Old Testament. Where, then, does it leave us with God's relation to everyman? Does God love some and not others? This question produces an ultimate tension in the Hebraic faith. Norman Snaith says:

> Either we must accept this idea of choice on the part of God with its necessary accompaniment of exclusiveness, or we have to hold to a doctrine of the love of God other than that which is biblical.[9]

While this is true to the Old Testament way of thinking with its roots in the experience of Israel as the people of God, it also raises the deepest issue in the faith of that people, and the failure to see

8. Martin Buber, 'The Power of the Spirit' in *Israel and the World* (New York: Schocken Books, 1948), p. 180.
9. Snaith, *op. cit.*, p. 139.

this can leave our view of the biblical witness in intolerable confusion. The problem is whether the God of Israel is the same loving, caring God in his dealing with all of his creation and with all nations? Snaith does not even raise that question, which is curious in one seeking to expound the logic of Israel's faith. For if God is faithful is he less faithful to other people than to this one?

H. Richard Niebuhr says, 'It does seem clear from any study of the Hebrew Scriptures that the history of Israel is marked by an almost continuous struggle between social henotheism and radical monotheism.'[10] Now radical monotheism is impossible unless the God to whom the people is covenanted is the one God who deserves and requires the loyalty of *all* creatures. Richard Niebuhr believes this principle was coming to recognition in the word which God speaks in Exodus, 'I am the I am,' and he agrees with Gilson and all catholic theology which has understood this text to say that, 'God is nothing less than being, and being is God, namely valuer and savior'.[11] Niebuhr quite rightly does not want to speak of this biblical statement as metaphysical, but it is clearly out of this conviction that the One God is the lord of all being that a doctrine of God's being in any way congruent with the biblical faith must come.

The implicit logic of the trust in God which Israel knows leads to God's universal concern expressed in the doctrine of creation. Here we must criticize the tendency in contemporary theology to discount the significance of the doctrine of creation for Israel. Karl Barth treats the theme of God's self-revelation in the creation as a 'side-line' in the Old Testament.[12] In Barth's view the fundamental theme is the covenant with Israel, and this is later read back into a doctrine of creation.[13]

Gerhard von Rad supports Barth's view in his commentary on the creation narrative in Genesis:

> The position of the creation story at the beginning of our Bible has often led to misunderstanding, as though the 'doctrine' of creation were a central subject of Old Testament faith. That is not the case. Neither here, nor in Deutero-Isaiah is the witness to creation given for its own sake. Faith in creation is neither the position nor the goal of the declarations in Genesis, chs. 1 and 2. Rather, the position of both the Yahwist

---

10. H. Richard Niebuhr, *Radical Monotheism and Western Culture* (New York: Harper & Row, 1960, p. 57; London: Faber & Faber, 1961).

11. *Ibid.*, pp. 42–3.

12. Karl Barth, *Nein: Antwort and Emil Brunner* (München, 1934).

13. Karl Barth, *Church Dogmatics*, Vol. III, Pt. 1, Sec. 41 (Edinburgh: T. & T. Clark).

and the Priestly document is basically faith in salvation and election They undergird this faith by the testimony that this Yahweh who made a covenant with Abraham and at Sinai, is also the creator of the world.[14]

But von Rad does not ask how this assertion that God is creator *does* undergrid the faith in salvation, indeed is absolutely essential to it. If Yahweh is not in control of the heavens and the earth, he cannot be the saving God. If there really are other gods, the claim for absolute trust in Yahweh breaks down. The doctrine of creation is essential to the relationship which Israel has with him. That surely is the implicit logic of the Old Testament. We should not forget that the men of the Old Testament were human beings with the same interest and concern about origins that men have shown in every culture. The final form of the creation narrative is late, but it shows quite clearly its rootage in mythological and primitive histories which gave form to the primordial intuitions of men reflecting upon their origin. The attempt of Barth and von Rad to relegate these elements to a position of unimportance is strained and unconvincing. It reflects the bias of contemporary theologies which have felt it necessary to try to show that Israel's faith had nothing in common with any other ancient outlook.

Israel's mature faith is clear about who Yahweh is: he is the creator of the world and every man. The story of Israel is set within the story of mankind, and both the care of God and the sin of man are known not only in Israel, but also as the ground theme of the whole human venture. The problem posed for the meaning of the love of God is, 'If the love of God is known in the election of Israel, what does it mean for God's dealing with the whole of mankind?' Has God created the world in love? Perhaps there is nothing in the Hebrew scripture which explicitly identifies God's act of creation as an act of love. Yet the creation of man in the divine image has the implicit undertone of God's recognition of the creation as good and of man as his handiwork. Universalistic passages which suggest that God's care for all nations is of the same character as that for Israel do occur as in Amos 9: 7, Ruth, Isaiah 19: 19–25, 42: 1–6, and 49: 6. This theme is also beautifully reflected in a Talmudic story. When the Egyptians are drowning at the Red Sea the angels want to sing, and God rebukes them: 'My handiwork is dying, and you wish to sing?'[15]

14. Gerhard von Rad, *Genesis: A Commentary* (Philadelphia: Westminster Press, 1961), pp. 43–44.

15. Lewis I. Newman, ed., *Talmudic Anthology* (New York: Behrman House, 1945), p. 144.

Of course there is one answer to the question of the relation of God's love for Israel to the other nations which appears formally satisfying. Through his elect people God will bless all. Whether this hope was put in form of imperialistic domination of the nations by Israel (Isaiah 60–1) or in more universalistic terms, it did serve to hold together the doctrine of election with the integrity of the divine character. In Abraham all generations of the earth should be blessed. But when we ask how this universal blessing is to come through Israel, we raise again the question of the place of love in redemption. In what sense does the hope for salvation rest upon the love of God? This question involves the complex and fascinating development of Israel's hope from the days of the exile and restoration to the time of Jesus with the rise of apocalyptic eschatologies and the messianic expectation. That God will right the world and fulfil his purpose in history is the constant theme. 'How?' and 'When?' are the perennial questions.

We find two contrasting tendencies in the development of Israel's salvation faith. They are interwoven themes and they cannot be neatly disentangled. By analysing them we may define the issues concerning love which concern us as we approach the New Testament doctrine.

One tendency is to interpret the redemptive action of God primarily in terms of the divine power. It is not a question of love, or of dealing with the wrongdoer as one who must be won back. It is the sheer assertion of the divine majesty in an act which restores the whole earth to its rightful obedience to the divine order. The prophetic faith looks forward to such an act of God, and it is not always asserted as a consequence of the divine love, or a necessary implication of what God has done in the past, but as the sheer fiat of the divine sovereignty in which the righteous God will do what he will do.

This expectation of the fulfilment of God's righteous purpose is the source of Israel's messianic hope. The messianic expectation has a complex history. The word messiah, God's 'anointed one', is used in the Old Testament for kings who rule through God's will and favour. There probably is no use of the word 'messiah' in the Old Testament to refer to a future messenger of God who will fulfil God's redemptive purpose. It is only gradually that the eschatological perspective becomes the significant content of the messianic prophecies. With the development of the apocalyptic pictures of the world's end in the period between the testaments, as in the book of Enoch and the Psalms of Solomon, the messianic hope is identified with the coming of the supernatural 'Son of Man' in a cosmic cataclysm which will bring God's reign as it ends history.[16]

These differences between the original forms of messianic hope and its later development are vital for understanding Israel's faith and for the New Testament assertion that Jesus is the Messiah. But our analysis here is focussed on a single point, the meaning of the love of God for redemption. It is clear that in the Old Testament the messianic figure brings salvation through the will and power of God to create a righteous order. He is never a suffering messiah in these visions. He is the effective agent of the divine power, fulfilling righteousness in history.

When this side of God's majesty is stressed, his power to save as he will, the perplexity is why God stays his omnipotent arm and does not act now. It is not an issue about the nature of God's love or its mode of working; but only the question, 'Why does he not do what his almighty power makes it possible for him to do?' and stop the perversion of justice. Habakkuk stands and waits, in faith, for salvation will surely come because God is just. In the book of Job the only answer which comes to the individual sufferer is God's assertion of his omnipotent power to create and to rule. Job is awed to silence, not by divine love, but by God's absolute power.

But alongside this power motif there is another theme more hidden and indirect, yet more profound. It is the theme of the salvation of God as a renewal of the marriage bond between God and Israel. This renewal is an expression of the faithful and forgiving love in which God has created the original covenant. Deutero-Isaiah makes use of the theme of the bride taken back by her husband with everlasting mercy.

> For your maker is your husband,
>   the Lord of hosts is his name;
> And the Holy One of Israel is your Redeemer,
>   the God of the whole earth he is called.
> For the Lord has called you
>   like a wife forsaken and grieved in spirit,
> like a wife of youth when she is cast off,
>   says your God.
> For a brief moment I forsook you,

---

16. Among the important discussions of the messianic idea are Martin Buber, *The Prophetic Faith* (New York: Macmillan, 1949); Rudolph Otto, *The Kingdom of God and the Son of Man*, new and revised Eng. ed. (Boston: Starr King Press, 1957); Sigmund Mowinckel, *He Who Cometh* (New York: Abingdon, 1954; Oxford: Basil Blackwell & Mott Ltd., 1958). T. W. Manson, *The Servant-Messiah* (Cambridge University Press, 1956); Reinhold Niebuhr, *The Nature and Destiny of Man*, Volume II (New York: Charles Scribner's Sons, 1943; London: James Nisbet & Co., 1943).

but with great compassion I will gather you.
In overflowing wrath for a moment
  I hid my face from you,
but with everlasting love I will have compassion on you,
  says the Lord, your Redeemer. (Isaiah 54:5–8)

Similarly Jeremiah's vision of the new covenant expresses God's power to create a new situation and to raise up a new and righteous people, but this requires a transformation of the heart (spirit) of men, and Jeremiah seems here close to envisioning a redemption of individuals rather than the people as a whole.

We see here, then, salvation depending upon the divine mercy which is the forgiveness and faithfulness of God and his care for his people. It is, therefore, an expression of the same love which Israel has known from the beginning of the marriage (covenant) relationship. But a new question appears. If God loves this erring people then does not the restoration and forgiveness involve the suffering which is a consequence of sin and the suffering of God who yearns for his people's redemption? If salvation is costly for a loving God does the suffering enter into the work of salvation? This problem of the divine suffering is of critical importance for a doctrine of love rooted in the biblical faith.

The general tendency of interpretation of the Hebraic faith seems against the idea that God suffers. He is 'long-suffering' indeed. That is, he is patient, and he withholds his righteous wrath. He yearns for and broods over his people. But God, the omnipotent Lord, does not suffer in the sense that he is hurt or shaken, or moved in his being by the action of men. The Old Testament is indeed reticent on this point. The passages which come close to suggesting the divine suffering such as Hosea's picture of God agonizing within himself over his beloved people are sometimes treated as too anthropomorphic to be taken with ultimate seriousness as they suggest that God can be in difficulty with his world.

It is usually held that the messianic expectation does not change this dominant picture. The messianic ruler of Isaiah 11 is just and compassionate; but he rules in the power of the Spirit. Through him God's righteousness becomes effectual in all the earth:

with righteousness he shall judge the poor,
and decide with equity for the meek of the earth;
and he shall smite the earth with the rod of his mouth,
and with the breath of his lips he shall slay the wicked. (Isaiah 11:4)

The messiah of God in the earlier apocalypses, for example in Enoch, does not suffer. It may be argued that pre-Christian Judaism never asserted a suffering messiah. The suffering servant of Deutero-Isaiah is in all probability not a messianic figure, however the servant is to be interpreted.

Yet two factors combine to make us look more closely at the theme of suffering love in the Hebrew faith. One is the result of researches in hellenistic Judaism, the results of which have been critically appraised by W. D. Davies in his *Paul and Rabbinic Judaism*. The other is the putting of the question about God's suffering in a new way, which is free of some of the rigid presuppositions about the being of God which have shaped later theology. This possibility is given a compelling statement by Abraham Heschel in his study, *The Prophets*, to which we shall turn in a moment.

It is at least possible that there was a conception of a suffering messiah in pre-Christian Judaism, so W. D. Davies holds.[17] He reminds us that there was the poignant awareness of the suffering of the prophets, and that their suffering was in many instances a constituent element in their witness. There is the classic example of Jeremiah's rebellion against the divine call. The Son of Man in Daniel, a pre-messianic figure, suffers. The Teacher of Righteousness in the Qumran community appears as a prototype of the leader killed by wicked men, the martyr who leaves a sacred and saving memory for the community.[18]

Certainly by the second century A.D. the figure of a suffering messiah was a familiar theme in Jewish teaching. Davies suggests that the element of offence in the Christian proclamation may have been, not the suffering or even the death of Jesus, but the shameful manner of the death.

The Suffering Servant of Deutero-Isaiah is usually taken as the most important anticipation in the Old Testament of the later doctrine of redemption through the vicarious sacrifice of God's man who bears the penalty of all man's sin. It is now argued by many New Testament scholars that Jesus himself did not identify himself with the Suffering Servant.[19] However, Paul and later Christianity certainly did make the identification. It is tempting to find here the deepest link between the Old Testament and the New in the understanding of how God redeems the world.

The problem here is one of the most fascinating and, so far, unresolved, of all the questions about the Old Testament faith. Who is the Servant, and whom does he represent? Whoever he is,

17. W. D. Davies, *Paul and Rabbinic Judaism* (London: S.P.C.K., 1948).

18. Matthew Black, *The Scrolls and Christian Origins* (London: Thomas Nelson & Sons Ltd., 1961; New York: Charles Scribner's Sons, 1961).

19. M. D. Hooker, *Jesus and the Servant* (London: S.P.C.K., 1959).

there is certainly a conception of vicarious sacrifice obliterating a penalty. 'Thou hast laid on him the iniquity of us all, and by his stripes we are healed.' (Isaiah 53: 5–6.) We know something about the historical development of this conception. The notion of the vicarious suffering of the King who atones for the sin of the people is a cardinal item in the ideology of sacral kingship all over the ancient Near East.[20] But the connection of this politico-religious imagery with the Servant Songs of the Old Testament is still obscure. Dr. James Muilenburg suggests that the Hebrew poet-prophet may have taken over a form of Akkadian liturgical speech in order to express his own vision.[21] We seem to be dealing with a conception which trembles on the verge of clarity but which remains obscure and in which the precise identification of the Servant cannot be made. It is as if the spirit of love is giving birth to a new form but is still in labour. In any case, if we ask, 'Is the suffering of the Servant the suffering of God?' we are not given an unequivocal answer in the text unless we read Isaiah 63: 9 in this way, 'in all their affliction he was afflicted,' but it is not certain what the text means. The Revised Standard Version translators, for example, read it: 'In all their affliction he did not afflict.' James Muilenburg thinks it possible that the affliction of the Servant is understood as being also the affliction of God.[22]

We are left, then, with a question about the understanding of God's love. Does divine love become suffering love in order to deal with the waywardness and suffering of the world? Does God's suffering become the way of his redemption of his people? Dr. Abraham Heschel, to whose book, *The Prophets*, we have referred, has given a radical and profound answer to this question. He suggests that we should remember as we read the prophets that they had a certain reticence about expressing the divine suffering directly. A sense of delicacy before the Holy prevented them from making it too explicit, and later rabbinic commentators sensed this.[23] For Heschel the divine pathos means God's involvement in history. It is the result of his personal participation in the life of his free and irresponsible people:

> Pathos, then, is not an attitude taken arbitrarily. Its inner law is the moral law; ethos is inherent in pathos. God is concerned about the

20. Ivan Engnell, *The 'Ebed Yahweh Songs and the Suffering Messiah in 'Deutero-Isaiah'*, Bulletin of the John Rylands Library, Manchester, V. 31, No. 1, Jan. 1948, p. 84.

21. James Muilenburg, Exegesis of Second Isaiah in the *Interpreter's Bible* (New York: Abingdon, 1954).

22. Muilenburg, *loc. cit.*   23. Heschel, *The Prophets*, p. 111.

world, and shares in its fate. Indeed this is the essence of God's moral nature: His willingness to be intimately involved in the history of man.[24]

We must realize that the Bible has strata of meaning which lie beneath the surface. Penetration to them is difficult, and we can never claim that we are grasping the ultimate themes. Yet some such conclusion as follows about the Hebraic witness to the love of God is necessary if we are to put the New Testament interpretation in its proper context.

In the Hebrew scripture God is known by Israel as the loving God who reveals himself in his actions toward the people with whom he has bound himself in a personal community of loving concern. His love takes on new expressions with the waywardness of his people. It becomes compassion, patience, a mourning for one who has turned away and the longing for his return. It takes form as merciful concern and the will to restoration of the familial bond. In consequence, man's concern for the other person, the giving of what is needful, and a just and merciful regard for every person are the human expression of love as ethical responsibility. All human passions and relationships have their ground form and criterion of judgment in this ethos.

God's dealing with his world does involve his own suffering. His love manifests itself in the communication of his longing, his agonizing over his world. His power remains sovereign, and its work will be done, but God does not live untouched by what happens. The insight that the work of love gets done in the world through the suffering of God's prophets, his messengers and finally his Messiah, begins to find its expression in the faith of Israel.

There is a final obscurity, however, about the way of the divine love which the Old Testament does not resolve. It concerns the question of whether and how the suffering of God becomes the decisive action through which he meets the need, not only of Israel, but of the whole creation. The problem of God's dealing with all of history still stands out as the unresolved source of tension in the Old Testament. Is the suffering of Israel the way in which the nations are finally made to know the love of God? We have no clear affirmation of this. Does God make the disclosure of his love the real meaning of the suffering of his Servant? We again do not have an unequivocal answer. How does the suffering of God in love become decisive for salvation? It is here that the New Testament begins.

24. *Ibid.*, p. 225.

CHAPTER III

LOVE IN THE NEW TESTAMENT

Love has a history, and a critical part of that history is the development from the faith of Judaism to the Christian faith. In this chapter we need to identify the most important features of that development. The faith that Jesus is the Messiah, the Redeemer, created a new understanding of what the love of God is and how God redeems. Our attention centres upon two main topics: first, the shift from the old covenant with the nation to the new covenant established through the one Elect Man who is recognized as the Messiah. The question about the universality of love and its relation to election is seen in this new context. Second, there is the meaning of the suffering of the Messiah, and consequently the question about the suffering of God as disclosure of the way love redeems.

A new and significant discussion between Christianity and Judaism should be possible. This chapter is not written with the view that Christianity answers every question raised in Judaism, or to prove that the Christian way of understanding God's redemptive work is superior to that of Judaism. The two faiths belong together while each has its distinctive outlook and its characteristic problems. We shall see how the unresolved issues in the New Testament witness have led to centuries of further search for the meaning of the love of God. Seymour Siegel has put the central issue for the two faiths concisely:

> For Judaism the problem is, with the world in the condition in which it is, why does not the Messiah come? For Christianity the question is, since the Messiah has come, why is the world in the condition that it is.[1]

(1)

THE CENTRALITY OF LOVE

The New Testament keeps the ground pattern of the Old in its assertion that the love of God is revealed in the election of a people

1. Seymour Siegel, 'Interfaith Concourse via Rome or Reconciliation?', *Saturday Review of Literature*, 42: 22–3, March 28, 1959.

to be his servant. It uses the family analogies of husband and bride and father and son. But in the New Testament the love of God is made manifest in his relation to His Son, Jesus, the Elect Man, and through him to the new people which are made a people through what God does through the Son. This, I am asserting, is the key to the New Testament doctrine of love. The failure to see that the understanding of love in Christian faith is given in the Father-Son relationship in God himself has vitiated many Christian theologies of love. However we take the doctrine of the Trinity, as ontological affirmation or as symbolic expression, it is essential to the way in which the New Testament sees the relation of God's love to his redemptive action in Jesus Christ.

Contemporary theology is indebted to this Christocentric emphasis as it has developed in the century and a half since Schleiermacher. Ritschl and other liberal theologians pressed further the position that the Christian knowledge of God is based upon the history of Jesus. Now Karl Barth has carried through in the most radical way the interpretation of Christian doctrine on the exclusive foundation of God's action in Jesus Christ. He finds here his solution of the meaning of election. Love as grasped in the Christian faith is inseparable from the history of Jesus of Nazareth. While I do not share Barth's exclusive view of revelation in history, I believe we must follow this insight that Jesus is the Elect Man to the end if we are to understand the meaning of love in the New Testament.[2]

Barth has seen that in the New Testament the theme of election is transposed from the nation, Israel, to the person, Jesus. The theme of Israel as God's beloved is fundamental for the Old Testament. The Septuagint translators used the Greek word meaning 'Son of his love' ($\dot{\eta}\gamma\alpha\pi\eta\mu\acute{\epsilon}\nu\sigma$) for Israel. In the New Testament this ascription is given to Christ. The term 'beloved' ($\dot{\alpha}\gamma\alpha\pi\eta\tau\acute{o}s$) had already appeared in messianic prophecies, as in the *Ascension of Isaiah*, and it does not always have a Christian source in that work. James Moffat says that the evidence of the quotation of the prophecy of Isaiah in Matthew 12: 18, 'Behold my servant whom I have chosen, my beloved in whom my soul is well pleased,' shows that 'Beloved' was interchangeable with 'Elect' as a description of Jesus. The same is shown by Luke's account of the transfiguration, 'This is my Son, my Chosen, listen to him'.[3]

Thus the love between God and his son is the pattern and ground of the communion of man with God. 'Love one another as I have

2. Karl Barth, *Church Dogmatics*, Vol. III, Pt. 1 (Edinburgh: T. & T. Clark).
3. James Moffat, *Love in the New Testament* (London: Hodder & Stoughton, 1929), p. 78.

loved you.' It is also characteristic of the Fourth Evangelist to see love as promised to those who obey Christ: 'If anyone loves me, he will obey my word, and my Father will love him, and we will come to him'[4] (John 14: 23).

We have taken two important steps in understanding the New Testament when we see the significance of the Christological theme for the meaning of love. First, love is known in its ultimate depth as the mystery of personal communion. The relation of Father and Son is the image of that communion in God. Love is being, the very being of God in an eternally outgoing, creative life. The spirit makes itself manifest as the form of personal communion. This is as far as our language can reach. We can no more exhaust its meaning than we can confine the life of God in a human pattern.

The second gain is to see that the meaning of love expressed in the life of Jesus becomes the basis of an ethic for human relationships. It gives the criterion of the ethical commandment to love. Thus the concrete human meaning of love is to have its final definition through the relationship of every human history to the history of Jesus. In one sense then the theme of election now takes on an even sharper tension than in the Old Testament. There is one elect man, and in some way all human history has to be interpreted from within his election. Jesus is the representative of God and of Everyman. All those who are to know God have been 'chosen in him, that is in Christ, before the world was founded, that we should be holy and blameless before him'. This 'predestining' is an act of love. 'He destined us in love to be his sons through Jesus Christ' (Ephesians 1: 4–5).

Who are the predestined? Is it all or some, and are some chosen for eternal life and some for eternal death? Here the tension in the meaning of election reaches its sharpest point; but now it is shifted from the question about a particular people to a question about the meaning of the one man who bears God's will for all. It is possible to hold that in thus concentrating the concept of election on the one man, the eternal son of God through whom all things are made, the New Testament actually universalizes the concept of election in a way different from the Old Testament. We can conclude as Karl Barth seems to do, that it is the sense of the New Testament that all are elected to salvation in Jesus Christ. The mystery of love in its relation to the lostness of men remains, and there is the long and dreary history of Christian theology on the theme of predestination. But it may be that the real direction of the New Testament is at last being brought to clearer light. The real sense of election is God's

4. *Ibid.*, p. 265.

loving communion between himself and his son. This is the spirit of love in God, and in his love God wills communion with all. The incarnate Christ represents God's love for everyman, and everyman's real situation before God. Love is the will to that communion between God and man and between every man and his neighbour which has its ontological ground expressed in the Trinitarian symbol of the love of the Father for His Son.

From this standpoint we can see why it is inadequate to describe the *agape* of God only as the spontaneous, unmotivated, uncalculated self-giving of the Holy God, regardless of the value of its object. *Agape* is first and primordially the spirit of communion willing the divine relationship between Father and Son as the ground and pattern of the fulfilment of all things.

Now, however, we have to take a further step and see that the love of God *becomes* the suffering, self-giving love of the merciful God for sinners, actualized when God gives his only son to share the human lot, to suffer the limitations of human existence and to die that the world might be reconciled to him. Love has a history in the very life of God as he deals with his recalcitrant creatures.

Without pressing too far the typological relationship of Old Testament and New Testament we can see here a repetition of the Old Testament experience of love. God's election love raises up his people into a covenanted fellowship. Then, in the history of their disloyalty, his love becomes a patient, merciful, redemptive sharing in the life of his people and the will to restoration. Love thus has its history in God's meeting of the concrete need of man.

So again in the New Testament, the love of God means the complete spiritual communion for which the human image of father and son offers the most important analogy. God loves his Son and he loves the world with an unshakeable will to communion (John 3:16). But the history of man is the history of his fall into loveless-ness. God has to deal with a humanity which can learn to love and be reached by love only through the divine self-giving and suffering. The story of Jesus is the story of the only begotten Son, the beloved, now fulfilling the divine purpose through enacting the life of love in the midst of the world's need. God's giving of his son is the decisive action in his revelation of his love. The character of the divine love is shown by Jesus' obedience, his acceptance of his vocation, and his giving of himself for all. 'God has shown his love for us, in that while we were yet sinners, Christ died for us' (Romans 5: 8).

In this history God's love has taken on the character of suffering for the sinner. When Jesus says, as in the Fourth Gospel's inter-pretative words, 'Love one another as I have loved you, greater love hath no man than this, that he lay down his life for his friends,' the very quality of the love which God has expressed through Jesus becomes the quality and character of suffering love poured out for another beyond the worthiness of that other.

This is the justification of Bishop Nygren's interpretation of *agape* in the New Testament. In the light of God's action in Christ we can think truly of the love of God only as we see it as forgiveness poured out for the sinner, the grace of God toward the unworthy. We sinning men do not know what the love of God is apart from this. But where Nygren's view is limited is that the love which is poured out in forgiveness is not only sheer forgiveness for the unworthy, it is God the Father's love for the Son. It is the fulfilled communion of spirit. The love which wills communion and shares it, becomes forgiving love in the light of the need of man. As Gregory of Nyssa says, God became man because it was man who was in trouble.[5]

We may ask if this gives us the right to speak of a 'motivation' in God. Does he love because men are in need, or in order to restore them to fellowship in the sense that there is some value to be added to God's being through his action? If God loves the world enough to give his son, does this mean that there is a calculated value in the result? All such language seems strangely out of place. The action of love is always the action of the spirit, creatively moving out to the other, without a mere calculation of results. Yet the action of God does create a new fellowship. It is motivated in the sense that love seeks out the other. That is surely a kind of motivation. There is no sense in denying motivation to the action of God any more than to the action of a human lover who desires reconciliation with another. Love can seek reconciliation without assurance of fulfilment.

There is a powerful theological tradition which settles this matter of the divine motivation in another way. God, it is said, is complete in his own being. He needs nothing and nothing can be added to him, hence whatever he does for man and the world in creation or redemption must be a sheer spontaneous act without any goal or purpose, for it can add nothing to God's being. We shall have much to say about this tradition later, but even in its extreme form, it does not reject the notion that God does will the reconciliation of the world to himself. The action of love is not a pointless fancy. It has an aim, the Kingdom of God.

(2)

LOVE AND FORGIVENESS

We have seen how the Old Testament faith understands that God's relation to his people in some way involved his suffering. There is the strange figure of the Servant in Second Isaiah whose suffering, even if it is not the suffering of God, is the way to redemption. We have said that the Hebrew faith does not come to a clear resolution of the question of how the suffering either of God or the Servant enters into the redemptive work of love.

On this theme the New Testament offers an answer, but the nature of that answer has led to some unresolved problems. We have come to the question of the meaning of Jesus' suffering as *atonement*. The New Testament makes the clear affirmation that it is through the suffering of Jesus that the way has been opened for the redemptive work of love. This is the centre of the New Testament faith. God's love has done its work through the life and suffering and death of the son. But the meaning of this action is embodied in a gallery of metaphors. Emil Brunner has distinguished five major themes in which the significance of the death of Christ is described.[6] There is the sacrifice, the ransom, the penal suffering, the victory over evil powers, and the symbol of the Paschal Lamb. All these metaphors have been worked into theories of the atonement in Christian history; but it is remarkable that no single doctrine of atonement has ever become the accepted theory to the exclusion of the others. It is as if at the centre of the Christian faith the redemptive action of God explodes all theories and formulas. The spirit breaks and creates many forms, and no one of them can contain it.[7]

The way in which the meaning of death is woven into the history of sin and reconciliation creates especially difficult problems in the doctrine of atonement. In the apocalyptic setting of late Jewish thought the idea of resurrection and personal immortality appears. In the New Testament death is sometimes represented as the penalty for sin, or it becomes the symbol for separation from God, and thus Christ's victory over sin is also the victory over death.

6. Emil Brunner, *The Christian Doctrine of Creation and Redemption* (Philadelphia: Westminster Press, 1952, pp. 283–5; London: Lutterworth Press, 1952).
7. Among important recent studies of the atonement are Gustaf Aulén, *Christus Victor* (London: S.P.C.K., 1931); William J. Wolf, *No Cross, No Crown* (New York: Doubleday, 1957); H. E. W. Turner, *The Patristic Doctrine of Redemption* (London: A. R. Mowbray, 1952).

The identification of death as the last enemy by Paul in I Corinthians 15 reflects the view that man has fallen into the hands of powers which must be broken by God's power. Dying with Christ means participating in his victory over everything that separates man from God. Forgiveness brings the promise of eternal life, and thus atonement and the eschatological hope are linked together. All this is said in images and metaphors which defy systematic analysis. Rudolph Bultmann uses somewhat drastic language but he puts our dilemma:

> The Jesus who was crucified was the pre-existent, incarnate Son of God, and as such he was without sin. He is the victim whose blood atones for our sins. He bears vicariously the sin of the world, and by enduring the punishment for sin on our behalf he delivers us from death. This mythological interpretation is a hotch-potch of sacrificial and juridical analogies, which have ceased to be tenable for us today. And in any case they fail to do justice to what the New Testament is trying to say.[8]

What then is the New Testament trying to say? Our concern is to see within the history of the atonement metaphors what happens to the understanding of God's love. The first answer must be that the conception of redemption as the work of God's love has often become obscured in the attempt to account for the suffering of Christ. The concepts of ransom, of vicarious suffering for the guilt of men, of propitiation and sacrifice all too easily turn into descriptions of how God is appeased through suffering, and thus the point that the atonement stems from his love is lost. Again, the victory over the powers of Death and Satan can be described in such military terms that the personal meaning of the forgiveness of God is lost in the drama of the divine conquest. Yet all the New Testament metaphors do have this in common, they see God's love involved in a real struggle with evil. Love's work must be done in a situation riddled with the consequences of man's separation from God. All the metaphors find a redemptive meaning in the suffering and death of the Christ, God's Son and Mediator. Here the theme that the love of God has a history receives its decisive expression in the Christian faith.

We may go beyond the traditional theories of atonement and ask a radical question: 'What account would be given of atonement if we were to interpret it from the standpoint of the most realistic analogies we know to human love when it deals with broken

8. Rudolph Bultmann, *New Testament and Mythology; The Mythological Element in the New Testament and the Problem of Its Re-interpretation.* English text in H. W. Bartsch, ed. *Kerygma and Myth* (London: S.P.C.K., 1953), pp. 35–6.

relationships and the consequent suffering?' We shall ask this question and try to find an answer in Chapter VII.

We have seen how the history of God's action in the world becomes reinterpreted in the New Testament as a history to be understood with Jesus Christ at its centre. It is now the history of humanity as lived under the impact of the new faith which is born out of response to Jesus, and through which a new 'people' has come into being which lives by the mercy God has shown in him. We have now to look at the New Testament teaching about the human expressions and forms of love.

(3)

LOVE AND ETHICS

The New Testament ethic of love has its foundation in the Old Testament. The two commandments, to love God and the neighbour, are at the centre of the mature tradition in Israel. In the New Testament love is affirmed, not as a new ethical principle, but as the spirit of a new relationship of man and God. The New Testament is marked by the radical insight that the spirit of love transcends every ethic of specific commandments and laws. Yet neither the law as Israel has known it, nor human laws are despised. New tensions appear as the history of love leads to new ethical forms. There are three vital points in the New Testament outlook on ethics.

First, there is the doctrine, especially as interpreted by Paul, that the spirit of love is the fulfilment of all righteousness, conjoined with a conception of the new life in Christ as committed to specific patterns of pure and responsible living. Paul sees love as the ground of ethical freedom. 'Neither circumcision, nor uncircumcision avails, but faith working through love.' 'Through love be servants one of another for the whole law is fulfilled in one word, "you shall love your neighbour as yourself".' Again, 'Bear ye one another's burdens and so fulfil the law of Christ' (Galatians 5: 6, 13–14; 6: 2). Yet Paul goes on to give scores of specific warnings and judgments against all kinds of unacceptable behaviour: impurity, jealousy, strife, party spirit, envy, drunkenness, carousing and the like (Galatians 5: 19–21). He gives practical injunctions concerning marriage, and the treatment of those who will not work. He advises concerning the attitudes of parents toward children, husband toward wife, master toward slave. Paul makes some qualifications concerning the adequacy of human judgment, even his own, in specific cases; but we see that commitment to the spirit of love as an alternative to legal obedience requires responsible living and the honouring of authentic forms of behaviour appropriate to the new life. So Paul repeats in his way the pattern in Jesus' teaching as recorded in the Synoptic Gospels. Jesus puts the command to love at the centre of the message of the Kingdom, and couples it with concrete judgments on forms of human exploitation, on the responsibilities of God's people in law courts, in marriage, in buying and selling, in religious duties. The ethic of love is not formless. When it comes into its full spiritual significance it begins to cut its own channels in human behaviour, but it has to cut them in the hard soil of human conditions. The freedom of the spirit is maintained so long as the meaning of ethical action is kept as response to the love of God rather than simply as obedience to law. The new commandment is to love one another as Christ has loved. That means the final ethical norm is in the action of God in the person of Jesus in whom the Spirit has become incarnate.[9]

In the New Testament the meaning of ethical love is given by the divine action in the history of Jesus. This is the second vital point in the New Testament ethic. When we ask what love is, or what is to be done in the spirit of love we are to look at the action of Christ in becoming the servant for the sake of the ungodly. 'Have this mind in you which was in Christ Jesus,' Paul says, as he adapts the kenotic hymn in which Christ who is equal to God humbles himself, takes the form of a servant, and becomes obedient unto death (Philippians 2: 5). Paul's conception of the Christian life is that we become conformed to the way of Christ. 'As therefore you received Christ Jesus the Lord, so live in him (Colossians 2: 6). Paul thinks of the sufferings of the life of faith as bearing in the body the dying of Jesus that his life might also be manifest (II Corinthians 4). This cruciform life is the meaning of the new creation. Paul speaks of the new life in the freedom of love as being itself the 'rule' (*canon*). 'Peace and mercy be upon all who walk by this rule, upon the Israel of God' (Galatians 6: 16).

We can sum up by saying that the ethical impulse in the spirit of love as released in the Gospel takes new forms and fulfils old demands because the spirit has become incarnate in the form of the Servant.

9. Our discussion may seem to by-pass the important question of how Jesus' teaching about love is related to that of the later Church. We are, however, concerned here with how the Church came to understand the meaning of love in the light of the revelation in Jesus. We can therefore characterize the Christian ethical outlook without attempting the perhaps impossible task of reconstructing the precise teaching of Jesus. For detailed studies of Jesus' teaching see Amos Wilder, *Eschatology and Ethics in the Teaching of Jesus*, revised edition (New York: Harper & Brothers, 1950; London: S.C.M. Press, 1954); and Ceslaus Spicq, *Agape dans le Nouveau Testament* (Paris: J. Gabalda, 1958–9), 3 vols.

What is given for the ethical life in Jesus Christ is not a law in the form of specific prescriptions, but an action which releases power to accept responsibility for that action which will serve the neighbour. This new form of being involves a radical new relation to all things. Paul sees the cross of Christ as the way in which the world has been crucified to us and we to the world (Galatians 6: 14). It is not only that a new idea of what love is has come into the world, though we need not deny there is something new in the way the idea of love will ever after be understood. The decisive matter is that the spirit of God has come into history in such a way as to plough up the old forms of human existence and to open the way to new human actions. The spirit has shattered the foundations of the old order of history in which man's lovelessness has the last word. A new history has begun.

We have, then, sufficient warning in the New Testament against letting any interpretation of the ethical life be turned into a set of objective rules which are simply to be obeyed as rules. We are to be prepared for the extravagance, the radical spontaneity, the unruliness of love in human existence. We say the warning is sufficient, yet legalism has plagued Christian life and ethics through the centuries. How is it possible for this radical new Gospel to be caught in the perennial forms of legalism?

We have to consider as part of the explanation the situation in which the ethic of love had to be appropriated. The world's history moves on in its worldly way, and the history of sin continues in the history of man. The issues of life remain. Men are born, grow, are taught, buy and sell, contend with one another as individuals, and fight as nations and people. Human loyalties are divided, human fears drive the spirit to self-protection and to desperation. Even the new spirituality brings its temptations with it. There is no absolute protection against turning spiritual wisdom and grace into pride. The history of the Christian community is a history of the old world being confronted by a new spirit. Here is a double reason why the forms of legalistic ethics remain. It is partly the sin of man's search for a moral security through obeying an imposed set of objective prescriptions. It is also the result of the necessity for some kinds of principles for the guidance of life, the organization of society, and the adjustment of the claims and counter claims in human living. Both the irresponsibility of sin, and the responsibility of love are involved in the struggle to realize an ethic conformable to the spirit of love.

It is sometimes held that the initial impulse of Christian ethics in its absolutizing of love was the search for a supernatural purity, and a refusal to compromise in any way the simplicity of the command-ment to love. Martin Buber says Paul sees faith as the only condition of salvation so that personal holiness and salvation become the sole concern, and the sphere of the person is separated from that of public affairs.[10]

Certainly Paul makes faith the sole condition of salvation. But Buber believes that Paul means by faith belief in a truth, a kind of objective knowledge, whereas surely for Paul faith in Christ is never separated from love to all the members of the body of Christ and to every man. The letters of Paul as well as the Gospel records show that the Christian community from the beginning made ethical decisions within the community and in relation to buying and selling in the market, and the problem of obedience to the state. There was indeed a brief period in the time following the experience of the resurrection when the believers expected the return of the Lord and the end of history so that a certain indifference to normal respon-sibilities in an ongoing history appears. This colours perhaps some of Paul's teaching about 'remaining in the calling wherein each is called'. What is remarkable is how quickly the need of the church to make ethical judgments on many problems entered into the shaping of the tradition, as appears to have happened with the modification of Jesus' word about marriage and the injunctions concerning the handling of disputes (Matthew 19: 7ff.; 18: 15ff.). In Romans 12 Paul writes about the state and its rightful powers in terms which have both guided and troubled the Christian conscience ever since. The pastoral epistles are filled with moral injunctions for wives, husbands, servants, teachers, philanthropists, ministers, citizens. 'Obey the emperor,' writes the author of the First Epistle of Peter (I Peter 2: 13). Love is the fulfilment of the law, but it does not provide answers to all of the laws' questions. Love has to cut some new channels as well as use those that are already present as it does its work in history.

The love which is to be given to the neighbour is the same love that God has given to us in Jesus Christ. The New Testament does sometimes use another word for love than *agape*, the word *philein*, as in 'Love one another earnestly from the heart' (I Peter 1: 22; I Thessalonians 4: 9). There is however no sharp difference in the usage of this word for love of the brother, as against the love spoken of as *agape*. Paul uses the forms of *agape* to express his love for the saints in Philippi (Philippians 4: 1). Both words are used in various contexts for all the dimensions of God's love for man, man's love

10. Martin Buber, *Two Types of Faith* (New York: Macmillan, 1951; London: Routledge & Kegan Paul, 1951). Harper Torchbooks edition, 1961, pp. 172, 173.

for God, and man's love for man.[11] The new ethical relationship demanded by the action of God's love in Christ is the giving of concrete help to the neighbour, the spirit of mercy and compassion, the creative concern which is the human analogue of what God has shown to man. It is an analogue which means the imitation of a divine pattern through participation in history.

We come to the third important dimension of New Testament ethics, the question of human affection and desire, and the relation of *agape* to the manifold human loves. We are to see every human love in the light of the central message about God's love in Christ. That is the way the New Testament approaches all human behaviour. It sees man in the spiritual crisis of repentance and the need for grace. It tells of what God does in that crisis, and in the light of that history all human experience is to be viewed. Certainly human experience is not ignored. All the human loves are there—family love, love for home and country, love of life and love of self, and also the perversions of love and its rejection.

Is there, however, a final and absolute gulf between the *agape* of God known in Christ and the love which rules human desire? That question must be asked, and it must be admitted that there is no clear answer to it. This is the critical issue about the relation of God's being to our being as creatures, and of God's love to finite creaturely desire, vitality and comradeship. Here the theologies have divided. We shall try to say in summary form how the New Testament presents the mystery and the dilemmas of love without wholly resolving them.

On one point we can be clear. There is no rejection of desire or passion or sexuality or the *eros* of the beautiful in the New Testament, though there are expressions and tendencies which could be used to support ascetic tendencies in later religious practice. Even in Paul's letters, where these tendencies appear, he keeps free from any identification of the body with evil, and from any disparagement of the natural loves. Paul uses the marriage metaphor of the Old Testament tradition as the image for the relationship of the Christian people to Christ. 'I betrothed you to Christ to present you as a pure bride to her husband' (II Corinthians 11: 2). It may be that the use of this image as the foundation for the interpretation of marriage in Ephesians 5 is not directly from Paul.

> For this reason a man shall leave his father and mother and be joined to his wife, and the two shall become one. This is a great mystery, and I take it to mean Christ and the church. (Ephesians 5: 31–2.)

11. Moffatt, *op. cit.*, pp. 46, 47.

But Paul has laid the foundation in the simpler injunction in Colossians:

> Wives be subject to your husbands as is fitting in the Lord. Husbands love your wives, and do not be harsh with them. (Colossians 3: 18–19.)

Paul calls the body the temple of the living God, and it is not therefore to be prostituted or otherwise misused (I Corinthians 6: 15). It is Paul again who opens the way to a Christian understanding of the creative good in human culture with its appreciation of excellence:

> Whatever is true, whatever is honourable, whatever is just, whatever is pure, whatever is lovely, whatever is gracious, if there is any excellence, if there is anything worthy of praise, think about these things. (Philippians 4: 8.)

We also find in the New Testament, beginning with the teaching of Jesus in the synoptic Gospels, the use of human analogies as parables of the divine love. The story of the prodigal son is a story of human love and loveless pride. It compares the mercy of God to the compassion of a father, and is told as a story about the relation of God's love to the human spirit. The story could be heard and understood by anyone who had experienced the depth of love in a family with its dilemmas and decisions, and Jesus uses it as a lesson about God which is reflected in the human situation. Karl Barth appears to hold that the New Testament would have us understand familial love only in the light of the divine love, but if this were the case, there would be no need for the parable. To be sure, the parables are understood more profoundly in the light of the full disclosure of *agape* in Christ; but that revelation illumines what is already pressing for recognition in human experiences of love. It simply is not true that the *agape* of the New Testament is nothing but the grace of God poured out without motive upon the unworthy. It is also the spirit of rejoicing, of friendship, and of the new life with its foretaste of the blessedness of life with God and with the brethren in the full freedom of love.

Nevertheless, when we have gone so far with the positive place of the creaturely loves in the Gospel, there does remain a profound and disturbing revolution in the New Testament faith. For the love which is made incarnate and powerful in Christ's presence among men is a love which involves a radical transformation of all earthly loves in the light of the Kingdom. It does not destroy the natural attachments and desires, nor does it count them as of no worth in the eyes of God; but it subjects them to a new judgment:

He who loves father or mother more than me is not worthy of me; and he who loves son or daughter more than me is not worthy of me, and he who does not take up his cross and follow me is not worthy of me. (Matthew 10: 37-8.)

The drastic character of these words is echoed by Paul:

But whatever gain I had, I counted as loss for the sake of Christ. Indeed I count everything as loss because of the surpassing worth of knowing Christ Jesus my Lord. For his sake I have suffered the loss of all things, and count them as refuse in order that I may gain Christ, and be found in him. (Philippians 3: 7-9a.)

God's new creation in Christ brings a commitment to an absolute good which makes everything else a temporary and relative good. Yet it is in this same letter that Paul goes on to the passage recommending all excellences to the Christians (Philippians 4: 8).

It might be said that this tension is resolved neatly by the full meaning of Jesus' injunction, 'Seek ye first the Kingdom of God and his righteousness and all these things will be added unto you'. But this does not resolve the tension in the life of *agape*. What things are to be given up? What becomes of the creative works of culture? What does it mean to seek the Kingdom first? We are not given directives, rather we are confronted with the issue. What did the new life mean for the first Christians in the realms of human desire, passion, creativity, knowledge, and love? The spirit of the New Testament community is perhaps most concretely expressed in the passage in Paul's letters in which he tries to answer the question as to whether Christians who are unmarried should remain so or not. He makes three points: first, each one should remain in that situation in which he was found by the Gospel. Even the slave can remain as he is though he need not; 'Were you a slave when called, never mind, but if you can attain your freedom, avail yourself of the opportunity. Are you bound to a wife; do not seek to be free. Are you free from a wife? Do not seek marriage' (I Corinthians 7: 21, 27). Paul tempers this reply—there is no sin in being married, but then, as if wrestling with an issue which cannot be settled by specific prescriptions, he gives his profoundest expression of what the new life means:

I mean, brothers, the appointed time has grown very short, from now on, let those who have wives live as though they had none, and those who mourn as though they were not mourning, and those who rejoice as though they were not rejoicing, and those who deal with the world as though they had no dealings with it. For the form of this world is passing away. (I Corinthians 7: 29-31.)

Here the tension between the new life and the old is strained as far as it can go without breaking. There is no seclusion from the world, and no asceticism or self-denial for its own sake. The Christian does not depart from the world as it is, but he has a certain detachment in regard to all present things. The reason is that 'the form of this world is passing away'. The imperfect tense is important. We are still within the old form. It has its demands and its responsibilities, but it has in itself no permanence.

Unquestionably the expectation of the imminent return of the Lord helped to shape the extreme form of this early Christian ethic. Paul's sense of the shortness of the time probably enters into his suggestion that each should remain in the 'calling wherein he was called'. It is all the more remarkable that even Paul draws back from absolutizing such injunctions. There is underneath it all the freedom to find what love requires and to do it.

We can sum up what actually did become the way of Christian living in the ancient world by saying that the Christians lived in the economic, political and social orders of their time seeking new patterns but conforming to the general requirements of the common life, and accepting constituted authority except when it required idolatrous worship. Some certainly refused military service. There was in some communities a practice of having all things in common, and there was practised for a time in some groups what Charles Williams has later called 'an experiment in dissociation', the living together of men and women with a complete renunciation of sex.[12] But these radical experiments never became normative for the churches. The suffering which came to the Christians came as a result of the refusal of emperor worship. They lived as witnesses to the Gospel, and their sufferings became marks of that witness, and a testing and tempering of the spirit. It is obvious not all maintained the pattern of sober, industrious life. Paul's letters are filled with injunctions against excesses and unseemly conduct. The call was clear to a sober, devout life, filled with a spirit different from that of the riotous passions and self-seeking lusts of the world. It was a joyful soberness:

> Now the works of the flesh are plain: immorality, impurity, licentious-ness, idolatry, sorcery, enmity, strife, jealousy, anger, selfishness, dis-sension, party spirit, envy, drunkenness, carousing and the like . . .

---

12. Charles Williams, *The Descent of the Dove* (London: Faber & Faber, 1950; New York: Living Age, 1956, pp. 11ff). On sexual ethics in the New Testament see William Graham Cole, *Sex and Love in the Bible* (New York: Association Press, 1959; London: Hodder & Stoughton, 1960).

But the fruit of the spirit is love, joy, peace, patience, kindness, goodness, faithfulness, gentleness, self-control, against such there is no law. (Galatians 5 : 19–23.)

Was this a new ethic, or simply a baptized and intensified form of stoic restraint and brotherliness? The virtues seem to be those of the decencies and ideals of a restrained reasonableness not different in form from the wisdom and integrity of traditional Hebraic or Greek values. The ethic of love did not create a wholly new pattern for human living. We see here a principle which runs through the entire history of love; the forms which express the spirit of love do not arise like some pure fountain from love alone. The forms are drawn from the tradition and experiences of men. They express a way of life which is congruent with the requirements of love, even though love itself finally will plough up and reshape them. That ploughing up of the old form takes a long time as the subsequent history shows.

We acknowledge, then, an important contrast in the New Testament community. On one hand it was committed to a radical break with the ways of an evil world, 'the worldly life which is the enemy of the cross of Christ. Their end is destruction, their God is the belly, and they glory in their shame, with minds set on earthly things' (Philippians 3: 18–19). The Christians drew apart from this. They belonged to a new order (Revelation 22: 5; II Timothy 2: 22; I Peter 4: 2; 5: 1). Yet the radical work of love implicit in the new ethic remains in a strange way hidden. Such issues as slavery, the status of women, and political freedom, the virtues of scientific honesty and integrity, the freedom of the spirit in worship, all such ethical concerns which have grown in significance throughout Christian history are in part at least implicit in the new life, but they are not explicit, and the reason for that must be sought in the historical situation into which the Gospel came. The revolution which the freedom of love meant is a permanent revolution which must work itself out in history.

But the seeds are there. Even a progressivist in his outlook on history like Alfred North Whitehead says that the greatness of early Christianity lay in its interim ethics, that is, in the way in which the ultimate moral demand was set free from a too immediate calculation of results.[13] This ethic was never wholly detached from concrete historical responsibility. It is significant that in the book of Revelation (a book Whitehead did not like because of its bloody and apocalyptic

13. Alfred North Whitehead, *Adventures of Ideas* (New York: Macmillan, 1933, p. 19; Cambridge University Press, 1933).

imagery), the vision of a new heavenly city at the end of time has the divine light shine so that the nations walk by it, and the 'kings of the earth shall bring their glory into it' (Revelation 21: 22ff.). Thus the Old Testament view of history as the redemption of the nations by the Lord of all things receives its Christian reiteration. The way is opened for the Christian mission to become involved in the problems of cultural and national existence. This is what did happen in Christianity. Had it not been so, Christianity would have become an esoteric sect, perhaps untroubled and uncomprised by, but certainly irrelevant to the issues of world history. That this did not happen is a fact, whatever view we take of the rise of the church to political and cultural power.

In concluding this chapter we must notice that something analogous to this acceptance and transformation of human ethics by love happened also in the realm of knowledge.

The *agape* of God in Christ brought a new wisdom, a new knowledge. Paul declares that this knowledge is his exclusive concern: 'I decided to know nothing among you except Jesus Christ and him crucified' (I Corinthians 2: 2). He goes on to speak of that which he imparts: 'a secret and hidden wisdom of God, which God decreed before the ages for our glorification' (I Corinthians 2: 7). Christ is the power of God and the wisdom of God to those who are called, but is a stumbling block and a scandal to the Jews and Greeks. Yet already in Paul's mind the forms of the Christian witness have begun to take on aspects derived from hellenistic culture. Paul uses the pattern of gnostic hymnody and liturgy to express the meaning of Christ. The full meeting of the Gospel with the mind of the Greeks must take place. This is the fateful intellectual event and the outcome will have a profound effect on the forms of interpretation of love. What did happen was that the Christian theologians began to work within the forms of Greek intellectuality. They sought to bring the Christian faith in God into intelligible relation to the Greek conceptions of the divine, of man, and of the world. Out of this came the Augustinian synthesis of the Greek conception of being with the Christian Gospel. Anders Nygren is quite right in saying that Augustine's conception of love shows the effects of this synthesis. The question is whether this distorted or compromised the meaning of *agape*, and that question remains one of the central issues for Christian thought and life.

The history of the Christian conception of love begins in the Old Testament, has its centre in the New Testament, and continues throughout the life of the church. What we have seen in the form and spirit of the biblical faith makes it clear how sharply different understandings of the meaning and requirements of love could arise. The later history shows three main ways in which the love of God made known in Christ was grasped and embodied as a Christian view of life. These are not simply three different concepts of love, but three total perspectives, each with its integrity, in which the meaning of the Gospel is worked out in thought and life. We shall call these three 'types' of the doctrine of love, and our next chapter seeks to characterize and contrast them.

CHAPTER IV

THREE FORMS OF LOVE

When we say that the interpretation of love has taken three major forms in the Christian tradition, we are not seeking to fit the entire history into a neat scheme, but rather to emphasize the fact that the interpretation of love has had a history. In this history three main perspectives have appeared as characteristic forms of the Christian life. Our typology is an instrument of analysis, and, hopefully, of vision. It is not a form to be imposed on the data. It is intended rather to sharpen and organize significant aspects of the data, and thus the analysis tends to produce 'ideal types', that is, forms which do not precisely correspond to any historical expression of the type.[1] We shall try to discover the underlying structures in the three types and we shall base each description upon specific historical sources: St. Augustine, St. Francis of Assisi, and Martin Luther.

A typology can have a further usefulness when the comparison of types with one another discloses relationships which might otherwise remain obscure. Two important insights will emerge from a typological analysis of the conceptions of love. The first is that the history of the Western concept of love has been influenced by the fact that St. Augustine worked out his interpretation of love in relation to the metaphysics of neo-platonism with its doctrine of God as being-itself, the absolute. In criticizing that Augustinian synthesis we are agreeing with Nygren that it is the critical point in the development of Christian doctrine. But where Nygren attacks the synthesis by isolating *agape* from *eros* as two utterly different conceptions of love, I shall try to show that he focusses on the wrong point. The real task is to see whether another ontological synthesis is possible, one freed from the neo-platonism which causes so much trouble for a genuinely historical view of God and man. Our analysis of the historical types will lead to the development of this possibility. The spirit transcends the forms; but the spirit can be obscured when the forms become hardened.

This leads to a second discovery. Each of the additional types has recreated itself in our era, but in each case it betrays an existential

1. A masterly use of typological method for theological clarification is H. R. Niebuhr's *Christ and Culture* (New York: Harper & Brothers, 1951; London: Faber & Faber, 1952).

restlessness. The classic types do not quite satisfy contemporary man's self-understanding. We shall examine the factors which have led three modern interpreters of love who stand within the main types to modify the traditional forms: Martin D'Arcy, Albert Schweitzer, and Reinhold Niebuhr. Thus the interpretation of love continues in a history where new forms break through the old.

Every Christian view of love involves the following themes: the meaning of the love of God in the history of Israel and in his action in Jesus Christ and the Church; the relations of faith and knowledge in the understanding of love; the question of the being of God in his relation to the world; the relation of the divine love to human loves and human self-expression; and the ethics of love as the basis of both personal and collective obligation. We shall characterize each type on these topics.

(1)

THE AUGUSTINIAN TYPE

St. Augustine formulated the conception of love at the critical point in the development of early Christianity, and his vision in some way informs all subsequent Christian thought in the West.[2]

Augustine weaves together two major themes. God is the Father of Jesus Christ, and Father and Son are united in the Spirit. The life of the Trinity is the life of absolute love. God graciously pours out his love upon the creation and through it he has come to men in the incarnation of his son for their redemption. This is the personal, active, redemptive side of the doctrine. But God is the fullness of being, 'being itself', as St. Augustine follows the neo-platonic doctrine. God is being, the ground, the ontological structure within

2. Augustine's doctrine of love is woven into all his writings. *The City of God* and *On the Trinity* are of major importance. Erich Przywara's *An Augustine Synthesis* (New York: Sheed and Ward, 1936) is a superb collection of texts. Where I have used this translation I have included the reference in Przywara's *Synthesis*. I have also used the translations in *The Basic Writings of St. Augustine* edited by Whitney J. Oates (New York: Random House, 1948).

On Augustine's doctrine of love the following are especially valuable: Anders Nygren, *Agape and Eros*, one volume with English translation partly revised by Philip S. Watson (London: S.P.C.K., 1953); J. Burnaby, *Amor Dei* (London: Hodder & Stoughton, 1938); Etienne Gilson, *The Christian Philosophy of St. Augustine* (New York: Random House, 1960). See also, *A Companion to the Study of St. Augustine*, ed. by Roy Battenhouse, introduction by D. D. Williams (New York: Oxford University Press, 1955); *St. Augustine* by M. C. D'Arcy *et al.* (New York, Meridian Books, 1957).

all beings. The world then is a system of structures and powers which exist through participation in God's being. The fulfilment of anything is the fulfilment of its being in God.

Hence for St. Augustine everything in the created universe shows on its positive side its participation in being. This is true of human knowledge. We can know ourselves as existing persons only through the act of knowing that we are, knowing that we know, and rejoicing in this knowledge; and here Augustine finds a reflection of the Trinity—the Father, the Son, and the Spirit. All knowledge, then, whether of logic and mathematics or of the good and the beautiful, is knowledge of patterns of being which participate in God. As the mind moves toward a fuller grasp of the truth it is led toward God. For Augustinians there is never an absolute disjunction between intellectual and mystical experience, for all experience has the power and truth of God's being as its ground. To know truly is to experience God. Rationalism and mysticism are not enemies but two sides of experience which reinforce one another.

The significance of love for knowledge becomes clearer when we consider the meaning of error and ignorance. Since the mind is properly directed toward being, error is a plunge toward non-being. Now to be is not only to know; it is to love, and indeed love is more fundamental than knowledge. Therefore St. Augustine sees all disorder in human existence as stemming from a disorder in the creature's love for God. This is why all hearts are restless until they find their rest in God. Love is the weight which bears the creature toward God.[3] Since God is to be loved above all else, a rightly ordered life can be founded only upon love for God, not for God as chief value among others, but as the ultimate and absolute good which underlies all the creaturely goods. Therefore the goal of love is the satisfaction and the culmination of the creature's life in God. This *fruitio dei* is the characteristic Augustinian expression of blessedness and peace in God.

An important consequence of Augustine's teaching is that to love anything, when that love is rightly ordered, is to love that thing or person in God. Nothing is self-sufficient but God. For Augustine, therefore, all truly human love is at the same time the love of God, and its natural uncorrupted intent is to seek the fruition of every finite and proximate love in the absoluteness of God's being. Augustine is often criticized for this doctrine on the ground that he depersonalizes human love by insisting that we do not love another person for himself alone. But Augustine's intention should be remembered. The fulfilment of every love is its destiny in the divine

3. *The City of God*, XI, p. 28.

life, which is the life of personal spirit, the Holy Trinity of Father, Son, and Spirit. St. Augustine's superb definition of sacrifice is well known:

> Every action which is performed with the aim of inhering in God in one holy society; whose purpose, that is, is to bring us to the end by which we can truly be made blessed.[4]

Augustine's God in whom all loves are completed is not impersonal. To love another in God is just to see that other as he truly is, as a participant in God's eternal life. The difficulties lie, I believe, not in the doctrine that we love others in God, but in Augustine's failure to develop a metaphysical view which provides for the fully social relationship of God and man.

St. Augustine's treatment of the love of beauty illustrates as clearly as anything in his philosophy his view of the pilgrimage of human loves. 'The soul has power to know eternal things as things to which it should cling fast (*inhaerendum*), but it has not at the same time the *power* to do so.'[5] What is the source of this weakness? Augustine explains that we love the beautiful, and beautiful things please by proportion, by number, and by rhythm. We love therefore what Augustine calls 'active performance' when the soul, reacting to the effects of its own body, becomes preoccupied with the pleasures of perception. It is diverted from the contemplation of eternal things and becomes restless, curious, and finally infected with anxiety. *Cura*, care or anxiety, replaces *securitas*.

Now there is much in Augustine about this tendency of the soul to turn toward preoccupation with temporal things, and much in condemnation of the body's lusts. Yet none of this is explained as caused by any inherent evil in the body or the material world. All things are good because they participate in the creation. Augustine never calls the body bad because it is body. He rejected that view when he rejected Manichaeism.

No, the real source of the soul's disorder is pride, 'the vice which made the soul prefer to imitate God rather than to serve God'.[6] Now pride is a failure in love's proper ordering. When he says that the soul must indeed find it 'easy to love God', Augustine is talking about the soul's created goodness and harmony with the divine order. The 'love of this world is far more laborious' for then we are

4. D'Arcy, *op. cit.*, p. 244.
5. *De Musica*, VI, xiii, 38. References to *De Musica* will be conveniently found in Albert Hofstadter and Richard Kuhns, *Philosophies of Art and Beauty* (New York: Modern Library, 1964), Translation by W. F. Jackson Knight.
6. *Ibid.*, VI, xiii, 40.

seeking fulfilment and peace and permanence where they are not to be found. The secret of rightly ordered love is to love our neighbour, 'the surest step towards an ability to cling to God'.[7] The source of disorder is the soul's turning toward the love of lesser things, and this comes from a desire to imitate God, that is, to be God, to dominate others, and to win honours and praise through our influence upon them. All this Augustine sees as the soul's movement away from being. To become distended with pride is to move toward what is outside the soul's real being and to become empty within, that is, to exist less and less fully, *quod est minus minusque esse.*[8]

With this doctrine of the fall from fullness of being Augustine combines another which for him is essential. Since God, being-itself, is immutable and changeless, the fall away from being is an attachment to the mutable. We turn away from pure eternity and toward non-being whenever the soul's affection is directed toward that which is changing. St. Augustine's attitude toward the pleasures of the body and toward human desire generally is profoundly affected by this doctrine. 'Therefore we must not place our joys in carnal pleasures nor in honour and tributes of praise; nor in our thought for anything extrinsic to our body, *forinsecus*; for we have God within us, and there all that we love is fixed and changeless.'[9]

While not absolutely disparaging the realm of the changing, Augustine has repeated the theme of Greek religion which seeks salvation in the changelessness of absolute being. Consequently the vision of a hierarchy of goods appears in which everything in the temporal world is contrasted with the superior value of the non-temporal order. Here a preoccupation with the eternal at the expense of this world has entered into the perspective on love itself. This is why Augustine's doctrine has at its foundation the distinction between the two loves, the love of God and the love of the world.[10] There is indeed a delicate balance in his thought and he believes he has perceived the right use of temporal things; but he is perilously close to saying that to love God is to turn away from love for whatever is changeable. Thus a kind of asceticism of the temporal is introduced into Christian theology, which has affected the whole course of the conception of love.[11]

The issues concerning this asceticism come out clearly in Augustine's view of sexual love. There is some point in the view that Augustine had much to do with fastening a negative and morbid attitude toward sexuality upon the Christian church, but we want

7. *De Musica*, VI, xiv, 47.
8. *Ibid.*, VI, xiii, 40.
9. *Ibid.*, VI, xiv, 48.
10. *The City of God*, XIV, p. 28.
11. Nygren, *op. cit.*, p. 650.

to find what it is in his view of love which led to this.[12] We have to go deeper than the familiar point that Augustine thought of the stain of original sin as transmitted through the act of procreation. We remember that Augustine never says the body is the source of evil. It is in the soul that evil arises. The body may weigh down the soul, but sinful actions result from the soul's misdirection of the body.[13] Further, Augustine can write beautifully upon the spiritual significance of marriage. When we compare him with such Fathers as Jerome and Tertullian he seems positively humane and liberal. The goods of marriage, he says, include the bearing and raising of children in the love of the Lord; the family loyalties of husband and wife, parents and children; and the sacramental unity of marriage. Augustine seems to give to sexual love the same power as that of other loves to participate in the fullness of being.[14]

We have further to allow to St. Augustine that some of his warnings about the dangers of moral distraction in the human loves come from an essential insight in the Gospel. Jesus' extreme words about hating father and mother cannot be forgotten in any Christian ethic (Luke 14: 26). Augustine seems to be giving sensible advice when he says that marriage is not always to be rejected for the sake of the Kingdom. Rather, he says:

> those who put their trust in these things, [i.e. marriage] who prefer them to God, who for the sake of these things are quick to offend God, these will perish. But those who either do not use these things or who use them as though they used them not, trusting more in Him who gave them than in the things given, understanding in them His consolation and mercy and who are not absorbed in these gifts lest they fall away from the giver, these are they whom the day will not overtake as a thief unprepared.[15]

Even Augustine's doctrine that procreation is the only morally acceptable goal of sexual intercourse is based in part on his concern lest the satisfactions of the world distract us from our first obligation to God. It must be admitted here however that along with all the Church Fathers he failed to see sexual expression within human love

12. Dorothea Krook, *Three Traditions of Moral Thought* (Cambridge University Press, 1959), pp. 271–5.

13. *City of God*, XIX, p. 27.

14. An admirable exposition and critique of Augustine's sexual ethics is in Thomas J. Bigham and Albert T. Mollegen, 'The Christian Ethic' in Battenhouse, *A Companion to the Study of St. Augustine*. See also D. S. Bailey, *The Man-Woman Relation in Christian Thought* (London: Longman, Green & Co., 1959; New York: Harper & Brothers, 1959).

15. *Enarrations on the Psalms*, cxx, p. 3.

as sustaining the personal relationship, and thus he fastened a doctrine of the unimportance of this personal function of sexual expression upon the catholic church which it is only now throwing off.[16]

The really serious problem in St. Augustine's view stems from something other than his concern about single-minded devotion to God. It lies in his view that since the love of God is the love of the immutable it relegates every other love to a lesser place in a system of values. Augustine moves from the unchallengeable Christian doctrine that nothing must stand in the way of love to God to the quite different doctrine that there must be a hierarchy of higher and lower loves. The love of God therefore is intrinsically one that can be expressed more adequately by refraining from sexual love. Here is the basis of Augustine's view that virginity is the highest human state, celibacy next, and that there is a scale of nobility in relation to continence after bereavement, with renunciation always receiving the highest honour.[17]

Here Augustine's theology of the Fall and the subsequent redemption of sufficient souls to replenish heaven further confuses his view of the meaning of sex. The divine command to Adam and Eve to be fruitful holds from the Fall until Christ, since the people of God must be propagated in history. But the coming of Christ makes procreation an optional and lesser good for the race. Celibacy can be recommended as the best way of life for all, for redemption is fulfilled in the church whether the race goes on or not.

Augustine does not lose his sense of the moral realities altogether in this glorification of virginity and celibacy. A humble Catholic wife is nearer God than a proud virgin. He allows that there can be a pardoning of sexual gratification sought for its own sake within marriage if it contributes to the happiness and security of the marriage state.[18] What disturbs us is that Augustine needs to hunt for this pragmatic justification of sexual fulfilment. His reason is that when all the loves are set within a hierarchy of values *any* love other than the love of God himself is a lesser love which can have only a relative justification.

It is important to trace this theological disparagement of sexual love to its source. The answer lies in the neo-platonic metaphysics which St. Augustine has taken into his doctrine of God. To love the absolutely immutable good which is above time and growth is

16. Vatican II, *Pastoral Constitution on The Church Today* (Gaudium et Spes), Pt. II, chap. 1, pp. 47–50.
17. Bigham and Mollegen, *loc. cit.*, p. 383.
18. *Ibid.*, p. 384; Augustine *On Marriage and Concupiscence* I, pp. 8, 15, 18.

of necessity to turn from the mutable and the temporal. Augustine cannot see it otherwise, given his presuppositions about God and the world. Hence he remains in the end double-minded about the human loves. They participate in God's being and may lead toward blessedness in him. Yet in themselves as directed toward this world, even toward the beloved in marriage, they are inferior to the love of God and therefore dispensable. No one can say that this doctrine is unheroic or without its insight into the issue of ultimate concern. But is it in truth the right appraisal of the human loves? Augustine never quite brings his view of sexual love within the range of his deepest insight as to what loving another in God means: turning the whole current of love for self and neighbour into the channel of the love of God 'which suffers no stream to be drawn off from itself by whose diversion its own volume would be diminished'.[19] To turn the human loves into the stream of devotion to God is one thing, to set devotion to God apart as one kind of love which makes others inferior is another. It is here that later Christian thought in the Reformation began to seek another solution.

Over against this disparagement of earthly loves it is also characteristic of Augustine's teaching that he declares the constructive power of love in the moral life. Virtue itself is 'nothing else than the perfect love of God' and the classic four virtues are rightly to be understood as four forms of love:

> Temperance is love giving itself entirely to that which is loved; fortitude is love readily bearing all things for the sake of the loved object; justice is love serving only the loved object, and therefore ruling rightly; prudence is love distinguishing with sagacity what hinders it and helps it.[20]

We see even more clearly why St. Augustine can speak with such freedom of love as the sole rule for the moral life. It is because love takes form in the virtues. It is their inner tendency and spirit. 'Our root is our charity, our fruits are our works."[21]

We are especially interested in the relation of love to justice since much modern discussion of theological ethics has turned upon this point. Reinhold Niebuhr in particular has pointed out how actual structures of justice in history represent balances of power informed by fear and self-defence as much as by any kind of love.

For St. Augustine it is clear where we must begin. Love as *caritas*, the love of God and neighbour, is inseparable from justice. 'The

19. *On Christian Doctrine*, I, xxii, p. 21.
20. *On the Morals of the Catholic Church*, XV.
21. *Psalms*, LI, p. 12 (Synthesis, sec. 607).

enlarging of the heart is the delight we take in justice.'[22] So Augustine has the interesting teaching that justice itself must be loved. As it is loved there is progress in the Christian life.

> Inchoate charity, therefore, is inchoate justice; progressing charity is progressing justice; great charity is great justice; perfect charity is perfect justice.[23]

Now the deep realism of this position comes into view. For the love which unites man with God must do its work in a humanity which has fallen away from God. There are two cities: one determined by love of God and one by man's self-love. Thus Augustine begins the *City of God*. What then are the requirements and possibilities of love in the history of the earthly city? Here St. Augustine's realistic view of political life is of such character that Reinhold Niebuhr can call him the wisest political philosopher in Christian history.[24] What St. Augustine does is to see the way of love in history as requiring the adjustment of life to political necessities. The two cities are mingled in history. A just state is possible, but only on terms in which the state can make demands upon the citizens whether they belong to the church or not:

> The celestial kingdom groans amid the citizens of the terrestrial kingdom; and sometimes the terrestrial kingdom . . . exacts service from the citizens of the Kingdom of heaven, and the Kingdom of Heaven exacts service from the citizens of the terrestrial kingdom.[25]

The principles which guide those who have begun to love God are justified in the service of love. It is St. Augustine who gives the most radical principle of freedom in all Christian ethics. 'Love and do as you will.' But to love is to be responsible, and human history is lived out under the conditions of the sinfulness of man. This means that society is involved in discovering and enforcing certain proper restraints in the common life. God intended equality among men; but 'private property, slavery, imperialism, the State itself, appear in post-Fall society as regulations of God to preserve nature, which is always being disrupted by sin'.[26] Justice thus appears as the rough, necessary, coerced order of human societies which is not wholly antithetical to love, since it serves the purpose of God in the

22. *Psalms*, CXVIII Serm. X, 6 (Synthesis, 601).
23. *On Nature and Grace*, LXX, 84 (Synthesis, 610).
24. Reinhold Niebuhr, *Christian Realism and Political Problems* (New York: Charles Scribner's Sons, 1953, pp. 120–1; London: Faber & Faber, 1954).
25. *Psalms* LII.
26. Bigham and Mollegen, *loc. cit.*, p. 391.

creation and history. But the actual enforcement of justice, and the struggle for it shows everywhere the tragic consequences of sin.

Yet St. Augustine does not quite leave the ethic of love in unresolvable dilemmas. History has a tendency, a direction. God's Kingdom is its goal. History moves toward the Kingdom, not as an irresistible progress in time; but as participating in the final resolution which God will bring about. Hence for St. Augustine there is a continual transformation taking place in life. Ceaselessly, surely, with infinite patience God remakes the world through his grace as the heavenly city grows and is fulfilled. The Church can undertake to convert the world and culture with an ultimate assurance. H. Richard Niebuhr sees St. Augustine as giving classic expression to the conversionist type of relation of Christ to culture.[27] Every level and type of human value is internally open to fulfilment through its relationship to God's goodness. There is nothing positively good in the world which cannot be incorporated into the life which loves God. Beauty, friendship, social justice are all material for the higher order which love seeks. Augustine is also willing to use the power of the state to bring heretics and schismatics into line. They cannot be converted by force, no one can; but there is a proper ordering of human life which should be carried out by the Church in the name of the heavenly city.

Human life displays everywhere a tragic disorder. Human loves are directed toward the self and the things that immediately gratify the self. Man allows himself to be borne away by his own weight from his true centre and life in God. This is so in spite of the fact that all man's knowing and loving, so far as it is an expression of his being, is a search for God. 'The learner who is questioned moves inwardly to God to understand immutable truth.'[28] Yet disaster overtakes him. Augustine sees sin as intervening in the movement toward God. Here is a paradox, for it is the very achievement of good, the sense of divinity, which tempts man to pride. Man overreaches himself. He becomes puffed up with knowledge and power. He forgets God and tries to make himself secure in his godlike qualities. The plunge into non-being can take the form of self-gratification and self-righteousness in the powerful and arrogant. But these momentary delights are empty and self-destructive.

Salvation which is the fulfilment of love cannot come from ourselves or our own will. It must come from God. Augustine understands God's incarnation in Jesus Christ as the act of the divine love coming to meet man, and reversing the destructive direction

27. H. Richard Niebuhr, *Christ and Culture*, Chapter 6.
28. Augustine, *De Musica*, Bk. 6, xii, 36.

which human love has taken. We have already seen that faith must be the foundation of a right understanding of the truth, and now we fully see why. The only disclosure of the truth which can rightly order the loves corrupted by sin is the divine humility which is displayed in Jesus Christ.

Augustine never tires of portraying the tremendous paradox of the incarnation. The almighty God has clothed himself in the rags of the humblest man:

> He is at once above, and below: above in Himself, below in His people; above with the Father, below in us. . . . So then Christ is rich and poor. As God he is rich, as Man poor. Yea, rich too now as Very Man, he hath ascended into heaven, and sitteth at the right hand of the Father; yet he is still poor here, is a-hungered and athirst and naked.[29]

The *agape* of God has come to us in a way which transcends our rational grasp and our human powers to respond. God's grace does what human power alone cannot do. Augustine's view of the way in which love does its work in the world is therefore a thoroughgoing doctrine of grace. He does not deny that there is a movement toward God in our existence in so far as we are drawn in some way toward the source of our being. Grace answers man's search for truth and beauty. But the human search has fallen into disarray and obscurity. The power of God alone can revolutionize our orientation and set us on the straight path.

The question of how God redeems us in Christ led to the later theories of atonement. Augustine has some suggestions in this direction but it is worth noting that he does not have what later systematic theology would call a fully developed Christology. Neither the incarnation nor atonement is given anything like a precise formulation. He knows the Church and its Sacraments as the channels of grace. In Baptism and the Eucharist the outward signs of invisible grace are present and effective mediators of the grace of Christ. While we speak of the mediation of grace we recognize that Augustine sees a profound tension between the immediacy of God and man's estrangement from him. This tension exists throughout the life of faith even as we are being ingrafted into Christ's body:

> We seek to attain God by loving Him; we attain to Him not by becoming entirely what He is, but in nearness to Him, and in wonderful and sensible contact with Him, and in being inwardly illuminated and occupied by His truth and holiness.[30]

---

29. Augustine, *Sermons* (de Script, N. T.), CXXIII, iv. 4 (*Synthesis*, 303).
30. *On the Morals of the Catholic Church*, I, xi, 18.

In Christ God gave the Spirit of his love to men. We grasp this by faith which only gradually and always imperfectly in this life becomes conformed to the Spirit of love. So there is a paradox in true holiness:

> Let whosoever shall have been delivered from sin remember what he was. . . . For then he beareth another man to be healed, if he shall remember that he himself was healed. Therefore let each call to mind what he was, and whether he be not still so; and he then will succour him that still is what he is no longer.[31]

It is the reality of grace present in Christ which is Augustine's constant theme. It is this which we lay hold upon in faith. But faith is possible only because love works beyond our deserving. We can begin to walk though feebly in the way of love because 'The Way has come to us'.[32]

(2)

AUGUSTINIAN EXISTENTIALISM

Father M. C. D'Arcy's penetrating study, *The Mind and Heart of Love*, shows how a contemporary Catholic doctrine which moves within the Augustinian and Thomist traditions discovers the inner tension and unresolved problems in the position.[33] The tension here occurs with variations in each of our three types. It stems from the fact that the tradition has had a too simple doctrine of man, and therefore the doctrines of love seem inadequate as man tries to cope with his existence in the world of the twentieth century. St. Augustine of course knows the depths in man. 'Is not man's heart an abyss? For what is there more profound than that abyss?'[34] This is why Augustine is read by existentialists with a profound sense of kinship. Yet Augustine has a security, both dialectical and spiritual, in his answers to the human questions which contemporary searchers cannot quite share.

The feeling that classic culture had a too simple view of man is related to both sides of the human situation, man's creativity and his chaotic freedom. There is a radical capacity in human freedom to create realms of meaning and reshape the world, but it can also

31. *Psalms*, XXV, p. 15.
32. *Sermons* (De Script. N.T.), CXLI iv, 4 (Synthesis, 329).
33. M. C. D'Arcy, S.J., *The Mind and Heart of Love* (London: Faber & Faber, 2nd rev. ed. 1954; New York: Henry Holt).
34. *Psalms*, XLI, 13. See the texts in Przywara, *op. cit.*, chapter XIV.

deny meaning to existence, reject God, and plunge toward self-destruction. In this uniqueness of human freedom, man's power to shape the meaning of life in his own image, there lies a seemingly unlimited capacity for sensing the absurdity, the futility, the ambiguities of existence, and for rejecting any unifying order in things. Man's reason becomes a conquering power in his dealing with nature, but it is a suspect and corruptible instrument, especially when man tries to understand himself. All the modern existentialisms have described this radically problematic and insecure situation of man, and have attacked the rational images of being. This has had a profound effect on how the human loves are seen. Some find the meaning of life in a present, intimate and manageable kind of human love, such as that for another person, or in the ecstasies of group belonging. For others love becomes a false value, a lie, and a deception. The history of man is viewed as a story of naked power, destructiveness and cruelty. Is love an option for man as he tries to wring some meaning out of a tangled mass of suffering and strife? Can any ethic of love cope with the politics of nuclear threat and population explosion? We shall see how within each of the three traditions of Christian love there is a search for an authentic realism about man and history which results in a strain upon the traditional forms.

Father D'Arcy's book takes the problem of the self as its centre, and seeks to interpret love in relation to the complex and dynamic view of selfhood which has emerged in modern psychology. D'Arcy moves into the problem by raising again a classic question in the medieval doctrine of man and his love. 'We want to know how a man who is by nature bound to love himself can also love God more than himself. If it can be shown that in loving himself truly he is in fact loving God more than himself then the difficulty is answered.' The question remains, D'Arcy points out, 'whether a human being imitates God by seeking itself and its own perfection or by going outside itself to want only God'.[35] There is a mystery here in the self-realizing love called *Eros* and the self-giving love called *Agape*. This mystery must be traced down into the existence of two loves within man. D'Arcy develops the doctrine of the two loves by identifying *eros* as belonging to the *essential* self. This love seeks fulfilment. It is possessive, masculine, imperious, and it denies the completion of personal being. It dominates the rational impulses and the will to understand. The other love is identified with the *existential* self. It is the love which seeks to give itself away. It is emotionally powerful in its heedlessness. It is feminine, intuitive,

35. D'Arcy, *op. cit.*, pp. 93, 98.

and spendthrift. It is the *agape* in the self. D'Arcy thus finds in human nature these structures which are used by and completed in the movement of divine love toward the fulfilment of life.

In insisting that there is a love in the self which lives by giving itself away to the other, D'Arcy asserts an Augustinian theme against the tendency toward intellectualism in St. Thomas, although D'Arcy's method of philosophical reflection remains close to St. Thomas. D'Arcy believes that this analysis of the two loves can encompass the complexity in the human self which has been exposed by modern existentialism. He gives attention to the work of Hunter Guthrie who combines essentialist and existentialist doctrines by distinguishing between the essential and existential Egos. The former looks within to its own becoming, the latter seeks an Absolute to which it can give itself. In consequence:

> In loving God there is no loss. The full love act, therefore if God so will, takes in both the ideal of the essential self and the existential self. There is the sheer giving and ecstatic happiness in being possessed by everlasting love, and concomitantly with this and fusing with it is the joy of possessing God as He is by means of the beatific vision.[36]

Without committing himself to an existentialist doctrine which gives primacy to the will over the intellect, D'Arcy is attracted to this position, for it fits in with his doctrine of the two loves. 'The love of self is a true love; it is necessary for the permanent selfhood and splendour of our finite beauty; it is not just a part of another love: it is a co-efficient with it; the *animus* (eros) and the *anima* (agape) give each other mutual assistance and love; the essential self and the existential self together make the "I", the person. Eros and Agape are not enemies but friends.'[37] This is D'Arcy's synthesis. He thus restates the Augustinian position beautifully in relation to a radical contemporary distinction between essence and existence, and the two movements of love in the self.

Some queries to D'Arcy bring out the essential problem which remains in this modern Augustinian solution. The internal tension in the Augustinian doctrine finally comes to the surface. We see that Augustine's metaphysics make the self-giving movement of love into a perplexity.

D'Arcy interprets the two loves in the following equation:

$$essence = mind = self \ love$$
$$existence = passion = other \ love$$

36. *Ibid.*, p. 273; cf. Hunter Guthrie, *Introduction au Problème de l'Histoire de la Philosophie* (Paris: Librairie Félix Alcan, 1937).
37. *Ibid.*, p. 304. (Parentheses mine).

This has consequences. One is that the mind is identified with self-seeking, and D'Arcy sees no way out of this.[38] All self-giving, therefore, has to come from something other than the mind. And second, since *eros*, the mind's love, is identified with essence, the striving, passionate, existential elements have to be formed elsewhere than in mind. This means that mind is something less than concrete existence. But are not intellectual passions just as 'existential' as any other? D'Arcy says, 'To be a person is to be essentially in search of a person. Love presupposes knowledge, but it can to some degree do without it; what it needs is the living and actual being itself.'[39] To some degree indeed love can do without knowledge; but only to a degree, hence the doctrine becomes unclear. If knowledge is essential to love, then knowledge and the mind's participation are as truly 'existential' as the passion of self-giving.

In the quotation we have given D'Arcy makes a suggestion that points to the real problem. Something, he says, must unify *eros* and *agape* as they work together so that they 'give each other mutual assistance and love'. But what is this love which unifies? Is it essential or existential? Clearly, it must be both. The distinction breaks down. St. Augustine would say, of course, that it is love itself, the love in God's being, which constitutes all essence and existence. D'Arcy holds to the essentially Augustinian doctrine that it is love in God which is the key to anthropology, the one love which is grounded in the being of God himself. But what is it in the being of God which makes it possible for love to be both self-giving and self-fulfilling? This is the real problem. D'Arcy does not carry through in his doctrine of God the radical suggestion of his own solution, that essential love in God's being involves a self-giving. The reason he does not, I suggest, is that he remains within the Augustinian metaphysical scheme even though he seeks a new anthropology. D'Arcy never questions the Augustinian-Thomist assumption of God's absoluteness as being-itself which receives no increment of value from the world. D'Arcy never reconsiders his position in the light of the analysis of *agape* to ask whether the love of God is also a participating and suffering love. He says, indeed, that the Christian revelation tells us that 'God has shown to us, *so far as is compatible with the unchanging plenitude of his nature*, a love like to that of self-donating and self-giving'.[40] But how far is this compatible? That is the decisive question which D'Arcy leaves unanswered as the whole Augustinian tradition leaves it. Again he says perceptively, to be a person is to be in search of a person.[41] But

38. *Ibid.*, p. 318.
39. *Ibid.*, p. 321.
40. *Ibid.*, p. 245 (italics mine).
41. *Ibid.*, p. 321.

this should lead to some consideration of what it means for God to be 'in search of man', to use Abraham Heschel's fine phrase. Notice that D'Arcy says search for the other person is *essential* to being a person. Must we not say that it is in the essence of the divine love to seek communion with the creature? Here a new perspective arises which the Augustinian type can never quite acknowledge.

The difficulty we have found in the Augustinian synthesis lies in its metaphysical doctrine. Both Nygren and D'Arcy seem to sense this though neither considers the question whether another metaphysical outlook might be compatible with the radical nature of love as grace, and with God's self-involvement in history. We return to this metaphysical issue in the next two chapters. Now, however, we consider the next major type of love in the Christian tradition. This type is serenely unconcerned with metaphysical problems. It seeks the spirit of love directly in the imitation of Christ. We call this type Franciscan, because it found its supreme expression in the medieval period in St. Francis of Assisi.

(3)

THE FRANCISCAN TYPE

The life and spirit of St. Francis of Assisi are well known, perhaps too well known through certain stereotyped images. There are paradoxes and perplexities in the Franciscan way of life no less than in other Christian ways and most of them appear at some point in Francis' own career. The difficulties in the Franciscan way arise, most of them, from the very directness, simplicity and absoluteness of the expression of love in human existence. It attempts to make a radical break with the forms of possession and privilege, and from all compromise with the world which eats away at the spirit. It is the imitation of him who had no place to lay his head, who went about doing good, asked forgiveness for his enemies, refused all special power and status, and who lived in communion with God the Father and with all men who would respond. For St. Francis this way is possible because it has been taken by Jesus. Thus the Franciscan lives in full dependence upon the incarnation, as does the Augustinian. But for St. Francis and his followers the spirit of love leads to radical nonconformity amid the patterns of culture with their structures of power and privilege. Love must take form in humble service and its source is personal union with the spirit of Jesus.

We can understand the freedom and radicalness of this Franciscan way when we see it within the spiritual expectancy which characterized the beginning of the thirteenth century. St. Augustine's view of history was ultimately optimistic since its end term is the Kingdom of God; but we have seen how this was adjusted to a patient and complex view of history in which the two cities of church and world are mingled in cultural creativity and conflict. St. Augustine died experiencing deep despair as the barbarians sacked Rome. In contrast St. Francis's age had an ecstatic hopefulness which found its prophetic voice in the strange mystic and biblical interpreter, the monk Joachim of Flora (1154–1202). Joachim meditated on the biblical texts and especially upon the signs of the passing away of the present age and the coming new age. He worked out a view of history in biblical terms in which the first period is that of the Father, characterized by the rigour of the law, and man's response of servile obedience and fear. The second period, that of the Son, is the rule of grace, marked by the requirement of filial obedience. Significantly, this period is dominated by the clerics. The third age is that of Spirit, the age of the plenitude of love, in which man responds in liberty and love. It is this third age which is trembling to be born, Joachim says. Indeed it is in some way already present. The ages interpenetrate in Joachim's thought, which is not without its subtleties.[42]

It is not certain that St. Francis knew Joachim's thought directly. Paul Sabatier thinks he probably did.[43] Certainly the radical freedom and expectancy of spirit which Joachim articulates is present in St. Francis. We find an illustration of the interpenetration of the two ages, as St. Francis experiences the frustration and perplexity of dealing with the powers of established institutions and finally has to compromise with temporal possessions and make his peace with the Church. The most important element in the Franciscan doctrine of love is related to Joachim's theme of radical freedom. The spirit of love breaks through the established institutions, the ethical order and personal relationships. It cuts its own channel with a cheerful abandon. It can despise the timidities and adjustments of ordinary existence. It creates human community where none was before through the directness of loving, humble action. The return to

42. George Williams, *Wilderness and Paradise in Christian Thought* (New York: Harper & Row, 1962), pp. 58ff. Cf. Herbert Grundman, *Neue Forschungen uber Joachim von Fiore* (Marburg: Simons Verlag, 1950).

43. Paul Sabatier, *The Life of St. Francis of Assisi* (New York: Charles Scribner's Sons, 1930), pp. 50–1. On the study of the Franciscan Sources see chapter by F. C. Burkitt in *St. Francis of Assissi, 1226–1926: Essays in Commemoration* (London: University of London Press, 1926), and Sabatier.

'evangelical simplicity' carries the explosive power of a new witness.

Underneath this simplicity and radical freedom there are decisions to be made. The world has to be dealt with and persuaded. Life involves relationships to things, to institutions, to the needs of people. Let us see how St. Francis meets these requirements, and compare his solutions with those of one who belongs to the Franciscan type but who lived in the twentieth century—Albert Schweitzer.

These are the main themes of the Franciscan way of love:

First, there is the directness and simplicity of the rule of love nowhere better expressed than in the first rule which Francis laid down for his order. Paul Sabatier sums up the spirit of the first rule:

> all is alive, free, spontaneous; it is a point of departure, an inspiration; it may be summed up in two phrases: the appeal of Jesus to man, 'Come follow me', the act of man, 'He left all and followed him'.[44]

This is a rule for a monastic order, and there are certain decisions which it requires. Love sets itself free by renouncing the kinds of obligations which would prevent its direct exercise. 'To buy love I have entirely renounced the world and myself,' St. Francis declares.[45]

This means the renunciation of grades of power and privilege and results in the attempt to create an essential equality and democracy in the order. It is true this democracy was never fully achieved, and one of St. Francis's temptations lay in the imperious use of his authority, but his intent is clear. 'As for me, I ask of God no privilege unless it be that I may have none.'[46] We note also the origin of the name 'Brothers Minor'. 'Let the brethren . . . never take an office which shall put them over others. . . .'[47]

The renunciation of privilege is less important (and less drastic) than the renunciation of possessions. The injunction to sell all that one has and give it to the poor is taken literally by St. Francis and is the rule for all members of his order. He even wanted the rule to keep the scriptural injunction for the traveller, 'take nothing for your journey, neither staff, nor scrip, nor bread, nor money' but this was omitted under pressures of necessity.[48] The brothers were to work to earn their bread; and if earnings were insufficient they might beg the little they needed. They owned the tools of their trades, but little else. Nothing illustrates more clearly the concrete meaning of the

---

44. Sabatier, *op. cit.*, p. 253.
45. Jöhannes Jorgensen, *St. Francis of Assisi* (London and New York: Longmans Green, 1954), Revₐ Ed., p. 78.
46. Quoted Sabatier, p. 204.
47. Quoted Sabatier, p. 117.   48. Jörgensen, *op. cit.*, p. 251.

Franciscan practice of love than the attitude toward wealth. It is renounced by those who choose the way, and it is denounced as an evil. St. Francis can speak of it as a sacrament 'of evil'.[49] Yet he does not call upon all men to give up their possessions. It is goodness and kindness, forgiveness, repentance, which can be asked of all. Those who become members of the order must indeed renounce all wealth, and thus the way of poverty will address its own message to those who are bound by their possessions. Francis does not say 'you cannot love and possess', but he does say, 'here is what love requires as we see it in the Lord'.

All force and violence are renounced. The way is the way of peace-making and this means renunciation of military service, and of all sharing in coercive enforcement of the state power. The third order was founded as a peacemaking order renouncing all military service.[50]

Is learning a possession which must also be renounced, or is it a good which can be pursued in love? The attitude of St. Francis here also is ruled by the spirit of renunciation for the sake of the purity of love. He does not command ignorance, but he does see in the search for learning and the intellectual life a temptation which must be exposed and chastened. We remember that humility is essential to love. Learning easily leads to pride, the worst of sins. St. Francis fears that in competition with the Dominicans his order will become another school dedicated to acquiring knowledge. 'A man's knowledge is just what he does' is a saying attributed to him,[51] a motto which has an important history in the philosophies of Western civilization.

The history of love is full of ironies and one of those is the Franciscan tradition that this non-intellectual faith with its directness and derogation of philosophy and learning produced a line of Christian philosophers which includes some of the great names in intellectual history: St. Bonaventura, Roger Bacon, Duns Scotus, and William of Ockham. One of Francis's sympathetic interpreters sees him as making incarnate in the integrity of loving action the essential Christian doctrines. 'All the highest intellectual conclusions of the Fathers appear in St. Francis under the aspect of reality, of deeds, of life.'[52]

49. Celano, *St Francis* II, ch. 35
50. Sabatier, pp. 267–8. Cf. Rigobert Koper, O.F.M., *Das Weltverständnis des Hl. Franziskus von Assisi* (Dietrich-Coelde-Verlag, 1959).
51. 'Franciscan Thought and Modern Philosophy' by Camillo Pellizi in *Essays in Commemoration, op. cit.*, p. 165. Cf. 'The First One Hundred Years of the Franciscan School of Oxford' by A. G. Little in the same volume.
52. Pellizi, *op. cit.*, p. 204.

For the first Franciscans the practice of the way was not through theological reflection but in preaching and healing and other forms of personal service. The ministry to the poor and sick is the cherished and familiar picture. The labour is manual labour. The deeds are the meeting of obvious human needs. The element of self-renunciation is clear. Marriage is renounced. There are mortifications of the flesh. The sense of identification with the sufferings of Jesus enters into the heart of religious devotion, as is witnessed by St. Francis's reception of the *stigmata*. Yet it is a joyful asceticism, and here we come upon one of the distinctive marks of the Franciscan type, its happy and lyric quality. It is the Franciscans who have linked the Gospel love with love of nature, the spirit of communion with the animals and the whole creation. We can discount some of the sentimentalities which have grown up around the image of St. Francis, but the genuineness of his delight in the created world, and the expression of interior joy in outward song is inescapable.[53]

As the new way found its form within the larger structure of the church the strain between Francis and the established powers becomes a familiar part of the history. He never separated himself from the *ecclesia* or its forms of worship. The way of love is sustained by the sacramental life. Daily mass is part of the rule.

The deepest note in the way, however, is sounded only when we come to the identification of the lover with Christ. It is the union of the servant with the master, of follower with leader, of forgiven sinner with the Lord of mercy. This union is the source of love's power. Just before he receives the stigmata Francis prays that he may feel in his own soul and body the suffering of Jesus, and, this is decisive for the meaning of love, that he may receive into his own heart that 'excessive charity by which thou, the son of God, wast inflamed, and which actuated thee willingly to suffer so much for us sinners'.[54]

The source of love is the personal bond with him who made love incarnate; and the bond is an immediate personal communion of spirit. This is the real sense of the imitation of Christ. It is being conformed to the love which informed the incarnate Lord. We may call this 'Christ-mysticism' if we wish. It is a mysticism which may culminate in such ecstatic signs as that experienced by St. Francis; but its essence is the personal union of spirit with the love of Christ in a way of life guided by the command of complete devotion.

The desire for freedom from compromise and restriction which

53. Jörgensen, *op. cit.*, p. 118.
54. From the *Actusbeat Francisci Fioretti* (The Little Flowers of St. Francis) in Jörgensen, *op. cit.*, pp. 297f.

breathes through the Franciscan spirit is not a solution of all problems. The history of St. Francis's life is filled with tension. His constant fear of the corruption of the order is part of the price paid for his attempt to keep free from all attachments which compromise love. In actual fact a continual series of adjustments had to be made to the authority of the Church. Further, this rigorous way is for those who can renounce the world to follow it; but it cannot be for all men. St. Francis seems quite clearly to accept this. Therefore the question of the possibility of the imitation of Christ in love is really not answered. Critical reflections also arise in connection with the psychological ambiguities of motivation. It is not a denial of the reality of love in the Franciscan way to point out that the will to power can take many forms and one of them may be the commitment to humility. St. Francis's self-knowledge seems to have brought this truth to consciousness for him as he sought to guide his order. As we read the words of his will we are struck by the combination of humility with the final attempt of the founder of a community to impose his decisions upon it for all time to come. He writes:

> I interdict absolutely by obedience all the brothers, clerics and laymen, to introduce glosses in the Rule or in this Will, under pretext of explaining it. But since the Lord has given me to speak and to write the Rule and these words in a clear and simple manner, without commentary, understand them in the same way, and put them in practice until the end.[55]

The will to be a servant can conceal an imperious desire to control. This is not to suggest that this form of love is more subject to pathological distortion than others; but only to say that the Franciscan type with its thirst for absolute love is subject to all the human temptations.

We can say, then, that the Franciscan type of expression of the love revealed in the Gospel has its characteristic forms. The very search for purity of spirit is itself one form of human expression. St. Francis shows the holy impatience of Gospel love to be free from stale compromise and lethargy, but he also has to find ways in which the life of simplicity and purity can take shape in the historical situation in which he lives. He must deal with the church, with the powers of a feudal society, and with the disciplines, temptations, and style of life of a monastic order, as he seeks heroically to have that order conform to the spirit of love.

The Franciscan type erupts perennially and unpredictably in history. There is something untameable in it. Personal dedication

55. Quoted in Sabatier, p. 339.

takes the form of dramatic protest and ethical judgment against an age or society. Our twentieth century has recognized its reappearance in a few lonely figures, and one of these of greatest ethical stature is Albert Schweitzer.

(4)

ALBERT SCHWEITZER: A MODERN FRANCISCAN

To characterize Albert Schweitzer as a twentieth-century Franciscan is not intended to establish a rigid parallelism between these two disparate lives in very different times. It is however relevant to the history of love to show that the force and mode of Schweitzer's life exhibits a fundamental kinship with the spirit of the Franciscan type. Schweitzer, the highly talented scholar and artist, renounced the privileges of life in European society to bring healing to people in the steaming jungle of Africa. Again the direct power of the example speaks for itself. Schweitzer responded in several ways to the question of why he went to Africa. His replies taken together suggest that he never really intended to give a reply. If one cannot see or feel the meaning of the act, there is no use trying to say it in words.[56]

Schweitzer's pattern of life exhibits much of the simplicity and impatience with organization that one finds in St. Francis. There is the same renunciation of the accepted structure of values in the world of affairs, and the same persistent problems of compromise and adjustment to necessities. His human relationships show the direct personal concern for hurt and suffering people. There is the same love of nature, and the principle of non-injury to life.

There appear to be two important respects in which Schweitzer's way differs from the Franciscan. The first is his high evaluation of intellectual and artistic creativity. In his love for music he shares with all the Franciscans the tradition of God's troubadors. But he also regarded his philosophy of civilization as an essential part of his life work. So the 'renaissance ideal' of creativity is upheld, and Schweitzer was explicitly conscious of his affinity with the renaissance spirit.[57]

The second fundamental difference is Schweitzer's independence of ecclesiastical order, and his freedom from identification with any

56. Of innumerable books on Schweitzer I believe the most illuminating and balanced from a theological point of view is Henry Clark, *The Ethical Mysticism of Albert Schweitzer* (Boston: Beacon Press, 1962).

57. Albert Schweitzer, 'Goethe, His Personality and His Work' in *Goethe and the Modern Age*, ed. by Arnold Bergstrasser (Chicago: Henry Regnery Co., 1950).

traditional pattern of religious life. He maintained the devotion of a Christian family worship in the hospital, and he never rejected the Christian tradition, but his life and work were not constituted within a religious order or sect, and he was responsible to no over-arching religious institution. Further, his philosophy of life appears to seek a universal perspective beyond the bounds of every religious tradition including the Christian.

The deepest affinity between Schweitzer and St. Francis lies in the interior religiousness which finds expression in the directness of the spirit of love. Schweitzer's radical demonstration of love in the form of unpretentious human service, under conditions which involve personal renunciation, corresponds directly to St. Francis's rule of love and humility as the authentic foundation of a way of life free from attachments of privilege and power. The act of service to the neighbour under conditions which require sacrifice marks the Franciscan protest against the world's tendency to trim love down to its own size. Schweitzer explicitly relates his doctrine to the tradition of ethical love. He says his principle of 'reverence for life' is broader and therefore more 'colourless' than what love has meant in the tradition, 'but it has the same energies within it'.[58]

We come then to Schweitzer's relationship to Jesus as the foundation and impulse of his way of life. We saw that for St. Francis personal identification with Jesus and dependence upon him is the centre of his being. The familiar closing words of Schweitzer's *Quest of the Historical Jesus* suggest a similar relationship:

> He comes to us as One unknown, without a name, as of old, by the lake-side, He came to those men who knew Him not. He speaks to us the same word: 'Follow thou me!' and sets us to the tasks which He has to fulfil for our time. He commands.
>
> And to those who obey Him, whether they be wise or simple, He will reveal Himself in the toils, the conflicts, the sufferings which they shall pass through in His fellowship, and, as an ineffable mystery, they shall learn in their own experience Who He is.[59]

Did this remain the source of Schweitzer's commitment, or is it a stage in a growth toward something beyond personal mysticism? Perhaps this question cannot be answered. The life speaks for itself, but there is enough to indicate that the carpenter of Nazareth was recognized as 'speaking the same word of command' in the Lambarene doctor's daily existence, even to his carpentering.

58. Albert Schweitzer, 'Ethics for Twentieth Century Man,' *The Saturday Review of Literature*, Vol. XXXVI, No. 24, June 13, 1953.

59. Albert Schweitzer, *The Quest of the Historical Jesus* (London: A. & C. Black, 1931), 2nd English ed. p. 401.

Schweitzer was an authentic saint, exhibiting the power of radical dedication to express the meaning of love. He was also an intellectual, a philosopher, and moralist who continued throughout his life wrestling with the issues of modern civilization. It is here that we find in Schweitzer a break with tradition similar to that which we found in D'Arcy. The traditional forms of ethical insight do not adequately comprehend the perplexity in which modern man finds himself when he tries to understand his place in nature, the dynamics of selfhood, and the ambiguities of history. Schweitzer shows how the Franciscan spirit in its very directness of attack on the problem of ethics finds perplexities which force a reappraisal of the foundations of ethical life. In a remarkable article in 1953 Schweitzer restated his reflections on the ethical tradition of Western man, and it is necessary to hear his argument.

Underneath man's quest for an ethical way of life Schweitzer sees a struggle which has not been sufficiently recognized, that between world-affirmation and world negation. The latter he finds in Hinduism, Buddhism, and in Ancient and Medieval Christianity. World affirmation he finds in the Hebrew prophets, the Chinese thinkers, in the Renaissance, and in modern thinkers. It is a large generalization, but the important point is the choice Schweitzer makes. 'Only the ethics which is allied to the affirmation of the world can be natural and complete.'[60] Christianity has never turned away from the world entirely; it has called for renunciation in order to transform the world and prepare for the Kingdom of God. Thus Schweitzer sees Jesus: 'In his ethics activity preserves all its rights and all its obligations.' Schweitzer then traces the history of ethics in the West, emphasizing the importance of the discovery that the ethics of love could be defended rationally, and the new enthusiasm this gave to philosophers. On the whole, he says, this confidence has dominated modern ethical theory until very recent times.

But now a perplexity has arisen in moral experience. The rational justification of compassion has become more difficult. Here Schweitzer discusses questions which critics of his position have often raised. How is it possible to have life at all without taking life? Does he not as a doctor take the life of bacteria, and does he not have to choose between saving a man and the animal who is attacking him? He must sometimes choose between the life of a mother and that of an unborn child. Here Schweitzer says we come into the realm of the arbitrary. We become guilty by necessity. This leads to an insight into the nature of the world process itself. The world as experienced offers no justification for compassion, because life is in conflict with

60. 'Ethics for Twentieth Century Man', *loc. cit.*

itself, 'Ethics can expect nothing from a true knowledge of the world'.

Schweitzer holds that the ethic of respect for life is based on the human will to live and that it follows we should respect the will to live wherever it exists. The good consists in preserving life, favouring it. Schweitzer now says this principle is even broader than love, for from it one may deduce the moral requirement of veracity, but this cannot be derived from love alone. We have then a universal obligation to enhance life, even though we find the creative process of the universe in conflict with itself. Schweitzer ends on a typically existentialist note, 'We live our existence instead of submitting to it'.

The new 'canticle of the sun' following Schweitzer would celebrate all living things, but recognize a dark mystery as well as beauty amidst the sun and stars and the struggle for life. The decision of the moral man requires the courage of risk in a world which does not yield a direct and obvious support of the principle of universal reverence. For the Christian this courageous decision is made in personal identification with the man Jesus, crucified for love. But again we have heard the contemporary note of perplexity struck. The Franciscan spirit finds itself less at home in the world than ever before, less able to give a direct assurance that such faith in love is the key to human existence. Yet in the dark insecurity of the world the light of a courageous and dedicated love may shine even more brightly.

(5)

THE EVANGELICAL WAY

The third way of love in the Christian tradition, like the Franciscan, intends a return to the purity of the Gospel. Like the Franciscan also it protests against the ecclesiastical order, a protest which appeals to the New Testament witness to Jesus Christ in judgment against the authority of the ecclesiastical tradition. But in contrast to the Franciscan way the Protestant Reformation understands the love of God as grace, as forgiveness given to man, rather than as a spirit which can be directly and immediately realized in man. Justification comes by faith in God's grace. It comes to man who is incapable of loving God and his neighbour through his own power or will. 'That which I would I do not, and that which I would not that I do. . . .' 'For I know that nothing good dwells within me, that is in my flesh. I can will what is right but I cannot do it. For I do not the good I want, but the evil I do not want is what I do. . . . Wretched man that I am! Who will deliver me from this body of death? Thanks be to God through Jesus Christ our Lord' (Romans 7: 18–19, 24–5).

Martin Luther's revolutionary conception of faith consists essentially in this, that the love of God which is man's hope and salvation has come to us in the form of the Servant which Christ has assumed. It comes only in this way to sinners. Hence the only form under which we can grasp the love of God is that which it takes when in faith we depend wholly upon God's mercy toward us. The way of love as a possibility for man rests wholly on faith in the divine forgiveness, and knowledge of the love of God comes only through that faith.

In his *Treatise on Christian Liberty* Luther interprets the Christological passage in Paul's letter to the Philippians, the great hymn of the incarnation, as the movement which takes place away from the equality with God which belonged rightly to Christ to the form of the Servant:

> Although Christ was filled with the form of God and rich in all good things, so that he needed no work and suffering to make him righteous and saved (for he had all this eternally), yet he was not puffed up by them and did not exalt himself above us and assume power over us, although he could rightly have done so; but, on the contrary, he so lived, laboured, worked, suffered, and died that he might be like other men and in fashion and in actions be nothing else than a man, just as if he had need of all these things and had nothing of the form of God. But he did all this for our sake, that he might serve us and that all things which he accomplished in this form of a servant might become ours.

So the form which love takes in Christ becomes also its form in us when we are joined to him in faith.

> So a Christian, like Christ his head, is filled and made rich by faith and should be content with this form of God which he has obtained by faith.[61]

The consequences which Luther and the other Reformers drew from this theme constitute the Protestant Reformation. It is by grace alone, and by faith alone that the love of God can be known, responded to, and expressed in love for the neighbour. Nothing in human effort or will, nothing in our human loves, distorted as they are by sin, can be relied upon as indications of the love of God.

61. Martin Luther, *The Freedom of a Christian*. Page references are to *Martin Luther; selections from his Writings*, ed. by John Dillenberger (New York: Doubleday, Anchor Books, 1961). The translation is by W. A. Lambert and Harold J. Grimm and is found in Luther's works, vol. 31, ed. by Harold Grimm (Philadelphia: Muhlenberg Press, 1957), pp. 74–5.

The image of God in man has been defaced, so that there remains only an awareness of God's power and law, and therefore of condemnation and wrath; but there is not in unregenerate man any power to know, express or share the love which alone can restore him to his true humanity. Self-love rules in actual man, and it contradicts the self-giving love which God has given in Christ. 'The dregs of the heart and the bilge of the old man remain, namely love of self (*amor sui ipsius*).' Luther continues:

> For none loves righteousness save this one, Christ, all others either love money, or comfort or honour, or else despising these things, they seek glory, or if they are the best of people they love themselves more than righteousness . . . thus while love of self remains, a man cannot love righteousness or do its works, though he may pretend to do so, and the consequence is that the so-called virtues of the philosophers, and indeed of all men, whether the lawyers or the theologians, may appear to be virtues, but are really only vices.[62]

The force of Luther's protest against the claims to authority of the established Church is to be found partly in the appeal to scripture, but also in this doctrine of man's condition and of the love of God as present only through God's grace. For notice, if this is the only way love can become known and powerful in human life, then all claims to possess or domesticate it, and all self-reliance on human virtue, power, and wisdom must be challenged in the name of the love of God. Thus the Protestant Reformation is a decisive moment in the history of the understanding of love, whether one accepts this position or not, for it raises in the sharpest possible way the question of the meaning of the human loves when seen in the light of the love of God as known to faith through Jesus. If love has a history then here is the point at which that history is shaped by a new understanding which claims to have its source in the history of Jesus.

Nygren's exposition of Luther as having recovered the pure motif of *agape* against all synthesis with *eros* does bring out the decisive aspect of Luther's treatment of love. Luther sets the *agape* of God sharply off against all human loves. Its character is its gracious outgoing, not to the desirable and lovely, but to the meeting of whatever need is present. Luther says, 'it (love) betakes itself not where it finds a good to enjoy but where it may confer good upon the poor and needy'. Nygren sees this as an obvious thrust at Augustine's 'fruition of love' in God.

62. Martin Luther, W.A. 57, 109.9; 110.3. They will be found in E. Gordon Rupp, *The Righteousness of God: Luther Studies* (London: Hodder & Stoughton, 1953), p. 203.

All that can be called Agape derives from God. From above his love comes down to us, and it must pass on through us to our neighbour. 'Amor crucis ex cruce natus' does not seek its own; and it has also left behind the idea of 'fruitio'.[63]

Nygren thus uses his doctrine of the contrasting motifs of *eros* and *agape* to point to what is distinctive in the Reformation conception of love, but he treats this as the only interpretation of love which really expresses the New Testament conception. We have found good reason to doubt that this extreme claim can be supported. There are several ways in which the relation of God's love and human love can be interpreted on the basis of the New Testament. What Nygren has shown is that the Reformers' doctrine of the gracious love of God as utterly beyond all calculation and analogy with human love establishes an aspect of New Testament faith which helps to shape every Christian perspective on love.

There are however certain characteristic issues which the Reformers' doctrine raises with other interpretations of love. Each type has to come to terms with persistent human problems in its own way, and the evangelical way has some especially acute tensions just because of its clear affirmation that the *agape* of God comes from the free grace of God beyond all human intent and capacity to grasp it.[64] Three major questions must be faced: how love comes to man; what love does; and how ethical decisions are possible in the life of faith.

As to the first of these questions, God's love comes to us in Jesus Christ, but we need to say how. Spirit and power are communicated but by what means? Love uses the means of grace in church and sacrament. Further, its communication is bound up in part with preaching. The Reformers probe this mystery, but never move from the view that love comes by grace alone, not by what men can think or prepare or grasp with their own power. It is received by faith alone, not by some answering love in man. In consequence God's

63. Nygren, *Agape and Eros*, p. 736 (London: S.P.C.K., rev. ed., 1953).

64. In confining attention to Luther and Calvin I am neglecting the 'left-wing' of the Reformation which adds a different note to the spiritual and ethical aspects of love. I am concerned with typology here and the ecstatic side of the Reformation, as manifest in the pietists and in such sects as the Diggers and Levellers belongs more nearly to the Franciscan type though it would require further analysis to support this. On this aspect of the Reformation with its importance for modern Protestantism see Reinhold Niebuhr, *The Nature and Destiny of Man*, Vol. II, Chap. 6, sec. III, and Ernst Troeltsch, *The Social Teaching of the Christian Churches* (London: Allen & Unwin, 1931; New York: Macmillan, 1931); George Hunston Williams, *Wilderness and Paradise in Christian Thought* (New York: Harper & Brothers, 1962), pp. 80–97.

love in his incarnate Word must be interpreted in fully personal terms but in a way which never permits any human power to contain it or control it.[65]

All the questions concerning the imputation of Christ's righteousness to sinners arise here. Is our new status as justified sinners one which can be understood dynamically as present transformation by the power of God, or is it sheer hope, relying upon the promise of God while we remain sinners? The positions of Reformation theology are varied and complex, but it is fair to say that Luther gives the central theme. Through the Word of God Incarnate in Jesus Christ, as that word is preached and heard, and with the clarifying and renewing power of the Holy Spirit at work in man, the believer begins to live by the promises of God. He is released from condemnation. The new life consists in becoming conformed to the image of Christ and joined in spirit with him. Love becomes effective through the personal relationship which God creates between the believer and Christ, and the believer's side of this relationship is faith which is casting his trust completely on to the grace of God.

Luther's expression of this relationship is full of metaphors, none of which is wholly adequate. Some are fully personal, some are analogies drawn from nature. There is the image of the seal impressed upon wax as Christ's image is impressed upon human nature. There is the glow of the iron which is heated in the fire. There is the well-known 'one cake' in which believer and Christ are 'baked' into union. In view of the importance of the analogy of marriage as used in the scripture it is noteworthy that Luther uses it freely:

> For if Christ is a bridegroom, he must take upon himself the things which are his bride's and bestow upon her the things that are his. If he gives her his body and very self, how shall he not give her all that is his? And if he takes the body of the bride, how shall he not take all that is hers? . . . Christ is God and man in one person. He has neither sinned nor died, and is not condemned, and he cannot sin, die, or be condemned; his righteousness, life and salvation are unconquerable, eternal, omnipotent. By the wedding ring of faith he shares in the sins, death and pains of hell which are his bride's. As a matter of fact he makes them his own. . . . He suffered, died, and descended into hell that he might overcome them all.[66]

Calvin's definition of faith is put with characteristic intellectual coolness and precision; but his doctrine of the Spirit as the present power of God making faith possible is clear:

65. Cf. Wilhelm Pauck, *The Heritage of the Reformation*, rev. and enlarged edition (Glencoe, Ill.: Free Press, 1961), Chaps. 3, 9–11.
66. *The Freedom of a Christian*, pp. 60–1.

Now we shall have a complete definition of faith, if we say, that it is a steady and certain knowledge of the Divine benevolence towards us, which, being founded on the truth of the gratuitous promise in Christ, is both revealed to our minds, and confirmed to our hearts, by the Holy Spirit.[67]

Calvin can also speak in personal and dynamic terms of the relation of the Christian to Christ. We are being transformed into his image:

Christ is not without us, but dwells within us; and not only adheres to us by an indissoluble connection of fellowship, but by a certain wonderful communion coalesces daily more and more into one body with us, till he becomes altogether one with us.[68]

These passages help us to grasp the meaning of the evangelical way. Later orthodoxies sometimes lost the significance of the re-making of the person through the relationship to the Person of Christ. Later pietism sometimes sentimentalized this relationship, making it depend upon emotional responsiveness, doctrinal correctness, or moralistic striving. For Luther and Calvin the key to the whole matter is that the love of God in Christ comes through the freedom of the Holy Spirit. It is grace, and its truth must be preached and received in faith. It depends upon no human law or pattern of life. It is the wind of God, blowing where it listeth. Yet the Reformers combined this radical freedom with the insistence that the new life is lived in the community of the church with its tradition, its scriptural authority and the celebration of the sacraments, for now the church is known as the community which God creates by his grace. Therefore the Church is itself subject to the judgment of God.

The second issue for the evangelical way concerns what the new life of faith requires of man. Man the sinner is utterly incapable of loving God or his neighbour. Sin is forgiven but not eliminated by grace. What then is to be the ethical expression of the new life?

We begin with Luther, whose picture of the redeemed life differs slightly from Calvin's. For Luther there is no question that a new life begins in faith. That life is the life of love to neighbour. Luther also speaks of love to God, and certainly of love to Christ, but neighbour love is the most prominent theme:

Behold from faith thus flow forth love and joy in the Lord, and from love a joyful, willing, and free mind that serves one's neighbour

67. John Calvin, *Institutes of the Christian Religion*, 7th American ed. (Philadelphia: Presbyterian Board of Christian Education, 1936), Book III, chap. 2, sec. 7.

68. *Ibid.*, Book III, chap. 2, sec. 29.

and takes no account of gratitude or ingratitude, or praise or blame, of gain or loss. . . .

Therefore if we recognize the great and precious things which are given us, as Paul says (Romans 5: 5) our hearts will be filled by the Holy Spirit with the love which makes us free, joyful, almighty workers and conquerors over all tribulations, servants of our neighbours, and yet lords of all.[69]

What, then, of the human loves, sex, play, artistic creativity? Are these to be displaced or transformed? As we read the Reformers today it is astonishing how little this question occurs in their writings. They do not seem to feel it as an acute problem. The reason may be that they have such a low view of man in his actuality. All his loves are but the refuse of a shattered original humanity, and it does not concern them what becomes of the ordinary human desires and attachments. One cannot deny that something of this attitude is present.

But there is a more important attitude, the 'secularizing' of the Christian life, and the refusal to make a distinction between a religious vocation and others. They accept the natural scene of life as the realm in which God works through every person. The relation here between the renaissance affirmation of human creativity and the reformation with its reliance on grace presents a complex and baffling problem. But we miss the real spirit of the reformation if we do not see the element of the renaissance with its acceptance of man's natural life as essentially good and the scene of his creative action. Luther and Calvin attack asceticism. They reject the necessity of celibacy or service in the church's ministry. The life of love is to be realized in the world of affairs.

Each one should do the works of his profession and station, not that by them he may strive after righteousness but that through them he may keep his body under control, be an example to others who also need to keep their bodies under control, and finally that by such works he may submit his will to that of others in the freedom of love.[70]

Calvin keeps this note of the uses of work as discipline in his doctrine of the Christian life. For Luther the tension between the freedom of love and the actuality of sin remains at a high pitch throughout. For Calvin there is more emphasis on ordered progress and growth in the redeemed life.[71]

We have said that the Reformation spirit accepts the natural scene

69. *The Freedom of a Christian*, p. 76.
70. *The Freedom of a Christian*, p. 78.
71. See *The Institutes*, Book III, chaps. 7–8.

of human life. This was given theological justification through the doctrine that grace comes through the personal relationship of God and man. The reformers of course did not reject the church, the sacraments, and the mediation of the witness through the scripture. They were not individualists. They did reject any view that grace is under the control of a human power, even that of the church. A man can be outside the sphere of grace even though he conforms to the objective requirements of the religious community. And he can remain inside the sphere of grace where he works in the secular community, for grace is not a special religious addition to the natural life of man. It is the personal presence of God in his mercy and forgiveness for every man as he is. The sacraments impart grace when faith is present and not otherwise.[72]

There is additional theological guidance for the life of the Christian in the world. God provides for the necessities of human living under the conditions of sin. Luther can boldly say that if all men were truly Christians there would be no need for 'secular sword or law'. There would still be need for work to meet human needs, but God has provided forms of law and government that man's life may be ordered, sin restrained, and the necessities of communal existence met. There are really two sides to Luther's doctrine:

> God has provided for non-Christians a different government outside the Christian estate and God's kingdom, and has subjected them to the sword, so that even though they would do so, they cannot practice their wickedness, and that, if they do they may not do it without fear nor in peace and prosperity. . . .[73]

But Luther joins to this special doctrine (and it is not clear just who he considers 'real' Christians), his more general view that God has made provision for all men in the orders of creation:

> Therefore you should cherish the sword or the government, even as the state of matrimony, or husbandry, or any other handiwork which God has instituted. As a man can serve God in the state of matrimony, in husbandry, or at trade, for the benefit of his fellow man, and must serve Him if necessity demand; just so he can serve God in the State and should serve him there.[74]

---

72. Martin Luther, *The Pagan Servitude of the Church*, Dillenberger edition, p. 300. The translation is from *The Reformation Writings of Martin Luther*, vol. 1, edited by Bertram Lee Woolf (London: Lutterworth Press, 1953).

73. Martin Luther, *Secular Authority: To What Extent It Should Be Obeyed*, Dillenberger edition, p. 370. Reprinted from *Works of Martin Luther*, vol. III (Philadelphia: A. J. Holman Co. and the Castle Press, 1930). Translation by J. J. Schindel.

74. *Ibid.*, p. 378.

This doctrine came to be called the 'Orders of creation'. It brings us to the third major issue in the Reformers' conception of love. The freedom of the Gospel is the freedom which makes love for the neighbour the criterion of all action and obligation. That is why Luther can say no law would be needed *if men were Christian*. But life, Christian or not, must be lived in the world as it is. What then are the criteria for Christian action in the world, in politics, in economics? Here the long history of the Protestant ethic begins. And it is here that new problems have emerged.

(6)

THE REFORMATION AND POLITICAL ETHICS

We have seen how in each of the other two types of doctrine of love contemporary experience raises questions which have forced a reconsideration of the meaning of love within that perspective. In the case of the Evangelical type the search for a political ethic has been one spiritual area in which the traditional formulations have proved inadequate, and we can explore this development. It is Reinhold Niebuhr in the twentieth century who, standing within the Reformation tradition, has become its foremost critic precisely at the point of the struggle for justice in history. Out of his reconsideration of the relation of the *agape* of the Gospel to political life he forged a new interpretation of the meaning of love in the Christian faith. He reaffirms the reformation views of the depth and persistence of sin, and the doctrine of justification by faith. But he seeks to show that these doctrines have a relevance to the contemporary experience of man, especially in his collective life, which the Reformers did not completely fathom. Niebuhr gives us, then, another example of the modification of the conception of love under the stress of contemporary experience.

In the background of Niebuhr's analysis there is Kierkegaard's view of anxiety as the source of man's temptation to pride and the flight from the self. With this clue to the nature of sin, Niebuhr has re-examined the actualities of man's political and economic behaviour. The result is a powerful description of the reality of sin which has few parallels in the history of Christian thought.[75]

75. The following summary is based upon Reinhold Niebuhr, *The Nature and Destiny of Man*, 2 vols. (New York: Charles Scribner's Sons, 1941; London: James Nisbet & Co., 1941–3). The analysis of sin is given mainly in Vol. I, chaps. 7–10; the criticism of traditional Christianity including that of the

Niebuhr believes the Reformers fell into two major errors. In Luther there is the danger of complacency about the established order, and a deflection of the Christian from radical reforming improvements in the struggle for justice. In Calvin there is the zeal to improve society; but there is a much too complacent view of the righteousness of Christians, and too little awareness of the elements of value and relative progress in the life of purely secular society. Thus Niebuhr combines an Augustinian sense of the elements of good and justice in the whole of creation with the Reformers' doctrine of the depth of human sin and the impossibility of man's virtue as justifying him before God. How Niebuhr has done this can be outlined in a brief characterization of his doctrine of love.

The search for a valid ethic is the core of Niebuhr's theological quest. Every rational analysis of the ethical situation tends to come out to the view that a harmony of interests held together in mutual regard and ultimately in the spirit of mutual love is the highest good conceivable and possible for man. Such a rational good would fulfil the demands of justice which flows from the ultimate principles of freedom and equality.

There are elements of mutual love in all human life. It is possible for one to take account of the needs of another, and there is a rational and a humanly sensitive concern about justice. Yet this drive toward mutual love and justice, so far as it is guided by man's rational estimate of his good, must always stop at the ideal of the mutual fulfilment of all. Mutual love must, according to Niebuhr, calculate the reciprocity of the other. It is not obligated to give more of the self than it can reasonably expect to be returned. Every concrete search for justice looks for that order in which my freedom and equality and that of my group are fulfilled along with that of all others.

In principle then mutual love works to fulfil life for all, but in actual history mutuality breaks down. It cannot fulfil itself. There are two reasons for this and they are related. There is, of course, the stark reality of life with its accidents and its tragedies, its misunderstanding and its end in death. There are all sorts of natural limitations on the fulfilment of an ordered community of mutuality. It is at best an ideal, not a direct possibility.

Reformers in Volume II, chaps. 5–7; and the doctrine of love in Vol. II, chap. 3, and *passim*. I have given a critical discussion of some aspects of Niebuhr's doctrine in Daniel D. Williams, *God's Grace and Man's Hope* (New York: Harper & Brothers, 1949), rev. ed. (Harper Chapelbooks, 1965), and in 'Niebuhr and Liberalism' in *Reinhold Niebuhr: His Religious, Social, and Political Thought*, ed. by Charles W. Kegley and Robert W. Bretall (New York: Macmillan, 1956),

But man does not live motivated by his ideal rational good alone. Man is sinner, living in an anxious freedom in which he can both imagine the highest possibilities of eternal fulfilment, and also sense the threats to his existence, his status, and his power which arise from the circumstances of life. Here Niebuhr makes full use of Kierkegaard's analysis of the nature of sin, and then brilliantly examines the actual way in which men estimate their own good and power and that of others.

The chief result of sin is that we overestimate the significance of our own good. We seek to achieve an absolute security for ourselves first, and thus our self-love is unmasked. *If* we loved our neighbour as ourselves we could regard the community of mutual love and the spirit which seeks it as the solution of the ethical problem. But Niebuhr denies that such a high ethical place is possible for man as he is. One of Niebuhr's most telling insights is that the claim to love the other equally usually is the mask of our inordinate self-love. The pretensions of righteousness reflect the inability of the self to be freed from its anxiety. Thus ethical 'love' becomes an ideology concealing the will to power. Niebuhr charges that all traditional doctrines, including those of the reformation, have insufficient realism about the persistence of self-love in the life of the redeemed.

Before we see how this analysis of love leads to a new consideration of the meaning of *agape* there is a complementary side of the ethical problem to be faced.

There are always at least minimal possibilities for the achievement of justice and a measure of brotherhood in human affairs. These do not depend upon the highest ethical commitments of which men are capable, but upon that mixture of human sympathy, rationality and self-interest which constitutes the basic pattern of human motivation. While Niebuhr is a realist about the possibilities of human justice, he has a strong concern for the social reformism in politics which characterizes modern democracy and the Christian social Gospel. Hence Niebuhr is quite unwilling to remain within the tradition of Lutheranism with its tendency to accept the established order, or with the early Calvinist view of the Christian reformation of the state. The struggle for political justice leads out beyond the power and vision of any present religious institution. That effort is compounded of many forces and powers. Every group has its interest, and must either conquer other groups or achieve some balance of rough justice with them. The motivation here is far from the love of the Gospel, yet the goods to be won through involvement in the stuff of history are genuine goods which must be affirmed in a Christian ethic.

Important as this struggle for relative justice is, it betrays the inadequacy of human ethics and human goodness to establish a righteous order. Every actual system of justice is compounded of rational order, a balance of power and the imposition of the will of one group upon another. Those who profit from the established order will estimate the degree of its justice more highly than those who suffer from it. Every order is precarious for it is subject to the violence of unreconciled forces. Thus the search for justice exposes man's real situation. Unless some principle higher than justice is found, even the effort for a minimally just order may end in despair. Those who strive for justice must finally be motivated by something higher than the securing of rights and freedom for all, for there will be demanded of them a self-sacrifice in which they do not see the fulfilment for which they give themselves.

Whether, then, we begin with the nature of brotherly love as a rational ethical ideal, or with the stuff of history as the scene of the conflicts out of which some kind of rough justice emerges, we are driven to the conclusion, Niebuhr says, that neither mutual love nor justice are ethical principles which can prove themselves viable in the course of human history. We begin to see that if history has a meaning there must be a transcendant ethical principle which stands above the relativities and wreckage of history.

Such an adequate answer to the ethical quest would be known by faith, not by rational analysis alone, as Niebuhr sees it. The Christian Gospel has its answer in the biblical witness to Jesus Christ. He reveals the love which is more than mutual love. It bears the unfinished tasks of history without claiming success in history. It is the love which gives itself for the other without rational calculation of results. It is sacrificial love, disclosed decisively in the story of Jesus, though there are intimations of it outside the Christian revelation.

This sacrificial love (*agape*) of which the Gospel speaks is the 'impossible possibility' for man. Niebuhr uses this paradoxical phrase in order to make it clear that even with the power of faith and the spirit man is still tempted by pride and self-love. Niebuhr will not however separate sacrificial love completely from mutual love or justice. *Agape* does not turn away from or despise the relative achievements of human ethical insight and effort. Niebuhr explicitly criticizes Nygren for making the distinction between *agape* and human love too sharp.[76]

In some respects, then, Niebuhr's doctrine does belong in the Augustinian type, with its complex acknowledgement of the signi-

76. Niebuhr, *op. cit.*, Vol. II, p. 84.

ficance of the relative values of existence as embodying a reflection of divine meaning. But ultimately Niebuhr is closer to the Reformers than to St. Augustine on the doctrine of love. He shares the Reformers' distrust of rational and metaphysical structure as stepping stones toward the pinnacle of Christian insight. Where Augustine's doctrine of love finds a synthesis of self-giving and mutuality in the being of the Trinity so that all loves participate directly in the structure of the divine being, for Niebuhr the depth and height of love transcend all rational analysis. Most important, Niebuhr asserts that sacrificial love, the *agape* of God, is a higher and different kind of love from that of mutuality.

While he does stand with the Reformers' position Niebuhr becomes the critic of the formulations of the sixteenth century and of later protestant orthodoxy. He is radically critical of the claims to righteousness on the part of the saved as well as the unsaved, both individually and collectively. Love in the Gospel sense is never a simple possibility, and there are new temptations with every spiritual achievement. At the same time, he wants to bring within the concern of love the struggles for freedom and equality which enjoy a margin of hope everywhere in human existence. For Niebuhr the *agape* of the Gospel, though symbolized by powerlessness in history, leads to involvement in the power conflicts of men for the sake of our humanity which can be rightly understood only from the standpoint of *agape*.

Our analysis of three types of the interpretation of love should make it clear there is no one way to express the meaning of love in the Christian faith. These conceptions of love have a history. The New Testament itself was born out of the concern to give meaning and structure to love as it had been experienced in the life of Israel and the life of Jesus. It is not only the conception of love which has a history; love itself, we are saying, has its history as God is dealing with his creation. If it is the work of love to create, to reconcile and to redeem, that work will be done in each age and life in ways which are shaped by the situations which love meets. Man's self-discovery is at the same time discovery of the infinite creativity of love in a history where there is freedom in the creatures and sovereign freedom in God.

The search for love always leads us back to the past, for we learn by recalling and reconceiving what love has done. But it is the task of each age to give its own account of the love which has brought us forth and under whose judgment we stand. In that account we try to say what we see, hoping that the love of God will break through our failures to understand.

In the following chapters we are seeking the meaning of love through an interpretation which emerges within the situation created by and now faced by all the traditional types. We shall try to re-state some conceptions so as to meet the problems which have led to the restlessness about love which we have discovered within each type.

We look for no synthesis of all these perspectives. That could lead only to superficiality and compromise. We begin rather with a critique of one aspect of St. Augustine's thought, his doctrine of God's being, for it is here, I shall argue, that some difficulties appear which have led to confusion in Christian thought about love.

CHAPTER V

A CRITIQUE OF ST. AUGUSTINE'S
DOCTRINE OF LOVE

Love has a history. The forms in which love is understood have grown and altered; and it is possible to see in this history the work of love creating new forms of its expression. We have reviewed the three outstanding types in which love has been grasped in the Christian tradition, and we have now to ask what this history means. We have seen tensions arise between the three types, and also have discovered within each one a restlessness born of the mystery and complexity in experience.

The sources of perplexity are clear enough. There is the psychological structure of the self with its two loves, the self-affirming drives and the self-giving drives, and the precarious freedom in which they must be held together. There is the anxious self which is something more than a rational soul dealing with a recalcitrant body. It is a new creation, existing on the boundary between life and death, being and nothingness. There are the possibilities and threats in man's new power to reshape life through technology. Nature seems less a nurturing mother, or a pattern to guide conduct, than a structured reservoir of power which can be bent to human ends. World politics require an increasingly delicate action of pragmatic statesmanship to meet the crises created by population explosion, poverty, the rise of new nations, and the power struggle between old nations, the intricacies of world economic policies, and the search for some form of collective security. In all this justice may still be pursued in the spirit of love, but the actualities put the love of neighbour in a setting never before experienced.

In the Christian faith such restlessness about the meaning and relevance of love should be understood as discovery that love has new work to do. God's work of love in history requires a reconception of its meaning, the discovery of new forms of its expression, and the transformation of those images of love which have become stereotyped and impotent in this epoch.

In Christian faith all thought about love leads to the nature of God, and therefore the reconception of love leads to the question of the being of God to which we now turn. A radical new possibility has opened up for theology. This is the interpretation of the love of

God in relation to a new metaphysical doctrine in which God is involved in time and becoming. In this conception of God's being it is possible to reconceive the relation of love to suffering and to consider what it means for God to act in history.

We have already noted the conflict which runs through most of Christian thought between the biblical vision of God as the creative and redemptive actor in the history of his creation, and the metaphysical doctrine inherited from the synthesis of the Christian faith with neo-platonic philosophy which conceives God as the impassible, non-temporal absolute. That synthesis has haunted Christian thought through the centuries. But it is by no means easy to see what doctrine of God's being can be more adequate to the biblical faith. It is worth our concentrated attention to see what is at stake here. One of the creative process philosophers, Charles Hartshorne, states in the beginning of *Man's Vision of God* his conviction that 'a magnificent intellectual content—far surpassing that of such systems as Thomism, Spinozism, German idealism, positivism (old or new) is implicit in the religious faith most briefly expressed in the three words, God is love'.[1] If this be true what is needed is not the discarding of metaphysics but the exploration of this new possibility in the doctrine of God's being.

(1)

GOD AND THE ABSOLUTE: THE METAPHYSICAL TRADITION

St. Augustine, as we have seen, expresses his doctrine of the meaning of love in the Trinity—God as Father, Son, and Holy Spirit—and in the metaphysical conception of God's being as the ground of all created things so that in the whole creation there is a reflection of the love which is the ultimate source of all things. Now we must examine St. Augustine's doctrine more closely, for it was he who made the decisive synthesis of the Gospel with the neo-platonic doctrine of God's being.

St. Augustine is overwhelmed with the greatness and majesty of the love of God. The Trinity is the very being of love. The Spirit is the bond which unites Father and Son. God's being is therefore the fullness and substance of love itself. Through participation in God the creatures have their existence. God is all goodness, all truth, all beauty. In so far as anything creaturely sees or exhibits

1. Charles Hartshorne, *Man's Vision of God* (New York: Harper & Brothers, 1941), p. ix.

these aspects of God's being it participates in the love of God and moves toward its own fulfilment. In so far as it is a creature it tends also toward nothingness, non-being. Sin is man's wilful turning to love the creature more than the Creator, that is turning away from the light to the darkness of non-being.

St. Augustine thus moves within the neo-platonic vision, but with a difference created by Christian faith. For the Platonists all love is yearning toward the good; it is spirit moving toward fullness of being. But for St. Augustine God himself is love, therefore love is not only aspiration, but is also the outpouring of the divine being toward the creatures.

St. Augustine sees love in man as the 'weight by which the soul is born wherever it is born'.[2] But God in his love seeks out the creatures and sheds his goodness upon them. Because of the fall into sin God comes into the world in his Son and gives himself to man so that the way may be opened for return to true being. To know the love of God, then, is to know the source and end of life. It is to be in pilgrimage toward eternal life, and to participate in the fullness of being itself.

So far all this may seem but a metaphysical rendering of the biblical doctrine, but St. Augustine wants to establish his conception of the being of God by answering many questions to which the Platonists have given their kind of answer. His own answers are attempts to combine the living God of the Bible with the changeless being of neo-platonic metaphysics.[3] What Augustine does is to conceive God the Creator and Redeemer with all the absolute aspects which neo-platonism had ascribed to the transcendent and changeless One. This was for Augustine and for all the Church Fathers not only an act of philosophic rationality, but also a confirmation of Christian piety as they ascribed to God all power, all completeness, all perfection of every kind.[4] Most important for our consideration was their conviction that all temporality, change, becoming, and passivity signify lack of perfection.

The result of this opposing of pure being to becoming was the doctrine of the divine impassibility, which has had throughout the centuries the approval of orthodox theology, both Catholic and Protestant. There is no question that the incarnate Son suffered on the cross. This was the foundation of all Christian theology. But did the Father suffer? The problem vexed the theologians. To say

2. St. Augustine, *Confessions*, xiii, 9–10.
3. John Burnaby, *Amor Dei*, p. 32 (London: Hodder & Stoughton, 1938).
4. See G. L. Prestige, *God in Patristic Thought* (London: S.P.C.K., 1956), chaps. 1–2.

that God did not suffer seemed a strange doctrine; yet to affirm it meant that he can be acted upon. To the Greeks this would mean that he is not really God. Cyril of Alexandria explains Christ's weeping at the tomb of Lazarus thus: 'He permitted his own flesh to weep a little, although it was in its nature tearless and incapable of grief.'[5] The critical issue lies in the assumption that temporality and passivity mean an inferior level of being. It is creatures who become and change. Their perishing is the sign of their dependence. Nothing less than the deity of God is at stake in the assertion of his changelessness, as St. Augustine sees it.

We must also acknowledge that the biblical affirmations of the absolute faithfulness of God, his changeless love, his sovereignty as Creator and Lord, could be taken to reinforce this metaphysical absolutism. God rules history and judges the nations. He will create new heavens and a new earth, and in the end be 'all in all' (I Corinthians 15). To the Fathers the use of neo-platonic language about God's perfection seemed a way of celebrating the majesty and faithfulness of God which they heard attested in the scripture. Let us see how St. Augustine unites this metaphysical doctrine with his faith that in Jesus Christ God has acted at a specific point in history to redeem man.

(2)

St. Augustine's Conception of Time

The problems involved for Christian faith come out clearly in St. Augustine's thought about the relation of the creation in its beginning, development and end to the changelessness of the creator. On one hand Augustine positively affirms the reality of time. It is not an illusion. The world has a beginning and end, and there is a real becoming and direction in the history of the world. He affirms this specifically against cyclical theories of time such as those of stoicism. The incarnation represents a decisive event in history, and this the platonists cannot understand.[6]

But the creative action of God cannot, for Augustine, qualify his 'unchangeableness'. Hence caution is the beginning of time and it happens all at once. Even in the face of the clear biblical statement that the creation took six days, St. Augustine's ontological presuppositions require him to say that for God to take time for

5. Cyril of Alexandria, *Commentary on John*, vii.
6. Confessions, VII, 9, 21.

creation would require a 'before and after' in God and this will not do. He says, 'For in the Eternal, properly speaking, there is neither anything past, as though it had passed away, nor anything future as though it were not as yet, but whatsoever is, only is'.[7] God, therefore, must have implanted all at once the seeds of things which are later to become in the world:

> Just as in that seed there were together (*simul*) invisibly all the things which would in time develop into the tree, so the world itself is to be thought to have had together—since God created all things together— all the things which were made in it and with it when the day was made, not only the heavens with the sun and the moon and the constellations . . . and the earth and the abysses . . . but also those things which the water and the earth produced potentially and causally, before they should rise in the course of time in the way we now know them, through those operations which God carries on even until now.[8]

Augustine could not be more explicit about the unity of all times in God: 'Thy today is eternity.'[9] He addresses God as 'Thou to whom nothing is to come'.[10]

But if 'nothing is to come', then the future must be present to God as well as the present and past, and Augustine explicitly affirms this. In his effort to grasp the unity of all time in God, he considers the experience of repeating a psalm which he comes to know better and better so that his knowledge of the psalm becomes a whole in which beginning and end are brought together. But strictly speaking even this will not do for an analogy of God's knowledge of past and future. 'Far more wonderfully and far more mysteriously dost thou know them.'[11]

Augustine's doctrine is that all times are co-present to God in one eternal vision. This is the *totum simul*. What is past, present and future for us is known to God all at once in his unchangeable vision.[12] St. Augustine acknowledges that what he says about time in God is beyond human understanding. Etienne Gilson sees that Augustine is confronted with a problem for which no philosophical answer can be given, for he is working with two modes of being which are absolutely heterogeneous. William Christian's comment is pertinent:

7. Augustine, lib. 83. quaest, qu. 19. Cf. William Christian, 'The Creation of the World' in Battenhouse, ed. *A Companion to the Study of St. Augustine* (New York: Oxford University Press, 1955).

8. *De. Gen. ad Litt.*, v. 23, Tr. by William Christian in Battenhouse, *op. cit.*, p. 330.

9. *Confessions*, XI, 16.   10. *Ibid.*, XI, 25.

11. *Confessions*, XI, 36, 41.   12. *On the Trinity*, XV, 7.

We are subject, even in our thought to the law of becoming. How then can we represent to ourselves the mode of being of that which is unchangeable? Here is a problem indeed and for it St. Augustine has no answer. What is worse, he is committed to saying that this unchangeable being, which he cannot adequately represent to himself, creates, knows, and administers a world of changing things. At this point Augustine is frank to say that no analogies can really help us.[13]

If what we are trying to understand here were only a peculiar intellectual difficulty in conceiving how time and eternity can be related, the problem would be an abstract one hardly worthy of special attention so far as the meaning of love is concerned. Problems of time and eternity, the changing and the changeless have their mysteries before which we can, like Augustine, only confess the limit of our sight. The real trouble is that Augustine and the classical theological tradition not only affirmed the mystery but also insisted that God's perfection requires his absolute changelessness. This determination to keep all time and becoming apart from God led to disastrous consequences for the understanding of God's love. We shall see the implications of his doctrine, which Augustine unflinchingly presses, until they constitute that dark and unlovely side of his theology which persists in much Christian theology since his time.

(3)

Consequences of Augustine's Doctrine

There is first, the consequence for human freedom. If all time is present to God then he knows the future. What is future for us is present for him. Here is Augustine's metaphysical basis for the teaching of predestination:

> In God all things are ordered and fixed; nor doth He anything, as by a sudden counsel, which He did not from eternity foreknow that He should do; but in the movements of the creature, which He wonderfully governeth, Himself not moved in time, in time is said to have done, as by a sudden will, what He disposed through the ordered causes of things in the unchangeableness of His most hidden counsels, whereby each several things, which in its appointed time comes to our knowledge, He both makes, when present, and, when future, had already made.[14]

That is, what God appears to do here and now, he really does in eternity.

The consequences of this doctrine for human freedom are well

13. Christian, *op. cit.*, p. 322.   14. *Psalms* 105, 45. sec. 35.

known, and have given theology much internal strain. Augustine disputed with Pelagius about free will, and generally Pelagianism has been viewed by the main stream of Christian thought as a heresy in which man's dependence upon grace for salvation is denied. It is now doubtful whether the usual view of Pelagius' doctrine is one he ever held. We know he did not reject the necessity of grace, but thought of it as leaving man free for co-operation with God.[15] But Augustine has always been given credit for having preserved the essential Christian doctrine that God's grace is necessary to give to man what he cannot give to himself, that is forgiveness, and the empowerment of his will to love God and his neighbour. Augustine thinks of freedom as the power to do what God wills, and man does not have this in his actual state of sin. Pelagius seems to think of man as having a 'neutral' nature in which his freedom has an open choice for or against God.[16]

Augustine's emphasis on grace is valid but it should not keep us from recognizing the difficulty in his teaching. It is not that he affirms that God must do something for man which man cannot do for himself; but that he combines this with assertion that God decides in eternity what will be done in every moment of time. This means that no decision of man makes any difference, for it is not really man's decision in the end. God has determined what every decision will be.

This is a very old debate, but we are concerned here with that aspect of it which flows from St. Augustine's metaphysical assumptions. In a universe where only God acts, and in which therefore he can in no way be acted upon, and where past, present and future are all telescoped into one simultaneous experience there can be no element of real freedom or spontaneity for the creatures. It becomes a puzzle how God can do anything new.

Augustine leaves no basis for conceiving any qualification of the absolute power of God over the creature. Thus he closes off the possibility that human decisions can alter history. Certainly every Christian theology will hold that man can never realize his goals apart from the prevenient grace and power of God. What God does man can never do, that is establish the conditions of freedom, including forgiveness, for man has misused and corrupted his will to love. But all this could be held without denying to man the freedom to make decisions and thus to make a difference in the future. The

15. Cf. Torgny Bohlin, *Die Theologie des Pelagius und Ihre Genesis* (Upsala Universitets Arskrift 1957: 9).

16. On the debate with Pelagius see Paul Lehmann, 'The Anti-Pelagian Writings' in Battenhouse, *op. cit.*

reason St. Augustine cannot allow this is, in the end, not his theological concern for the grace of God, but his metaphysical commitment to the absolute. God has to be the cause of every action. John Calvin under Augustine's influence explicitly says that God wills every event.[17] The criticism we are making of St. Augustine can be made from more than one philosophical point of view. Karl Löwith says Augustine failed to relate God as primary cause to the secondary causes.[18] John Burnaby says pointedly: 'Augustine never realized that his own conception of grace required nothing less than a revolution in his thought of the divine omnipotence.'[19] In assessing the consequences of this classical position it must be remembered that man's wrong or evil choices are as fully determined as the right ones. Thus Augustine says God not only foreknows but ordains the fall of Adam. God selects those to be saved in relation to the number of fallen angels, and the eternal punishment of hell is prepared for the condemned and therefore unrepentant sinners. Yet this is all the work of love for God is love. Dante is fully in accord with the orthodoxy of Augustinian and medieval Christianity when he sees inscribed over the gate of hell:

> Justice moved my High Maker; Divine Power made me, Wisdom Supreme and Primal Love, . . . leave all hope ye that enter.[20]

The discrepancy between the orthodox teaching of an eternity of punishment for those predestined to damnation and the belief in God's love is one of the too rarely examined problems in traditional Christian doctrine. The present debate about universalism, in which Karl Barth's thought plays an important part as he seemingly moves toward a doctrine of universal salvation, shows that there is something here which the Christian mind has not yet fully adjusted in its doctrine of God.[21]

There is a second consequence of the doctrine of the absoluteness of God over against all temporality and change. It introduces into the human loves a division between love of temporal things and love of the eternal which tends to a devaluation of this world and of creaturely humanity.

17. Calvin, Institutes, Bk. I, chap. 16; 'Not a drop of rain falls but at the express command of God'.
18. Karl Löwith, *Meaning in History* (Chicago: University of Chicago Press, 1949), p. 172.
19. Burnaby, *Amor Dei*, p. 230.
20. Dante Alighieri, *The Divine Comedy, Inferno,* Canto III.
21. Karl Barth, *Church Dogmatics* II/2; IV/3. Cf. criticism by Emil Brunner, *The Christian Doctrine of God* (London: Lutterworth Press; Philadelphia: Westminster Press, 1950, pp. 346–52). Cf. Burnaby, *Amor Dei*, chap. vii.

Now surely St. Augustine is defending something very important in his doctrine that we love other things and other men *in God*. This must be so, in his view, for all things have their being through participation in God. What we seek and know in another person is not him alone, but him in relation to his creator and to all other things. We know ourselves not just in ourselves, but as participants in the power of being. We truly know ourselves only *in God*. Hence love has a tangent within it which moves through the other person toward the fullness of being which is God himself. Charles Williams speaks rightly of the Augustinian theme of the 'in-godding' of the self.[22]

Anders Nygren criticizes Augustine for this doctrine and says that it depersonalizes the neighbour.[23] We do not see him as he is in himself, but only as a reflection of the divine. If there is a depersonalization in Augustine's view, however, it does not lie in the doctrine that we love others *in God*. It lies in the way Augustine conceives of God's being and its relation to the creatures. For God's being, Augustine believes, has its perfection in its *immutability*. Part of the inferiority of the creatures is that they are temporal and they change. They can suffer and be acted upon. Hence the conclusion is drawn that love of what is unchanging is higher than love of what changes. It is this platonic theme which devaluates the world of creatures and requires that we love the creatures *only* for the sake of a perfection which in no way suffers or is moved. The dangerous implication is that when we love the neighbour as a suffering, growing, becoming being, we love him only as one who points our love to another order of reality. Augustine says:

> Give me a lover, he will feel what I speak of; give me one who longs, who hungers, who is the thirsty pilgrim in this wilderness, sighing after the springs of his eternal homeland; give me such a man, and he will know what I mean.[24]

Thus the heart of love is its longing for eternity. But, we must ask, does this mean that love should never be given to what is concretely involved in history? We need not reject Augustine's teaching altogether. He knows that the depth of love is never concentrated solely on a person; but always has a hunger for the full being of that person which means his being in God. But surely this does not require a devaluation of creaturely being just because there is suffering in existence. The real difficulty is Augustine's equating of God's

22. Charles Williams, *Religion and Love in Dante* (London: A. & C. Black Ltd., 1941), p. 40.
23. Nygren, *Agape and Eros*, pp. 549ff.
24. *Joan. Evang.*, xl, 10.

perfection with immutability which introduces this unnatural discrepancy between love of God and love of the neighbour. In the previous chapter we noted one consequence in Augustine's view of sex in which he justifies sexual abstinence because the giving up of temporal love for love of the eternal is an act of prudence in view of the superiority of the eternal.[25]

We come then to the critical issue of the suffering of Christ as atonement for sin. Here if anywhere we should see what place suffering has in love. Augustine gives us no formal doctrine of atonement. He uses many images. Aulén is undoubtedly right in aligning Augustine with the classical motif of God's victory over the satanic powers which he wins by sending Jesus to the Cross.[26] Augustine uses vivid terms to describe the conflict of God with Satan including the well-known 'baiting of the hook' which catches the devil as he snatches at Christ. Augustine usually speaks of the suffering of Christ in relation to the humility in which God assumed our condition so as to lead us out of pride and despair toward himself. This assumption of our flesh is an act of love. 'If God did not love sinners, He would not have come down from heaven to earth.'[27] The suffering of Christ results from his assumption of our humanity. He is our salvation because in him God reverses the direction of our pride and self-love, and shows the way to blessedness:

> The Teacher of humility, the partaker of our infirmity, giving us to partake of His own divinity, coming down for the purpose that He might teach the way and become the way (cf. John xiv, 6) deigned to recommend chiefly His own humility to us.[28]

And Augustine believes 'there is nothing more powerful than the humility of God:[29]

> To what doth He exhort thee? To imitate Him in those works which He could not have done had He not been made man. For how could He endure sufferings unless he had become man: How could he otherwise have died, been crucified, been humbled? Thus then do thou, when thou sufferest the troubles of this world. . . . Be strong, be long suffering, thou shalt abide under the protection of the Most High.[30]

Redemption in Christ is incorporation into His Body the Church, and love is the bond of the Church:

25. Cf. Nygren, pp. 494–5.
26. Gustaf Aulén, *Christus Victor* (New York: Macmillan, 1931; London: S.P.C.K., 1931).
27. *Joan. Evangel.*, xlix, 5.
28. *Psalms*, LVIII, i, 7 (*Synthesis*, 340).
29. *Ep.* CCXXXII, 5–6.
30. *Psalms*, XC, Sermo. i, 1 (*Synthesis*, 337).

> The whole Christ is Head and Body, . . . the Head is our Saviour Himself. . . . For the whole Church, which consists of all the faithful, since all the faithful are members of Christ, hath that Head set in Heaven, and it governeth His body. And although it is separated from our vision, yet it is joined together in charity. Hence the whole Christ is Head and its body.[31]

We ask now if this divine self-emptying and involvement in our human lot does not reveal the nature of love itself? Here is the issue: what does the incarnation tell us about love? If the incarnation satisfies our longing for the fullness of being, is it not because 'fullness of being' involves suffering with and for the other, a participation in life which has becoming and freedom within it? But in Augustine's theology, God as being-itself cannot suffer.

It is here in its account of the love revealed in Jesus that the discrepancy in the classical theology lies.

Anders Nygren has identified the difficulty. We can put it most bluntly by asking whether Augustine does not come close to glorifying a certain 'complacency' in the divine love. Nygren uses the word 'ego-centricity'. This may be too strong, but it points to the issue. Nygren says Augustine is not interested in the causal analysis of the incarnation, that is, in the way in which it accomplishes God's purpose, but only in the teleological analysis, the end which it is said to accomplish. Nygren sees the difficulty, but he has not traced it to its source.

If Augustine identifies love with a sheer rest in being, enjoying the fullness of self rather than self-giving, why does he do so? I propose that a metaphysical analysis of what he meant by being throws light on the answer. It is not simply that Augustine has mixed up the Christian *agape-love* with the self-seeking *eros* of Greek religion. He sees far more deeply into Christian doctrine than that. What he does is to combine the God of the Bible with the absolute of neo-platonic metaphysics. The result is that the active, temporal, creating, suffering side of God's being does not come sufficiently into view. It cannot do so because it contradicts the absolutist doctrine of perfection.

Nygren gives an important suggestion about the history of doctrine when he says that the Church Fathers were saved from falling completely into a Greek pattern of thought by the three biblical assertions of Creation, Incarnation, and Resurrection.[32] But rather than conclude, as Nygren does, that these themes require us to reject all metaphysics, why not say that they require us to reconsider

31. *Psalms* LVI, 1 (Synthesis, 371).
32. Nygren, *op. cit.*, pp. 276–87.

our metaphysics? All three ideas point to a relationship of God to the world which differs from the Greek view. God creates the world and acts to redeem it. These actions involve time. They involve God's relationship to the needs, suffering and decisions of his creatures. Nygren can include election in his list of the themes which keep the dynamic aspect of the Christian doctrine of God, for election, as we have seen, means God's self-disclosure to a people at a point in history, his creation of a new relationship and the assuming of its consequences. Nygren, however, is not concerned with metaphysical analysis. He emphasizes the affirmation of the goodness of the material world, the refusal to regard the body as evil, and the significance of the resurrection doctrine in opposition to the Greek views of the immortality of the soul. These are all significant topics, but surely they cry out for metaphysical interpretation. What is real and what is not? How are freedom and human destiny bound up with time and becoming in the world? How does God act in the world and upon it?

To sum up, great as the structure of the interpretation of love is in St. Augustine, it exposes a discrepancy between the reality of the loving and acting God and the metaphysical vision of perfect completion and impassibility. Let us state the essence of Augustine's position.

Love is the key to being. It fulfils all the special forms of being, and it fulfils the quest for knowledge of being. The disorder in human loves is the central fact about man's plight. The saving and reconstruction of a truly human existence depend upon a revolution in the direction and content of all our loves, and that revolution comes through what God has shown in Christ, through a love which condescends to us. All this is fundamental to Christian faith and St. Augustine has given its theological foundations.

Further, we find in him a tough-minded realism about the actualities of human history as the mingling of the divine love and disordered human love. He describes with great accuracy the necessities of Christian existence in which love is the meaning of all knowledge and action, but in which man must cope with vast and threatening powers and institutions which are ruled by the distorted and misdirected passions of the corrupt human spirit. Augustine never lets us forget that we live in two cities at the same time, the City of God, and the City of Man which is infected with sin. Therefore all human life must become a pilgrimage, a turning about of the soul to a new way in a mysterious life which does not yield its secret all at once. The light has come to us, and we can walk by it, but only as those who have to find their way in an unfinished and complex world. The pilgrimage is a progress toward the truth, not a sheer possession of it.

Augustine's doctrine of love leaves us in difficulty through its tendency to put love ultimately beyond all tension and suffering. Love is completed by being beyond tension, beyond the risks of freedom in the dialogue of God and man in history. But I shall argue that love cannot breathe in such a 'block universe'.[33] For St. Augustine all things are caught in the predetermined web of God's absolute, non-temporal, impassible, unchanging power. He bequeathed that doctrine to later theology. St. Thomas does not depart from it in any essential point so far as his doctrine of the being of God is concerned. Luther and Calvin, in spite of their rejection of the scholastic metaphysics, have this neo-platonic God in the foundation of their thinking. At no point do they question the doctrines of the divine perfection, impassibility and non-temporality. Both are as predestinarian as St. Augustine when it comes to the question of freedom. They try unsuccessfully to assert man's freedom in spite of the divine foreknowledge of every event.[34] They explicitly reject the view that the Father suffers. It is on these fundamental points that theological reconstruction must focus its attention.

(4)

A METAPHYSICAL ALTERNATIVE

We have observed an existential restlessness within the traditional conceptions of love. We now see one important source of that restlessness. It is the radical historical consciousness of contemporary man. He thinks of his life and world as involving a real freedom, possibilities as yet unrealized, an open-ended future which he shapes partly by his own decisions. As one discerning interpreter says:

> Modern man can only define himself as a *being in history* (*zoon historikon*), a being with a past, a present, and a future . . . all schools of contemporary thought share the realization that truth, understanding, and reality have the character of events rather than of things.[35]

33. William James's well-known phrase.
34. Martin Luther, *On the Bondage of the Will*, review of Erasmus, preface. Dillenberger ed., p. 181.
35. Paul Schubert, 'The Twentieth Century West and the Ancient Near-East', *The Idea of History in the Ancient Near East*, ed. by Robert C. Dentan (New Haven: Yale University Press, 1955), pp. 314–15.

It is not necessary to review here the many factors which have gone into the making of this historical consciousness; but it is more than an incident in our intellectual history; it is a revolution in our sense of life. Existentialist philosophy may push the revolution to its limit as in Sartre's doctrine that man creates himself out of nothing, and this 'nothing' is at the heart of man's freedom.[36] There are more balanced views, but we cannot escape the fact that our sense of time and becoming has created a new understanding of what it means to be.

The evolutionary world picture with its eons of time for the emergence of life and mind is now the setting in which we think. The scientific way of knowing depends upon taking the world as a series of processes or events, whose structures are abstract patterns manifest in activity. Karl Jaspers accurately describes the significance of the new scientific attitude toward the 'reason' in things:

> Quite different is the new impulse to keep minds open to the boundlessness of the created universe. This tends to steer cognition toward the very realities which do not tally with known orders and laws. The *logos* itself constantly urges man to trip himself—not in order to give up, however, but to regain his footing on a higher, broader, more fulfilled level, and to continue this steady progress toward unfulfillable infinity. This kind of science springs from a *logos* which is *not self-contained* but *open* to the *alogon*.[37]

This 'unfulfillable infinity' is the key to the modern consciousness. There is always more to know, always a new set of problems to meet. On one point especially we should be clear. This sense of history does not depend on a progressive conception of life. The idea of progress was one form in which the new historical sense came to birth; but the historical consciousness can also be nihilistic, pessimistic, or realistic. Radical freedom may be man's possibility of shaping his future, but also of destroying his life. What has changed is not the increase of historical hopefulness; but the sense of what kind of options there are and where we must find meaning if any is to be found.

The new sense of time has direct bearing on the meaning of love.

36. Jean-Paul Sartre, *Being and Nothingness* (New York: Philosophical Library, 1956, Part II, chap. 1, esp. p. 79; cf. pp. 591–2; London: Methuen & Co., 1957). Sartre says in his autobiographical *The Words* (New York: Fawcett World Library, 1964, 'I keep creating myself: I am the giver and the gift', p. 20; London: Hamish Hamilton, 1964).

37. Karl Jaspers, *Nietzsche and Christianity* (Chicago: H. Regnery, 1961), pp. 70–1.

If human existence is reconceived in a radical historical consciousness, then the forms of love must be reconceived also. Human loves
viewed in a purely secular way take on new meanings with the
growth of the democratic ideal, new relationships of the sexes, the
freedom of youth, the discovery of the dynamics of emotional
growth, the possibilities and threats of technological control, the
world-wide social and political revolution.

The history of the conception of love is also the history of the
conception of God. In the biblical perspective God works and
reveals himself in every generation. It is conceivable that aspects
of the biblical witness to the love of God have been obscured in
the tradition, and that some of the traditional interpretations are
no longer tenable. This means that through the internal creativity
of the biblical perspective, joined with the modern historical consciousness which it helped to create, a new possibility has been
opened up for reconceiving the meaning of God's being in relation
to time and history. It is that possibility which we consider in what
follows in this book. We conclude this chapter by stating the main
thesis put forth by process philosophy which proposes nothing less
than a revolution in metaphysics and theology. This will lay the
foundation for a re-examination of the meaning of love.

Process philosophy is a term which designates a broad movement
in modern philosophy and more particularly a group of thinkers
who have set out to reconsider the metaphysical problem on the
basis of the evolutionary world-view and the temporal flow of
experience. Process thought developed in the evolutionary philosophies of the late nineteenth century, and has a kinship with the
'emergent revolutionary' theorists.[38] The process philosophers are
interested not only in an evolutionary description of the cosmos,
but in what happens to all the traditional metaphysical problems
when time is seen as an ingredient of being itself. Henri Bergson's
philosophy is one of the first and most radical statements of this
new metaphysics. Samuel Alexander developed a realistic process
doctrine in *Space, Time and Deity*. Both Bergson and Alexander
influenced Alfred North Whitehead, whose scientific and philosophical genius created the major work in process thought, *Process*

38. For the background of the movement see Lloyd Morgan, *Emergent
Evolution* (New York: Henry Holt, 1926); John Dewey, *The Influence of Darwin
on Philosophy and other Essays in Contemporary Thought* (New York: Henry
Holt, 1910); Philip Wiener, *Evolution and the Founders of Pragmatism* (Harvard
University Press, 1949); John Herman Randall, Jr., 'The Changing Impact of
Darwin on Philosophy', *Jrnl. History of Ideas*, Vol. XXII, No. 4, pp. 435–62;
Alfred North Whitehead, *Science and the Modern World* (New York: Macmillan,
1931; Cambridge University Press, 2nd ed., 1936).

and Reality.[39] There are close affinities between the process philosophers and American pragmatism. William James, Charles Peirce, John Dewey, and George Herbert Mead have much in common with the process metaphysicians.

All the process philosophers have been concerned with religion, and Bergson, Alexander and Whitehead developed metaphysical doctrines of God. Whitehead's outstanding interpreter in the mid-twentieth century is Charles Hartshorne, who has given a lifetime of attention to the metaphysical conception of God implied in process thought.[40]

While all these we have mentioned remained philosophers, a group of Christian theologians have seen in the new metaphysics a possibility for rethinking the theological doctrine of God in relation to a contemporary view of nature and the new historical consciousness. Theologians have developed the new insight in radically different contexts. Henry Nelson Wieman began with the Whiteheadian metaphysics and moved to a radical empiricism in theology.[41] His student, Bernard Meland, has remained closer to Whitehead's metaphysical outlook and has given a searching interpretation of the nature of faith and the meaning of the Christian faith.[42] The Anglican Lionel Thornton took Whitehead's ideas developed in *Science and the Modern World* and used them in the construction of a Christology in *The Incarnate Lord*.[43] Thornton kept Whitehead's radical conceptions in a subordinate place in his theological structure and his later thought has moved away from this attempt at a

39. Henri Bergson, *An Introduction to Metaphysics*, tr. by T. E. Hulme (New York: G. P. Putman's Sons, 1912; London: H. Jonas & Co. Ltd.); *Creative Evolution*, tr. by Arthur Mitchell (London: Macmillan & Co., 1911; New York: Henry Holt, 1911); Samuel Alexander, *Space, Time, and Deity* (London: Macmillan, 1927); Alfred North Whitehead, *Process and Reality* (New York: Macmillan, 1929).

40. Charles Hartshorne, *Man's Vision of God* (New York: Harper & Brothers, 1941); *Reality as Social Process* (Glencoe, Ill.: Free Press, 1953); *The Divine Relativity* (New Haven: Yale University Press, 1948); *Process and Divinity: Philosophical Essays Presented to Charles Hartshorne*, ed. by William L. Reese and Eugene Freeman (La Salle, Ill.: Open Court, 1964).

41. Henry Nelson Wieman, *The Wrestle of Religion with Truth* (New York: Macmillan, 1937); *The Source of Human Good* (Chicago: University of Chicago Press, 1946); *Man's Ultimate Commitment* (Carbondale: Southern Ill. University Press, 1958). Cf. *The Empirical Theology of Henry Nelson Wieman*, ed. by Robert Bretall (New York: Macmillan, 1963).

42. Bernard E. Meland, *Faith and Culture* (New York: Oxford Press, 1953; London: Allen & Unwin, 1955). *The Realities of Faith* (New York: Oxford Press, 1962); cf. Daniel D. Williams, 'The Theology of Bernard E. Meland', in *Criterion*, the Divinity School of the University of Chicago, Summer, 1964.

43. Lionel Thornton, *The Incarnate Lord* (London: Longmans Green, 1928).

philosophical theology. Something similar might be said of William Temple who adopted aspects of Whitehead's thought concerning the evolutionary process, but kept within an idealistic structure.[44]

In more recent years under the stimulus of Whitehead's thought and the constructive work of Charles Hartshorne, certain theologians have been developing 'process theology' as a systematic theological outlook. Norman Pittenger is the first theologian to work out a Christology incorporating the process view of God and man in his *The Word Incarnate*. Schubert Ogden and John Cobb, Jr., as well as the present writer, have committed their theological attention to the interpretation of the new metaphysic for Christian faith.[45] For these theologians, no philosophy is sufficient for Christian faith. Theology interprets the life of faith which needs philosophical structure for its intelligibility, but Christian faith is existential commitment and participation in the church which is a community of historical experience having its origin and centre in the New Testament witness to Jesus Christ.

The relation between philosophy and theology is a perennial problem for Christian thought, and the debate about methodology never ends. In the last analysis the test of a method is whether it illuminates concrete problems in life. The present book is an attempt to think theologically about the meanings of love with the resources contributed by process thought. The justification for such a method would be that it commends itself by making some sense out of the meaning of the love of God and the loves of men. Process thinkers do not claim to 'have all the answers'. One of our cardinal tenets is the tentativeness of all structures of interpretation. We are trying to grasp the meaning of love in the Christian faith in responsible relationship to the scripture, to the classical tradition, and to a contemporary scientific and rational understanding of our existence.[46]

Process philosophy opens up for Christian theology a way of

44. William Temple, *Nature, Man, and God* (London: Macmillan, 1949).

45. I have given a brief account of process theology in *What Present Day Theologians are Thinking*, second revised edition (New York: Harper & Row, 1966). Cf. Schubert Ogden, *Christ Without Myth* (New York: Harper & Row, 1961; London: William Collins Sons & Co., 1962); *The Reality of God* (New York: Harper & Row, 1966); John Cobb, Jr., *A Christian Natural Theology* (Philadelphia: Westminster Press, 1965); W. Norman Pittenger, *The Word Incarnate* (New York: Harper & Row, 1959; London: James Nisbet & Co.). Cf. Dr. Pittenger's article 'A Contemporary Trend in North American Theology: Process Thought and Christian Faith', *Religion in Life*, Vol. 34, 1964–5, pp. 500–510.

46. I have given an outline of a theological method of this type in 'Truth in the Theological Perspective', *Journal of Religion*, Vol. XXVIII, No. 4, Oct. 1948.

conceiving the being of God in historical-temporal terms. What it proposes is akin to the existentialist search for radical freedom for man, and the acceptance of the risks of being; but process philosophy is closer than existentialism to the classical philosophies in its search for an intelligible metaphysics. It seeks the *logos* of being. Process theologians believe that we can recapture aspects of the biblical message which have been obscured throughout the history of the tradition. The biblical God acts in a history where men have freedom which they can misuse. He is at work in time, and it is just this which the theological tradition, conditioned by neo-platonic metaphysics, has never been able to encompass.

In the next chapter we shall examine the specific ideas of process philosophy with respect to the nature of love. Here I introduce that exploration with a brief characterization of the metaphysical position especially as it is stated by Alfred North Whitehead; Whitehead's is the seminal mind which provided the main structure of thought which is process philosophy.[47] Whitehead has a close affinity to the classical metaphysical tradition. He sees the structure of being as the eternal order in the mind of God, but he wants to conceive reality including God himself as exhibiting a real history of concrete happenings.

Whitehead the philosopher used the instrument of metaphysical analysis for a critique of traditional theology. His most telling statement against the tradition is that 'the Church gave God the attributes which belonged exclusively to Caesar'.[48] He held that the monarchical element in the Semitic concept of deity had been joined to the Unmoved Mover theme in Aristotle and as the neo-platonists developed it. The metaphysical result was the God who does not suffer, who is unaffected by what happens in time, the God of absolute predestination and unfreedom. Whitehead believed that this doctrine had confused the mind of the church about the nature of the love disclosed in Jesus. Whitehead saw an ultimate ethical contrast between brute force or coercion and persuasive love. The Gospel presents the figure of the Christ as the expression of a non-

47. A. N. Whitehead, *Process and Reality*, p. 520. Cf. his *Religion in the Making* (New York: Macmillan, 1926). The best general account of Whitehead's philosophy is Victor Lowe, *Understanding Whitehead* (Baltimore: The Johns Hopkins Press, 1962). For analysis of Whitehead's doctrine of God see the chapter by Charles Hartshorne in *The Philosophy of Alfred North Whitehead*, ed. by Paul Schilpp (Chicago: Northwestern University Press, 1941); William Christian, *Whitehead's Metaphysics* (New Haven: Yale University Press, 1959).

48. *Process and Reality*, p. 520. Cf. Daniel D. Williams, 'Deity, Monarchy, and Metaphysics; Whitehead's Critique of the Theological Tradition' in *The Relevance of Whitehead*, ed. by Ivor Leclerc (New York: Macmillan, 1961).

coercive love which draws the world in its freedom toward a finer community of being.[49] As Whitehead envisions the Christian message, Christ taught, lived, and died with the authority of a supreme ideal. His words were not metaphysical reflections, but the most direct and intuitive communication of which language is capable. Thus Christianity has been a religion seeking a metaphysic in contrast to Buddhism, which is a metaphysic generating a religion.[50] Whitehead therefore is not substituting philosophy for religion and faith. He regards philosophy as a never finished essay in fathoming the intelligibility of things, and it is always mistaken when it claims completeness for its conclusions. Philosophy is an instrument of vision. It should be the guide of life, not merely a technical exercise in the analysis of logical problems, but a bold attempt to grasp the structures of reality within the limits of human knowledge and frailty.

What Whitehead thus provides for us in the search for the meaning of love is a perspective on the world which opens new possibilities for conceiving the divine love and human loves. He articulates a world view which combines the classic search for being with the radical historical and temporal consciousness of the twentieth century. We can say that Whitehead sees his interpretation of the doctrine of God's being within the pattern of St. Augustine's 'faith seeking understanding', provided by faith we do not understand the acceptance of dogma; but the religious intuition born out of the impact of Jesus upon the world.

We can here indicate the main outline of Whitehead's doctrine of God as a basis for reconsidering the meaning of love.

There are two aspects of the divine nature. The first Whitehead calls the primordial nature of God. This is the ordered realm of abstract structure which embraces all the patterns of the possible meanings and values relevant to existence. Whitehead holds that this side of God's being does not change. It is present in him in one perfect, timeless vision. It is God as the eternal orderer of the world. This aspect of God's nature has all the attributes which the tradition ascribed to him. It is eternal, it cannot be acted upon, it cannot suffer. It simply is, because if there is a meaningful world of time and process, then there must be an order which makes it a world and which sets the boundaries of how things can be related to one another.

God's primordial nature is the structure of possibilities; his

49. A. N. Whitehead, *Adventures of Ideas* (New York: Macmillan, 1933; Cambridge University Press), chap. X.
50. A. N. Whitehead, *Religion in the Making*, p. 50.

concrete nature is his participation with his creatures in the society of being. Whitehead calls this God's consequent nature. God's actuality involves concrete process. God shares with the creatures the power of his being, allowing them a measure of freedom and spontaneity so that God's temporal interaction with the creatures is a real history of inter-communication and action. What happens in this world makes a difference to God. He responds concretely to every new event by taking it as a datum into a new phase of his own life and adjusting it within the harmony of his vision. What remains fixed for God is the absolute integrity of his aim which looks toward fullness of life for the whole creation. To move the world toward this fulfilment, God shares in the concreteness of events. We avoid here one of the curious consequences of the Augustinian ontology which is that the world can add nothing to God. How can you add anything to absolute perfection? But in Whitehead's doctrine every achievement of good, of value, of meaning in the world increases the richness of God's being. God is not the world process. God is the eternal structure and power which makes a world possible and which participates in each moment of the world's becoming, for the world is nothing without him. As concrete life God is conscious, personal being.

Metaphysical outlooks are not provable as mathematical theorems. They are visions of the world which are to be judged, as Whitehead says, by their comprehensiveness and their adequacy to illuminate our actual experience.

There are three important consequences of this process metaphysics. First, it makes freedom and history intelligible as real aspects of being. In the classical metaphysics all temporal things are something less than real, because in being-itself all time and process are overcome. In the process view the spontaneity, originality and freedom of which we have some fragmentary experience is a clue to the nature of being. God's function in the world is not to make time disappear, or to make the future as certain as the past and the present. It is to give an ordered pattern to the creative life of the world and to bring new possibilities into existence in a real future. Those who are seeking for the 'secular' meaning of the Gospel could well turn to Whitehead's doctrine of the secular functions of God.[51] God holds the world together by offering his eternal structure of value to every particular experience so that everything happens in significant relation to the world order and the community of beings. But God's function as cosmic orderer does not destroy the freedom of the creatures within the order.

51. A. N. Whitehead, *Process and Reality*, p. 315.

The second major point in the process doctrine is that it deals with the significance of evil in a manner different from the tradition. Process metaphysics does not explain evil away. It is under no necessity of doing so because it does not make God the sole cause of every happening. He exercises his creativity in a real world which has elements of spontaneity, of chance, and, at the higher levels, of moral freedom within it. Metaphysics does not explain why the world is this way; but it can describe a cosmic society of freedom which involves tangled cross histories. Life histories interfere with one another, as when a virus inhabits an animal body and causes disease. Process doctrines can go the whole way with existentialism in recognizing that man in his freedom may plunge into self-worship, or self-destruction; but this is because the real world has this risk within it, not because God wills that any creature should lose the meaning of life or decrees that any person should lose his possibility of knowing the good and doing it.

The third consequence of the process doctrine is a new analysis of the meaning of love, both the love of God and the human loves. This is our central concern, and we shall give the next chapter to the philosophical aspect of this analysis.

CHAPTER VI

LOVE AND BEING

Being and loving are united in human life. Persons come into the world through an act which may be an expression of love. The child grows under the nurture of love which is first experienced through physical contact which is as necessary to life as food. We are told that 'lonely infants fed and cared for regularly and with sterile impersonal efficiency do not live into childhood'.[1] Growth to maturity consists in discovering what and whom we love and how we respond to the love of others. We would not know how to tell what it means to be human without an account of love.

In this chapter we ask a very old question, as old as Empedocles and Plato's *Symposium*, 'What light does our understanding of love throw upon what it means to *be*?' We saw that for St. Augustine love and being are ultimately one, but we also saw that he has difficulty making freedom and, therefore, human love intelligible. We are in search of an alternative understanding of love and being in which the freedom and creativity of human loves have their place and in which the love of God is understood in his involvement with a real history. We are in need of a metaphysical doctrine in which we understand reality in the light of the existence of loving beings within it.

Our thesis in this chapter is that it is possible to gain metaphysical insight through an analysis of love. We do not undertake a complete defence of the possibility of metaphysical knowledge. The issue as to whether we can have an intelligible account of 'being' is indeed vigorously discussed in philosophy today, and we cannot treat with indifference the serious questions raised by modern analytic philosophy about the meaning of statements about being. But I see no other way to a defence of metaphysical thought than to exhibit its power to illuminate human experience. What we undertake here is a very modest segment of the total enterprise. It is simply to ask what kinds of structures we find present in the human experience of love. We can then reflect upon what implications our account of these structures may have for a doctrine of God's being and his relationship to the world.

1. Quoted from Phyllis Greenacre in Karl Menninger, *The Theory of Psychoanalytic Technique* (New York: Basic Books, 1962, p. 78; London: Hogarth Press, 1958).

The question of what we are doing when we reflect metaphysically about love is so important that a brief account of the relation of our method here to other metaphysical methods is in order. In the philosophical tradition the metaphysicians have usually taken one of two opposing routes to the knowledge of what it means to be. The platonists and idealists turned to reason and the human spirit to find a higher order of being which transcends space, time and matter. They tried to reach a realm of being which is the foundation of the world but which transcends all the limitations of finite existence. The naturalists on the other hand, with a powerful impetus from Aristotle, took the categories of physics and biology such as form and matter, time and space, cause and effect, and sought real being in that which man shares with all nature. Descartes' attempt to put the two methods together with a doctrine of two modes of being, extended substance and thinking substance, is an uneasy and ultimately unworkable compromise.

A third way to metaphysical knowledge is being explored in contemporary philosophy. Here process philosophy finds something in common with the phenomenologists and the existentialists. The new method represents in one sense a much more modest approach to metaphysics. It does not seek a complete scheme and final knowledge. It proposes to describe significant aspects of human experience in order to gain some illuminating perspectives on the nature of the whole to which man belongs. Thus Martin Heidegger begins his search for 'being' with the analysis of *Da-sein*, man's *being there*, his concrete existence in space and time with the attendant realities of care, anxiety, freedom, working, using, deciding and dying. Alfred North Whitehead has much more concern than Heidegger for the problems of the new scientific world-views but he is not so different in his metaphysical method as he takes his departure from immediate human experience, establishes the category of feeling as his major clue to being and then seeks to elaborate the structures of human experience such as perceiving, remembering, valuing, becoming, and dying as giving us the structural scheme for interpreting all experience.[2]

What we may thus attain is not absolute truth in a total vision of reality but illumination of those aspects of our being which are determinative of all experience but are so easily overlooked. Human existence is one form of being and our interpretation must be such

2. Cf. A. N. Whitehead, *Process and Reality*, Pt. I, chap. 1. I am speaking of Heidegger's method in *Sein und Zeit* which I find more convincing as an approach to metaphysics than his later phase where poetic mysticism seems to replace dialectical analysis.

as to make human experience intelligible. Whatever is present in the inescapable structures of human experience must be present in 'being-itself' to use that as a synonym for ultimate reality. Indeed, except as sheer mystery, 'being-itself' has no meaning apart from the forms of being we encounter. If there are other aspects of being we have no way of knowing them. Being includes more than the human, all experience tells us that, but being is that which creates, and shapes human existence. In proposing then a description of the essential structures present in human love we are doing something akin to what Plato did without being committed to projecting these forms of experience into some absolutely transcendent realm. It is characteristic of Plato to begin with some question out of human experience such as 'what is justice?' and to pursue the analysis dialectically until that structure of being appears which makes the human experience of justice intelligible. The Form of the Good in the *Republic* is the category which makes justice, temperance, courage and wisdom intelligible. In the *Symposium* Plato used this method of getting at the nature of being by analysing love, and he there laid down the lines of a metaphysical method for interpreting love and being in a way which will prove relevant for us. Later Platonism and Neo-platonism became preoccupied with the dialectical problems of the Parmenides, and tended to lose the concreteness of Plato's humanistic method.[3] We are to probe the meaning of being through considering the forms of human love. At the very least, such a method might open up certain possibilities for metaphysical understanding which have been overlooked. This I believe can be shown to be the case.

We shall concentrate our attention on interpersonal love, and thus accept a certain restriction on the range of our method. We speak of love in many relations. Animals may love their masters and be loved by them. A man can love innumerable things, his tools, his play, his country, the landscape, food, music, silence. Our concentration on interpersonal love focusses attention on a particular form of experience. We can raise later the question of the relation of love of persons to other loves.

It is important to recognize that we do not restrict our inquiry to sexual love. It is arguable that all human loves have a sexual factor, but this certainly is not the definitive element in all. The categorial conditions for which we are searching may be the same for all human loves, whether sexual or not. Sexuality raises as many questions

3. For a penetrating survey of the philosophical discussion of love see Richard McKeon, 'Love and Philosophical Analysis' in his *Thought, Action, and Passion* (Chicago: University of Chicago Press, 1954).

about the possibility of human love as it settles. It is noteworthy that Jean-Paul Sartre, a masterly phenomenologist, sees the structure of love as more fundamental than sexuality in man's existence. But Sartre's analysis leads to the conclusion that each individual is enclosed within himself and going out of oneself to the other, which is the meaning of love, is really impossible.[4] If, against Sartre, we say that love is possible, what would be the conditions of being which it would require?

(1)

THE CATEGORIES OF LOVE

I propose five categories as necessary for love:

1. *Individuality, and taking account of the other*

Love requires real individuals, unique beings, each bringing to the relationship something which no other can bring. The individuals must be capable of taking account of one another in their unique individuality. In Leibnitzian language, there must be monads, but they must have 'windows'. This 'taking account of the other' means that each brings to the relationship an originality which belongs to him alone and each finds in the other an originality which belongs to that other alone. The individual who takes account of the other cannot see him merely as the illustration of a type. There will be in every experience of love forms and qualities which are experienced by countless others; but unless these universal forms are known in what makes the beloved this individual and no other, that which gives authenticity to love is not present. This position helps to un-cover one aspect of the confusion in much popular language about love which treats it as a universal experience which is merely illus-trated in particular cases.

We can see the necessity of this categorical obligation to preserve individuality if we consider the standpoint of one who is the receiver of love from another. If I am loved merely as one who illustrates a general type, then I know *I* am really not loved at all. I dissolve into a universal who is 'loved' by another universal. But persons are not universals; they are unique and irreplaceable subjects who exemplify abstract universals, but whose being is never wholly contained by them.

4. Jean-Paul Sartre, *Being and Nothingness*, pp. 408, 297, 615. Critical analysis of Sartre's doctrine in Paul Ramsey, *Nine Modern Moralists* (Englewood Cliffs, N.J.: Prentice-Hall, 1962).

It is a corollary of this analysis that if love be possible at all, then a non-defensive relationship to another is possible without destroying the individuality either of the lover or the beloved. Put positively, this means that relationship to the other can be a *concern* for the other which does not negate the selfhood of the lover or destroy the uniqueness of the one who is loved.

Experience in the psychological clinic shows the great importance of this doctrine. The fear of loving another or of being loved by another in anxiety for loss of self is a common neurotic symptom. All human love must overcome this fear, for in love two unique beings undergo a transformation through what each gives and receives, and this always involves a threat to the self *as it is*. Hence one of the categorical conditions of love is that there be a transforming relationship without destruction of individuality. To anticipate briefly, this gives us ground for criticism of many distortions of religious love, both love for God and love for man. The religious and ethical love which begins as response to God's love can very easily become depersonalized. But it is persons who love, and they risk being changed if they really love.

2. *Freedom*

There is a familiar image of 'falling in love' which sees love as fate, not freedom. To find oneself 'in love' is a state from which no act of will can extricate us, and for which no decision of ours is an explanation.

There is surely something here which belongs in any description of the conditions of love. There is no absolute freedom in human experience, and elements of arbitrariness, accident, and determinism enter into any relationship. But when we consider not only the beginnings of love but its full course, we must affirm freedom as one of its categorical conditions. This point needs to be developed. There are three aspects of the matter.

First, love always has an historical context. The 'not yet' is always an element in the experience of love, the future which has certain ineluctable features and yet which in its concreteness is unknown. Take the example of death. If Heidegger is right we are always dimly aware that life runs toward death, yet only in special circumstances are we able to know precisely about our own death.[5] This means that every commitment in the relationship of love is made in a history with risk and uncertainty. Our freedom in love consists in

5. Martin Heidegger, *Being and Time*, Eng. Tr. by John Macquarrie and Edward Robinson of *Sein und Zeit* (London: S.C.M. Press, 1962).

the way in which we accept, face, and interpret that risk. It may be assumed and faced or denied and repressed, but we cannot give ourselves authentically to another in love without the will to assume the demands and risks which are present. How we accept and deal with these demands is never purely impersonal and automatic, no matter how 'fated' or compelling the initial emotion or circumstances may be. We learn what it means to love not from initial attraction, but from the decisions which have to be made in the new life history into which love bids us enter.

The second aspect of the categorical demand of freedom is that to love is to affirm and accept the freedom of the other. It is not only the future course of life which holds the risk and promise of the unknown. The 'Other' makes his decisions about that future and in that history. To love is to accept another who makes his own decisions, including that of the love relationship itself. In loving I make the history of another's freedom my history. The refusal to accept the other's freedom to be and to decide is a failure in love, for we deny that in the other which is essential to love itself.

The decisive point concerning freedom is that if in love we will to be loved by another, then we must will the other's freedom to love or not to love. Nothing is more pathetic than the attempt to compel or coerce the love of another, for it carries self-defeat within it. That which is coerced cannot be love, hence in love we will that the other give his love freely. At the heart of every human love there is a dependence upon freedom which cannot be either bought or compelled.

The ability to love implies, thirdly, that we risk our existence in a relationship where predestination, in the sense of determination by something less than personal will, would destroy the meaning of love. Certainly the desire, the longing and concern for the love of the other is present, but this is subject to the absolute categorial condition that the other be free.

If freedom is never absent from love, neither is it ever unconditional freedom. It is qualified by the physical, emotional, and historical circumstances in which love exists. Further, all love has a history in the self, a beginning, a growth, a confrontation with crisis and decision, and such freedom as we have must be found within this history. We are free to make a commitment, but once it is made we are not free with respect to its having been made. We inherit emotional patterns and physical qualities, as well as cultural conditioning. One of the marks of authentic love is growth in freedom to acknowledge the realities, and to keep the integrity of the self within those realities.

3. *Action and Suffering*

To love is to act. Loving involves feelings, emotions, cravings, valuations and sharing, and all these require a movement toward the other, whether it be overt physical movement or the movement of the spirit. The power to act is a condition of love; but it follows that the capacity to be acted upon, to be moved by another, is also required; for to act in love is to respond, and to have one's action shaped by the other. It is this latter side of love which is often overlooked or misinterpreted, and it is of especial importance. It is the other side of the category of individuality. In love we give of our personal being and uniqueness. But we do not love unless our personal being is transformed through the relation to the other.

This means that there can be no love without suffering. Suffering in its widest sense means the capacity to be acted upon, to be changed, moved, transformed by the action of or in relation to another. The active side of love requires that we allow the field of our action and its meaning to be defined by what the other requires. To be completed in and by another is to be acted upon by that other. To be fulfilled in human love is to have one's freedom circumscribed (not destroyed) by the other's freedom. This meaning of suffering as being acted upon is essential here entirely apart from suffering as the undergoing of pain, although of course pain is one form of suffering.

It is one of the conditions of love that suffering enters into the texture and meaning of the relationship. It is by what is suffered as well as by what is given that love is recognized and its quality affirmed. Any experience of love includes the discovery of the other through what the other suffers for, with, and because of me. The evidence of love is nowhere deeper than this. 'Greater love hath no man than this: that he lay down his life for his friend.'

Suffering therefore is not something incidental or external to love; but it enters into the new life which love creates between persons. It is not only that in committing oneself to another we take the risks of certain kinds of suffering. It is that we accept the inevitability of being conformed to the other. When we love, we enter a history in which suffering is one condition of the relationship. We are to be conformed to the need of another. The sacraments of love, the giving and receiving, the shattering of self-centredness in authentic love, the refusal to possess without the free acceptance of the other, all disclose the significance of suffering as a constituent aspect of love.

Suffering has the power of communication. An examination of this power leads us further into the nature of love.

The forms of suffering are innumerable. There is destructive suffering, accidental suffering, apparently meaningless suffering. There is suffering which leads to growth, which becomes a source of creativity, and which challenges response. Suffering can lead to ugliness or to beauty. It can unite and divide. Any form of suffering can be a means of expression; a communication from spirit to spirit. It becomes a language of feeling and of caring and that is its importance for love. It can also be used as a weapon against the spirit. It can be used to create status and to tyrannize over others. But its great service to love is as the means by which one spirit reveals itself to another. This is why art or drama which describes love without suffering is trivial. The great literature of love is filled with suffering. Without suffering we are not spoken to in the depths. There is something more profound than catharsis in the aesthetic experience. It is the reconstituting of our being through the truth communicated through suffering.

The theme of humour in love belongs here at least in part. Humour is communicative and one reason is that it is very close to suffering. We are not speaking of the bitter and destructive humour that accompanies much conventional description of sexual love, romantic attachment, and marriage. We are speaking of humour which is enjoyed in love. Some is the humour of sheer play and delight. Some rises from what makes really profound humour, the sense of limitations, the ironies of fate, the recognition of our common humanity in this strange and incomprehensible existence. To say that without humour there can be no love may be to forget the element of temperament; but there is no doubt that there is a communication in love which involves the play and laughter which come from suffering together the human condition.

Our thesis that in the relationship of love suffering becomes a means of communication from spirit to spirit will enter into our consideration of how the divine love is expressed when we discuss the atonement.

4. *Causality*

Something must be said at this point about the way in which the categories involve one another. Each needs the other for its full explication. What we have said about action, suffering and communication implies causality. Since Buber and Nygren want to speak about love in 'non-causal' terms our alternative analysis of this category is especially necessary.[6] I argue against Buber and Nygren

6. See Anders Nygren, *Agape and Eros*, Pt. I, and Martin Buber, *I and Thou* (New York: Charles Scribner's Sons, 1958, 2nd ed., pp. 51ff.; Edinburgh: T. & T. Clark).

that love is meaningless without causality. Unless the actions and suffering of one move the other to action and suffering, the relationship is futile. But we must see the nature of this 'moving'. There are complexities in the relation of love to causality.

Love implies that there is a causal relationship which is compatible with freedom and with concern for the other's freedom. Mechanical causality is present in nature and in all human action, but mechanical causality must be superseded by another type where love is actualized. By mechanical causality I mean that which operates without any purpose of valuation except immediate and habitual response to a particular stimulus.

In love the kind of causality must be operative in which intentions are alterable in the very process of their exercise. We have stressed the role of the future in the commitment of love to the other. To love is to enter relationship in which the growth of love transforms the initial motivation. Dante's pilgrimage toward the vision of God which begins with the love of Beatrice is an archetypal account of this pilgrimage. Preoccupation with origins is fatal to love. This means that the causation which occurs in love must be of such sort that the growth and alteration of the persons and of the meaning of their love must be possible within the structure of causality which love exemplifies. That is to say, any absolute determinism is excluded.

Causality in love involves not only the prehension of the past but response to possibilities in the future.[7] Human freedom depends on real openness to the future. It follows that some future possibility can function as a cause, and in such a way that our decisions regarding the future have an element of freedom. Of course this does not require absolute freedom, whatever that would be. It is the requirement that for the reality of love human decisions must enter into the determination of the future.

We see that the causality operative in love does not exclude coercion. The issue here is ethical as well as metaphysical. In love we impose conditions upon one another both intentionally and unintentionally. We restrain one another, oppose our wills to the other's use of his freedom. We set conditions, pass judgments, and make demands. All these are aspects of human relationships which are intensified where there is love. But so long as love is present all such demands and conditions are intended for the sake of the other and for the growth of love. Certainly the condition 'so long as love is present' is supremely difficult. Much of sin gets into the human spirit under the guise of love; but the sin is not always the coercion of the other,

7. 'Prehension' is Whitehead's word for 'organic taking account of'.

it is the perversion of goals, the misuse of power, and the self-justification which grows not from love but from its absence.

One corollary of this view is that creativity in human relationship can never be the sheer imposition of one will upon another. It must be the kind of action, with whatever coercion is involved, which so far as possible leaves the other more free to respond. The goals of teaching, nurture, persuasion, punishment, when pursued in love mean the search in freedom for more freedom.

Love is often spoken of as being itself a cause, an effective power. The problems here involve many metaphysical questions about cause and power. One aspect of the power of human love can be singled out here. The discovery that we are loved does have a causally efficacious power which creates through that experience the transformation of the self. This is one of the most important themes in the psychoanalytic doctrine of love, not only in the Freudian school but also in all depth psychology. The attitudes and responses which the self finds in others are powerful factors in moving the self. Being loved creates a new person. We can make the general statement that inter-personal relations constitute a field of force in which action in any part of the field alters the structure of the field and all the elements within it. Psychology and other inquiries must fill in the empirical details here, complex and mysterious as they are. The decisive point is that there are several types of causality in inter-personal relations, and that there are unique aspects of causality between persons which reveal both the efficacy of love and its distortions.

It is to be observed that Aristotle's doctrine of final causation, whatever its place in the order of love, is a relevant if inadequate way to describe the dynamics of personal relationship. We are drawn toward what is yet to be. And it is not only being drawn to an object of desire which is at work in love, but also the transforming experience of coming within the orbit of the love of another.

5. *Impartial Judgment in Loving Concern for the Other*

Love is often described in terms which contradict impartiality and exclude any kind of evaluation. This is the case not only in descriptions of romantic love as unhinging the reason, but even the highest love is sometimes so interpreted. For example, Martin Buber and Anders Nygren put the highest love in tension with and even in opposition to rational calculation and objective evaluation. I propose a counter thesis, that there can be no real love without the rational function which aims to transcend personal bias, and which assesses objectively the human situation, including that of the lover, the beloved, and their relationship.

Consider that if love is concern for the other as he really is, then objective knowledge must enter the experience of what it means to commit oneself to the other. It is the sheerest sentimentality to suppose that love can dispense with objective knowledge. To be is to be involved in particular structures of existence, and to be a person is to respect the precise relationships of body, culture, and spirit in which we stand to others. For example, to love another person in the commitment of marriage is to deal with all that person's relationships, ancestry, family, vocation and life history, 'for richer for poorer, in sickness and in health'. To love is to accept responsibility for assessing the real situation in which we love, and that means self-discovery and discovery of the other. This does indeed require more than reason. Love contributes to knowledge and loving is in a sense a way of knowing; yet love does not yield knowledge by itself, but only in relation to the objective analysis of experience. The demand for impartiality in judgment then is not a contradiction of love; but the high tribute which love pays to the other, the tribute of seeking the truth in the other and the other in the truth.

This same point may be put in relation to the discovery of the 'needs' of the other. Even the most radical assertions that the divine love is 'uncalculating' usually come with the concession that love is concern for the need of the neighbour. But how shall we discover needs except by realistic appraisal and understanding? It is the precise trick of emotional bias to make us believe we are exercising love because we are giving the other what we think he needs. We may be ignorant of the real need and actually be satisfying ourselves instead of the other. It is not loving concern alone which tells us what needs are; the structures of human existence, and their discernment require impartial, loving judgment, united with critical reflection.

The settlement of claims in the light of an objective standard available to all is the meaning of equity, and equity is not the contradiction of love but one of the principles by which love respects the actualities of life. Without love we do fall below the standard of equity, and without forgiveness we miss that element in love which transcends purely rational justice. But love without equity becomes depersonalized. Charles Hartshorne says: 'Love is the effort to act upon adequate awareness of others, awareness at least as adequate ideally as one has of oneself.'[8]

One of the real dilemmas of human love appears here since love

8. Charles Hartshorne, *Man's Vision of God*, p. 165.

always seems to require concentration of concern upon some and not upon others. This produces a tension in every judgment of human need. Parents protect their children at the expense of other children. Sin enters here quite readily and easily amidst genuine moral dilemmas. But if the claim of justice is one of the structures of existence, then the being of the other is violated if this claim is not honoured, even in love. We see why in the strongest human loves concern for the other will be tempered with concern for the larger causes of justice which both must respect. This is in part, at least, what St. Augustine means by loving the other 'in God'. Only as we love the fullness of God's purpose more than any other by himself can we really love at all.

(2)

GOD'S LOVE AND HUMAN LOVE: THE PROBLEM OF ANALOGY

We come to the question of what use we can make of this analysis of human love when we speak of the love of God. Is not the heart of faith the recognition that God is utterly different from man? God is creator and not creature; Lord and sovereign, not dependent and limited by the conditions of our existence. Our knowledge of the love of God must come from his self-disclosure. It is not a projection from our human loves.

We have seen in our study of the biblical view of love that if we say human experience throws no light on the meaning of the divine love, we are departing from the biblical mode of speaking about God. The Bible uses many human images and analogies: master and servant, husband and bride, father and son. It is not only philosophers who have tried to think of God through human analogies, it is the way of the biblical witness.

Let us put the point in another way. It may be that all human analogies fail in describing the love of God. But the question of what God's love means requires us still to interpret the scriptural language. We have seen that the interpretation of love in the biblical faith has taken several directions in history. We have also seen that the traditional Christian interpretations of love have been largely influenced by one kind of philosophical thought about being. It is surely conceivable that another analysis of love in human experience might open up possibilities of understanding the meaning of the love of God testified to in the Bible in a way which breaks through traditional concepts. The spirit of love is greater than any of its forms of expression or comprehension.

I am arguing then for a revolution in ontological thinking, if we are to speak more clearly about love. On the strictest biblical terms there must be something in common between the words we use to speak about God's being and about our being, otherwise it is impossible to see how language about God the Father, and God the Son can be meaningful at all. What language could be more humanly relevant? The doctrine that there is a 'community of attributes' between God and the creatures is found in St. Augustine in his doctrine of the analogy of being.[9] The central point St. Thomas makes is that any rational justification for such statements about God as that he is one, good, intelligent, wise, and so on, is that the being of the creator is reflected in the being of the creatures.[10] Even Karl Barth, who once called the doctrine of the *analogia entis* the invention of the anti-Christ, has more recently acknowledged that there can be speech about God's being which is analogical but which is not bound up with all the classic metaphysical doctrines.[11] Barth has developed his own doctrine of analogy which, to be sure, he claims is based solely on the biblical revelation.

A full defence of the analogical mode of thinking about God would require an elaborate discussion. What I shall do here is to consider the consequences of applying to the doctrine of God the results of the analysis of the categorical conditions of human love. I shall try to show that this mode of thinking illuminates our experience of all love, and leads to a relevant interpretation of the biblical assertions about God and his revelation in Jesus Christ. In the end, the only justification for metaphysical thinking is that it throws light on human experience in its widest and deepest ranges.[12] Proof is out of place in speech about God, but we can seek insight where the tradition has left us in confusions and obscurity.

(3)

GOD AND THE CATEGORIES

If individuality, freedom, action and suffering, causality, and impartiality are categorical conditions of human love, then there is an initial presumption for Christian thought that the being of God,

9. Augustine, *Confessions*, VII, xi, 17.
10. St. Thomas Aquinas, *Summa Theologica*, Pt. I, Qu. 13, Art. 1–5.
11. Karl Barth, *Church Dogmatics*, I/1, Preface, p. x; III/1; III/2, §29.
12. A. N. Whitehead, 'The ultimate test is always widespread, recurrent experience'. *Process and Reality*, p. 25.

who is love, is in some way reflected in these structures of our existence. There is no good reason for taking away from love all that constitutes its distinctively human aspects and using the remainder to construct a doctrine of love in God.

It is often argued, to be sure, that many of the structures we have designated, such as suffering, the limitation of power by another's freedom, the involvement in risk, constitute deprivations of being, and hence are not appropriate tokens of the divine nature. But this is precisely the issue to be discussed. Are they merely deprivations, or are they positive and constituent elements of love? Suppose love is the capacity to will the freedom of the other, whatever that freedom may mean for the one who loves? Is this any less a positive element in the being and value of love than its other attributes, such as power or goodness? Charles Hartshorne says that the notion that God is more perfect the more completely he is removed from change, time, and risk, is a prejudice which simply contradicts our experience of human love.[13] What we have to look for is some explanation of why the tradition that perfect love is beyond suffering has such a powerful hold.

If the categorial analysis of love explodes the notion that the conception of God must require absolute simplicity, unchangingness, and impassibility then the analogy of being may be understood so as to affirm a creative, temporal, and relational aspect in God's being. In this metaphysical outlook we can really carry through the analogy between human love and the love which is in God. It will still be analogy. We acknowledge our situation and our limitations when we use human categories in our speech about God. If we seek a doctrine of being, it is clear that God as the reality which is necessary to all being cannot sustain exactly the same relationship to time, space and change, which the creatures exhibit. God's being is that on which all being depends. All times are embraced in his everlastingness but the future is really future for him also. The power of being in the creature is not the power of being itself, but a derived and limited power. God does not come to be or pass away, but he can be involved in the changes in a world where there is coming into being and passing away.

The problem of a metaphysical theology is to carry through the analogy of being with full justice both to the structures of experience and to the transmutation of structures as they apply to the being of God.[14] Whitehead, for example, who declares that in rational

13. Charles Hartshorne, *Man's Vision of God* (pp. 114–120).
14. St. Thomas's doctrine of analogy has been criticized because in the analogy of proportionality we are left with the assertion of some relationship

metaphysics God must exemplify the first principles of being, still has to allow for categorial differences between God's way of being and that of the finite actual occasions. God is necessary to every finite being, but no particular finite being is necessary to God. Love in God must involve what is required for love among the creatures and between God and the creatures, yet God remains God, involved in the history of the creatures as the being upon whom they all depend.

Let us put what this means for the relation of love and being in the metaphysical aspect of theology in a summary statement.

If God is love and the ground of the structure of love, then he remains in the absolute integrity of his being what he is throughout all time and all circumstance. His love is what ours never is, steadfast, adequate to his purpose, complete in concern for all others. Yet God constitutes with his creatures the metaphysical situation in which their love can be real, and in which love between himself and the creatures can be actualized. This means that our categories of individuality and communion with the other, freedom, action and suffering, causality which leaves the other free to be moved by the other, and impartiality of judgment have their analogues in the being of God. This means that God is not non-temporal in all respects, beyond causality, beyond any of the structural requirements which make love between beings possible. Rather he exemplifies these categories as positive structures of his love.

This constitutes such a considerable revision of the traditional doctrine of God that its very radicalness may argue there must be something wrong with it. I think this reaction is mitigated if we remember that in spite of much of the formal ontological language about God in traditional theology, the language of devotion has been modelled very largely on the acceptance of God's hearing, responding, sharing, and suffering with his creatures:

> I waited patiently for the Lord;
> He inclined to me and heard my cry.
> He drew me up from the desolate pit,
>   out of the miry bog,
> and set my feet upon a rock,
>   making my steps secure (Psalms 40: 1–2).

between God's being and finite being, but we do not know what this means for God's being. See Dorothy Emmet, *The Nature of Metaphysical Thinking* (London: Macmillan, 1946). The agnostic note certainly creeps into St. Thomas's doctrine and one reason is that he saw the paradoxes involved in combining the view of God as simple, immutable, and impassible with the biblical language about God as Father, Son, and Spirit, begetting the Son, and Creating and Redeeming the World. Process metaphysics proposes analogies in which the Creator-Redeemer God of the Bible is really conceived as creative being.

> And after you have suffered a little while, the God of all grace who has called you to his eternal glory in Christ, will himself restore, establish, and strengthen you.   (I Peter 5: 10)

> In this is love, not that we loved God, but that he loved us and sent his Son to be the expiation for our sins.   (I John 4: 10)

To review all the categories with a full discussion of their analogical application and transmutation is a very large task. Let us indicate the main lines which this inquiry will follow.

1. *The Individual*

God who loves has the integrity of individuality. He relates himself to others in a communality of being. So far this assertion is in harmony with the traditional theological standpoint. God is one, and other than any creatures. All things are brought into being through his will. He loves, he can be addressed, and he can be loved.

The doctrine of the trinity raises the problem of individuality as well as other ontological issues. It has been often observed that the doctrine provides for a community of being in God himself within which love as action and response can be meaningful. This may be one way in which the tradition has recognized that an absolutely solitary individual can neither love nor be loved. But let us leave the logic of the divine individuality in relation to the doctrine of the trinity and pass to another issue.

The necessity for 'individuality in relation' in all love does make it difficult to see how God as 'being itself' can love at all. 'Being-itself' is either the absolutely alone ONE, utterly beyond all categories, or it is the synthesis of all structures and beings. But can a synthesis of all structures be a loving being, or a source of love? This onto-logical problem of God's being in relation to love seems to me the critical point for the Augustinian-Tillichian tradition. For while God cannot be simply one being among many, his individuality as one in relation to others is implied by the assertion that he loves. 'Being-itself' is an inadequate expression for God. 'Being which is the source of the community of beings' is better.[15]

2. *Freedom*

If love means willing the freedom of the other, then the possibility of combining love with predestination or absolute determinism is swept away. If God wills to love, and, above all, if he wills to *be* loved he cannot determine the love of the other, even though it be

15. Daniel D. Williams, 'Tillich's Doctrine of God', *The Philosophical Forum*, Vol. XVIII, 1960-1.

the determination of the creature by the creator. This doctrine of radical freedom does not mean that every possible meaning of the doctrine of predestination is negated. If destiny is the shape of a possible future which must be actualized in freedom, then God is the supreme predestinator. Every destiny is shaped by him. But destiny without freedom is meaningless. That is, even God cannot absolutely predetermine a future which has a loving community within it.

Again, we have seen that coercion is one instrument of love, but it must be coercion for the sake of winning freedom for the other, and freedom is personal decision, not automatic response. Therefore this approach to the doctrine of God means a revision of the traditional view of the exercise of the divine sovereignty. It rejects the doctrine that since God is love he must in the end win every creature's response. If he loves, he risks the refusal of love.

It should be added that the assertion of limited freedom for the creatures also involves the assertion of all the freedom in God compatible with the freedom of the creatures. God is the supreme instance of freedom to love. He never refuses to love, but the specific action of his love lies within the mystery of his being which no ontological analysis can fully penetrate or exhaust.

3. Action and Suffering

A third consequence of our analysis is the rejection of impassibility in God. To love is to be in a relationship where the action of the other alters one's own experience. Impassibility makes love meaningless. In asserting this thesis, familiar in process philosophy, I wish to stress the analogical situation when we speak of God's suffering.

Suffering in human experience always suggests and may well include some destruction of our being. It always threatens our poise if not our integrity. It can deaden sensitivity. We may say that these things result when our love is not strong enough, but that is not the whole story. Our finitude has its price. There may be more than we can stand. Life takes us beyond the limits of our strength. To love is to recognize that there will be destruction in time of what is humanly precious.

Suffering in God cannot be regarded in just the same way. It is not a pain or deprivation which threatens his integrity. It must be the acceptance in the divine of the tragic element in the creation, a patience and bearing with the loss and failure, and ever renewed acceptance of the need for redemptive action. Suffering always threatens our being. It never threatens the being of God, but is an element in the history of his accomplishment of his will. It may involve a threat to the completion of his purpose in a given occasion, but not a deflection of his purpose.

Again, suffering is what it is for us in part because we do not see its full consequences. In our doctrine of God, even God's knowledge does not encompass all the specific aspects of future free decisions. But God's being includes his knowledge of all possible outcomes. He knows the boundaries of all tragedy, just as he knows the infinite resources for dealing with every evil. Suffering is thus transmuted in God without being eliminated. God participates in the world's suffering, but without all the limitations which beset finite sufferers.

We remain close, but not too close, to the tradition when we say that there is that in God which does not suffer at all. The invulnerability in God is the integrity of his being, his creative vision and function which is his sovereign majesty. This is not acted upon, it is not moved or altered. But God in his creativity works in and through creatures who do suffer and who become occasions of his suffering. The traditional doctrine that the Son suffers but not the Father seems a hopeless compromise. It makes the relation between the Father and the Son utterly different from love, and the non-suffering Father an unbelievable being remote from anything which makes being good.

4. Causality

What the analogy of causality excludes from the doctrine of God is his exercise of sheer power to create without becoming involved with the creature, and without being subject to the suffering which follows upon the creature's freedom. Causality without involvement is incompatible with love. The traditional assertion that the will of God is the ultimate cause of every event cannot be preserved without qualification, because a will which allows no effective power to any other cannot be a loving will.

Here the ontological approach to love in relation to causality leads a little way toward the solution of a persistent theological problem. How does God act upon the world? How does his love move the sun and the other stars, and human hearts?[16]

We have seen that the act of love toward the other may elicit the response and transformation of the other. Nygren thinks of all *eros* love in the pattern of the soul's being drawn towards the object of desire. But the analysis of the human *eros* reveals that something more is involved. The power of love is evoked not only by the presentation of the desirable, but by experiencing the attitude and

16. I have elaborated this point in 'How Does God Act' in Reese and Freeman, eds., *Process and Divinity* (La Salle: Open Court, 1964).

disposition of love toward the self from another. This is a human analogue of what the biblical faith testifies, that God's self-communication through historical experience has power to evoke and reconstruct a human response. The divine action need not be thought of as a matter of super-casuality behind the scenes through which everything happens; but as the continual divine self-communication, presenting to the creatures not only the good to which they may aspire, but also the support and recreative power of the sustaining and loving reality which is in the depths of all things.

All metaphysical analysis is abstract. It seeks only those aspects of being which constitute its structural necessities and forms. No metaphysics can give us the fullness of being, that of a blade of grass or the smallest unit of matter. Contemporary metaphysical thought recognizes these limitations. The analysis of structures, however, can enable us to see the concrete more clearly and this constitutes the sole justification of metaphysical thought. We are seeking an interpretation of the love of God and the loves of man in the light of the biblical faith and in relation to human experience. We have gained some ground in this alternative to the classical way of speaking about God's being, and we see that this suggests some fundamental clues concerning how God's love is communicated to us. We look now at three major themes of Christian theology using the instrument of this vision of God's being. The three themes are: God and man, the history of freedom and sin; Jesus Christ, God's action in the incarnation; and redemption, the meaning of atonement.

CHAPTER VII

GOD AND MAN

In his great essay, *The Fire Next Time*, James Baldwin describes his youth in New York City's Harlem:

> Yes, it does indeed mean something—something unspeakable—to be born, in a white country, an Anglo-Teutonic, anti-sexual country, black. You very soon, without knowing it, give up all hope of communion. Black people, mainly, look down or look up but do not look at each other, not at you, and white people, mainly, look away. . . . The universe which is not merely the stars and the moon and the planets, flowers, grass, and trees, but *other people*, has evolved no terms for your existence, has made no room for you, and if love will not swing wide the gates no other power will or can.[1]

The situation Baldwin describes has its specific context in the racial problem, but within it he has discovered the crux of the human situation. Communion is another word for love. Man is created for communion but he loses it and he loses the power to recover it. If we believe that in spite of man's failure love can be recovered we have the triple theme of the Christian Gospel. Man bears the image of God who is love. Man's love falls into disorder; but there is a work of God which restores man's integrity and his power to enter into communion. Every Christian theology is an elaboration of this theme. Man is a battlefield upon which many loves clash. His self-love may become so powerful that it can over-rule every other force. Man is the source of love's perversion, the speaker of the kindly word which covers the vicious evil, the wearer of the mask of pride. Man falls into unlove, and experiences the boredom and horror of life without meaning. Man is captured by some loves to the exclusion of others. He is the sensualist for whom the flesh becomes God, or the moral idealist for whom 'love of mankind' is drained of all emotion and there is neither concern nor pity for real human beings. Yet man must find love in and with others for it is the only fulfilment life offers. He is the being whom no earthly love satisfies, until it becomes a way to the love of God. When man's love fails or becomes distorted, the final resource in the love of God is a creative act of

1. James Baldwin, *The Fire Next Time* (New York: Dial Press, 1963, p. 44; London: Michael Joseph, 1963).

healing. Love is disclosed as grace. In this and the two succeeding chapters we examine these major assertions of Christian faith in the light of our interpretation of love as spirit at work in history.

(1)

LOVE AND THE IMAGE OF GOD IN MAN

In the biblical faith man's greatness is understood in the light of of the image of God which he bears. If God is love the image of God in man defines the forms of love in human existence. Yet the image is defaced, distorted, 'ruined', so the Reformers said, by man's wilful self-separation from God. Can we get light on the nature of the divine love from man's distorted experience of love? This question of what happens to the image of God through sin underlies some of the most critical issues in the Christian interpretation of love and it will be worthwhile to give some attention to the history of this theme and its development in contemporary theology.

The traditional Roman Catholic doctrine is derived from Irenaeus, who noted that two words, *tselem* and *demuth* are used in Genesis I to assert that God has created man in his image. Irenaeus therefore made a distinction between the *image* of God which is man's distinctive endowment of reason, his dominion over nature, and his creaturely dignity; and the *similitude* to God which is faith, hope and love, that is, the full and righteous relation which man is supposed to enjoy as God's creature. For Irenaeus it is this *similitude* which is lost in the fall but the image remains relatively intact. This has formed the ground plan of all subsequent Catholic theology with its formula of 'grace completing nature' as the pattern of redemption. The *similitude* must be restored to the *imago*. There are, of course, many qualifications to be made of this brief characterization, but it is essentially the traditional Catholic position.[2]

The Protestant Reformers attacked this structure. They said that not only is the similitude lost in the fall, but the whole image of God is left in 'ruins'. Nothing in human nature is left intact after sin. The reformers wanted to show that the corruption of the fall extends to the whole man. They believed that the Catholic pattern leads to an unjustified confidence in human reason which is subject

2. Full critical discussion of the history of the doctrine of the *imago dei* in Emil Brunner, *Man in Revolt* (London: Lutterworth Press, 1939; New York: Charles Scribner's Sons, 1939), Appendix 1. David Cairns, *The Image of God in Man* (New York: Philosophical Library, 1953).

to pride and demonry. They saw the image of God as constituted by the 'original righteousness' with which God endowed Adam. They said this righteousness, which is man's right relation to God, has been lost almost completely. We say 'almost' because Luther and Calvin had to make some qualification concerning the effects of the fall. Neither they nor their followers in Protestant orthodoxy believed that man has lost all sense of God or of moral obligation. Something constructive must be left in human reason and conscience if man is to have a basis for a collective life with a measure of justice and sanity. Thus Calvin asserts that the capacity for 'civic righteousness' remains in fallen man.[3]

Whichever of these traditional positions we take, we see that our view of the place of love in human existence is at stake. The Catholic doctrine makes the love of God one of the three supernatural virtues, and says that in the fall faith, hope and love are lost. But can the love of God be lost without profound effect upon the whole of man's life ? When St. Augustine says that without faith and love the reason cannot be rightly ordered in the world or rightly directed toward God he seems closer to the Reformers than to St. Thomas. On the other hand, the Catholic tradition contends for a truth which must not be surrendered, that there are in fallen man capacities for reason, conscience, and creativity which are not wholly destroyed by sin.

Theology in the twentieth century has been interpreting the *imago dei* in a way which expresses the personal and historical nature of the relation between God and man. Thus the foundation is laid for a theology which understands love as the centre of human existence. Since it is the Christian faith that God is love, it is curious that theology has been so late in taking love as the key to the Christian doctrine of man. Let us see what this new direction involves for an understanding of human love and the divine love.

In a well-known controversy Karl Barth and Emil Brunner debated Brunner's thesis that the *imago dei* remains in fallen man *formally*, but that it is lost *materially*. To this Karl Barth replied, 'Nein'.[4] Subsequently both Barth and Brunner explicated their positions in ways which not only brought their views closer together, but which may avoid the compromise of the reformers with the 'relic' of the imago, and the dubious simplicity of the Catholic view that sin leaves the *humanum* relatively intact.

Karl Barth now speaks of the *imago dei* as the distinctive form of human existence, that is, life in community. Following a suggestion

3. Calvin, *Institutes*, Bk. II, 2, xiii.
4. Eng. Tr. of the debate in *Natural Theology*, a translation by Peter Fraenkel of the principal texts (London: G. Bles, 1946).

made by Dietrich Bonhoeffer, Barth says that the connection in Genesis between the *imago dei* and the creation 'male and female' is not incidental, but that this primary form of human community indicates the meaning of the image of God in man. Barth analyses man's life in community in four 'categories of the distinctively human'. These are:

(1) Being in encounter is a being in which one man looks another in the eye.
(2) There is mutual speaking and hearing.
(3) We render mutual assistance in the act of being.
(4) All the occurrence so far described as the basic form of humanity stands under the sign that it is done on both sides with gladness.[5]

In this structure of community Barth sees a reflection of the divine community, the Trinity. Barth reminds us that God says, 'Let *us* make man in *our* image'. Barth thus gives his own version of St. Augustine's bold suggestion that in the being of man there is a reflection of the holy Trinity, God's being as Creator, the Father; the knowledge of his being, the Logos; and the rejoicing in that knowledge, the Spirit. Barth here continues the tradition of 'metaphysical' theology except for one very important difference. Barth says this 'image of God' does not give man any knowledge of God whatever. Man does not know God. His human existence does not point him toward God. All man's religion is false and idolatrous. Thus Barth seems in the end to maintain the position he asserted against Brunner: there is nothing in man as he actually is which in any way discloses his origin in God.

It is hard to see how Barth's ambivalent position here can be defended. If the form of man's life in community is derived from the being of God, then there is something in man which does point toward the true God, however obscurely it may be known. Process theologians make this criticism of Barth. They believe man has an awareness of his God-relationship, however confused it becomes.

Apart from the special issue concerning Barth's doctrine of sexuality as the key to the *imago dei*, there is something like a consensus in contemporary theology concerning the theme of the *imago dei*. What we are coming to see is that it is a mistake to define the *imago dei* as any set of attributes or qualities which man may possess. The *imago dei* needs to be conceived in dynamic terms as the relatedness which God has established between himself and man and to which man can respond. Karl Barth sees the *imago* in the forms

5. Karl Barth, *Church Dogmatics*, III/2, No. 45, 2.

of human interaction, the life of personal communication in sharing and rejoicing. Emil Brunner stresses the theme of responsibility.[6] Man is the being who can respond to the claim of the other, and give himself to the other. James Muilenburg interprets the Genesis in similar terms:

> This is characteristic of Old Testament thought, everywhere; divine revelation is revelation which places man before a choice, a decision which must be made. The highest purpose of man—his supreme task and function—is to do the will of God. It is not coincidence that Christian faith sees the Son of God wrestling in the torment of decision before he goes to the cross. . . . It is the image of God in man which makes him a decision-making person. His ability to choose, the freedom implied in his choice, his sense of difference and value, these surely are aspects of what is divine in him.[7]

All these converge on the view that the *imago dei* should not be conceived as a special quality, but as the relationship for which man is created with his neighbour before God. The image of God is reflected in every aspect of man's being, not as a special entity but as the meaning of the life of man in its essential integrity. But surely this can be most clearly grasped if we say that love is the meaning of the *imago dei*. In this way we can recognize in man that which underlies his special capacities such as reason, moral judgment, artistic creativity, and religious awareness. All these find their meaning in life which is created for communion, that is personal existence in community with others. This is the universal fact of facts, deeper than reason and the integrating reality in life.

This thesis that the *imago dei* is the form of creation for life fulfilled in love gives us our basis for the interpretation of sin. The root of sin is failure to realize life in love. The cleft in man which results from sin is more than the loss of a supernatural endowment. It is disorder in the roots of his being. It is the disaster resulting from twisted, impotent or perverted love. Sin infects the whole man. It does not at once destroy the reasoning powers, though in extremity it may do even that. It does not completely take away conscience, though the loss of love may finally result in the disappearance of conscience. It does not eliminate creativity from man's life, though it may turn that creativity into demonic self-destructiveness. It does not leave man without any sense of God or knowledge of the holy, though it may distort this sense, turning man's worship into idolatry and leaving him without hope and seemingly without God.

6. Emil Brunner, *Man in Revolt, passim.*
7. James Muilenburg, unpublished paper, *The Doctrine of Man in the Image of God*, p. 6.

If this analysis be correct all human loves have something in them which pulls them on a tangent toward the love of God. They reflect their origin in God. A doctrine of man following this clue will search in the human loves, even in their incredible distortions, for that which reveals man's relationship to the loving God who is his Creator. The love of God can be present whether it is overtly recognized or not.

In this way contemporary theology has moved to a dynamic interpretation of the image of God, its loss and restoration. The process theology which informs our interpretation of Christian faith agrees wholeheartedly with this view of the image of God in man; but it proposes a distinctive addition to the doctrine, for process theology sees love disclosed in a history in which the spirit of God creates new forms. In this history God is involved with the world both as its eternal ground and as the supreme participant in the suffering which his creativity involves. In process theology therefore the 'analogy of being' which holds between God and the creatures must be related to a fully historical conception of what being is. Man bears the image of God in his temporality as well as his participation in eternity, in suffering as well as in peace. His loves are in process. There are three implications of this way of understanding the image of God in man, which have important consequences for our understanding of man's estrangement from God and the consequent disorder in his existence.

(2)

God's Creativity and Man's

God's love is creative power bringing the worlds into being, and working with them for the fulfilment of an ever new creative order of life. The Kingdom of God is the goal of his creation, but we need not conceive the Kingdom as a fixed 'state of being' toward which things tend. The Kingdom of God is the fulfilment of God's being in relation to every creature, and if being is love, then the Kingdom must be an infinite realm of creative life.

Man's creation in the image of God is his call to participate in creativity, in its splendour and its suffering. Creativity is at work in all things, and certainly in what we call the secular orders. To love is to become responsible for doing what needs to be done to make the world a more tolerable place which reflects more fully the glory of its origin. When we love God we love the infinite creative source of being. God's work is everywhere and needs no state of completion for its meaning is endless creative life. To love God is to love the one who sets the ultimate boundaries to life, boundaries which are not defined by a final state of affairs, but by ever new possibilities of growth.

The second implication of this doctrine has to do with the metaphysical truth that to be is to respond. We have seen that passivity to the other, setting the other free, and the will to have one's own existence shaped by the other as well as to give oneself creatively constitutes one of the categorial conditions of love. If then life in communion is the essential nature of man, this includes transformation by participation with the other, and the acceptance of suffering with and for the other. It is not the essence of man to try to make himself invulnerable. That is sin. It is the essence of man to find the meaning of his life in a community of mutual responsiveness and sharing.

This doctrine exactly reverses Jean-Paul Sartre's view that what marks human existence is the impossibility of breaking through to the other or being reached by the other. The tragedy is indeed where Sartre sees it, in the way we do become 'walled off' from one another. But this is tragic because it contradicts man's essential being, which is his will to communion.

We also find here a resolution of the problem which D'Arcy has posed in the tension between the two loves of self-affirmation and self-giving. Something has to link these two loves, and in D'Arcy's structure as we saw it there would have to be still a third love. But in the process view there is no need for that complication. Both self-affirmation and self-giving are aspects of the essential love which is the will to communion. Self-affirmation without response is deadly. That is why egoism so often becomes desperate. Self-giving without self-affirmation is meaningless. That is why much of what appears to be self-giving love is really self-destruction. What we need to see is that self-affirmation and self-giving are united in the essence of love which is communion. Tensions are present indeed, and the failure to reconcile them constitutes the dark side of the human condition, but there is no contradiction in the essential pattern of love.

We are speaking of the *imago dei*, and this means that the love which God gives to man and which man may return to God bears some analogy to the human will to participation. God makes himself vulnerable to receive into his being what the world does in its freedom, and to respond to the world's action. We acknowledge always a drastic limitation in speaking of the being of God and his love.

What it means for God to love the world, to suffer, to give freedom to the creatures and to will communion with them is the very mystery of existence. We must not equate our being with God's and say that love, suffering, freedom, and creativity mean for him precisely what they mean for us. What we can do, however, within the perspective of Christian faith, is to give an account of the love of God which does not make nonsense out of the profoundest aspects of love in human experience. If we say that the *imago dei* in man is his creation for communion with God and the creatures, we mean that God wills communion on terms of man's real freedom and responsiveness. It is to know that the love God offers is responsive love, in which he takes into himself the consequences of human actions, bears with the world, and urges all things toward a society of real freedom in communion.

This doctrine in no way negates the great assurance of the New Testament of the steadfastness and the inexorableness of the love of God. Paul's hymn at the close of Romans 8 expresses the ground of Christian faith:

I am persuaded . . . that nothing can separate us from the love of God.

So also does his assertion that love never passes away (I Corinthians 13). What God gives is his absolute faithfulness, his everlastingness in unceasing love. The meaning of existence lies in the possibility of communion in freedom; this is what is assured to faith.

The power of God, however, is not that of absolute omnipotence to do anything. It is the power to do everything that the loving ground of all being can do to express and to communicate and fulfil the society of loving beings. God's power expresses his love, it does not violate it. Therefore it is the kind of power which holds the world together in one society, setting limits to the freedom of the creatures without destroying that freedom. Whitehead remarks, 'The power of God is the worship He inspires'.[8]

If this view of the relation of love and power be accepted the book of Job must be read as a half-way point on the way to clarification of the meaning of God's power. To be stunned into silence before the sheer might of God's creativity is indeed one dimension of man's discovery of his place in things. The power of God stretches beyond all imagination and description. We cannot solve the riddle of why things are as they are. But the biblical doctrine of God does not remain with man abased before omnipotence. It asserts that man is

8. A. N. Whitehead, *Science and the Modern World* (New York: Macmillan, 1927, p. 276; Cambridge University Press, 1936).

given knowledge of God by the way God gives himself in his en-counter with the world's evil. He ·persuades the world by an act of suffering love with the kind of power which leaves its object free to respond in humility and love.

Love does not put everything at rest; it puts everything in motion. Love does not end all risk, it accepts every risk which is necessary for its work. Love does not resolve every conflict; it accepts conflict as the arena in which the work of love is to be done. Love does not neatly separate the good people from the bad, bestowing endless bliss on one, and endless torment on the other. Love seeks the reconciliation of every life so that it may share with all the others. If a man or a culture is finally lost, it is not because love wills that lostness, but because we have condemned ourselves to separation and refuse reconciliation. We make our hells and we cling to them in our lovelessness.

Much conventional religiousness, born of a mixture of piety and anxiety, conceives love as a special power which will bring every problem to resolution and every life to completion. There is, how-ever, a subtle error in the view that love's goal is to bring life to rest. In the name of love it deifies the power of absolute disposal. It makes the goal the peace of completion rather than the peace of openness to new experience in a shared community. It makes love a special kind of power which renders all others impotent, whereas love is just the power of being, using, shaping, eliciting, and recon-ciling all the special powers in the creative movement of life. Many distortions of religious devotion and ethical life come from a too simple view of what the love of God is, and from the use of love as escape from the risks of life, rather than as the will and power to accept them.

Here, then, is the first consequence of the doctrine of God's being as love in process. Man, created in God's image, is created for participation in the infinite life of communion within the everlasting creativity of God.

(3)

The Love of God and the Love of His Creatures

A second consequence of the process doctrine of God is that while the distinction is preserved between man's love for God and man's love for the neighbour, this is not the distinction between love for what is merely temporal and love for what is eternal. We can distinguish between love for the eternal source of creativity which works in the temporal world, and love for the creatures whose being involves their participation both in God's eternal structure and in his temporal creativity. This point is worth our especial attention. Much confusion about love results from the supposition that what is in time and unfinished cannot be loved as fully as that which is complete.

We have seen how St. Augustine, in spite of his clear teaching of the goodness of the creation, asserted the superiority of loving God to loving the world because God is eternal and the world is temporal.[9] This devaluation of the temporal world is a remnant of platonism. Our present doctrine seeks to counteract it.

We say that God has both an eternal and temporal dimension in his being. To love eternal being as a different kind of being is to miss the real point about God's love, that it is manifest not only in his eternity, but in his temporality. It is the essence of God to move the world toward new possibilities, and his being is 'complete' only as an infinite series of creative acts, each of which enriches, modifies, and shapes the whole society of being.

God's being abides. This is the supreme contrast between his mode of being and ours. Augustine is so far right. God is not at the mercy of time. His love remains constant in its intention. He does not pass away. All times are in his hands. There is indeed a dimension in the love of God which differs from human love, and the platonists and many mystics have seen it. To discover or be discovered by the love of God is in one sense to find the unchanging, perfect and final meaning of all things. This is that aspect of rest in love which finds its completion only in the love of God. But that is only one side of the truth. The other side is that the love of God not only creates the temporal world, but shares in its temporality and its becoming.

The true contrast between God and the world is not that between timeless eternity and the temporality of the creatures. It is the contrast between the supremely creative temporal life of God and the fragmentary, limited creativity of the creatures. To love God, then, is to set the highest value on temporality as well as on eternality, for in this view temporality is a dimension of all value.

It is this explicit evaluation of temporality which is the critical point. The creatures are not to be contrasted with perfection because they are temporal; but only because their creativity is fragmented, distorted and partial. To love God is to do more than love the creatures, but it is not to turn away from the creatures. It is to rejoice as fully in temporality as in eternality. The Kingdom of God is not a static state, but an everlastingly rich process of becoming.

9. *Supra*, chapter 5.

In this view we can still accept St. Augustine's doctrine that we love others in God. Nothing has its being solely in itself. To love another is to seek that person as he is, in all the dimensions of his life, and in all that makes him a person. It is to love the bond which makes us one with him, that is to love God. The Christian doctrine here presents a sharp contrast to all humanism. If Christianity is true, there is no such thing as loving another only for himself, for every person is a participant in the society of being. He bears the image of God and he is loved as one who belongs in communion with God and with his fellows.

This doctrine that we love others 'in God' has been criticized as leading to depersonalizing of love. To love another 'in God' seems to suggest that the other is devalued. He is merely an illustration of being so it is not really the person that we love, but God.

We have seen this danger in St. Augustine's version of the doctrine; but the danger lies in Augustine's presupposition about the contrast between God's being and the being of the creatures. To love another in God does depersonalize, *if we make God's eternity the key to his perfection in contrast to the creatures*. Then another person can only be a pointer toward the eternal which is superior to all temporality. But in process doctrine the meaning of God's being is his creative communion with the creatures. God values each person in himself, and as a participant in the creative history of the world. Thus to love another in God is to acknowledge in the divine love that which affirms the unique value of the person. Once we break through the traditional deification of timelessness for its own sake, the meaning of the *imago dei* takes on a new dimension.

(4)

HUMAN CREATIVITY

The third important consequence of this doctrine is the affirmation of human creativity as implicit in the *imago dei*. Man bears power and responsibility to reconstruct his world, reshape his life, and create new value.

This theme, to be sure, is not altogether absent from the traditional doctrines of the *imago dei*. Christian theology has always asserted some margin for man's creative self-expression. The *imago dei* includes reason, and the power of reason to grasp meaning involves creative expression of that meaning. Aesthetic creativity is shown in the uniqueness and greatness of human culture. As C. N. Cochrane says in his *Christianity and Classical Culture*, the Christian faith discovered a depth in human personality which classical culture had not envisaged.[10]

In the modern period the potential creativity of man has been disclosed in ways beyond the imagination of every previous culture. Man can reshape the conditions of his life, change the face of nature, eliminate killing diseases, reconstruct the human body, control the growth of population in ways beyond anything remotely conceivable before the twentieth century. Natural disasters are still present in flood and earthquake, yet to an increasing degree man changes the conditions of the earth, his homeland. Now he begins to explore the far universe, lengthen his life span, discover unlimited sources of energies in the atom, and crack the genetic code.

Creativity can be demonic as well as productive. The new powers of man bring possibilities of total self-destruction. Man can end his existence on this planet. He can dehumanize as well as create. All this means that the significance of the *imago dei* must be reassessed. God sets limits to life, but those limits include much wider possibilities than we have known. Man's cultural development produces a raging despair as he contemplates the possibilities for self-destruction, and also the megalomania of complete self-confidence compounded by the fanaticisms of groups and national passions. In this new historical situation love has to do its work.

(5)

THE IMAGO DEI AND SIN

An account of evil can be given from many points of view—medical, psychological, and political—but an account of the evil called sin implies belief in man's spiritual freedom and therefore in his guilt. Only a creature who bears the image of God and is capable of loving God and his neighbour can 'sin' in the Christian sense of that word.

An account of sin, then, must describe the career of the human spirit in its freedom. How can such an account be given? It is a plausible position that nothing can be said about sin except to confess it, for it cannot be objectified. It is life turning away from life in communion. It is man's wilful violation of his essential and created goodness. What more can be said? Karl Barth spends little

10. Charles N. Cochrane, *Christianity and Classical Culture* (Oxford University Press, 1940).

time in his vast dogmatic system on the discussion of the nature of sin. It is, he says, the 'surd' in existence. It should not be there. It has no metaphysical status. It cannot be rationally conceived. Every attempt to describe it may easily fall into an 'explanation' which does not explain.[11]

Yet to leave the matter here would be to pass over two important aspects of the meaning of sin. One is that just as the spirit of love can be seen as reflected in its forms, so the forms of sin may be described even though their roots are hidden. The second point is that just as the spirit of love has its history in the creation of new forms, so we can try to clarify the meaning of sin through analysis of the forms in which men have acknowledged sin in different historical situations.

These two observations lead to a third. The history of love and the history of sin are the same history. This is the biblical perspective. The Bible gives four principal images of sin:

The creation story and the fall, in Genesis;
The covenant story and the unfaithfulness of Israel to Yahweh;
The incarnation story and the crucifixion of the man of love;
Paul's account in Romans 1 of man's initial knowledge of God, his refusal to honour God, and his fall into the disorder of sin.

All four accounts begin with the original communion between man and God. In each case man disrupts the relationship. He refuses to love, trust, and honour the Creator who gives him life. In all four accounts there is a resulting failure of love of the neighbour, a fall into a disordered life where all the loves are perverted by disunity and discord.

The history of sin's primordial appearance can be variously recounted in the faith which has the story of Israel and of Jesus at its centre, but the meaning of sin is always a refusal of love. This is why the identification of sin with its particular forms is always mistaken. It is the error of legalism. The *centre* of sin is not in the various forms of transgression but in the personal history of man who is created for communion and refuses it.

The descriptions of the particular forms of sin which theologies give are largely attempts to recognize sin in its second or objectified stage. It cannot make sense that we put ourselves in the place of God in pride, or plunge into the nothingness of sensuality in despair, unless something has been disrupted in that communion which makes us human. Disobedience or the breaking of the law of God is conceivable only if in some way we have already become lawless. This

11. Barth, *Church Dogmatics*, II/2, p. 185.

is the point which moralists and legalists who identify sin with
specific acts generally overlook.

Further, if creation for freedom to love is the image of God in
man, sin is a perversion of man's essential being. It draws its power
from what man really is. There can be no sin without love, either
love perverted, love distorted, or, and here we peer into a deeper
depth, love destroyed by a revengeful unlove which turns against
life itself. There is a tradition in theology which holds that nothing
is done without love. Etienne Gilson states it for the medieval
theologians:

> Even in the midst of the lowest pleasure, the most abandoned
> voluptuary is still seeking God; nay more, as far as regards what is
> positive in his acts, that is to say in all that makes them an analogue
> of the true Love, it is God Himself Who, in him and for him, seeks
> Himself.[12]

The seven deadly sins have traditionally been interpreted in their
relation to love: pride, envy, and anger are perverted love, for we
take delight in what should grieve us; sloth is deficiency of love,
and avarice, gluttony, and lust are excessive love.[13]

(6)

THE EXISTENTIALIST ANALYSIS OF SIN

Modern theology has tried to go beyond the traditional ways of
interpreting the forms of sin to achieve some further insight into its
roots and its manifestations. The movement begins with Kierkegaard,
who tries to do two things: to give a phenomenological description
of anxiety as the occasion (not the cause) of sin, and to give a
phenomenological account of the forms which result from man's
fall such as loss of selfhood, impersonal objectivism, and despair.
Kierkegaard does indeed say that sin cannot be described, it can
only be spoken about in faith. What he says about the forms of
human despair and the sickness of the spirit is not intended as
objective description of sin. But in several major works he gives a
phenomenological description of the forms of man's fall away from
the authentic selfhood with which God has endowed him. The
existentialist movement inaugurated by Kierkegaard has become

12. Etienne Gilson, *The Spirit of Medieval Philosophy*, tr. by A. H. C. Downes
(New York: Charles Scribner's Sons, 1936), p. 274.
13. Dante Alighieri, *The Divine Comedy*, Carlyle-Wicksteed, Tr. (New York:
Modern Library, 1932).

philosophically creative as it has described man's loss of his *essential* humanity. Theology, as Dr. Tillich says, needs this existentialist analysis.[14] It is a means of insight and confession for our age. Each age reveals itself to itself in its account of good and evil. In the twentieth century, 'the age of the Grotesque', as Dürrenmatt has called it, we must try to give an account of man which in some way can encompass the monstrous evils, the horrors of mass murder, the idolatry of nation and race, the plunge into the meaningless, the fascination of evil, and the abyss of despair in innumerable lives.[15]

Theologians inspired by Kierkegaard's analysis have been trying to give an account of the internal history of the fall into sin. The key supplied by Kierkegaard is found in his analysis of anxiety. Man as a creature has a depth within him which stretches his imagination to infinity. He can desire eternity, yet he knows that he dies.[16] 'Anxiety is the dizziness of freedom!'[17] As creatures with a sense of the infinite, we grasp for absolute security and know we do not have it. Now this situation is not sin, but it is temptation to sin, to try to overcome our anxiety and in a fake or dishonest way to get out of the threatened state. We try either to seize security or to escape from the struggle for it.

Reinhold Niebuhr has given one of the most searching descriptions of this inward history of the fall of man. In *The Nature and Destiny of Man* his chapters on sin are masterly analyses of individual and group pride and of sensuality. For Niebuhr self-love is the primal form of sin. Therefore it is a disorder or failure in man's love which is the heart of the fall from original righteousness. Niebuhr tends to see pride as the most fundamental and persistent form of sin. Pride appears as pride of power, pride of intellect, pride of moral achievement and spiritual pride which finds in religion its convenient vehicle. Thus religion becomes the final battleground on which the issues of spiritual life and death are met.

Niebuhr's analysis of sensuality is equally astute. The anxious self can make its own self-gratification the sole object of desire, or sensuality becomes a convenient means of escape from the self's agony through the obliteration of feeling, the plunge into nothingness.

Niebuhr sees the fall into sin as inevitable, viewed from one side, because in man's situation as creature in a threatening world he is

14. Paul Tillich, *Systematic Theology*, vol. II, pp. 19–28.
15. Eric Bentley, ed., *The Storm Over The Deputy* (New York: Grove Press, 1964), pp. 104, 108–9.
16. S. Kierkegaard, *The Concept of Dread*, tr. by Walter Lowrie (Princeton: Princeton University Press, 1946).
17. The phrase is Reinhold Niebuhr's.

always tempted to try to make himself more secure than he can be. Yet Niebuhr holds to responsibility despite inevitability. This is a paradox which reason cannot unravel. In all pride and self-love man bears responsibility. His freedom is corrupted from within.[18]

Paul Tillich's description of the forms of sin varies somewhat from Niebuhr's.[19] Tillich reviews the three major descriptions of sin in the theological tradition: Sin as unbelief, as *hubris*, and as concupiscence. Each of these tries to get at the inward and personal root of sin. Sin as concupiscence is the turning of the self in upon itself, the *cor incorvatus in se*. It is not merely self-gratification or 'selfishness'. It is a distortion of love, an inversion of the self's true direction, so that everything to which the self should be given in love is now sought as a possession. It is the power of love transformed into the will to become absolute. Sartre sees this drive for divinity at the centre of man's existence. 'To be man means to reach toward being God. Or, if you prefer, man fundamentally is the desire to be God.'[20] But it is an inevitably frustrated desire. Therefore the love of being finds it must destroy its own ultimate object. Nietzsche understood and expressed the frustration of one who wills to be God but cannot. So Nietzsche must proclaim the death of God, his murder by the 'ugliest man'. It is this dialectic of the love which cannot accept communion with another, but tries to become absolute which lies in the depths of sin as *hubris*. Luther and Kierkegaard give us classic expression of the struggle with the temptation to hate God.

The Reformers stressed the theme of sin as unbelief, and Tillich gives it central importance. Unbelief here does not mean rejection of dogma, though it is subject to that distorted interpretation. Unbelief means refusal to trust God. It is the spirit's disloyalty to its creator. The Genesis story finds in the serpent's temptation of Eve the suggestion that God is not to be trusted; he has lied to man about the fruit of the tree (Genesis 3: 4).

Luther says, in his *Treatise on Christian Liberty*, 'The beginning of all sin is to depart from God and not to trust him'.

From the standpoint of process theology this view of the core of sin as unbelief or refusal to trust is the profoundest point reached in the tradition. It suggests an interpretation of sin in relation to the doctrine of the image of God as man's creation for freedom in communion. Anxiety is temptation to refuse life in communion. The forms of sin are ways of seizing substitutes for communion or of smothering anxiety about its loss. The existentialist tradition

18. Reinhold Niebuhr, *The Nature and Destiny of Man*, Vol. I, chapters 7–10.
19. Paul Tillich, *Systematic Theology*, Vol. II, pp. 44–59.
20. Sartre, Jean-Paul, *Being and Nothingness*, p. 694.

which Reinhold Niebuhr and Paul Tillich have interpreted so profoundly in their theologies, I am now proposing to say, becomes even more illuminating when we take not simply the will to be, but the will to *belong* as the key to human action and feeling. Acknowledging great indebtedness to the theologies just briefly reviewed I shall try to show what a functional analysis of man as created for communion may do to illuminate our experience of the forms which unlove takes.

(7)

SIN AND THE WILL TO BELONG

Begin with the assertion that the fundamental human craving is to belong, to count in the community of being, to have one's freedom in and with the response of others, to enjoy God as one who makes us members of one society. Out of the Civil Rights movement has come a good English phrase for this, 'a sense of somebodyness'.[21] If we begin here we can say that the root anxiety is that of 'not-belonging', of not counting. Men are not afraid of not existing nearly so much as they are afraid of not being wanted. This is proved daily when death is risked, or even sought for the sake of a love, a loyalty or a protest. Here then we make one qualification of Tillich's doctrine that matters of ultimate concern are those which determine our being or our non-being. When we ask what really constitutes being for man the answer is that it is belonging, or communion which constitutes its heart.

If this perspective on the nature of man has validity it will throw some light on the experience of lostness, revolt against life, and despair in the twentieth century. There are two facts about contemporary culture which rise starkly before us. First, the abandonment of personal freedom and judgment to the passions of group loyalty and idolatry; and second, the cruel and wanton destruction of human life.

Albert Camus, in his brilliant *L'Homme Revolté*, has pointed out that the crime of crimes in our time is murder. The ruthless taking of human life is one of the perennial facts of history, but the twentieth century has experienced perhaps its worst example, the concentration camps.[22] Irving Stone says:

21. The phrase has been used by Martin Luther King.
22. Albert Camus, *The Rebel*, Pt. V (London: Hamish Hamilton, 1953; New York: Vintage Books, 1959).

That one set of human beings could do this to another set condemns our whole species. There are savages within us against whom we must be on our guard.[23]

It is the word 'savages' here which needs critical analysis. It usually refers to the uncivilized and unrefined stages of culture. It is tempting to see the wanton violence and cruelty in human history as a 'throw back' to what is primitive and undisciplined in human nature. Shirley Jackson Case, who held an optimistic view of history, attributed the cruelty in human nature to an inheritance from 'Neanderthal man'.[24] But the question is whether we can explain this side of human history as regression. Do we not have to see the real problem in the highest reaches of the human spirit rather than the lowest? No animal is as cruel as man or as destructive. No primitive mind could invent the equivalent of the Nazi concentration camps. No savage could articulate the exquisite self-justification of the kindly and paternal White Supremacist. A theological student working for Civil Rights in the South, himself a Southerner, described the opposition of some white people in the community in which he was working. He reported that the depth of passionate hatred directed against those who were trying to affirm racial equality was 'simply unbelievable'.

The pathology of the spirit is indeed 'unbelievable', but its roots can be probed. We have to perceive in the dark side of human history not only the persistence of savage passions, but we have to see the distortion in the very height of human nature. The power of love and the craving for love has turned against itself.

To be human is to desire to belong, to have the security of being recognized in a group which accepts us, speaks our language, holds our values, gives us our freedom to move as we will. There is a natural love for our people in the intimate family group and in the larger community. This is the natural foundation of love of homeland, love of country, love of 'ours'. But this love is always a troubled love, for no group can give all the security we crave. No human community can be as completely fulfilling as we wish, and moreover there are the threats to its existence both from within and from without. Whatever threatens my group threatens me. The threat may be overt or it may be subtle, such as the threat of sheer difference in colour, religion, language, taste, or morals. Any non-conformity is a warning signal that my group is challenged. In the resulting

23. Irving Stone, 'What Some People Have Forgotten About God's Deputy', in *The Storm Over The Deputy* (New York: Grove Press, 1964), p. 236.

24. S. J. Case, *The Christian Philosophy of History* (Chicago: University of Chicago Press, 1943), p. 213.

anxiety we are tempted to reject the other's claim to our concern, and to absolutize ourselves. The will to belong becomes the will to preserve our way against every other. Since this can never be wholly justified rationally, we seek justification by identifying our way with the absolute good.

Thus the passion of the will to belong becomes the passion of self-deification. The superior must defend itself against the evil and inferior. Human history proves that there is literally no limit to the wanton cruelty and destruction of others of which some men are capable. This is not to say that all group pride is without a sense of perspective. The problem is complicated by the fact that there are real issues of justice and defence of values in any important conflict. Elements of sanity remain. We are describing the pathology of the spirit, not its residual element of health. We see however that the will to belong can be perverted into absolute hatred and destructiveness of anyone or anything which threatens the security of our belonging.

Certainly innumerable factors of economic, social and political history enter into the causes of human conflict.[25] The love for the group can be deliberately and cynically exploited by those in a position to control and to persuade. But the demonic passions unleashed in history lead to the theological question, 'How does the powerful and creative love in the human spirit turn into brutal and destructive cruelty?' The answer we suggest lies in the anxiety of not-belonging.

The fury of racial and national hatreds is indeed beyond explanation, but we recognize two ways in which the power of love is appropriated in these passions. On one side the threats to present security drive us to desperate defence of what we have. The fear of losing the community we now enjoy draws strength from our present love as we resist every threat to its existence, or to its alteration. On the other hand we do not ever completely kill the longing for the larger community. Therefore our self defence becomes desperate partly because we must resist our need to come into relationship with the other whom we reject. The more deeply we crave a human relationship to those excluded from the present circle of love, the more powerful must be the resistance to it. The fury of hatred is born in part out of the need to resist in the self what we really crave in love and communion. This dialectic of feeling operates powerfully in the experience of racial prejudice. The recognition of the other as a human being who might be loved must be denied

25. Cf. Gordon Allport, *The Nature of Prejudice* (Cambridge, Mass.: Addison Wesley, 1954). Anchor Books edition, 1958, pp. 476ff.

else the whole structure of our present prejudice would be swept away. One possible disguise of the real situation is to persuade ourselves that we really do love the other in his place and at the social distance we prescribe.

With this analysis we can also anticipate the nature of the healing which must come to human loves. Something must re-create the capacity to belong in the society of God's creatures so that man finds his security in giving himself to the service and enjoyment of God and His Kingdom as the ultimate context of every human love.

Another aspect of the sin which results from man's failure to love, is self-destruction. We are not primarily concerned here with the question about suicide, for suicide occurs in many circumstances which cannot be easily categorized. It is the turning of man against his humanity with which we are concerned, the self-sought de-humanization manifest in so much individual and social pathology in our century. Conformity explains much of the success of the Nazi mass murder programme. Also political imperialism and cynical power-seeking help to explain it; but there is something even more sinister, the turning of man against himself. It is that strand in Nietzsche's thought which consists in despising man as he is. It is the disfiguring of humanity in the worship of evil which Genet describes in his novels and plays.[26]

The ultimate mystery of evil is that man in becoming human denies that which makes him human, his freedom in communion. How does this happen? How can it happen? Here the existentialist philosophy has developed Kierkegaard's analysis in a significant way which throws light upon the nature of love.

In modern existentialism the 'Fall' is something which takes place inside each individual soul. It can be described in this way: there are two ways of existing, the authentic and the inauthentic. The authentic way is to be ourselves, to affirm our humanity, make our choices, and take life as it comes, feel it as it is, not lie to ourselves about how we do feel and think. The one truth to which authentic life must hold is that we are free to tell the truth about life, and to choose how we shall take it. Sometimes this is put with a kind of stoic resignation. We can only choose how we will take life, not whether we can alter any of its arrangements. Sometimes it is put with more of the sense of freedom to make life over. The so-called 'death of God' theologians have made much of this shift from stoicism to optimism.[27] But the essential point of this humanist

26. Jean Genet, *The Balcony* (London: Faber & Faber, 1958).
27. William Hamilton, 'The New Optimism from Prufrock to Ringo', in

doctrine of authenticity is that we can 'be ourselves' using our individuality for shaping our lives, and that is authentic existence. As Jean-Paul Sartre says it, 'authenticity consists in having a true and lucid consciousness of the situation, in assuming the responsibilities and risks that it involves, in accepting it in pride or humiliation, sometimes in horror and hate'.[28]

Inauthentic existence is the fall from inner self-determination. We allow ourselves to be moulded by what others expect of us. We feel what the advertisers want us to feel, to respond as the propagandists intend us to respond. We tell ourselves that we really do feel what we are expected to feel. We allow our self-image to be constructed by others. We are sunk in the mass, as Heidegger sees us. Such existence is inauthentic precisely because it is not *our* existence. Note that this is *inauthentic* life no matter how high the ideals which society or church may press upon us. We are fallen because we have become less than free men.

Dr. Carl Rogers' psychological researches provide significant analogies to this view of the fall. He describes it as the separation of our conscious experience from our organic feelings. We are cleft inside. We hold a picture of who we are which will not allow us to admit our real fears and desires. We become literally separated within ourselves, and this inner cleft is the beginning of the fall into self-rejection. Rogers is not an existentialist, but he remarks:

> I have been astonished to find how accurately the Danish philosopher, Soren Kierkegaard, pictured the dilemma of the individual more than a century ago with keen psychological insight. He points out that the most common despair is to be in despair at not choosing or willing to be oneself; but that the deepest form of despair is to 'choose' to be another than himself'.[29]

A Christian doctrine of sin will appropriate the insight expressed in existentialism, and which, in the case of Kierkegaard, is derived from Christian sources. What needs to be emphasized is that in this fall within the self some sort of *self-betrayal* is involved. It is not—notice—that we betray our *best* self; that is a moralistic way to put it. We betray our *real* self, with its struggling, its hopes and fears. We refuse to trust ourselves in our real relation to anything. We refuse to believe that life is good and worthy for us as we really are,

William Hamilton and Thomas J. Altizer, *Radical Theology and the Death of God* (New York: Bobbs Merrill 1966).,

28. Jean-Paul Sartre, *Anti-Semite and Jew*, (New York: Schocken Books, 1948), p. 90.

29. Carl Rogers, *On Becoming a Person, a Therapist's View of Psychotherapy* (Boston: Houghton Mifflin, 1961, p. 110; London: Constable & Co. Ltd.).

that our small margin of freedom with all its risks makes the difference between fulfilling life and destroying it. Sin is unbelief and here it is unbelief in ourselves.

It seems only a short step from this discovery that we do betray ourselves to the fact that in all such betrayal we are destroying not only ourselves, but—*Man*, yet this is a step which many find it difficult to take. Most of the existentialists do not take it. For them the fall is wholly an individual affair within each man. There is no human nature to be betrayed, no *Man* as such; for this they say is an abstraction, a mere idea and unreal.

But existentialism reveals its own instability here. If there is no 'human nature', that is, no universal principle of human existence in which all are involved, then how can we make a distinction between authentic and inauthentic existence? If, as Sartre seems to say, each of us makes himself up as he goes along, creates his world out of nothing, how can anyone say of another that his way of life is inauthentic? By what standard? If you say 'by the standard that each one should choose his way of life', then you are stating a universal principle of what it means to be human.

The awesome fact is that in every human attitude and choice we make, we are taking an attitude toward EVERYMAN. In choosing our way we take a position in relation to every way.

This point bears upon racial and class intolerance. People who put other human beings in a lower class or treat others as inferiors degrade their own humanity. What I do to another I accept as a possibility in his treatment of me. This is usually denied by those who discriminate against other groups, but it is the logic of the matter. Whatever I do to another human being, that in principle I do to myself. This logic proves itself in life, for once the spell of the sense of superiority is broken, we discover that those who despise other people create a cleft within their own personalities. They destroy part of themselves in destroying others. The *imago dei*, our common humanity, cannot be wholly eradicated.

Here is one illustration of how the violation of certain human relationships discloses the wrong in which we are all implicated.

In recent years there have been revelations of scandals in college sports. Young men's lives have been ruined in sell-outs to gamblers. Mass dismissals from schools of national importance have taken place. Who was responsible? Many people involved in no direct way discovered they had an uneasy conscience. Back of the pressure on the players was not merely the evil design of gamblers. There was the 'exploitation of the hero' in modern athletics. There was the greed and desperation of institutions trying to make money and prestige out of athletics. And there was the compensation for our insecurities in hero-worship. The strong man, the winner, is the reliever of our own frustrations and the surrogate for our vindictiveness against opponents. With sure insight Arthur Miller has Willie Loman in *The Death of a Salesman* relieve his sense of failure in daydreams of his son carrying the ball over the goal line before a hundred thousand cheering spectators.

As a result of the scandals in athletics the student editors of a school paper in Canada decided that they bore a direct share of guilt, and announced they would publish no more athletic news with the following declaration as reported in the Press: 'We have helped make campus heroes out of football players. We have contributed to making university sport into big business and big business the yardstick of education.' The quoted comment of the coach in this particular school was: 'I'm amazed. I'm speechless.' One knows however that there are many coaches, athletic directors, and athletes who saw the cost of exploitation long before the rest of us did.

To this analysis of sin we must make two additional points.

The first is that a theological interpretation of man's existence is not an alternative to its analysis in economic, political and psychological terms. Human history is infinitely complex. Every life is shaped by the struggle for survival, the accidents of history, and the power of cultural symbols and traditions. We do not know what human life would be without the distortions produced by sin. It is always difficult if not dangerous to try to assign in a simple way the element of real sin and guilt in human actions. When some advertising men set out to reconstruct the American woman's self-image and make her identify herself as housewife in order to sell more pie-mix, how can responsibility for this violation of communion between persons be justly assessed?[30] Certainly there is sin in the society which makes this possible, but it is sin in the context of the struggle for existence, and the insecurities of men and women in a society where the terms of sexual equality and fulfilment remain obscure. A theological anthropology is no substitute for empirical cultural analysis. But without the theological dimension we miss what finally distinguishes man, his search for dignity as spiritual being.

Our second qualification is that the omnipresence of sin should not obscure the positive good in human life and human loves. Without the essential structure of goodness there would be no knowledge of sin, and indeed no meaning in speaking of it. It is

30. Betty Friedan, *The Feminine Mystique*, chapter 9 (New York: W. W. Norton, 1963; London: Victor Gollancz Ltd., 1963).

even possible to assert that human life can know a genuine recovery of innocence in spite of evil. Without a glimpse of innocence in moments of spontaneous renewal and creativity life would be intolerable.

But we lose our innocence, and we lose our freedom to love. Deep within the history of this loss there is the paradoxical fact that we lose our freedom in trying to make certain that we belong to a group or a power in which we can be free. We cannot give a final explanation of why this happens. But we can summarize our theological account of what happens in this way:

We are created for communion with God and our neighbour in a life which offers communion on terms which require courage and trust in a future we cannot see, which postpones fulfilment and does not allow every kind of immediate gratification. When we discover the risks involved in being human in the great community we are anxious, and when we do not find the hope of communion we are desperate. We willingly deny the fullness of our humanity in order to gratify some part of it. We choose to be human on terms which are immediately satisfying, self-protective and comfortable. But this choice can be an act of self-destruction, and in the depths of our being we know it. Like Albert Camus' Jean Baptiste in *The Fall*, we have refused to respond to the cry of another human being, and we are now less than the persons we must be if we are to accept life.

It is not a long step in the logic of emotion to will to destroy the sensitivity of life itself, to turn against ourselves and everything which symbolizes full humanity. We kill what we love because we refuse to love on the terms which life gives. Hannah Arendt speaks in her study of the Eichmann trial of the 'banality' of evil. The secret of that banality is here. Human evil is in some sense a rejection of life, that is, a rejection of what makes us truly human beings.[31] To be human is to search for the terms on which the self can be itself in relation to every other self.

In the structure of personal relationships there is a 'humanity' between us which is more than what we now are, but in which alone we can be human. We shall call this the Christological structure of human life. There is 'man' between us and our neighbour; and there is 'man' between us and ourselves, and between us and God. This

31. Hannah Arendt, *Eichmann in Jerusalem, A Report on the Banality of Evil*, Rev. Ed. 1964 (New York: Viking Press; London: Faber & Faber). Miss Arendt has been criticized for use of the term 'banality' here on the ground that it minimizes the monstrous character of the crimes, but the critics seem to me to miss the point. It is the dreary and pointless inhumanity of evil which she perceives and exposes.

'man' is not an impersonal principle, but is the formal possibility of our being in communion with the whole creation and the Creator.

The way of redemption must be the restoration with power of this humanity which is between us and yet beyond us. There must be re-created the actuality of our humanity in communion. The restoration of the hope for communion is not something we do, but what God has done and continues to do. It is this assertion that God's healing grace has become decisively present in Jesus Christ which we have now to explore.

CHAPTER VIII

THE INCARNATION

The meaning of love in the biblical faith is revealed in God's actions in history through his relationship to Israel and the giving of his Son to the world that all things might be reconciled to him. Yet in the Church's doctrine of the incarnation: the Person of Christ, and of the atonement: the Work of Christ, the love of God seems rarely to be given central importance. The meaning of Jesus' relation to God becomes debated as the relation of divine and human natures, and the traditional doctrines of atonement, except Abelard's, are shot through with metaphors from law court, battlefield, and penitential office which express the theme of love only indirectly, if at all. What would happen to traditional doctrines if the love of God were made the criterion for our understanding who Jesus is and what he has done?

In this chapter we ask what it means to understand the relation of God and Jesus as an expression of love, and in the next chapter we try to give an account of atonement which takes love as its centre and substance.

Certainly to understand love in the Christian way is to grasp what God has done in Christ, and to see what God has done in Christ is to understand love. We work within this circle not outside it, and do not claim a ready-made conception of love which unlocks all the mysteries of Christ. We are, however, insisting that however we interpret that mystery, our central clue is that God's being is love and our human situation bears the need for the restoration and fulfilment of life in love.

Consider, then, this approach to the meaning of the incarnation.

The Christian faith is that a decisive action of God in a human life has brought redemption, and has begun a new history of reconciled and fulfilled life. In Jesus Christ God has given what is needed to heal the disorders in the human spirit, and to inaugurate a new possibility for every life. Human history, and indeed the history of the whole creation, can now be understood from the perspective created by this action of God in Jesus.

The Church has never considered this assertion as self-interpreting. There is always more to be said in exploring its meaning and mystery. The New Testament itself grew out of continuing reflection on the meaning of Christ. Faith has sought understanding, not to dispel the mystery, but to keep it from false interpretation, and to find its coherence with a critical rational understanding of existence. Is the Christian assertion about Jesus Christ the imperialism of one more parochial faith, or does it really fulfil man's search for understanding? Is the meaning of God's presence in Jesus removed from all human understanding, or does it display a connection with the structure of every man's search for himself and for God?

We must first state our presuppositions about our knowledge of Jesus and the redemption accomplished in him.

(1)

THE HISTORICAL JESUS

We are speaking first of all about an historical person, Jesus of Nazareth, who lived and died in Palestine about the years 4 B.C. to A.D. 30. We date our Christian era from him. It is in this life, lived out on the soil of a small country in the eastern edge of the Mediterranean Sea, that the central act of God's dealing with human history took place. Such is the Christian assertion. Our knowledge of this action of God is bound to concrete historical data. The New Testament speaks about one who was born, grew, lived and taught, encountered religious and political opposition, and was crucified in the punishment often meted out in his time to criminals and to those charged with political subversion.

What can we know about Jesus of Nazareth? The records about him are the result of decades of remembrance, the preaching of a new faith, the growth of a tradition and its interpretation, in which categories are used which come from several Judaic traditions and from Greek and Hellenistic religion and philosophy.

The position I accept is that the Gospels are a synthesis of faith and fact and the two elements cannot be completely separated by any human research or reflection.[1] This can also be expressed in John Knox's terms, that Jesus was remembered, he was interpreted, and he was known still.[2] The Gospel record of Jesus is the witness

1. Cf. Paul Tillich, *Systematic Theology*, Vol. II, pp. 101–18.
2. John Knox, *Jesus Lord and Christ* (New York: Harper & Row, 1958). Knox's analysis of the historical problem seems to me the clearest in contemporary biblical scholarship. I have discussed his position in 'John Knox's View of History' in *Christian History and Interpretation*, ed. by W. R. Former, (Cambridge University Press, 1967), and the general problem in *What Present Day Theologians are Thinking*, 2nd rev. ed. (New York: Harper & Row, 1967), chap. IV.

to the meaning of life as held in the living memory of the community, and communicated in a process of tradition, reflection and interpretation.

When we speak of Jesus Christ, therefore, we are speaking of Jesus as the Church has re-examined, criticized, and reflected upon its remembrance of who he was. The fact that it is an historical memory of an actual person is as much a part of the remembering as are the great Christological reflections, such as the identification of Jesus with the Logos, the Eternal Word of God in the Creation. The words reported in the Gospels as spoken by him are there because Jesus spoke these or similar words, or words which gave rise to other words—yet we never have indisputable proof that he said this and not that. Certainly the New Testament record shows that Jesus' words have been added to, qualified and reinterpreted.

Every interpretation of Jesus of Nazareth grows out of the meaning of his life as it is rooted in history, but it is a history which has the memory and growth of a tradition as an ineradicable part of that history. It is impossible therefore to separate all the original empirical facts from later interpretation. We must try to read the New Testament as an account of what the man Jesus of Nazareth was heard, understood, and recognized to be by those who had their faith reborn through his impact upon them, either directly or through the hearing of the Gospel message preached.

It is a fair question why we need to bother with historical criticism at all if in the end we cannot separate faith and fact. The answer is that it is necessary in order to keep faith from taking flight from history and creating a picture of the Christian revelation which distorts historical fact. For example, New Testament criticism has enabled us to keep the picture of Jesus of history from becoming historically unintelligible when Jesus' self-interpretation as given in the Fourth Gospel cannot be integrated with the self-interpretation we find in the Synoptic Gospels. In Mark's Gospel, to take one instance, Jesus keeps the Messianic secret to himself until almost the end; in John it is proclaimed publicly from the beginning.

Again, there is always the danger of treating the suffering and death of Jesus as a purely 'spiritual' action, resulting from 'sin' but without concrete historical causes. Historical research points to the facts of the resistance of the authorities to his message of judgment, Jesus' concern for the poor, and his strictures against the exploiters. Historical research expresses the fidelity of the Church to history. When the question is raised about the 'historicity of Jesus' the meaning of the question requires discussion with the secular historian and a recognition of his methods.

We recognize and hold to the historical sources of the Gospel, but we are dealing with the meaning of Jesus as person and that is never something wholly objective. Practically all historical writing contains interpretation of motives which go beyond direct evidence. We have no picture of the inner life of Jesus save a few hints, and we should not try to reconstruct it. We cannot know Jesus' precise conception of the messianic mission, but only that he did not set the question of messiahship aside in preaching the Gospel of the Kingdom.

The nature of our knowledge of the historical Jesus, and the meaning of the phrase 'the historical Jesus', is indeed a critical issue for theology in our century. The interpretation given here of love as the meaning of the incarnation does not depend on any one solution of the problem of historical knowledge, but is, I believe, compatible with every view which accepts the main outlines of modern historical criticism and its methods. We shall now try to see if by focussing attention on love as the centre of the Gospel, we can gain a viable interpretation of the meaning of the Incarnation.

(2)

THE PROBLEM OF TRADITIONAL CHRISTOLOGY

It is well known that the traditional doctrine of the person of Christ was developed as an answer to the question, 'How are the human and the divine nature together in one Person?' In the context of the word 'nature' there was partly the Hebraic contrast of God the Lord with man his creature, subject to the passage of time and death. There was also the Greek metaphysical contrast between the eternal, divine, unchanging being of God and the temporal, finite mode of being of the world.

The Church Fathers saw clearly what was at stake. God must be fully present in Jesus else there is no real redemption. That is why Arianism was rejected. Christ was of one substance with the Father. But also Jesus has to be fully man, else there is no redemption, for our human condition must be penetrated to be redeemed.

The struggle to find a proper Christological language was not, therefore, a meaningless debate; but an attempt to guard the truth of the Gospel by finding terms which would not compromise either the divine or human side of the incarnation. The formula achieved at Chalcedon succeeded at least in setting the boundaries within which Christological thought must move. The two natures, divine and human, are together, unmixed, unconfused, inseparable, and undivided in one Person. The one Person is Jesus Christ, the Eternal Son, the second person of the Trinity who has taken human nature upon himself.

I have said this marks the boundaries within which Christological thought must move, but let us add a qualification, *so long as the terms of the problem are set in the relationship of two metaphysically contrasted 'natures' defined as the Greeks conceived them.* We can now see that the entire discussion in the first centuries was dominated by assumptions about divine and human nature which are open to question. It is a fact, for example, that on both sides of the dispute between the Alexandrines and the Antiochenes there was a constant fear of introducing any element of suffering or temporality into God. The Antiochenes, Theodore of Mopsuestia and Nestorius, had perhaps the stronger sense for the humanity of Jesus. They wanted to assure his moral personality, and the reality of his humanity which grew in wisdom and stature. They looked for formulas for joining divine and human which would protect full humanity. The relation of God and Jesus was a union of grace, Theodore said, which is analogous, though *only* analogous, to the union of love in marriage.[3]

From their point of view one of the Antiochenes strong arguments was that they were protecting theology from any suggestion of God's involvement in temporality or suffering. He is joined in a moral union, in fellowship with Jesus, but he is not, so to speak, metaphysically touched by the suffering of the man. The Alexandrines by contrast were accused of having to accept in their formulation the view that God has assumed the suffering of man for the one Person is a union of the two natures.

Cyril of Alexandria saw the problem acutely, and it is most instructive to see him struggle with it. If Jesus Christ, the God-man dying upon the Cross, is 'the One Person (hypostasis) incarnate of the Word', then is not God there suffering and dying? Cyril's answer which we have already quoted shows how desperately the Fathers sensed this dilemma.[4] God allows himself the signs of grief though he remains really impassible. It may strike us of a later time as curious that so much effort was expended to make certain that Jesus' death on the cross could not *really* mean suffering for God. The reason lies in the Greek conviction that only a God who is beyond

3. An important recent study is Rowan Greer, *Theodore of Mopsuestia* (London: The Faith Press, 1961).
4. *Supra*, p. 93.

all movement, impervious to all influence from beyond himself, and therefore free from the possibility of suffering can really be God.

We need not deny that something important is being protected here; but is it being wisely protected? Suppose we reverse the Greek assumption and hold that God's capacity to involve himself in the suffering of his creatures and of his incarnate Son is the supreme manifestation of his divinity. His suffering is the exhibition of his perfection, which is not that of impassible being but of love which cannot be impassible.

With all respect to the Chalcedonian achievement it strangely sets the theme of divine love to one side in arriving at the agreed upon formula. It is true that the Chalcedonian statement begins with a rehearsal of the Nicene-Constantinopolitan Creed with its affirmation of God's becoming man for our sakes, and this is recognized as the action of divine love. Yet curiously little is said about the mode of redemption in the discussion, and nothing is said about the love of Father and Son in the formula of the incarnation.

What is wrong here is not that metaphysics has replaced confessional theology. It is that a metaphysics in which love between God and man cannot be intelligible is presupposed in the very attempt to say that God has shown his love in taking the form of a servant, and sharing our human lot even to death.

If love constitutes God's being, and if man is created in the image of God, then the key to man's being and to God's being is the capacity for free, self-giving mutuality and concern for the other. This leads us to fundamental convictions about the meaning of the incarnation.

(3)

JESUS AS GOD'S ELECT MAN

In the New Testament faith Jesus is God's Elect Man. He is the beloved Son made flesh. The life and death of Jesus are set within a specific action of God. Here we have the New Testament parallel to the Old Testament faith in which election love appears in the creation of the covenant relationship. God elects his Servant, his Beloved.

The conception of the incarnation as an act of grace appears early and persists throughout Christian history even though it seems close to adoptionism, the condemned heresy which held that God selected the man Jesus at a particular time in his career to become the Christ. St. Augustine, for example, boldly says:

> The Saviour, the Man Christ Jesus, is Himself the brightest illustration of predestination and grace. Every man, from the commencement of his faith, becomes a Christian by the same grace by which *that* Man from his formation became Christ.[5]

Augustine is not, to be sure, committed to adoptionism by this accent on the electing grace of God giving his Messiah to the world. The New Testament thinks of election as hidden in the mystery of God's purpose. 'He chose us in him before the world was founded' (Ephesians 1: 4). The whole of Jesus' life is the expression of the divine action. He has a vocation, a summons from God, to respond to the divine will as the one who incarnates God's love.

We noted the distinction in the Old Testament between God's election love by which he establishes his covenant with his people and his *chesed,* the love which becomes compassion, forgiveness and redemptive concern for his people in dealing with their faithlessness. In the New Testament account of the incarnation both aspects of the divine love are present. God's election love is his love of the Son, and through him his call to abundant life for all his people. There is an ancient discussion in theology as to whether God would have become incarnate had there been no sin. St. Thomas Aquinas obviously finds the view attractive although he concludes, on biblical grounds, that it was because of sin that the Word was made man. He immediately adds, however, 'And yet the power of God is not limited to this;—even had sin not existed, God *could* have become incarnate'.[6] The incarnation fulfils the purpose of the good creation. It is the expression of God's creative will to raise up his people and establish his Kingdom.

But the history of man is the history of the good creation invaded by sin. The love which becomes incarnate as Jesus takes upon himself the suffering of the world is the merciful, compassionate love of God. The meaning of incarnation incorporates the taking on of the burden of sin. Paul boldly says Christ was made to be sin for us (2 Corinthians 5: 21). The love which God expresses in Jesus is love taking the form required by the situation it meets. The creative divine love becomes suffering, redemptive love for the sake of the world. The spirit of love required a new form to meet man's need.

So far we are speaking of the incarnation as the action of God's prevenient grace. God who has created man now enters human life in a new way to transform it, but it remains human life. Jesus, the incarnate Lord, is real man. How the union of God and man can

5. Augustine, *On the Predestination of the Saints*, I, xv.
6. Thomas Aquinas, *Summa Theologica*, Part III, Qu. 1, art. 3.

be understood so that the humanity is not merely a form or appearance has been the most difficult issue in Christian theology.

Let us see what happens to our conception of the incarnation if we say that the relation between God and Jesus is determined by love.

Love means to will the freedom of the other, the acceptance of the consequences of relationship to another, and the vulnerability which goes with that acceptance. If there is real humanity in the incarnation, then there is a real human will with human freedom. It may be remarked that the Church had to face very early the issue of whether there was one will or two in the incarnate Lord, and the Sixth Ecumenical Council finally affirmed in 680 that the two natures involve two wills.

This doctrine that love is the meaning of the divine-human relationship in the incarnation leads to a way of interpreting the incarnation. The union of God and man in Jesus Christ is the communion of God with the man Jesus. It is a communion in which the deity of God and the humanity of Jesus are joined in the freedom of love. God in his grace created a humanity which becomes responsive to him and committed utterly to him. This communion enacted in concrete history discloses the mystery of love in God's being. It is the mystery symbolized in the Trinitarian language of God as Father, Son, and Spirit. Jesus of Nazareth as known in the experience of the Church is the human exemplifier of the spirit of God.

We must remember our limitations in speaking about the incarnation. The New Testament does not reveal the 'inner life' of Jesus. In his great book, *The Communion of the Christian with God*, Wilhelm Hermann fails to be convincing when he tries to say that the Christian knows in his experience the communion which Jesus had with God.[7] We cannot delimit another's experience by ours. Least of all can we fit Jesus' experience to our limited understanding. What we can do is to see that the essential elements of humanity are preserved in our understanding of the incarnation, and that means that whatever is necessary to love is present there.

Using this test we see the incarnation as an action of the freedom of God accepting and releasing the freedom of man. Without freedom Jesus would not be man. His freedom is not a contradiction to the power of God but the condition of that humanity which God seeks in love. To love is to accept the freedom of the other with all its consequences, even for God.

It follows that as Jesus witnessed to God's love he experienced the risks, dilemmas and decisions of a real human being, living and

7. Wilhelm Hermann, *The Communion of the Christian with God* (London: Williams & Norgate, 1895).

growing in a particular culture with its political and religious situation. His mind was shaped by the tradition he inherited, and his language communicated in the forms which were appropriate and available in that time and place. He lived as a man, in dependence upon God, his mind open to the question of God's purpose for him, wrestling with the temptations of human flesh and knowing all of them. His interpretation of his vocation to serve God could grow and could be altered by new experience. He could believe God would do certain things which did not happen as he expected. Whatever special powers he had, he found limits set to them. However clearly he preached his message, and however powerful his spirit of love to persuade and to win men, he encountered opposition, misunderstanding and hatred. He experienced human love in his family and for his companions. He wept and grieved with them and rejoiced with them. He knew that his life ran toward death, and that he could be killed. It also follows that Jesus' life was remembered in the human way. The record of his life exhibits the accidents and vagaries of human tradition-making. He has been understood and misunderstood in innumerable ways. Men have debated whether he existed or not. Such is the human condition and the risk of love's work in it.

If the things just bluntly said sound strange, it is because in spite of the Church's clear assertion of Jesus' humanity, and in spite of the New Testament record, we may find it harder to think clearly of his humanity than of his deity. The reason for this lies deep in a misunderstanding about the impassibility of the love of God which has shaped our tradition for centuries.

There is nothing just said about Jesus' humanity which is not explicitly asserted in the Gospel record. He grows in wisdom and stature (Luke 2: 52). He is tempted in all points as we are. He marvelled at the unbelief he found, and discovered his powers were limited (Mark 6: 5). He apparently expected the end of history and the beginning of the Kingdom of God before the preaching of his disciples was finished (Matthew 10: 23). There are many indications as to Jesus' thought of his relationship to the messianic expectations of his time, to be sure in texts which leave room for much interpretation. And there is the cry from the cross, 'My God, my God, why hast thou forsaken me?' which surely may arise from the spirit in its freedom giving voice to agony over the silence of God (Matthew 27: 46).

The Gospels picture Jesus as living a life of dependence upon God expressed in continuing acts of prayer and devotion. Perhaps in prayer freedom reaches its deepest point, the freedom to open life to God, to protest to God (as in the prayer in the Garden), to seek the will of God, and to acknowledge absolute dependence upon him. Jesus of Nazareth prayed. The incarnation fulfilled and did not negate human freedom.

It may be objected that this is only one side of the New Testament picture of Jesus. The mystery of the incarnation is precisely that while he was man, he was God incarnate; and the New Testament is filled with the signs of Jesus' uniqueness. There is the Virgin Birth. In the temptations Christ meets Satan face to face, which seems to put his experience into a dimension different from that of other men. There are the miracles of healing, subduing the storm, raising the dead, and the decisive importance of the Resurrection in the rebirth of faith.

It is not to our purpose here to explore all the complex questions associated with the miracles. If we hold the conviction that it is God's love which is at work in Jesus, then whatever the miracles are as events they point to the love of God, not to a power which by-passes the involvements of love. It is a mistake to rely upon the miracles as the decisive key to who Jesus was. While the miracles are manifestations of the divine power, they did not conquer the human resistance to Jesus. They did not convince everyone of his divine mission. No miracle occurred that he might escape loneliness, agony, and death. We shall come shortly to the special significance of the Resurrection, but the point we are insisting upon is that the New Testament account of Jesus does not allow miraculous power to overshadow the real man, suffering, teaching, rejoicing and dying. To put the point categorically: if God is love, then the means he uses to communicate with man will leave man free, as he seeks to persuade, not to coerce the human spirit. Miracles are signs of divine power, but they do not coerce belief.

Just what powers were released in God's action in Jesus does indeed exceed our understanding. The creative God may work in new ways. It is not for us to say what God could or could not do, or precisely what powers Jesus possessed. It is essential however to see that faith rests upon more than miracles.[8]

We must now ask about the perfection of Jesus Christ, and the assertion that he was sinless. This is indeed an extraordinary claim to make. Does it not set Jesus apart from all other men? And does our redemption depend upon its truth?

The tradition is clear. Jesus is God's beloved Son. He is tempted to reject his vocation both at the beginning of his ministry and the end, but at no point is Jesus represented as asking for forgiveness.

8. The history of religions is filled with miracles, including many 'saviours' who have more extraordinary things recorded about them than does Jesus.

The New Testament picture is that of an unbroken communion between Father and Son. This surely is what the assertion of Jesus' sinlessness must mean. There was given to those who knew him and to those who heard the message about him, the meaning of life in unbroken communion with God. It is the life of complete dedication, of acceptance of vocation, of taking the consequences of doing the will of God and the suffering which that involves. Sin, we must emphasize, is not primarily particular acts of transgression or moments of human weakness and failure. It is the rupture of the communion between God and man. Through Jesus we see the meaning of a life in which this communion remains unbroken.

But does the image correspond to the reality? We can reasonably argue that it must correspond in a fundamental way, else we would never have been given the image. This is the answer to all suggestions that the picture of Jesus is an historical accident or a creation of the human mind. He so loved that men remembered him this way. Unless he so loved, it is unbelievable that he would be so remembered.

At the same time we need not make assertions about every moment and action in the life of Jesus, or give an account of his temptations and his variable psychological states. How could this possibly be done, and on what kind of evidence would it rest? The claim about sinlessness should never be made as an assertion about the experience of Jesus, as if we had to prove that he never knew humility or the need for confession. It means that in him there is an enactment of what life is when communion with God is unbroken. That is the only meaning of the sinlessness of Jesus which is essential to the message of salvation through him. The sinlessness of Jesus cannot be made a matter of empirical historical description.

In the incarnation God has won man's response without destroying his freedom. Man's freedom is finite and dependent, and is fulfilled only in obedience to the will of God. God's freedom is the power of his being as creator, judge, and lord of history. But the freedom is real in both God and man, and the incarnation does not set it aside.

(4)

THE SUFFERING OF JESUS

Love involves suffering, the freedom to be acted upon by the other. Suffering does not mean only anguish of body or spirit. It means being acted upon, and responding to the other in his freedom. In this perspective we take a position about the incarnation which the orthodox tradition has denied, at least formally, and that is that the incarnation involves not only the suffering of the man Jesus, but also the suffering of God the Father. How can we speak of love between Father and Son if the Father is unmoved by the Son's suffering? Process theology holds that love is disclosed in the incarnation precisely because the freedom of God and man are there so united that the man conforms to God's will, and God responds to the concrete decisions and suffering of the man. This does not mean that God's love for man is contingent upon what man does but the form which love takes is contingent upon man's need. God enters into and takes into himself the situation created by the sin of man. As Jesus suffers in his love with and for sinners, he discloses the suffering love of God.

The Christian Gospel asserts that history is changed by what Jesus has done. The new humanity includes Jesus' dedication. Where the tradition has gotten into trouble is in suggesting that God withholds his love until Jesus has suffered to pay the penalty of sin. In our view God never withholds his love, but the release of love's creative power was made possible in a decisive way through Jesus' acceptance of suffering in his identification with man's condition. Thus through his suffering Jesus is the centre of the history in which love has taken a new form.

We have, then, a perspective in which to consider what it is that Jesus' suffering means and how it enters into reconciliation between man and God. Our next chapter will deal exclusively with that question. Already we have declared for one important qualification of the way in which the suffering of Jesus has usually been represented. The tendency of traditional theology has been to say that it is in the miraculous displays of extraordinary power that Jesus' divinity is manifest, and that in suffering, hunger and thirst and dying his humanity is manifest. This is explicitly said in Pope Leo's Tome, which was the substantial basis for the Chalcedonian formula. Leo wrote:

> To hunger, to thirst, to be weary, and to sleep is evidently human. But to feed five thousand men with five loaves—to walk on the surface of the sea with feet that sink not, and by rebuking the storm to bring down the 'uplifted waves' is unquestionably divine. . . . It does not belong to the same nature to weep with feelings of pity over a dead friend and, after the mass of stone had been removed from the grave where he had lain four days, by a voice of command to raise him to life again.[9]

---

9. ' The Tome of Leo ' in *Christology of the Later Fathers*, E. R. Hardy and C. C. Richardson, eds., *The Library of Christian Classics* (Philadelphia: Westminster, 1954), p. 365.

Thus power is divine but pity is human. It seemed to the fathers that any suggestion of God's suffering would compromise his deity. How could we speak of God as dying? The doctrine of the Incarnation we are defending does not assert that God dies. Nor does he experience hunger, doubts and trials as we do. There is a sense in which man's sufferings belong only to man. But we still say that in man's suffering God also suffers. The disclosure of who God is has come through Jesus not primarily in miraculous powers, but in his self-identification with the suffering of the world for the sake of love. But if Jesus, for the sake of love, accepts suffering, surely God the Father, united with him in the fullness of love, accepts this suffering for himself. God does not surrender his deity, his everlastingness, the perfection of his power and love. God remains God. But if God is love he does his creative and redemptive work by involving himself in the history of human freedom with its tragedy. God's deity is manifest supremely at the very point where Leo sees only humanity, that is in the weakness, suffering, and dying of Jesus. We acknowledge certainly the mystery of revelation. God is hidden in his self-manifestation. But God is hidden in the whole being of Jesus Christ, not just in part. God is both revealed and hidden in the extraordinary events, the miraculous signs. So also God is both hidden and revealed in the suffering of Jesus. He is hidden in the mystery of love's burden, its vulnerability to misunderstanding, its initial powerlessness which becomes powerfully redemptive. God is revealed in Jesus' suffering because in him suffering is the authentic expression and communication of love. 'We know the love of God in this, that while we were yet sinners, Christ died for us' (Romans 5: 8). There could be no more concise statement than the Apostle Paul's of the love that is disclosed in Jesus in his involvement with human suffering and need.

God works in the new situation created by his freedom and the freedom of Jesus. God now has a new history to deal with because it is history with Jesus' action in it, with all the consequences of that action and of God's response to it. The New Testament uses several metaphors and images in declaring that God the Creator has created again in Christ. There is the assertion that 'if any man be in Christ he is a new creation' (2 Corinthians 5: 17). Paul thus speaks of the new creation through Christ, although he does not speak here of Christ himself as a new creation. Paul thinks of Christ the eternal Son of God as existing before all worlds. But it is remarkable that along with the belief in Christ as the eternally-begotten Son, Paul and the whole New Testament can speak in a daring way of a 'New Being' in the incarnation. Since this assertion is connected with the resurrection, we must give especial attention to this part of the Gospel record.

(5)

THE RESURRECTION AND THE NEW CREATION

The resurrection of Jesus is God's act, not man's. The theme of the divine prevenience underlies the whole account. It is Jesus who is raised from the dead, and all that he was and did is involved in what God does in the resurrection. It is the act of God, completing the history of his beloved Son, and inaugurating a new situation in human existence. There is even the radical suggestion in one strand of the New Testament that it is in the act of resurrection that God has made Jesus Lord and Christ. Peter says in the sermon recorded in Acts:

> Let the house of Israel therefore know assuredly that God has made him both Lord and Christ, this Jesus whom you crucified (Acts 2:36).

Paul speaks of the resurrection as the decisive action through which God has brought new life into the world, and hope for overcoming death and sin. 'The first man, Adam, became a living being, the last Adam became a life-giving spirit' (I Corinthians 15: 45). Christ is the 'first fruits' in the redemptive act of God. 'For as in Adam all die, so also in Christ, shall all be made alive. But each in its own order: Christ the first fruits, then at his coming those who belong to Christ' (I Corinthians 15: 20-3). Paul declares the same theme in Romans 5 where the accent is upon the justification brought by Christ to set aside the condemnation which has fallen upon all Adam's sin. 'So one man's act of righteousness leads to acquittal and life for all men' (Romans 5: 18). Paul characteristically unites the bestowing of forgiveness with the overcoming of death. Romans 6 makes this plain:

> Do you know that all of us who have been baptized into Christ Jesus were baptized into his death? We were buried therefore with him by baptism into death, so that as Christ was raised from the dead, by the glory of the Father, we too might walk in newness of life.
>
> For if we have been united with him in a death like his, we shall certainly be united with him in a resurrection like his. We know that our old self was crucified with him so that the sinful body might be destroyed, and we might no longer be enslaved to sin. For he who has died is freed from sin. But if we have died with Christ, we believe that we shall also live with him.

The incarnation is a new act of creation receiving its final sign in the experience of the Risen Christ. Here the themes of election love and covenant are fused. The redemptive action which expresses God's forgiveness and his will to reconcile sinful man to himself is at the same time the expression of God's election of his Son and all those joined to him through the power of incarnate love. Thus election not only underlies the eternal purpose of love, but it appears in the will to create a new covenant when the old has been broken. The mystery of love embraces both creation and redemption, and the redemption is a new creation.

Resurrection here means the action of God completed in the disciples' experience of the risen Jesus as the sign of the new life inaugurated in him. Many different interpretations of the Gospel record are possible. However we understand these particular events, they meant for the disciples the confirmation of God's power and presence in Jesus, and of the new existence which he bestows. There are innumerable resurrections in the history of religions, and we may well believe that conventional forms of miraculous expectation have entered into the present Gospel tradition. But it is the resurrection of *Jesus* which Christian faith affirms. To have faith in his resurrection is to have faith that the spirit of love incarnate in him has created a new body for its life in the world. The new life is a life of trust in God, and hope for eternal communion with him. It is a new form of human experience which is the beginning of putting on the form of Christ. The resurrection is a mystery of faith, but it is not a collection of esoteric happenings. It has its analogues in the human experiences of forgiveness, the renewal of love, and the rebirth of hope. It means release from fear for the self, and its entrustment to God in life and in death. Whether we live or die we are the Lord's (Romans 14: 8).[10]

(6)

IMAGO DEI AND IMAGO CHRISTI

The doctrine of the image of God receives a new meaning in the New Testament assertion that we are being transformed into the image of Christ. The humanity which God intends for us has been

10. I have discussed the question of Jesus' 'identity' in relation to the resurrection faith in a comment on a paper by Professor Hans Frei, 'Theological Reflections on the Accounts of Jesus' Death and Resurrection' in *The Christian Scholar*, Vol. XLIX, No. 4, Winter, 1966.

given a new form in the love of Christ as he has dealt with sin. In one sense this is a restoration of the original image, but it is more. It is love taking new form in history. We know our humanity not in looking back tò a lost perfection, but in looking forward towards the consummation of the new creation.

There are at least four implications of this doctrine that the *imago dei* is fulfilled in the *imago Christi.*

First, the restoration and renewal of the *imago dei* in the image of Christ means that our *humanness* belongs to the goodness of the creation. Theologies which have stressed incarnation have usually had a strong humanist accent. The Incarnation reveals a new humanity which fulfils the intention of creation. Here all the positive affirmation in the Christian view of Jesus' life is based: Jesus, the incarnate Lord, affirms the essential goodness of man as he experiences all the needs of body and mind, and enters into human comradeship and rejoicing.

The discovery of the ethos of the Qumran community, which had many elements prototypical of the Gospel, serves to underline one decisive difference between the spirit of Jesus and the ideals of the desert sect. There is no asceticism in Jesus or his message, no renouncing of the world for the sake of a cloistered purity, no rejection of eating, drinking, marriage, beauty, or laughter. 'Consider the lilies of the field how they grow, they neither toil nor spin, yet I tell you even Solomon in all his glory was not arrayed like one of these' (Matthew 6: 28). 'I came that they may have life, and have it abundantly' (John 10: 10). When the young man asked about the way to inherit the Kingdom, Jesus looked upon him and loved him (Mark 10: 21).

There is to be sure a powerful counterpoint in the Gospel. While Jesus discovers faith in some, he denounces a faithless generation. He acknowledges those who are not far off from the Kingdom, but he excoriates the hypocritical exploiters of man's bodies and spirits. He calls disciples and commits his cause to them, yet they fail him at the decisive moment. The incarnation is the history of the contention of the love of God with the ambiguity of man who both sees and does not see where his true good lies. In spite of the ambiguity, the image of God which has now become the image of Christ implies the essential goodness of man's existence, the dignity and spiritual significance of the human, the possibility in human flesh for fulfilled life.

A second implication of the *Imago Christi* theme is that the joining of the believer with Christ involves his sharing the suffering of Christ. The disciple must appropriate, internalize, and bear the cross for himself. The *imago Christi* is authentic only as 'carrying in the body the death of Jesus' (2 Corinthians 4: 10).

Central to this perspective on love is the conviction that the *imago Christi* is not the form of an otherworldly perfection to be suddenly realized in history. It is the perfection of love which grapples with this existence and is freely given in the unloveliness of the world's guilt and travail. The imitation of Christ embraces many patterns of life. Authentic love in the Christ image will never be able to prove itself overwhelmingly attractive, powerful, and adequate. It is a sign of love to accept the disfiguring, the misunderstanding, and even the ridiculousness in human eyes of what it undertakes (2 Corinthians 6: ff.). Final judgment as to what is really love belongs to God alone. 'There was no form or comeliness by which we might desire him' (Isaiah 53: 2). The Christ image lies in the shadows as well as the light of human experience.

The third aspect of the life which is conformed to Christ is that it is not simply a having but a becoming. The New Testament speaks of Jesus as the new Adam who restores man to fullness of life; but this restoration comes in a history. We are to be conformed to his image, Paul says (Romans 8: 29). 'For now we see in a mirror dimly, but then face to face' (I Corinthians 13: 12). The new reality is in conflict with the old. Paul counts himself not to have attained (Philippians 3: 12). 'The whole creation has been groaning in travail together until now, and not only the creation but we ourselves, who have the first fruits of the Spirit, groan inwardly as we wait for our adoption as sons, the redemption of our bodies. For in this hope we were saved' (Romans 8: 22–4).

These powerful paradoxes of the Christian life are essential to its description. To have the light of the knowledge of God's glory is to walk by faith and not by sight (2 Corinthians 4: 6; 5: 7). Paul exhorts the Galatians to stand in the freedom wherein they have been set free, yet he addresses them as 'my little children with whom I am again in travail until Christ be formed in you' (Galatians 4: 19). He 'toils mightily to present every man mature in Christ' (Colossians 1: 28–9).

Where then is the peace and assurance of the Christian life if it is born in such tension? The Protestant Reformers found their answer to this question again in Paul. 'Bearing about in the body the dying of Christ' is not a matter of turning attention to the self at all. Faith is not assurance about our private state of holiness, but confidence in the saving power of God. We have faith, not in faith, but in the God who offers life and compassion.

There is a sense then in which the *imago dei* is expected, not possessed. Humanity, in the Christian view, is prospective, not retrospective. This is why Christianity shares our openness to the future with the existentialists. Man has yet to become what God is preparing him to be. 'Beloved, we are God's children now: it does not yet appear what we shall be (I John 3: 2).

Finally, in the new relationship to the incarnate Lord we have new knowledge of what love is. The *imago Christi* is the form love takes when the spirit becomes the servant. The image of God includes the structures of human existence, but it points toward new forms which God's creative purpose brings forth. Created in God's image we may confess the sin which defaces that image, and hear the invitation to walk through the valley of death in a new way.

Such a view of the Incarnation holds that the Holy God achieves his will in the world, not by overriding the conditions of human existence, but by communicating his love in a personal life lived out in actual history. No account of the incarnation can penetrate the mystery of that life. It can only recognize the way in which Jesus gave witness to the love of God, and confess him as the one through whom we know who we really are: creatures who can love one another and God and share our being with all his wondrous creation.

Jesus revealed the love of God in a bloody first-hand encounter with the sin and evil in the world. The traditional name for what he did in that encounter is atonement. We turn now to the atonement as the victory of love.

CHAPTER IX

THE ATONEMENT

The spirit of love takes form as love meets the other and his need. The spirit has taken the form of a Servant in the incarnation, and the Servant has met humanity in the depths of its separation from God. The two marks of this separation are sin and death. Their defeat in the Servant's death on the cross is the atonement. In the Christian faith it is the atonement which discloses the ultimate resource of God's love. Reinhold Niebuhr says, 'The Atonement is the significant content of the Incarnation'.[1] Certainly it is the central action in the incarnation.

It is well known that there has never been an orthodox doctrine of the atonement. The New Testament uses a number of images and metaphors, and never confines the meaning of the cross in a formal definition. The theme is too vast for any single interpretation. All the powers which assail man's being and hope are met in the Cross —sin, death, the demonic powers, the judgment of the law, and despair at fulfilling it, the weight of guilt, the mystery of dying, the tragedy of history. The way of redemption is told in unfathomable images, the life of preaching and healing, the little group of disciples, the hunger of the crowds, the opposition of the powerful, the last meal with the institution of a sacrament of remembrance, the betrayal, the trial and agony, the disciples' desertion, and the death, and then the strange and variously described experiences of the resurrection. Strangest of all from the standpoint of faith is the fact that although the word from the cross, 'it is finished', has been spoken, the history of sin and death goes on. Mankind carries the burden of guilt and the anxiety of dying in a humanity misshapen and bewildered by its own creations. Life in faith and in the Church remains life under judgment. What indeed has been accomplished in the work of God in Jesus Christ? Every theology of atonement arises in the history where we continue to search for an adequate expression of the truth. Theologies are instruments of vision, not resting places for the mind and heart of faith.

Nevertheless, from the beginning of the Christian Church, there have been accounts of the atonement which explored the scriptural metaphors and expanded or reinterpreted them. They use concepts

1. Reinhold Niebuhr, *The Nature and Destiny of Man*, Vol. II, p. 55.

drawn from many areas of human experience. I believe it is a defect of most traditional theories of atonement that they obscure the centrality of love in redemption. In order to show this we must look briefly at the major types of interpretation of atonement. The essential point to observe is that every interpretation has used some pattern or image drawn from human experience and religious devotion.

We noted in Chapter III Emil Brunner's classification of the metaphors of atonement in five types: Sacrifice, the first of these, derives from a form of religious worship and devotion. The Suffering Servant figure is based upon the concept of penal suffering for wrong. The ransom payment means literal ransom or the purchase of freedom. The contest of God against Satan is based upon the image of warfare. The historical symbol of the Passover Lamb comes from the history of Israel's deliverance preserved in a ritual of remembrance. To Dr. Brunner's five types we can add the theme Paul finds in the mystery religions, the God who dies and rises again that his followers may have immortality.

Later theology never remained wholly bound to these traditional images, though all of them are repeated in the Fathers, in St. Anselm, and elsewhere. Anselm asks the question, 'Cur Deus Homo', 'Why did God become man?' His answer is a synthesis of the theme of offence against the divine honour based on the analogy of the feudal lordship and the sacramental practice of penance with its suffering proportionate to the extent of guilt. Abelard's less systematized doctrine stresses the persuasive power of the divine love, and has been traditionally called, not very illuminatingly, the 'moral influence theory'. Abelard, the professor, uses the image of the 'persuasive teacher' and interprets Christ's suffering as divine instruction about love. For Schleiermacher Christ saves man through the perfection of his God-consciousness, which is the existence of God in him and which must be restored to man. For Albrecht Ritschl, Christ saves man by fulfilling his vocation to establish the universal ethical community in which the spirit is victorious over the resistance of nature.[2] Thus every theology seeks a pattern in which the atonement can be understood.

2. A bibliography of the historic doctrines is unnecessary here. R. S. Franks, *A History of the Doctrine of the Work of Christ* (New York: Hodder & Stoughton, 1918), is standard. Gustaf Aulén, *Christus Victor* (London: S.P.C.K., 1931) is very important. H. E. W. Turner, *The Patristic Doctrine of Redemption* (London: A. R. Mowbray, 1952), and William Wolf, *No Cross, No Crown*, supplement Aulén's analysis. D. F. E. Schleiermacher, *The Christian Faith* (Edinburgh: T. & T. Clark, 1928), and Albrecht Ritschl, *The Christian Doctrine of Justification and Reconciliation* (Edinburgh: T. & T. Clark, 1900), are major works in modern

When we say that these patterns of experience have been used in doctrines of atonement, we do not mean that the theologians have tried to reduce the meaning of God's saving work to forms of human experience. Most have recognized they are using analogies. Shailer Mathews once accurately described most theories of atonement as 'transcendentalized politics'.[3] It is God who redeems man, and what God does cannot be identified with any human experience or form, though it penetrates human understanding.

One of the important books on the atonement in the twentieth century is Gustaf Aulén's *Christus Victor* in which he finds three major *motifs* in the tradition: the classic theme of Christ as victor in combat with Satan and the demonic powers of sin, death, and the law; the Latin theory, stated most adequately in Anselm, in which Jesus as man pays the penalty incurred by sin, a sufficient payment since he is the Son of God; and the moral influence theory in Abelard. Aulén holds that Luther rescues the classic motif from the deficiencies in Anselm's and other views, and it is this classic theory which most adequately expresses the New Testament faith.

Aulén gives several reasons for preferring the *Christus Victor* theme.[4] God is both the reconciler and the reconciled. Christ's death and resurrection is the overcoming of the powers which assail man, sin, death, the curse of the Law. In all these the power of Satan is present and must be broken. The cosmic dimensions of the conflict of God with evil are thus recognized. Further, the incarnation and atonement are one continuous and integral action of God. Here Aulén finds special significance in Irenaeus' doctrine of the divine action as a reconstituting (recapitulating) of humanity's history of creation and fall and the restoration of man's rightful maturity and direction.

Every profound theory of the atonement has its existential aspect, that is, its way of expressing the concrete human situation and what redeems us from futility. If this were not so the theory would not persist. The 'classic' theory as expounded by Aulén is often criticized for neglecting the existential dimension of atonement. The contest of God and the demonic powers takes place in a cosmic dimension 'above man's head', so to speak. How this ultimate victory of Christ becomes our victory is not clear. It should be said however that

---

theology. British theological studies by Rashdall and Moberley are well known. The most recent study, and one of especial insight, is F. W. Dillistone, *The Christian Understanding of Atonement* (London: James Nisbet & Co., 1968).

3. Shailer Mathews, *The Atonement and the Social Process* (New York: Macmillan, 1930).

4. Aulén, *Christus Victor* (London: S.P.C.K., 1931).

Aulén's version of the classic motif keeps one existential aspect of importance. It reveals the experience of sin and death as personal bondage. The theme of the God-man confronting Satan himself and defeating him expresses the liberation which comes when the paralysis of fear is broken and freedom of the spirit becomes a present possibility.

As Dr. Tillich has pointed out, the Latin theory of the satisfaction of the divine honour through the death of Jesus has always gripped men because it meets the burden of guilt, the experience of moral failure, and the impossibility of 'making up' for what we have done. The moral influence theory points to the power which the example of suffering love can have. It can reach the depths of the self where there is still the possibility of responding to persuasion.

There is, however, a remarkable fact which appears when we look at the history of the doctrine of atonement. It is this—that none of the traditional theories has taken as its point of departure and its key an experiential analysis of the work of love. Every doctrine recognizes that it is the love of God which has been shown in Jesus Christ and his cross and which is the source of redemption. But in interpreting the 'how' of redemption, the question has too rarely been asked, 'What is the meaning of atonement as love doing its distinctive work in dealing with guilt and self-destruction?'

If God's work is reconciliation, that is, personal restoration of his people to the community of love and the renewal of the 'marriage bond', one would suppose that the profoundest insight into the 'how' of reconciliation would come from the experience of reconciliation between persons. Yet this has rarely been given full scope in theology. Is the human experience of love and forgiveness too intimate to become objectified as a theory of God's way of working? Perhaps the dimension of the divine is so different from the human that we need remote analogies rather than personal ones. We can counter by asking why political transactions, or forms of religious sacrifice, or ransom payments are more able to bear the freight of the divine meaning than are the personal relationships of love, betrayal and forgiveness. In any case, we can only seek to tell how God's saving power comes into life.

Let us look again at the atonement as the New Testament witnesses to it, and as the centuries of Christian experience have wrestled with it. Our clue is that if the atonement means God doing what needs to be done to reconcile the world to himself, then the human experiences which may reflect this work of God must be those of personal reconciliation. Now giving an account of personal reconciliation is very difficult. The healing of broken relationships takes many forms. We seem to know much more about how we fall into disruptive conflict and hatred than about how these are overcome. Betrayal is easier to describe than forgiveness.

As we seek to keep close to experience we also keep attention fixed upon the experience of reconciliation in the New Testament witness to Jesus. The New Testament message deals with human experience and throws its revealing light on human motives, desires, and action. God has made his love known in the way a man lived and died. Without this involvement in experience no Christian account of redemption will be anything but a dream in an unreal world.

What we seek is a personal, experiential interpretation of atonement through analysis of reconciliation in human life. Love takes a new form in the work of reconciliation. We could not think at all without the traditional doctrines, but we can hope to shift our angle of vision slightly as we look again upon the mystery.

(1)

DISCLOSURE

What happens when there is a break in human relationships and an actual reconciliation? We can distinguish four phases. These four do not constitute a chronological sequence. They interpenetrate, as four aspects of one history.

The first is disclosure. This beginning seems obvious. We have to know that there is a rupture in communication with one another in our mutuality and our love if we are to be reconciled. But to know this in the sense of being aware of conflict and disorder is one thing; to know it in the sense of seeing clearly its depths and its roots, and confessing it as real is profoundly difficult. Nothing is more common in human relationships, both for individuals and groups, than the belief that we are men of goodwill and all the ill will lies in the other. The history of human pretences, self-deception, and failure to see our hostility and resentment of the other is a constant theme of the world's literature, and its consequences are strewn throughout history in politics, revolution, and all the tragedies of human hatred. The forms of peace in the conscience are infinitely varied and they are so satisfying that exposing them can only be the work of grace.

It is a fair proposition that all sin involves some kind of dishonesty, a self-deception about our real motives, and a distortion of the truth about others. We know through the psychological clinics something more about the mechanisms which operate when the human spirit is anxious and self-protective. Our capacity to shut out reality is very great, because the risk of the truth is so great. Whitehead is speaking out of a high idealism when he says, 'it is the blunt truth we want'.[5] Usually it is the last thing we want.

Disclosure to the self is the first painful work of love. One of the assured results of modern psychological therapy is that unless there is some offer of security, some removal of the threat of the rejection we fear, we cannot face the depths of our hurt and guilt. The first service, therefore, of grace as forgiveness is service to the truth. It makes possible the beginning of confession. We see then that disclosure is not simply a prologue to reconciliation, but a continuing and essential aspect of the whole history.

The Gospel account of Jesus' ministry can be read as the history of the disclosure of man's sin. The exposure of guilt is one dimension of his work of reconciliation. Dr. John Bennett remarks in his discussion of the Gospel record that the recorded words of judgment spoken by Jesus against the faithless generation, the exploiting groups, and the pride of the 'righteous' are more prominent than the words of forgiveness.[6]

> For John came to you in the way of righteousness and you did not believe him, but the tax collectors and the harlots believed him; and even when you saw it, you did not afterward repent and believe him. . . .
>
> I tell you the Kingdom of God will be taken away from you and given to a nation producing the fruits of it. . . .
>
> When the chief priests and the Pharisees heard his parables, they perceived that he was speaking about them.
>
> (Matthew 21: 32, 43, 45)

Words of judgment do not necessarily achieve self-disclosure for those who will not see. Disclosure involves confession which cannot be compelled. Nevertheless, the history of Jesus puts him clearly in the prophetic tradition of blunt speech concerning God's judgment upon sin. He calls the names of crimes and points to the unjust and the exploiters, and to the viciousness and destructiveness of men.

Disclosure comes not only through exposure of wrong, but also in demonstration of right. The parables of the Good Samaritan and the humble tax collector expose the pride of the self-righteous and the unlove of those who pass by on the other side. The human spirit is a proving ground for the truth against the lie. We should remember

---

5. A. N. Whitehead, *Adventures of Ideas*, p. 321.

6. John Bennett, *Christian Realism* (New York: Charles Scribner's Sons, 1941), p. 41.

that a not inconsiderable part of Jesus' ministry was spent in controversy over specific issues of law and ethical practice. What is proper on the sabbath? What about paying taxes to Caesar? What are the conditions of preparation for the Kingdom? Who sinned that this man suffers? Honest analysis can be a work of reconciliation. The ultimate hope for man is that the truth will be known:

> Beware of the leaven of the Pharisees which is hypocrisy. Nothing is covered up that will not be revealed, or hidden that will not be made known. Whatever you have said in the dark shall be heard in the light, and what you have whispered in private rooms shall be proclaimed upon the housetops (Luke 12: 1–3)

This is to be sure an eschatological promise. The final disclosure of the truth is not given in history; it is something expected at the end of the history of reconciliation. But there are anticipations and fragmentary realizations of the truth. And at the centre of history we begin to know our real humanity illuminated by the humanity of Jesus. Love has multiple strategies in disclosing the truth. That there can be no reconciliation without the foundation of truth is the first statement about it.

While the truth may become clear, it is rarely simple. Men are conditioned by historical circumstances. Pathological conditions in society or the individual block communication. Charles E. Silberman has analysed the problem of communication in racial relations. He describes the feelings of Negroes who find that all decisions are made for them. One black nationalist leader said to him, 'You whites have always decided everything, you even decided when to set us free'. Silberman points out that 'Negroes want to achieve their aims by their own efforts, not as a result of white beneficence'. He continues:

> The crux of the matter may be summed up in the difference between the words 'conversation' and 'negotiation'. Whites are accustomed to holding conversations with Negroes, in which they sound out the latter's views or acquaint them with decisions they have taken. But Negroes insist more and more on negotiations—on discussions, as equals, designed to reach an agreement. . . . To negotiate means to recognize the other party's power. When Whites negotiate with Negroes therefore, it not only helps to solve the Negro's 'Negro problem' it helps solve the white man's 'Negro problem' as well; for whites begin to see Negroes in a different light—as equals, as men.[7]

---

7. Charles E. Silberman, *Crisis in Black and White* (New York: Random House, 1964), pp. 193, 198. Lillian Smith's *Killers of the Dream* is a powerful description of the pathology of insecurity and its effect on human communication (New York: W. W. Norton, 1949).

The notion that love for fellow man is a substitute for what Silberman here calls 'negotiation' is the sentimentality which needs to be exposed and eliminated. And when no way to negotiation seems open love will maintain loyalty to the discovered humanity which lies waiting to be set free.

To love is to will to find the conditions of human community whatever they may be. The search for knowledge of our actual predicament at whatever risk to our self-image, our pride, and our privilege is the first requirement in the reconciling action.

(2)

LOYALTY AND SUFFERING

The second requirement for reconciliation is an action which renews loyalty to the broken community in spite of the rupture of disloyalty. A new deed is required, an affirmation that man is bound to man in communion in spite of separation. Atonement requires constructive recommitment in the midst of disaster.

One of the searching interpretations of atonement in the twentieth century was given by the philosopher Josiah Royce in *The Problem of Christianity*.[8] Royce's philosophic idealism was built upon the tragic aspect of life and what he called the 'moral burden of the individual'. Royce sought to interpret human existence as the search for loyalty to an adequate cause. Sin is disloyalty to the one really adequate cause, the world of loyal men. Disloyalty is universal. We seek self-affirmation against the community, and this fall into disloyalty is irrevocable. Time is movement from the past toward the future, and the past cannot be changed. The burden of guilt persists. Thus Royce affirmed the reality of time and, at least in *The Problem of Christianity*, seems to say that God has a temporal aspect. He sees the problem of history, then, as the recovery of meaning in the face of the burden of moral guilt.

Royce now interprets Christianity as the faith that the moral burden of past wrong has been so dealt with in the history of Jesus recorded in the New Testament that the way is re-opened to unlimited creative growth for the human community. Thus an infinite hope overcomes the tragedy of man's self-betrayal. Royce is clearer than Hegel about the creativity of history. He was aided in this by

8. Josiah Royce, *The Problem of Christianity*, 2 vols. (New York: Macmillan, 1914). Valuable interpretation in John E. Smith, *Royce's Social Infinite* (New York: Liberals Arts Press, 1950).

Charles Peirce's theory of interpretation as the structure of historical existence. Interpretation is a triadic process. Someone interprets a sign to someone. It is a temporal process. The present interpreter interprets the past, which has become objectively given and remembered, to the mind which receives the new interpretation. Thus with each interpretation the process moves into a new state of affairs.[9] In idealist fashion Royce sees human existence as this infinitely expanding community of interpretation. The relevance to the atonement is that the past can take on new meaning when the burden of guilt is lifted through a new act of loyalty. Royce believed he had here found a way to interpret the Christian community's affirmation about Jesus. In its memory of Jesus the Church has the foundation of its existence in the memory of the deed of Jesus who acted in absolute loyalty to the community in the midst of its disloyalty.

If historical actions were only isolated events the life and death of Jesus would be just an incident without effect or power; but if history is constituted by remembered and interpreted events, then what Jesus has done enters into the texture of history. The Christian community is in intention the community which lives by its remembrance of Jesus' loyalty to the whole community of being. For Royce then human history is the story of man's fall into guilt and its overcoming by atonement. Thus Christianity in essence knows the meaning of life as unlimited loyalty to the community of interpretation and interpreters.

In this philosophy of loyalty Royce is interpreting the meaning of love so that the power of love's dealing with guilt is brought to the fore. Atonement is that working of love in which the meaning of being human is made plain. Thus the idealist philosopher illuminates the doctrine of atonement. He has gone beyond the traditional doctrines by drawing his metaphor from within the action of loyalty when it deals with the broken community. He has described the human process of reconciliation.

Royce's doctrine gives especial importance to the Church as the community which remembers Jesus. His classic definition of the church is 'the community of memory and of hope'. The atonement works in history through the living memory of the community. It is initiated in the life of Jesus, but it is an action which reverberates in every subsequent action. Atonement is the continuing action of God restoring the world to its right mind and spirit. Jesus' loyalty is the concrete deed which opens the way to an infinitely creative universal community.

We can incorporate Royce's analysis of atonement into our

9. Royce, *op. cit.*, Vol. II, chaps. 11–14.

doctrine of love in process theology. But in *The Problem of Christianity* Royce has curiously little to say about the *action* of God. His community of interpretation seems a little 'bloodless' and over-intellectualized. We need further theological interpretation of the biblical witness to Jesus' suffering and death as revelation of God's suffering love.

The metaphysical doctrine of God in process theology can appropriate but extend Royce's view. Jesus' suffering witnesses to God's love bearing with his world. It is an act of human loyalty which discloses the divine loyalty. We can avoid the idealist error, which Royce does not escape, of trying to prove that in the end everything is really as it should be, since atonement overcomes guilt. Royce held the interesting view that the atoning deed must not only heal the community but it must leave the community better than it was before the rupture of disloyalty.[10] This is a remnant of the idealistic attempt to prove that the world is really better because of sin. (St. Augustine makes the same claim.) I cannot see that such a proof is necessary or possible. What is more to the point is to ask how the suffering of Jesus achieves reconciliation and new good, not to calculate its amount.

We have come to the question of suffering in human experience as we try to understand atonement. What does suffering accomplish?

Suffering has many meanings and functions. We think of suffering as pain of body or mind, and as the bearing of the consequences of some illness or wrong. It does of course include these things. But if suffering means being acted upon or being conformed to another in a relationship, then its diversity and complexity begin to appear. The suffering of a beginner learning to play the piano is not the same as the suffering of the accomplished artist playing a recital, or reading critical reviews after a performance. The suffering of a child who does not understand his parents' orders is different from the suffering of the parent who must make requirements he cannot fully explain. And the suffering which comes from the obligations of love is far different from the suffering which comes from love's refusal or frustration.

Suffering can only be understood in the context of the personal history where it occurs. This means that the suffering involved in reconciliation must be understood in its existential function and situation. The traditional doctrines of atonement understand Jesus' suffering as penal or sacrificial. It is the price exacted for sin or the consequence of sin. Surely this is an inescapable aspect of the truth. The consequences of moral and other evil have to be born, and this

10. Royce, *op. cit.*, Vol. I, p. 308.

truth underlies what is valid in the atonement theories. But these theories have given too little attention to the positive function of suffering in human relationships which I hope to show is bound up with *communication* between persons.

Human suffering is always a symptom of a problem, a difficulty, a tragedy, a commitment, or a hope. Suffering discloses a need, a yearning or a disruption. The power of suffering is the power to communicate the spirit's anguish. The truth here is so familiar it seems a commonplace. Yet we know that the deepest discovery in love is that the other suffers for us, and we discover that we love when we suffer for and with the other. Suffering's greatest work is to become the vehicle of human expression. Suffering is not an emotion, but it is an ingredient in all emotion, even the emotion of laughter. Whether suffering always is experienced as pain is debatable. It does always involve some bearing of a situation, a way of experiencing the world and being reshaped by it. That is why suffering even in its most terrible forms has the potential of self-disclosure and knowledge of others. This is attested in the experience of concentration camp survivors.[11] This power of revelation is the power of communication. The experience of suffering enters into the syntax of human expression.

We do not say that suffering always has a constructive function, or that it provides infallible communication between man and man. There are vast stretches of suffering in human life which, empirically viewed, seems to be nothing more than accidents of biological and social history. Suffering can be self-destructive to the point of shattering any hope of finding a meaning in existence. The mystery of evil is not the mystery of suffering *per se*, but the mystery of destructive, apparently senseless suffering. What we can say is that some suffering becomes a source of growth in love.

Suffering becomes constructive when it exposes the truth. In the New Testament interpretation of Jesus' suffering, this theme is perhaps most sharply expressed in the letter to the Colossians. On the cross Jesus has exposed the principalities and powers, made a public spectacle of them (Colossians 2: 15). In the New Testament picture of the Christ the sufferings of Jesus are signs of his vocation to preach the Kingdom, his love for God and for man, his contention with evil, and his conflict with the established powers.

Jesus' suffering not only exposed the sources of evil, but it communicated the loving will to oppose those evils and to seek the reconciliation of mankind. It is a common misunderstanding of love

11. Julia de Beausobre, *The Woman Who Could Not Die* (New York: Viking Press, 1938).

religiously viewed that it must always try to create immediate peace and harmony. Nothing could be further from the picture of love in the New Testament. Jesus' acceptance in love of his vocation to expose human iniquity leads to open conflict. It leads to misunderstanding and violence. It stiffens human defences as men begin to know the judgment against them.

The suffering which creates resistance can also open the way to a new response in love. This power of communication through suffering can never be fully known in an impersonal way. One of the most mysterious and powerful of all forces is the understanding which comes in interpersonal communication. All schools of psychotherapy seem to agree on this point, that the interpersonal relationship is the most powerful force in restoring psychic health.[12] The victories in psychological therapy are dramatic instances of what takes place continually in human relationships. We know one another through the personal responses which involve the taking into the self of the attitudes and emotions of the other. This process is partially blocked, incomplete, and frustrated. We are moved by the weakness, hatred, and indifference of others as well as by their love. The critical point is that it is in this dynamic field of personal interaction that love becomes effective. What happens goes far deeper than the conscious level of understanding, and only in continuing reflection do we discover what the other person has communicated to us.

What is valid in the moral influence theory can be preserved by a fuller interpretation of what the communication of love involves. The 'moral influence theory' is so named because it appears to stress the 'power of example'. It suggests the image of Jesus as the teacher who instructs or persuades men concerning the meaning of love. But 'example' is too weak a term to describe the personal communication of love through suffering. Jesus' suffering has transforming power not merely as a demonstration of a truth but as an action which creates a new field of force in which forgiven men can be changed.

Josiah Royce saw that the deed of the loyal man brings a new community of understanding into existence. We can now add to Royce's view the insight that the reconciliation which creates the new community comes by way of suffering. Jesus suffering becomes the very word and speech of love finding bodily, historical expression and creating a new possibility of communion.

12. Karl Menninger, *The Theory of Psycho-analytic Technique* (London: Hogarth Press, 1958; New York: Science Editions, 1961—Menninger monograph series). The same theme is developed from a different theoretic position in Bernard Steinzor, *The Healing Partnership* (New York: Harper & Row, 1967); cf. Don S. Browning *Atonement and Psychotherapy* (Philadelphia: Westminster Press, 1966).

We come to the deepest mystery when we see in the suffering of Jesus a disclosure of the suffering of God. We have seen how the traditional doctrines of atonement tend to resist this conclusion. They try to keep from saying that the Father suffers. But the inevitable consequence is that the suffering of Jesus must then be viewed as some kind of price exacted by God for his forgiveness. We have traced this doctrine to its origin in the metaphysics of neo-platonism. It cannot survive a clear analysis of what love is. If being and love are inseparable, then being and suffering are inseparable. God is involved in the history of his creatures because he loves the world. His self-disclosure is an action which means suffering. He takes into his own being the consequences of the actions of love in the world.

The incarnation, we have said, is the communion of God with the man whose vocation is to enact love in the world. That communion requires the communication of love from God to man and through man. What Jesus reveals on the cross surely is not that human love suffers while the divine love does not. What he reveals is the love which does not shirk suffering, and that love is God himself at work.

We acknowledge that in denying the suffering of God the tradition tried to protect a truth, but it protected it in an unfortunate way. The truth of impassibility is that God's love is the everlasting power and spirit of deity. He is Lord. Unlimited love belongs to him as it belongs to no creature. God's love is absolute in its integrity forever. In this sense his love is invulnerable. That 'nothing can separate us from the love of God' is the assurance of faith. It is natural for us to associate suffering with finitude, the threat to being, the disruption of spirit. Whatever suffering means in God, it is for him consonant with his deity and with the integrity of the divine spirit.

The doctrine that God suffers does not bring God down to man's level, but brings our understanding of God up to the level of the faith that God has revealed himself in Jesus Christ. The claim that God communicates his spirit to us through the person is not a claim that God's being is knowable completely in our human categories. We have to use the forms we have. We should speak therefore of the meaning of suffering in God with the greatest restraint. But something crucial is at stake in our understanding of what it means to say that God is love. If God does not suffer then his love is separated completely from the profoundest human experiences of love, and the suffering of Jesus is unintelligible as the communication of God's love to man.

We say, then, that the suffering and dying of Jesus is at the centre of the redemptive action we call atonement. The cause of Jesus' suffering is sin and the human predicament. He meets that situation by bearing what has to be born that the work of love may get done. God in Jesus Christ suffers with his world, not meaninglessly but redemptively. He has inaugurated a new history by an action which, restores the possibility of loyalty in this broken, suffering, yet still hopeful human community.

(3)

I AND THOU

We are trying to see how reconciliation takes place. Personal communication comes through action; but it also comes through speech. The philosophies of the I-Thou relationship have rightly insisted that there is a primary word which is spoken from one free subject to another, in the freedom of the personal relationship. The rupture of sin is a break in personal trust and fidelity. That is why sin can never be fully defined by reference to transgression of objective law. It means personal separation, and it can be healed only by personal reconciliation. There is a point in personal relationship where only the direct word, spoken and heard, can be adequate for the forgiveness and renewal of reconciliation.[13] Language here does not mean any one form of speech. It can be spoken words, gestures, or signs. Personal communication often finds spoken words unnecessary. Yet the spoken word is always present in the context of personal existence. One of the consequences of sin is the corruption of speech in the trivializing, sentimentalizing, false ornamentation, and obfuscation of our talk.

God's creative action in history works in human language to make it the vehicle of truth instead of lies, and of reconciliation instead of hurt and destructive bitterness.[14] In Jesus' work of atonement he spoke the words of forgiveness and reconciliation and he spoke them

13. Martin Buber, *I and Thou*, 2nd ed. (New York: Charles Scribner's Sons, 1958; Edinburgh: T. & T. Clark).

14. The relation of language to religion and the redemptive process deserves especial attention. H. Wheeler Robinson, *Redemption and Revelation* (London: James Nisbet & Co., 1942; New York: Harper & Brothers, 1942), is valuable. There is renewed interest in J. G. Hamann's insight. See Ronald Gregor Smith, *J. G. Hamann, 1730–1788*, with selections from his writings (London: Collins, 1960). Martin Heidegger's philosophy continues to stimulate philosophic and theological discussion on this topic. See Heidegger on poetry and revelation in *Existence and Being* (Chicago: Henry Regnery, 1949; London: Vision Press, 2nd ed., 1956).

as indicatives and imperatives of the spirit. The word from the cross, 'Father, forgive them for they know not what they do', gathers up many prior words in his teaching: 'forgive us our debts as we forgive'; the declaration of forgiveness to the paralytic (Matthew 9: 1–7); the word which is still part of the Gospel though a late addition to the Gospel record, 'neither do I condemn thee, go and sin no more' (John 8: 11). And there is the discussion with Peter, recorded in Matthew's Gospel about forgiving seventy times seven (Matthew 18: 22).

Any word can be corrupted in human usage, including the word 'forgiveness'. It can be used to proclaim our moral superiority over another, used as a moralistic club, sentimentalized and debased. But the word can be spoken and heard in the authentic experience of reconciliation, and it stands in the language of the Gospel as the Word of God clothing itself in human speech and opening the way for the language of redemption to be spoken between God and man.

(4)

THE NEW COMMUNITY

Atonement involves both the action of God and the participating action of man. It is the work of love dealing with the situation in which love has been twisted, blocked, and lost. We tend to think of atonement only as the prologue to a new relationship. After one 'atones for his deed' by so much suffering or penance the new life begins. But this falsifies the real situation. Atonement is creation. The new community brought into being through the renewal of love has in its structure the experience which brings about the renewal. The quality of the new community is founded on the remembered, present and anticipated work of reconciliation. This leads to an analysis of the doctrine of the Church, which concludes our exploration of the personal meaning of reconciliation.

God's loving action in Jesus Christ is the creation of a new humanity and a new community in history. The new humanity is constituted by how it has been brought into being through love which suffers and forgives. The doctrine of the Church as the community which bears the meaning of reconciliation in history is not then an addendum to the doctrine of atonement. The Church is the creation of the atoning action of God. This reconciling action continues and is known wherever God's love transforms the disfigured life of humanity with the power of a loyal and forgiving spirit. Failure to understand that the Church exists by continual participation in the atoning action of God in Jesus underlies many of the illusions in conventional images of the Church. Let us describe the Church as the community which lives by participation in the atonement.

The first consequence is that the Church is the form of the new creation, the new being, in history. Christian existence is never isolated existence. It is existence in a new community founded on faith in the divine action of reconciliation. God has created a new humanity in history whose form is life in the one Body with many members. The Gospel does not proclaim merely an ideal or a hope, but a victory which has been won and through which a new life has come into existence.

We have seen that the resurrection experience was the sign which re-created the hope of the disciples. The power of the resurrection was the establishment of the faith that in Jesus God's Messiah has appeared with redemptive power, and God's Holy Spirit is present to bring men into the new life for which Jesus has opened the way. The resurrection was the sign that the separation from God which has been exposed in the death of the man of God at the hands of sinful men is overcome now and forever. A new life reconciled to God has been made present with power in history.

It is true that the resurrection faith is connected with personal destiny beyond death and that it became the symbol of hope for universal resurrection and eternal life. But resurrection has the meaning of God's victory not only over death but over sin. The New Testament sees the final issue in history between God's holy love and the lovelessness of satanic pride, legalism, and self-centredness. Resurrection points to the expectation both of divine judgment and of eternal life. Therefore Paul explicitly connects the resurrection with the overcoming of sin: 'If Christ has not been raised, your faith is futile, and you are still in your sins' (I Corinthians 15: 17). W. D. Davies has suggested that in the earliest tradition Jesus appears first to Peter because it is Peter who had denied his Lord and for whom therefore the assurance of forgiveness was most explicitly bound up with the possibility of a new life in grace.[15]

This meaning of the resurrection for faith can be held with various views of the resurrection experiences. Christian faith in the victory of love does not depend on any single interpretation of the events following the crucifixion. It does depend on the connection between Jesus dying for sinners and the new life which God makes possible through him. In faith the Church knows itself as founded upon what God has done in the human situation riddled with betrayal. He has

15. W. D. Davies in a sermon preached in James Chapel, Union Theological Seminary, New York.

moved within the betrayal to show his love as reconciling power. The Gospel is that this love can be trusted absolutely and cannot be destroyed.

> Blessed be the God and Father of our Lord Jesus Christ! By his great mercy we have been born anew to a living hope through the resurrection of Jesus Christ from the dead, and to an inheritance which is imperishable, undefiled, and unfading, kept in heaven for you, who by God's power are guarded through faith for a salvation ready to be revealed at the last time (I Peter 1: 3–5).

> Nothing can separate us from the love of God which is in Jesus Christ our Lord (Romans 8:39).

This assurance bears the clear implication that since the Church exists through the prior and present action of God's grace its dependence upon that action ought to be its distinguishing mark. The Church should never think of itself as possessing grace, but as participating in it, and that participation is above all dependence upon grace as forgiveness.

The Church incorporates in its memory and its hope the reconciling work of God which is unfinished. So the New Testament joins with the assurance of redemption the powerful counterpoint of the summons to repentance and faith:

> Be sober, be watchful. Your adversary the devil prowls around like a roaring lion, seeking someone to devour. Resist him, firm in your faith, knowing that the same experience of suffering is required of your brotherhood throughout the world. And after you have suffered a little while, the God of grace who has called you to his eternal glory in Christ, will himself restore, establish, and strengthen you (I Peter 5: 8–10).

The New Testament is filled with such injunctions. Memory and hope belong together. Church history shows love in a continuing but hopeful struggle with the sin and pride which infect sometimes with greater virulence those who professedly live by love. God's suffering continues in his contention with the Church. This is decisive for an honest doctrine of the new community.

In the sacramental life of the Church, Baptism is given once for all; but Holy Communion, the Lord's Supper, is a continually repeated sacramental action. There are many theologies of the sacraments and the Catholic, Orthodox, and Protestant doctrines show important differences. In the light of the atonement we see certain elements essential to a Christian view of the sacraments.

The Eucharist, Holy Communion, the Lord's Supper, is a memorial, a representation of the events in the history which brought the faith of the church into existence. But it is not only a memorial of the past. It is the celebration of the continuing action of God who gave his Son for the world, who continually offers men the mercy of forgiveness, and calls them to become members of the living body of their Lord. The sacrament does not repeat the sacrifice of Jesus. That was once for all. But there is an important truth in the traditional Catholic language about 'repetition'. The suffering, atoning, and redeeming love of God is remembered and represented ever anew when the sacrament is celebrated, and, we most certainly add, when it is received in faith. The suffering of the church and the suffering of God are involved in one history. The suffering of the church results from love, and from failure to realize the authentic community of love. The suffering of God is his involvement as he contends with men both within and outside his church.

The sacrament of Baptism means incorporation into the body of Christist. Whether we accept Baptism for infants or not, we should not think of it as merely a decorous ceremony of formal acceptance into the church. We are baptized into Christ's death, and receive here the sign of God's grace and mercy. The sacraments are actions within the history of love's work. They are forms created by and for expression of the love which redeems. They can be empty forms, or vehicles of the Spirit in all its depth and wonder.[16]

The Christian understanding of the Holy Spirit is inseparable from the meaning of atonement, for it is in the action of Jesus Christ that the Spirit, which is God's quickening power and presence, has created the new form of human existence. In Christ the Spirit is known as the love which is *agape*. Certainly the work of the Holy Spirit is not confined to one strand of history. God has not left himself without witness in any land (Acts 14: 17). Wherever the human spirit is moved by love in preparation, knowledge, or fulfilment there the Holy Spirit is finding a response. But those who in faith participate in the community established by the atoning action of Jesus experience the Spirit creating a new body for its expression in the world.

The knowledge of the Holy Spirit as given in the atonement ought to guard the Church against the sin of claiming to exhibit unambiguously the holiness of God, but sadly this sin persists and may even find reinforcement in the claim to possess the Holy Spirit. Such a claim means that the meaning of atonement has been obscured. The Spirit which renews the broken community is that which the community cannot command for itself, but which it receives by grace. Therefore

16. I have a brief discussion of contemporary sacramental theory in *What Present Day Theologians are Thinking*, 3rd ed. (New York: Harper & Row, 1967), chapter VI.

when we look for the marks of the presence of the Holy Spirit we should include humility about claims for its possession. Such humility does not exclude the ecstatic joy of receiving the Spirit of God, or the peace of *agape* with God and the neighbour, but it is joy and peace made possible within love's work of forgiveness. The Holy Spirit and the human spirit remain two, not one.

Our interpretation of atonement has been developed from its christological centre. It points to that work of God in history which has brought the new community founded on the Spirit of forgiving love into being. The Church in its intentionality is this new historical reality, a body of living, suffering, working, dying people who have been brought into a new relationship with God and one another. Luther puts it daringly: 'We are to be little Christs for one another'.[17]

There is always the danger of parochialism in an account of Christian faith which moves from its centre in Christ outward toward all experience. By describing the atonement as the action which we see in the history of Jesus we in no way deny the working of the gracious love of God outside the Christian circle. Wherever men experience their self-betrayal, and their loveless divisions and find a new power to love one another and discover a deeper human community there we see analogies to what we have experienced decisively in Jesus Christ. To believe in atonement as the revelation of the love which fulfils and reconciles all human loves is to see all history in a new way. Human life is the search for the love which fulfils the will to belong, and which has passed through the story of love's betrayal and found a new possibility of hope.

As we take our description of love as known in Jesus Christ into some concrete areas of human living we are not only trying to see human experience in the light of the *agape* of God but also seeking to understand more fully what all loves really are. We do not first know love and then apply our knowledge. We love, grow, and suffer, and perhaps the truth of *agape* becomes clearer. We shall examine four areas of human living: the way of self-giving, sexuality and love, the struggle for justice, and love in the intellectual life. We bring to the analysis whatever we have gained from our interpretation of the central disclosure of God's love in Jesus Christ, and we bring to it also the illumination we have found in the doctrine that God's life is in process as he involves himself in the growth, becoming and travail of the world. It is our hope that this new perspective will throw light on persistent human problems, and open the way to some new assessment of the forms which the spirit of love may be taking in contemporary life.

17. Martin Luther: *Treatise on Christian Liberty*, p. 76.

CHAPTER X

LOVE AND SELF-SACRIFICE

'It is only necessary to know that love is a direction and not a state of the soul. If one is unaware of this, one falls into despair at the first onslaught of affliction' (Simone Weil).

There is a familiar portrayal of Francis of Assisi in which the saint stands rapt in meditation, his eyes fixed upon the skull which he holds in his right hand. In his left hand he has a cross. He is absorbed in the contemplation of death, his own and that of Jesus. St. Francis accepted the drastic transformation of the self and its loves by the Gospel. 'He who saveth his life will lose it; but he who loses his life for the sake of the Gospel will save it.' But if the love of God and neighbour means complete self-giving, what becomes of all the loves which constitute human selfhood, and what becomes of the self? In this chapter we consider the meaning of self-sacrifice. God's love must transform without destroying human desires, strivings, and search for selfhood. How is this possible? This is the central problem for every Christian interpretation of love, and it underlies all the special ethical questions such as those dealing with the sexual life, with the struggle for justice, and the intellectual life which we are to consider in later chapters.

(1)

Selfhood and Self-sacrifice, the Issue between Christianity and Its Critics

Christianity has a double problem in attaining clarity about the meaning of self-sacrifice. Granted all the Christian premises, it is still difficult to see how the self can maintain its vitality as a growing, self-affirming free spirit, and yet be giving itself away. Many powerful critics of Christianity hold that the love it offers negates life.

It is easy to find texts which apparently support this view. St. John of the Cross says:

The soul that is to ascend this mount of perfection, to commune with God, must not only renounce all things and leave them below, but must not even allow the desires, which are the beasts, to pasture over against

192

this mount—that is, upon other things which are not purely God, in Whom every desire ceases: that is, in the state of perfection.

By this we are to understand that the love of God must never fail in the soul, so that the soul may be a worthy altar, and also that *no other love must be mingled with it.*[1]

Simone Weil, twentieth-century mystic, puts the radical demand:

We participate in the creation of the world by decreating ourselves. . . . May God grant that I become nothing.
In so far as I become nothing, God loves himself through me.[2]

Dag Hammarskjöld's *Markings*, one of the great examples of self-examination, is all the more striking as it comes from his life of public responsibility. Hammarskjöld repeatedly contrasts self-seeking and self-sacrifice:

Your life is without a foundation, if, in any matter, you choose on your own behalf.

Of Jesus he says:

Assenting to his possibility—why? Does he sacrifice himself for others, *yet for his own sake*—in megalomania? Or does he realize himself for the sake of others? The difference is that between a monster and a man. 'A new commandment I give unto you; that ye love one another.'[3]

Reinhold Niebuhr says that sacrificial love, the *agape* of the Gospel, must transcend mutual love. *Agape* is given freely for the sake of the other and is heedless of reward or response. Only *agape* leads to fulfilment, but the fulfilment must be the unintended result, otherwise love masks our self-seeking and then the goal is lost. Niebuhr argues that sacrificial love is the 'impossible possibility', and he has exposed in a masterly way the sin in our pretences of morality and brotherhood. It is grace alone, with the forgiveness it holds, which can release us to recognize and in some fragmentary way begin to live in self-giving love for God and neighbour.[4]

Many secular critics attack this view of love as self-sacrifice in all its Christian forms. They see it as a devaluation of man, a repression of the self's vital impulses, and an unwillingness to affirm its creative

1. St. John of the Cross, *The Ascent of Mt. Carmel, Works,* Vol. I, Eng. trans. (London: Burns Oates & Washbourne, 1934), Bk. I, ch. 5, paragraphs 6–7.

2. Simone Weil, *Gravity and Grace* (New York: G. P. Putnam's Sons, 1952; London: Routledge & Kegan Paul), p. 80.

3. Dag Hammarskjöld, *Markings,* tr. by Leif Sjöberg and W. E. Auden (New York: Alfred A. Knopf, 1964, pp. 93, 69; London: Faber & Faber, 1964).

4. Reinhold Niebuhr, *The Nature and Destiny of Man,* Vol. I, pp. 287–95; Vol. II, chap. 3.

194   THE SPIRIT AND THE FORMS OF LOVE

power. It postpones self-realization to an eschatological future and thus draws energies away from the present tasks of history. Amos Wilder has put the critics' point concisely:

> The Christian has not made clear for himself the paradox of world denial and abundance of life. He has lodged in an otherworldliness that has seemed, whether to a Nietzsche or a Lawrence, a blasphemy against the natural creation, or in a compromise with life that has lost any creative appeal, and so deserved the apostasy of those thirsty for reality.[5]

Erich Fromm's criticism of Christian ethics is fairly representative of the point of view of many who find the basis for a philosophy of self-realization in psychology. He says that the Christian faith in God has restrained freedom and repressed productive love, and his strictures are especially directed at the Protestant Reformers:

> Luther's relationship to God was one of complete submission. In psychological terms his concept of faith means: if you completely submit, if you accept your individual insignificance, then the all-powerful God may be willing to love you and save you. If you get rid of your individual self with all its shortcomings and doubts by utmost self-effacement, you free yourself from the feeling of your own nothingness and can participate in God's glory.[6]

For Fromm, man's only hope lies in the discovery within himself of the productive powers of love. He should achieve an ethical outlook based on human nature, and overcome the distortions and illusions which bind his spirit. He must become 'man for himself'.

It is instructive that in Fromm's recent book, *The Heart of Man, its Genius for Good and Evil*, he seeks to answer the criticism of his optimistic view of man.[7] He traces all the sources of human evil to some factor in the developing life of the person which has become fixed, and blocks normal activity. The temptations of freedom itself, its anxieties and insecurities, and the possibility of the spirit's self-corruption are never admitted by Fromm. Christianity, he believes, has missed the real key to human fulfilment. It has a false understanding of the roots of evil, and its ideal of life is incompatible with the free development of man.

5. Amos Wilder, *The Spiritual Aspects of the New Poetry* (New York: Harper & Brothers, 1940), p. 164.

6. Erich Fromm, *Escape from Freedom* (New York: Holt, Rinehart and Winston, 1941), p. 81. For a more judicious estimate of Luther by a psychiatrist see Erik Erikson, *Young Man Luther* (New York: Norton, 1958; London: Faber & Faber, 1959).

7. Erich Fromm, *The Heart of Man, its Genius for Good and Evil* (New York: Harper & Row, 1964).

Albert Camus is one of the most powerful of the contemporary critics of Christianity. His view differs sharply from Fromm's, for Camus sees the tragic element in human existence. Man's world holds untold suffering and evil. Human effort to roll the stone up the hill only results in a roll down again and the endless repetition of this heroic effort. Yet Camus has denied that his *Myth of Sisyphus* is pessimism. Man can recognize his limits. He can hear the human cry for help and respond to it. He can rebel against the evil in existence even if he cannot eliminate it.[8]

Christianity's failure as Camus sees it, is that it avoids the human dilemma by promising fulfilment in another world, the hereafter. It conceals the tragedy of life with a pseudo-solution. Whatever fulfilment men can have, Camus believes, must be found in this life. This challenges man's will, his decision, and his heroism, but these belong to his humanity, and he does not need the support of faith in God.[9]

Camus's affirmation that humanity can get along without God in an ethical way of life defines the critical issue which a Christian doctrine of love must meet. Why is not the power man finds within himself enough? If man turns to the love of God for help, does he not inevitably become confused about human love? Why is the love which God gives so necessary to man?

The way to an answer leads through the mystery of self-giving and the paradox of the Gospel as we try to understand the relation of the love of God to the human loves. The crux is the meaning of self-renunciation in *agape*. How is it compatible with the loves which constitute human selfhood, and how may it transform them?

Self-denial has been interpreted in three ways. There is, first, the monastic way with its realistic facing of the problem of love in the world, and its heroic answer of renunciation. It may be described as the institutionalization of the Franciscan spirit. It begins with the conviction that the absolute way of love cannot be realized directly amid the involvements of family responsibility, political power, and economic acquisition. Some therefore are called by God to express the purity of love by separating themselves from worldly commitments. They take vows of poverty, chastity and obedience, and commit themselves to the way of love in a dedicated community as their sacrificial participation in the body of Christ and his service in the world. There is no claim to perfection, only the striving for it.

8. Albert Camus, *The Myth of Sisyphus*, tr. by Justin O'Brien (London: Hamish Hamilton, 1955; New York: Knopf, 1955).

9. Albert Camus, *The Rebel* (London: Hamish Hamilton, 1953; New York: Vintage Books, 1959, p. 303).

There is obedience to the injunction to seek first the Kingdom of God, an obedience which is not possible without this drastic self-renunciation. Therefore the whole body of Christ, the Church, lives in partial dependence upon the merit achieved in the special vocation of the 'religious' orders.

Surely there is something permanently valid in this view of the Christian life. There are special calls to a way of life which breaks with established structures and privileges in society. Without renunciation the work of love would not get done in the world. The incarnation keeps this before us. The Son of Man 'had no place to lay his head'. In fulfilling his vocation he refused the ties of marriage, the status and power of political responsibility. The imitation of Christ will always lead some to an analogous self-denial as the way of love.

A careful historical judgment of the monastic solution must be that it is not the sole answer. It has its own difficulties. Individual poverty became collective wealth. Personal self-denial of status and privilege may create collective power and prestige. There is no evidence whatever that renunciation of worldly loves and family ties controls the passions and perversions of *eros* in the soul. I side with the Protestant Reformers here and say that in spite of its authentic heroism the monastic way wins its victory over the world too easily. If love gives meaning to life it must create a valid way of life for all, not only those in especially constituted orders. Monasticism undoubtedly offers a way for some, but it is not the only way to the sacrificial life of love.

The Reformers' alternative conception of the way of love in the world begins with the insight that the tendency of man is to seek self-justification and to think of ethical perfection as an achievement of human freedom. Against this the Reformers assert that the real significance of *agape* lies in forgiveness. The concern for moral self-justification before God always falsifies our situation. So long as we seek some 'right pattern' to express the way of love, we are seeking to prove ourselves righteous, and we shall certainly fail. God's love is his mercy toward us in spite of sin, and it remains mercy and forgiveness throughout the whole of life. It is this gracious love by which the justified man lives. Here Luther and Calvin try to put the ethical life on the bedrock of the New Testament estimate of our actual situation before God. The way of love involves repentance for what we are, not proof that we love as we should.

But to leave the matter there is not sufficient. There must be a way of life for the Christian. For Luther the Christian is one who, being released from self-righteousness, is ready to give himself to his neighbour. Thus a powerful tension appears in Luther's description of the Christian life. The Christian needs no law for he lives in the spirit of love. To be sure, there are very few Christians, but Luther believes there are some. The spirit of Christianity is this:

> I will do nothing in this life except what I see is necessary, profitable, and salutary to my neighbour, since through faith I have an abundance of all good things in Christ.[10]

But the Christian lives in the world with its law, its needs, and its demands. Strictly speaking the law would not be necessary if all were Christian, but God gives it for the restraint of those whose hearts are not governed by the Holy Spirit, including those who are nominally Christian, but who do not live by faith and love. Hence the Christian strenuously gives himself to the needs of the common life and becomes obedient to law, for in this way he does what is necessary for service to the neighbour.[11] Luther says:

> That is what makes caring for the body a Christian work, that through its health and comfort we may be able to work, to acquire, and lay by funds with which to aid those who are in need.[12]

The Christian upholds the law of the state and supports its defence against others when justice is at stake. Again Luther:

> [If a foreign government is your opponent, then you should first offer justice and peace, but if this is refused then defend yourself by force against force. . . .] And in such a war it is a Christian act and an act of love confidently to kill, rob, and pillage the enemy, and to do everything that can injure him until one has conquered him according to the methods of war.[13]

Much has been said in criticism of Luther's doctrine here, and there are many issues concerning the later development of the Christian ethic in relation to war and social justice; but our immediate concern is to understand Luther's faith that it is possible for the Christian to live the life of *agape* in the midst of the world's affairs and conflicts. Luther believes, and Calvin agrees, that there is a right use of the things of this world, and that every man is called by God to respond in faith and love in the situation in which he finds himself.[14] That is, everyone who knows the Word of God finds

10. Martin Luther, *Treatise on Christian Liberty*, Anchor Books ed. by John Dillenberger (1961), p. 75.
11. Martin Luther, *Secular Authority: To What Extent it Should be Obeyed.*
12. Martin Luther, *Treatise*, pp. 73–4.
13. Luther, *Secular Authority*, p. 398.
14. Calvin, *Institutes*, Bk. III, chap. 10, 'The right use of the present life and its supports'.

that he has a vocation to service in the world, a calling from God. One can live in the spirit of the Gospel in so far as he uses everything in the world as a means of preparation for and service to the neighbour.

We must ask, however, whether with all the realism of the Reformers in their doctrine of vocation, they solved the problem of self-sacrifice in the spirit of *agape*. It is especially interesting that Luther with his sense of the persistence of sin in the redeemed, and his absolute reliance on justification by faith, still makes a rather neat distinction between those who are truly Christian and those who are not. He says less than we would expect about the temptations, especially the new temptations, which come within the Christian life. While Calvin seems to see more clearly than Luther the need for reforming the orders of the world guided by love and justice, both Reformers see the organization of society in terms which we know are far too simple in the light of the later history of democratic forms of political life.

The Reformers' great achievement was the insight that the way of *agape* can be actualized in secular existence with all its issues and decisions. The spirit of *agape* leads to action to meet the needs of men in the world as it is. But the radical terms of this actualization, with its persistent problems, have come more fully into view in later generations. We are somewhat more aware of the complexity of motives, especially those of the 'good'. The unmasking of the soul in the modern concept of ideology has exposed the pretences of good people in a way which must enter into a critical understanding of religions. The task of actualizing justice is far more complex than the Reformers saw it. The involvements and dilemmas of social policy forbid any simple doctrine of the righteousness of the ways we take in the world, however honestly we take them in the name of love.

We should not be surprised, therefore, nor should it prompt us to cynicism, that ordinary Christian life and practice achieves a kind of common-sense acknowledgement of the realities of human motives along with the demand for self-sacrifice, and does not seek to inhibit too much the natural cravings and drives. The prudent soul makes a concordat between the many loves and the love of God. It acknowledges the demand for complete self-giving, and then makes allowances for ordinary motives, the needs of the flesh, the importance of not aiming too high, and the requirement for sensible self-protection in getting along. This, I hold, is a more honest settlement than one which makes only the pretence and admits no need of compromise. But it is a settlement which means the domestication of the soul and the eventual destruction of the spirit's high calling. Is any other way possible?

Søren Kierkegaard believes that it is possible to hold together the *agape* of the Gospel and the earthly loves. His way to this, whether we find it acceptable or not, should prove instructive to the modern spirit which has become acutely conscious of the false masks of piety. Kierkegaard's *Work of Love*, along with many other writings, gives a marvellous example of spiritual surgery which penetrates the pretences of the self. Kierkegaard sees quite plainly that there can be a pseudo-self-denial:

> *A merely human self-denial* thinks as follows: give up your selfish wishes, desires and plans—then you will be honoured and respected and loved as just and wise. It is easy to see that this sort of self-denial does not lay hold of God or the God-relationship, but remains on the worldly plane of a relationship between men. *The Christian self-denial thinks:* give up your selfish wishes and desires, give up your selfish plans and purposes in order to work for the good in true disinterestedness—and then prepare to find yourself, just on that account, hated, scorned and mocked, and even executed as a criminal; or rather, do not prepare to find yourself in this situation, for that may become necessary, but choose it of your own free will. For Christian self-denial knows beforehand that these things will happen, and chooses them freely.[15]

But Kierkegaard, for all his insight, has not taken the full measure of the problem of love. He comes precariously close to accepting an external and legalistic criterion for the presence of love. Unless love leads to a specific kind of rejection the spirit is not really loving, this is what he seems to hold. But is this so? This would make the life of love impossible within the established orders of the world. Kierkegaard, it should be remembered, rejected marriage responsibilities for himself. The decisive renunciation in his life is his breaking his engagement to Regina. It is never made very clear what went into this decision; but we can reflect upon it in the light of a passage in *Works of Love*:

> The point at issue between the poet and Christianity can be quite accurately defined in this way: Earthly love and friendship are partiality and the passion of partiality; Christian love is self-denying love, therefore it vouches for this 'shalt'. To exhaust these passions is bewildering. But the extreme passionate limits of partiality lie in exclusiveness, in loving only one; the extreme limits of self-denial lie in self-sacrifice, in not excluding a single one.

---

15. S. Kierkegaard, *Works of Love*, tr. by D. F. and L. M. Swenson (Princeton: Princeton University Press, 1949, pp. 157–8; London: William Collins Sons & Co., 1962).

He goes on indeed to say that Christianity does not reject sensuality or marriage. But he reiterates his theme:

> Christianity harbours a suspicion about earthly love and friendship, because partiality in passion, or passionate partiality, is really another form of selfishness.[16]

Kierkegaard rightly identifies here the perplexity in the Christian view of love. To love every neighbour and yet to commit oneself to a beloved person makes abiding tensions and poses difficult decisions. Kierkegaard seems to allow his first answer of renunciation and the answer of the Reformers to stand side by side without any clear resolution of the two perspectives. In his meditation on 'Thou shalt love thy neighbour' he writes in the spirit of the Reformers as he tells us not to give up love of wives and children but 'preserve in your earthly love and friendship your love for your neighbour'.[17] Certainly the suspicion about the earthly loves remains, and Kierkegaard rightly brings it into the open. But what he fails to see clearly is that earthly loves may themselves come into the service of God. Failure to love the neighbour may be born in the failure of love in the family. If Kierkegaard sees this he does not make it a part of his reconciliation of *agape* and the earthly loves. The point may be put another way. The sexual relationship and the family loves can become blocked and corroded when there is no outgoing love toward the neighbour. We should add this point to Kierkegaard's word: 'The concept of the neighbour is precisely the middle term of self-abnegation, which enters between the I and I of selfishness but also between the I and the other I of earthly love and friendship.'[18] It is not only self-abnegation but also fulfilment which the outgoing love of *agape* offers to love as affection, and affection may be the first school of *agape*.

One other aspect of Kierkegaard's view of love deserves special attention. His individualism is such that he overlooks how social structures separate men from one another. Kierkegaard lacked a social ethical doctrine of *agape* which is no less concerned to break through to the neighbour, but is less naive about how social orders corrupt human relationships. Kierkegaard sees that 'purity of heart is to will one thing', to use the title of one of his meditations; but he does not fully see that purity of heart requires responsible participation in the common life. He discusses the Gospel demand for equality, and he realistically knows that we must love the neighbour 'while allowing the earthly differenced to continue'.[19]

16. *Ibid.*, pp. 43–4.   17. *Ibid.*, p. 51.
18. *Ibid.*, p. 45.   19. *Ibid.*, p. 69.

But should all differences in the *status quo* continue? Kierkegaard says:

> He who loves his neighbour is calm. He is calm through being satisfied with the conditions of earthly life assigned to him, be they those of distinction or of poverty, and for the rest, he allows every earthly distinction to retain its power, and to pass for what it is and ought to be here in this life.

To be fair to Kierkegaard, he acknowledges the good intentions of the social reformers' drive toward equality, although 'worldly equality, even if it were possible, is not Christian equality'.[20] He criticizes the caste system.[21] Despite these concessions to the need for social justice Kierkegaard's doctrine remains inadequate. It must be said of his view what has been said of the monastic and the Reformers' solution, that it solves the relationship of self-sacrifice to human loves too easily. Kierkegaard makes such a complete break between the purity of the love which wills only an eternal good, and the involvements of the common life that the real task of *agape* to come to terms with responsibility in the world never gets quite into focus. Surely the deepest work of love occurs just where it cannot remain 'calmly untouched' in the established orders, but is constrained to challenge, reform, or deny them. The tension between friendship and the universal love of neighbour is present in all love in a way which Kierkegaard saw but never fully resolved.

The love of the eternal is not a wholly different kind of love from love of the temporal. The real problem is that the human loves and the love God has made present in Christ are together in the self which must find the way to eternal life in the struggles and passions of history. That is why there will always be Augustinian, Franciscan, and Evangelical forms of Christian living.

Whatever it has been in past centuries, love takes form in our century as participation in shaping a new world order. Self-giving means to witness and labour where the lives of innumerable human beings are at stake. Life can be given for the sake of the Gospel in mass movements, in political revolution, in complex social strategies and cultural creativity. Sacrificial love requires a perception of the relation between the ultimate claims of *agape* and the complexity of human motives. Love can be humbly present in the passion, conflict and world-shaping creativity of life. The Incarnate Lord who bears the life of Everyman seems to touch history at a tangent; but the tangent intersects with the realities of collective existence. Jesus was not crucified for preaching a pure love unsullied by contact with

20. *Ibid.*, p. 60. 21. *Ibid.*, p. 57.

social issues, but for relating the message of love to the critique of social privilege and power.

Simone Weil had much in common with Kierkegaard. She was a deeply introspective, lonely, agonizingly sensitive wrestler with God. But her search for the authentic way of love took her into the midst of the social struggle. Born in France in 1909, she was five years old when the First World War began. When she discovered that the French soldiers at the front had no sugar she refused to eat sugar at home. Trained as a teacher and possessing an exceptional intellect, she added to her teaching duties in a French manufacturing town an interest in the problems of workers and the unemployed. She walked in picket lines and shared her too scanty supply of food. In an attempt further to identify her life with factory workers, she worked in an automobile factory, a job which taxed her frail strength to the limit. She went to Spain during the civil war, determined to lend support to the Loyalists' cause, though as part of her ethical commitment she refused to fire a gun.

During the Second World War strenuous work in the vineyards of Southern France caused another breakdown in health. After making her way to England, she prepared for the French Government an analysis of problems of reconstruction after the war, a report published under the title, *The Need for Roots*. It is filled with ripe wisdom. In the war days in England she refused to eat more food than was being allowed on the ration of her countrymen in France. The strain was too much for her frail constitution and she died in 1943 at the age of thirty-three.[22]

This is the outward story. The inner spiritual experience is that of the mystical discovery of God, and a movement toward the centre of Roman Catholic faith. She came into a close relationship to Catholic sacramental piety and yet never became a Catholic. Part of her stated reason for remaining outside the church was that she feared elements of demonic collective passion might be corrupting the widespread enthusiasm for the church, and she wanted to make clear that the love of Christ is something essentially different from the feeling of security which comes from belonging to a group. As her biographer says, 'she remained crouching on the threshold of the church for the love of all of us who are not inside'.[23]

If we take such a life with its freight of personal psychological struggle and try to make it our example of what the love of God

22. Biographical sketch by Leslie Fiedler in his introduction to *Waiting on God* (London: Routledge & Kegan Paul, 1951; New York: G. P. Putnam's Sons, 1951).
23. *Ibid.*, p. 28.

means, we only do violence to that life and make ourselves ridiculous in trying to imitate it. This was itself no repetition of the story of Christ. It exhibits the obvious relativities of human choices. There are some interesting examples of this. Simone Weil, late in life, confessed that one of her youthful demonstrations of solidarity with the poor (I think in this case the refusal to wear stockings) was really prompted by a desire to plague her mother. And one of her few friends, a person who admired her deeply, remarked that he had never once known her to yield a point in an argument! Every life has its ambiguities in the light of love.

While we cannot make a universal ethical pattern out of Simone Weil's life, she does, like Kierkegaard, point to where the problem of the relation of love to self-realization lies. Nothing less than complete love to God and neighbour fulfils the self. In a life of such dedication, all neat theories of self-realization through social adjustment have their shallowness exposed. The only self fit for the community God intends is that which has learned to give itself away. But what is given away? And what happens to human loves in the giving? We have quoted what Simone Weil says of the need to 'de-create our egos'. But surely the ego must also be re-created. Human existence is existence in desire, in the self-affirmation of life craving more life, and the aggressiveness of the spirit. Selflessness with no *eros*, no vital impulse, no love of life, is not real selfhood. Jesus saying, 'He who loves father or mother more than me is not worthy of me' (Matthew 10: 37) may suggest that human loves are not destroyed but transcended in the higher loyalty.

Is self-sacrifice an ultimate limit toward which the self may move, but which it can never quite reach, or is there a union of sacrificial love with the self's growth into its full stature which can be realized, though certainly only through grace? It may be that this question brings us to the limit of analysis of self denial. Each one must live through to his answer as he is and where he is. Yet the matter is so critical for the Christian meaning of love that we should try to face the meaning of self-sacrifice as clearly as possible. We need to cut through our illusions and our pretences. A sense of reality about the love we know in Christ is easily lost or confused. If there are those who do not find it so, then this book must appear to them as pointless and irrelevant. But for the rest, it may be that the paradox of losing life and finding it may be seen in clearer light if we get a more adequate view of what the self is. Our sense of reality about love will be helped if we see the self not as a fixed object but as becoming, a career. In the final section of this chapter I will expand this suggestion in the outline of a theory of the self, not to dispose of the mystery of self-sacrifice, but, if possible, to bring its issues into clearer focus.

(2)

SELFHOOD AND SELF-SACRIFICE

All the human loves: sexual love, comradely love, humanitarian love, and the religious love of the good and the beautiful, belong in the fulfilled self. They will be transformed in self-giving, yet they must live, for they constitute personal life. Our question is how the love of God, *agape*, with its absolute self-giving, can fulfil the human loves without destroying them.

The thesis I propose is that the human loves have two aspects which make them a preparation for *agape*. They have the power to open up the self, and thus to begin to show the requirement of self-giving. Second, they reach the limits of self-fulfilment, and thus prepare for the acknowledgement that only a love which transcends the human loves can fulfil the self.

This thesis specifically rejects the position that *agape* is a complete contradiction of human love. At the same time it does not identify *agape* with the form of any human love, and it does not expect human loves to move toward *agape* in a direct and simple way.

This thesis of the essential relatedness of all the loves can be defended only if we see the self as a becoming, not as a fixed entity. If the self is not a becoming, but a substance with a fixed structure, then those who separate *agape* completely from the human loves are surely right. Then *agape* hovers above the human loves on another plane, and it will come as an utterly foreign element into the natural life of the self. But if the self is a becoming, then the full meaning of selfhood lies in a personal history and not in a completed structure. To be a self is to move toward being, not simply to possess being in a certain way. In this understanding of the self we can ask how all the human loves and *agape* itself, enter into growth toward selfhood. There can be dynamic relationships which bring *agape* and the human loves into a genuine interaction. We must examine self-sacrifice with the time dimension in view.

There is, to be sure, no magic in the word 'becoming'. The mystery of selfhood and of the work of *agape* remains. We are seeking the meaning of personal existence which has its corruption in sin and sickness. We know every love, including *agape* as it is refracted in the dark mirror of life. But it makes a great difference whether we look for love's meaning in static formal structures, or as the spirit at work in a history where there is freedom, growth, and decision, and where new forms are created.

In the following discussion I use the term *agape* to refer to the self-giving and forgiving love which God has decisively expressed in the world in his redemptive activity in Jesus. I mean by 'the human loves' all our experiences of organic feeling and sympathetic attachment for things and persons in the world. This includes self-love.

There are three aspects of the growth of the self and its loves. First, there is the will to belong which is the core of selfhood. Second, there is the discovery that belonging requires self-giving as well as receiving and the consequent search for an adequate object of love. Finally, there is the dimension of hope which the self must find in its loves. We learn to love in history, and 'it does not yet appear what we shall be'. In all three aspects, love as *agape* comes as the transforming fulfilment of the search in human love. It is not that we discover the meaning of *agape* by going into the depths of the self; but that we discover in the depths of the self a hunger born of the self's own loves which only *agape* can satisfy.

The self is a *will to belong*. We have stated the doctrine of the *imago dei* as the will to communion. Here we are on the track of the meaning of self-sacrifice, and we need to analyse the will to belong more fully. I suggest the 'will to belong' as more fundamental than either the 'will to power' (Hocking) or 'ultimate concern', in Tillich's sense of that which determines our being or non-being. The reason is that the 'will to belong' designates more precisely that psychic and organic craving which constitutes our humanity. Of course any conceptions of the nature of selfhood can be validated only by appeal to our fundamental intuitions. We have no absolute precision or dogmatic finality here. But the 'will to belong' does point to what we observe in human motives, cravings, sacrifices, satisfactions, and perversities.

When John Donne says 'no man is an island' he is not lecturing us to have consideration for others, but is stating the fact which constitutes our existence, that we are bound in one bundle of life. The self is thrown into an incomprehensibly vast creation, a world teeming with other creatures, and other selves. Each self tries to find where it fits in this immense and threatening confusion. The primordial sense of the need to belong appears. It is both physical and psychological. It is the search for at-homeness, for knowing where we are and who we are as we grow in freedom to deal with the environment. The power and stubbornness of the self to maintain its being against the onslaughts of an overpowering world is one of its most amazing characteristics. It will grasp at anything, use anything, defend anything in struggling to maintain its poise and strength. Some views of child development stress an early phase of self-centredness and narcissism as essential in the growth of the personality. Certainly this is one part of the story. But self-centredness is the centre of something more than the self; it is the centre of the world in which the self must get along. There is, therefore, in all self-assertion and self-centredness both the pole of autonomy, the affirmation of self-integrity and independence, and the pole of symbiosis, which requires conformity and relatedness to the other.

Both autonomy and symbiosis require communication and response. The autonomous self wants to be recognized as a self, and it seeks response in the other. Belonging involves communication and no self can exist without some fulfilment of this fundamental need.

There is, therefore, a kind of self-giving in the most elementary level of selfhood. It is the self-giving which offers communication to the other, and craves, waits for, and is rewarded by the response of another. We need not endow this 'self-giving' with ethical quality any more than we would the craving for food or warmth. The self must participate in being with its environment and thus begin to belong.

Primary evidence that this is a valid account of the self is found in what we recognize in many incipient illnesses of the personality. Excessive autonomy without regard for the other, and the lack of power to communicate are pathological, just as symbiosis in which the self no longer 'belongs' because it loses its identity in the other is pathological. The point we are making does not require a precise definition of 'normal' adjustment or balance between autonomy and symbiosis. Every self is unique. Creativity appears in extraordinary forms. Some imbalance in personal relationships may contribute to it. We can say that the limits within which sane selfhood must exist require the self's participation in a real world and in a community of selves where there is communication in some form of speaking and hearing. In Martin Buber's language, there can be no I without a Thou, though the forms of communication between I and Thou are indefinitely diverse and open to creativity.

As the self grows and emerges from this primordial self-relatedness a new aspect of self-giving appears. For the self can grow only by overcoming fixation at any point in its becoming. The self seeks integrity; but there can be no integrity without change. This is the hard lesson. It means that in every becoming there is some surrender of present satisfactions, defences and securities to a new demand. The past is not rejected. It remains a dynamic part of the personality, even when lost from conscious memory. But no past is sufficient for the new present, and no past form of the self's being can be preserved unaltered. This may seem a commonplace, yet it is the source of the desperate battle of the self for life, and it is here that temptation enters. Change means risk, and risk is painful. We are willing to grow provided we know we can maintain or increase our present security, but this can never be absolutely known. We begin to 'save our life' by holding on to it as it is. It is the first manifestation of the Fall.

The objective self at a given moment is largely the deposit of experience as shaped by our self-understanding. This given self bears its freight of hurt and hope, its creativity and anxiety, its self-seeking, and its groping for love. We cling to this self as it is. We fear it is all we have. Even its sufferings are familiar and we clutch them because their very familiarity is comforting, and saves us from facing the deeper suffering hidden underneath. We usually would rather live with our present frustrations than risk acquiring new ones. Yet so long as we aim at the maintenance of this present self, as we now conceive it, we cannot enter the larger selfhood which is pressing for life. This natural resistance of the self to becoming is not in itself sin. It is a self-protective device of the human spirit; but when it becomes an invitation to use our freedom against the risk of becoming it is temptation to sin. The meaning of sin is usually not that we try to make ourselves the centre of everything. That may happen, but it is a monstrous perversion. We are usually more subtle. We make our present state of selfhood the meaning of existence, and thus refuse the deeper meaning which lies within and beyond this present. When that refusal becomes refusal to trust in the giver of life and the greater community he is creating it is sin. The good we cling to may be noble in itself. Whitehead's comment is pertinent:

> Good people of narrow sympathies are apt to be unfeeling and un-progressive, enjoying their egotistical goodness. Their case, on a higher level, is analogous to that of the man completely degraded to a hog. They have reached a state of stable goodness, so far as their own interior life is concerned. This type of moral correctitude is, on a larger view, so like evil that the distinction is trivial.[24]

Beyond this need to grow there is the third discovery in every love. It is the distinction between love and possession. We have already encountered this in our analysis of the categories of being. The freedom of the other to be and to respond is part of what love

24. A. N. Whitehead, *Religion in the Making* (New York: Macmillan, 1927), p. 98.

wills. We affirm the principle that all human loves bear the possibility of learning to 'let go'. We must speak of *possibility*; for of all the lessons of love this is the most difficult. Here indeed sin enters every life and threatens destruction. Yet any authentic discovery of human love involves the will to affirm the other's being whatever that may cost. The lover learns to let the other become himself. This is the farthest pole from indifference. It is the will to love, but only in the freedom of the spirit. Parents have to learn that love for children involves letting them be and grow in their way. This is true no matter how great the responsibility of parents to guide, discipline and educate. Love respects the margin of freedom in every self, and remains loyal even when rejected or misunderstood.

It may clarify and reinforce the point here to observe that a similar principle applies in other than interpersonal loves. The creative artist loves the work he does. He loves his tools, his materials, the aesthetic vision which he seeks to make present and make palpable. As artist he learns that love requires the self to discipline its desires and satisfactions for the sake of the objective truth and beauty which it seeks. Anders Nygren seems to me to describe the corruption of the aesthetic *eros*, not its positive nature, when he calls it self-centred. The aesthetic *eros* requires a man to live beyond self-gratification and to accept a realm of meaning with its organizing principles which imposes itself on the process of creativity.

An artist may remain a self-centred and self-seeking person, but he has learned something of self-giving so far as he experiences aesthetic creativity. This applies not only to ecstatic moments but also to the plodding discipline. The delight and the discipline in the aesthetic experience are nicely recorded by Pablo Picasso and Georges Braque, two of the greatest modern painters. Picasso says:

> It is my misfortune—and probably my delight—to use things as my passions tell me. . . . How awful for a painter who loathes apples to have to use them all the time because they go so well with the cloth. I put all the things I like into my pictures. The things—so much the worse for them—they just have to put up with it.

And Braque:

> Emotion should not be rendered by an excited trembling; it can neither be added on nor be imitated. It is the seed, the work is the flower. I like the rule that corrects the emotion.[25]

We should remember that ecstasy in its root meaning is *ecstasis*, being taken out of one's place. Without the breaking of the shell of

25. Quoted in Robert Goldwater and Marco Treves, *Artists on Art*, 2nd ed. (New York: Pantheon Books, 1947), pp. 419, 423.

self-centredness there can be no real art. Love is not possession, but participation. Theology should not look down its nose at the realm of aesthetic creativity, but seek to understand that here also there can be preparation for the spirit of *agape*.

There is then a kind of self-giving which is inescapably present even when we resist it. I believe that Father D'Arcy is quite right in finding in the self both the love which seeks to grasp reality and the love which wants to give itself away. But I do not believe we need to invoke two different loves for this. The two movements are two aspects of what is essentially and existentially one, the growth of love through discovering its claims, its demands, and its fulfilment in the spirit of participation rather than possession.

The self-giving or self-sacrifice we have so far described, is not yet the self-giving which is claimed by the Gospel. We have found analogues to losing one's life in order to save it, but only analogues. For every particular love contains an implicit question of which we become gradually aware, and which may come into sharp focus only in crisis: 'where is the absolute and trustworthy fulfilment of the self's will to belong?' The will to belong cannot stop short of an absolute which fulfils it. William Ernest Hocking stated this truth in his *Human Nature and Its Remaking*.[26] It is the decisive point in a theological anthropology. Karl Barth restricts the image of God in man to man's community with his fellows. But man seeks community with the source of his being. It is the God relationship which makes a man a man. Man is linked with the whole of things, with eternity and time, with the open future as well as the past, with the source and end of his being as well as with his most intensely satisfying present loves. The self craves the completely trustworthy fulfilment of the will to belong. Only to whatever fulfils our being can we give ourselves without despair.

The Christian Gospel asserts the reality of such an absolute in the Kingdom of God. We are created to find ourselves in belonging, and we really belong to that which makes us lovers. The only commitment which can sustain an absolute trust is that which accepts what we are in all the conditions of finitude, and yet offers participation in the infinitely creative life which takes our present loves beyond themselves into the service of God. It is the trivial faiths and pseudo-religions which offer satisfaction to the self as it is, or as it ideally projects its wishes. The truth in the Gospel which cuts into all our loves is that every love must be offered up to the creative transformation which God is bringing about in the whole creation.

26. William Ernest Hocking, *Human Nature and its Remaking*, rev. ed. (New Haven: Yale University Press, 1923), chaps. 27, 47.

Henry Nelson Wieman's important distinction between creat*ed* good and creat*ive* good can help us state this crucial point.[27] Every human love is a created good and is directed to some created good, that is, some structure of meaning, person, or value. The *creative* good is the present working of God, bringing new structures into existence. That working is terrible in its power to shatter old structures. It can be threatening and painful in what it demands of the self and its present forms of good. It breaks open every present form for the sake of a new, and more inclusive community of meaning. Now the creative good is itself 'good', but in a peculiar way. It is good not as objective form, but as the source of new structures of value. The love it commands is not directed toward a given object or structure; it is openness to the working of the creative spirit which is the source of all good. The ultimate issue in self-giving is 'given for what?' Men give themselves for all kinds of things, good and bad, creative and destructive, for fame, money, infatuation, homeland, religion, dogmas, prejudices. There is no limit to the kinds of self-giving of which we are capable. But the sacrifice of self in the love which is *agape* challenges every claim but one. It does not displace the human loves, but it transmutes them by giving them a new context. 'He who loves father and mother more than me is not worthy of me.'

Agape thus challenges the claim to absoluteness of every other love since what it offers transcends every private satisfaction, desire, or value. *Agape* offers the reconstituting of life so that every human love participates in a love greater than itself.

We now see human loves in a new light. *Agape* is not another love which is added to the others. Neither is it their contradiction. It is the love which underlies all others, leads them toward the discovery of their limits, and releases a new possibility in the self which is created for communion.

God discloses himself as *agape*. We do not discover his love welling up within us. We discover it at the boundary of our existence, in the experience of crisis, and in the overwhelming goodness for which we give thanks, or at the abyss of despair toward which we plunge. *Agape* is the affirmation of life, the forgiveness of sin, the spirit in which the self can give itself away and yet be fulfilled.

In this way, then, we affirm the radical self-denial in *agape* while preserving the creative significance of human loves. The deepest mystery of love is not simply the power of self-denial but the capacity in every love to learn self-giving and thus within the vital impulses

27. Henry Nelson Wieman, *The Source of Human Good* (Chicago: University of Chicago Press, 1946), chap. 3.

of creaturely existence to prepare for the claim of God upon the spirit. No human love can redirect itself by its own power toward the Kingdom of God; but no human love is without its potential service to the work of the Kingdom when it comes to full self-understanding.

This view may seem perfectionistic and too remote from the realities of passion, the narrowness and perversions of our loves. The reason is that we know human love only in its ambiguity. Every experience of love participates in the goodness of the creation, but also in the distorted life which results from sin. The darkness of evil lurks in all existence. Human loves can be constructive, releasing, and even innocent; but they can also be destructive, idolatrous, twisted with hatred, feeding our blinding and demonic rage. Even 'acts of self-sacrifice' can be nothing but vengeful attacks on others. More commonly we exhibit our 'sacrificial' spirit as a means of coercing or deluding others to do our will. 'After all that I've done for you,' we say in our tyrannous distortion of self-giving. There is no rational explanation for the depth of evil of which we are capable. The cruelties of history are beyond belief.

Our doctrine, then, makes no claim that we are really good and loving beings. But it does throw some light upon the dark side of the human story if we see human cruelties and destructiveness as corruptions of the power to love, and thus as belonging not to the norm of human nature but to its pathology. The need to belong, to be secure in relationship to the other, to find the self fulfilled and loved is so great that when it is blocked the power of love bursts into the demonic passion of fanaticism, self-worship, arrogance and superiority toward those who threaten our little securities. Paul Tillich has defined the demonic as the 'form-destroying eruption of the creative basis of things'.[28] In part, at least, the perversity of man exploits the good in his humanity. The need for the love which he cannot escape when unfilled, becomes his torment, his agony, the source of his self-destruction and his violence.

Where and how, then, does the love of God move in the human loves? The answer is, everywhere, within the mystery of grace. 'The wind bloweth where it listeth', and no form can define the way in which the spirit of *agape* makes its way into our human pilgrimage. It comes when in living, loving and dying we are brought to the boundary of our existence. It may come in the ecstasy of rejoicing in human love, and it may come in the breaking of our self-confidence and our security when we reach our limits. Above all, it may come

28. Paul Tillich, *The Interpretation of History* (New York: Charles Scribner's Son, 1936), p. 85.

when the idolatry and self-centredness in the human loves are exposed and we discover the meaning of God's forgiveness freely given, offering us acceptance and new life. The word of God which became flesh in Jesus Christ moves in human life, often secretly, often unrecognized, yet persistently becoming the luminous word through which we begin to understand what every love really is.

(3)

LOVE AND HOPE

Agape transforms the hope in the self's pilgrimage. We cannot fully know the meaning of love until it has done all its work. Without the eschatological dimension in love we do not see it as it is. It is the mark of love to be willing to await consummation, not to seize it. *Agape* indeed bears an assurance for every future. It overcomes the fear of death and defeat. 'Nothing can separate us from the love of God.' Love never disappears. But what love may do and will do, what creative and redemptive work lies ahead, can only be known partially in the history of love until the 'end'.

Here our theme that love has a history reaches its culmination and its limit. The decisive expression of *agape* has been given in the history of Jesus, and what God has begun in him is not finished (I Corinthians 15). God does not set aside the conditions of human existence. He works in history to reconstitute it, but that is a process, not a complete action.

From this vantage point we get a new perspective on self-sacrifice as the ultimate expression of *agape*. The self is constituted by its entire history. To be a self is to belong in the great society of being, and belonging is not destroyed by death. Hence the self can give itself away knowing that its being is not completed in a moment of time. We recall the temporal dimension of the Gospel paradox concerning self-sacrifice. 'He that saveth his life *will* lose it, and he that loseth his life for my sake and the Gospel *will* save it.' The reference is not primarily to some future event, though it embraces an eschatological hope. The future for the self is the whole of its meaning in the everlasting life.

This is why we cannot define the limits of the work of *agape*. We may never be able to point to an act of self-sacrifice as the decisive moment in which the self is controlled by *agape*. We may experience no such moment in life, and perhaps in most lives there never is such a moment. But there is in faith the beginning of *agape's* formation of the human spirit. There is the hope and prayer that it may be so. Since *agape* always includes forgiveness for what we are, there is a sense in which even to begin to discover its meaning is to be born again. But we are reborn to hope. All acts of 'self-sacrifice' have the poignant element of 'not knowing' the end. Love does not demand to know.

As St. Francis stands with the symbols of death and self-sacrifice in his hands, so stands every life of faith. This is no morbid theme, but the assurance of the Gospel that just as there is the ultimate demand of self-giving, so is there no real life or fulfilment without learning that he who loves can give himself up for God since God has given himself for us.

CHAPTER XI

LOVE AND SEXUALITY

Sexuality prepares the way for human love, but, in order to pass from sexuality to love, an act of inversion, and of dying to the self is necessary (Jean Guitton).

Love and sexuality are linked in human experience, though sex is not love, and love is not always sexual. The loves which are linked with sexuality seem to be the extreme case of the ambiguity in human loves when they are judged in the light of *agape*. Sexual love has the power of ecstatic self-giving. At the same time it seems possessive, self-centred, demanding of immediate gratification, heedless of the self-denial and the dedication which goes with enlistment in the service of the Kingdom of God. The doctrine that *agape* fulfils the human loves has a critical test in interpreting the sexual life, not because of the earthiness of sexual love, but because of its power to drive the spirit in seeming disregard of God or neighbour.

Our purpose in this chapter is twofold; first, to understand why Christianity with its positive view of the goodness of the creation has come to a crisis in its understanding of sexuality; and second, to consider a theological view of sexual existence which sees its place in life which is fulfilled by the love of God.

There is a widespread revolt against traditional Christian standards of morality in sex. This revolt reflects a new consciousness of what sexuality is, and a conviction that the Christian tradition has misunderstood and rejected the creative function of sex. One Christian commentator remarks:

> If sexuality seems to be marking the twentieth century with its stamp, it is certainly not that man has changed but simply that he has a different consciousness of sex, and has given it a place of its own in his scale of values. [1]

Jean Guitton has astutely observed the new situation. In the primitive state sex and love were on the plane of instinct. But when knowledge enters 'consciousness has moved away from instinct'. He continues:

1. Menie Grégoire, 'A Final Word About Love' in *Sexuality and the Modern World*, a Symposium in *Cross Currents*, Vol. XIV, No. 2 Spring, 1964, p. 258. (Further reference to this symposium will be indicated, *Cross Currents Symposium*.)

The intellect comprehends what life enjoys; much more than that, it apprehends the mystery of the mechanism. It is mistress of creation and of love. Formerly, even when the means for the control of life were known, they were screened by ignorance and secrecy. The nineteenth century dared to approach these forbidden shores; it defined the elements of a kind of *positive sexology* capable of totally transforming the economy of love, the status of the family, custom and even morality itself.[2]

(1)

SEX IN THE CHRISTIAN TRADITION

How did Christianity get identified with a repressive, morbid, and banal attitude toward sexuality?

This history is especially puzzling when we recall the spiritual dignity which the Bible gives to man's physical and mental powers. The creation is good. Men and women are made for one another, to be fruitful and replenish the earth, and to have dominion over it. The love, joy, and fidelity of sexual union furnish the most important biblical image for God's faithfulness to his people. Both the Old Testament and the New reject an ascetic attitude toward the sexual life. The *Song of Songs* gives exquisite lyric expression to the beauty and delight of human love. Jesus blesses a wedding feast. Nowhere does he assign merit to sexual abstinence for its own sake. He does indeed teach the rigorous requirement for purity of motive; but there is forgiveness for those who sin in this area as in any other, and his severest judgments are reserved for the proud, the exploiters, and the self-righteous. St. Paul, for all his apparent negativism about sex in the Christian life, gives the fulfilment of married love the highest possible place by making it a parable of the union of Christ and his church. The body is the temple of the living God. For this reason, and for this alone, its members should not be misused, that is, 'joined to a harlot' (I Corinthians 6: 16).

Yet there developed very early in the church a strain of asceticism which treated sexuality as a concession to the weakness of the flesh. Virginity was exalted as the highest way of life, and the conception of 'merit' was connected with sexual abstinence. St. Augustine teaches that the stain of original sin is transmitted through the sexual act. Some of the Greek Fathers, such as Gregory of Nyssa, say that God created Adam and Eve sexless and that the phrase 'male and female

2. Jean Guitton, *Essay on Human Love,* tr. by Melville Chaning-Pearce (New York: Philosophical Library, 1951), p. 5.

created he them' referred to a subsequent act necessitated by Adam's disobedience. Apart from sin, propagation would have been by some harmless mode of vegetation.[3]

Some Christian commentators suggest that the biblical view of sex was corrupted by Greek dualism. Thus Reinhold Niebuhr remarks:

> Perhaps the negative attitude is due to the influence of Platonic dualism, the distinction between man's body and soul. If so, Christian sex ethics defies the truth—ostensibly its dearest truth—about the psychosomatic unity of man. Perhaps the eschatological element in biblical faith determines the negative attitude toward what was clearly a force of nature, but also though not so clearly, a force of the spirit.[4]

Paul Ricoeur takes a similar view. The original Christian cosmovital notion of the sacred was attacked by 'orphic and gnostic dualism' before it could create a culture equal to itself.

> Suddenly man forgets he is 'flesh', indivisibly Word, Desire, and Image; he 'knows' himself as a separate Soul, lost and a prisoner in a body; at the same time he 'knows' his body as Other, an evil Enemy. This 'gnosis' of Soul and Body, and of Duality in general, infiltrates Christianity, sterilizes its sense of creation, perverts its confession of evil, and limits its hope of total reconciliation to the horizon of a narrowed and bloodless spiritualism.[5]

Both statements are relevant, but we should not conclude too soon that it was all a corruption of the biblical outlook. The question still arises, how did gnosticism and dualism infiltrate Christianity so easily if they are essentially alien to it? Ricoeur's picture of man's sudden forgetfulness of the link of body and soul is not too convincing. Would this happen just because a new philosophy was encountered?

Niebuhr and Ricoeur do indicate however where we should look for a source of the tendency in Christian thought about sexuality. The biblical understanding of life never had a chance to shape its own culture and ethic, and thus to create a context for sexuality within a Christian style of life. Ricoeur points out that the Christian view of the unity of body and mind had no opportunity to 'create a culture for itself'. One might object this does not apply to the Hebrew community which had ample time to form its own culture. But the Hebraic ethic applied to one people for whom faith and

3. Cf. Robert Briffault, *The Mothers* (New York: Macmillan, 1927, Vol. III, pp. 372–5; London: Allen & Unwin, 1960).

4. Reinhold Niebuhr, 'Christian Attitudes Toward Sex and Family', *Christianity and Crisis*, April 27, 1964, p. 74.

5. Paul Ricoeur, 'Wonder, Eroticism, and Enigma', in *Sexuality and the Modern World, Cross Currents Symposium*, p. 135.

ethics formed in principle an organic whole. The Christian church had to express its formative power in many cultures as it sought to create a universal community. This is much more complex than the regulation of the life of one people. It may well be that the Jewish community has so far achieved a more balanced and integral view of the sexual life than has Christianity.

The Christian community began as a small group expecting the end of history, and enjoying a certain indifference to the secular orders. It then became the religion of a world empire, having to maintain its integrity in the hellenistic world as it interpreted, borrowed, and adjusted to the values of a cosmopolitan culture. This is why Christianity has yet to develop the real significance of the view of sexuality, family-relationship, and human creativity which the Bible makes possible.

The Protestant Reformation attacked certain elements in the Catholic tradition, its exaltation of celibacy above marriage, its conception of the religious vocation as of greater merit than secular life with family responsibility. In Luther especially, and also, we note, in the early Puritans, we find a positive view of the life of married love as a glorification of God and its joy as a celebration of God's goodness. On this point Roland Mushat Frye's studies are valuable. He says:

> In the course of a wide reading of Puritan and other Protestant writers in the sixteenth and early seventeenth centuries, I have found nothing but opposition to this type of ascetic 'perfection'.[6]

> It should be clear by now that early Puritanism consciously taught the purity, legality, and even obligation of physical love in marriage. 'Whose bed is undefiled and chast pronounc't', as Milton wrote in his great marriage hymn (Paradise Lost, IV, 761) or, as the anonymous *Office of Christian Parents* puts it, two who are made one by marriage 'may joyfully giue due benevolence one to the other; as two musicall instruments rightly fitted, doe make a most pleasant and sweet harmonie in a well tuned consort'.[7]

While this corrects the popular notion of puritanism, we still must ask how the term 'puritan' acquired its repressive connotation. If in Protestantism we find acceptance of sexuality as a creative and pure aspect of human life and as finding its ultimate freedom and honour in married love, where has the tradition failed?

Part of the answer is found precisely in what the Puritans did not

6. Roland Mushat Frye, *The Teachings of Classical Puritanism on Conjugal Love:* Studies in the Renaissance, Vol. II, 9 (1955).

7. Quoted by Frye, *loc. cit.*, pp. 155–6, from *The Office of Christian Parents* (Cambridge, 1616), p. 140.

say. They had a high view of sexual fulfilment within marriage; but said little about sexuality in the whole life of the person. There is very little attention to infancy, adolescence, and preparation for marriage. There is nothing about the situation of those who cannot be married. This is like describing health with no reference to its conditions and development or to disease. There are two important factors which have restricted the development of an adequate view of sex. One implication of this silence and repression was that sexuality has no place or meaning outside of marriage. Everything else is defilement. Second, there was a conspiracy of silence as to how sexuality enters into human growth. One consequence has been the appalling failure of both church and home in sexual education. The unspoken assumption has been that sexuality has all problems solved within the bonds of marriage, and that nothing can or need be understood about it except in the rules for marriage. The consequences of this combination of repression and ignorance are too well known to need recounting here.

Walter Lippmann has suggested that the church was serving itself in providing narrow channels for sexual expression. It dammed up the emotional energies to bring them into the service of the institution.[8] Of course this assumes that the sexual energies can be thus sublimated, but the relation of these energies to human creativity is an enormously complex question upon which we have little dependable light.

We see where a Christian theology of sex needs to begin. The question is the meaning of sexuality in human existence. We need a sexual ethic, but its valid principles can only be derived as we understand what we are dealing with.

The deficiency in Christian teaching in the area of sex is analogous to the theological reaction to the development of scientific knowledge. The Church never opposed science. Its doctrine of creation and faith in the dependability of God contributed to the rise of modern science, as Whitehead has persuasively shown.[9] Yet the scientific method had to make its way against a heavy weight of ecclesiastical opposition. The relation between Christian faith and the scientific way of understanding nature involves many complex and unresolved issues, but the plain fact is that scientific understanding had to grow largely under secular auspices, with too little encouragement and understanding from the religious tradition.

8. Walter Lippmann, *A Preface to Morals* (New York: Macmillan, 1929; London: Allen & Unwin, 1929).
9. A. N. Whitehead, *Science and the Modern World* (Cambridge University Press, 1936); Mentor Books ed. (New York: New American Library, 1948).

Our need for understanding sexuality is in a somewhat similar case. Of course knowledge of sexuality requires more than scientific understanding, though it has its scientific and technological side. The modern exploration of sexuality has required anthropological, biological, psychological and literary investigation. The knowledge explosion and new freedom of communication have had profound effect. The Freudian revolution has altered the form of man's self understanding. The Kinsey studies, for all their narrowing of attention to sex as biological function, have few parallels in man's search for objective knowledge of himself. D. H. Lawrence can stand as the pioneer representative of those who have used the literary art to explore human emotion and to protest and prophesy against the repression and devaluation of the sexual life. Now the world of art, literature, motion pictures, is in a volcano-like eruption of sexual expression, exploitation, adventure, perversion, criticism and reflection.

We need not claim that some great new revelation has come out of all this. It may be so, but that is not the point to be argued here. The critical matter for those who want to take a responsible position is how to participate in this new discussion of sexuality. Is this one realm where God is at work to reveal the meaning of love? Can we understand the spirit and forms of *agape* more deeply through insight into the sexual *eros*? Is there Christian insight into sexuality through a reflection on the work of *agape* in the sexual life with its frustrations, idolatries, and creative powers? These are decisive theological questions.

If Christianity is to show the relevance of its doctrine of love to contemporary man it must make clear that in sex as in science the Christian view of the world is not confined to first century concepts. Christian anthropology can incorporate new experience and new knowledge. I have sometimes thought that if religious and moral teachers would only admit that sex is interesting, that it challenges to new discovery and is replete with unanswered questions, the confession would create a new climate for this critically important discussion. What is required is not fearful retreat into dogmatism, or instant acceptance of every new idea about sexuality; but an informed theological reconsideration of the nature of man, including the function of sexuality. Here I suggest only an outline of where I believe such a theological investigation would lead.

(2)

SEX AND HUMAN EXISTENCE

I offer five assertions about the place of sexuality in human life. These are all, I believe, implicit in the biblical view of man, but they need to be made explicit. It is not enough to treat sex as a mystery, which it is, or as something about which everyone knows, which in a sense it is. We need to achieve a more adequate view of the sexual experience in personal life. We can appeal only to our common understanding and intuitive judgment. This is neither science nor dogma, but a phenomenology of the sexual life. Whatever its validity or limitations, it represents the type of analysis which the theological tradition has for the most part avoided.

First, sexuality enters into the whole of man's life and qualifies all human reactions. The discovery that this is so belongs in its empirically documented form to fairly recent times. In all human growth, in the relation of infants and parents, in the developing life of the child, and the search for identity with its special crisis in adolescence, in maturity and senescence, sexuality is in the core of the personality. Its energies, psychic qualities, disturbances, and affective tone may modify, alter, enrich, or debase everything in experience. This is not a doctrine of pan-sexuality as the secret of all human behaviour. We can recognize the omnipresence of sex without asserting its omnipotence.

This view does not commit us to any one theory of infantile sexuality such as the Freudian. We are a long way from understanding how sex enters into the child's growth, and the significance of human differences. What we do know from clinical experience is that personal interrelationships with their sexual dynamics reflect the whole life history.

One special consequence of sexuality concerns the differences in the experience of men and women. Those differences are enormously complicated by cultural conditioning, and every aspect of the matter is being discussed at the present time. But masculinity and femininity as primordially given, and later conditioned, by cultural, social and economic relationships are fundamental determinants in every life. Theologians should remember that nearly all the theology has been written by men. A woman theologian, Dr. Valerie Goldstein, says this has given a certain caste to all Christian doctrine, particularly the doctrine of sin:

For the temptations of woman *as woman* are not the same as the temptations of man *as man*. . . . [The woman's] temptations have a quality which can never be encompassed by such terms as 'pride' and 'will-to-power'. They are better suggested by such terms as triviality, distractibility, and diffuseness; lack of an organizing centre or focus; dependence on others for one's own self-definition; tolerance at the expense of standards of excellence; inability to respect the boundaries of privacy; sentimentality, gossipy sociability, and mistrust of reason—in short, underdevelopment or negation of the self.[10]

Menie Grégoire says:

Tied to the service of the species, feminine sexuality differs essentially from man's; man is free, instantly released. He belongs to himself, he is absolute act, and the unfailing self-possession of his body is the greatest astonishment for woman. For her, there is never any true self-possession, never a moment which does not belong, if not to eternity, at least to that passage of time which, for agnostics, strongly resembles it. Her body is, by definition, a fetter. It is made to break loose from, to change, to become deformed; it assaults her balance, her life, her strength, and her freedom.[11]

As a male I may remark that I find male self-possession somewhat exaggerated in this statement. But there is no question that the sexual dimension, expressed or repressed, creative or destructive, is a qualifier of all experience. Therefore a sexual ethic which offers only the prohibition of overt sexual behaviour except under certain regulated circumstances is woefully incomplete. The obligations and possibilities of human sexuality are present and have to be handled in the whole of life. Consider, for example, how sex enters into religious feeling, and how the religious community must reckon with the sexual dynamics in pious emotion.

Our second assertion is that sex is one of the important languages of mankind. It is one way the self seeks and communicates with another self.

The will to belong, we have said, is fundamental in human existence. This will finds in sexuality one of its powerful opportunities, challenges, and frustrations. Human belonging does not mean physical possession alone; indeed the language of possession violates the spirit of belonging. The will to belong is the will to communicate, to express oneself and to find a response. Thus the search for belonging becomes in large measure a search for language which will open

10. Valerie Saving Goldstein, 'The Human Situation: A Feminine Viewpoint', in Simon Doniger, ed., *The Nature of Man* (New York: Harper & Brothers, 1962), p. 165.

11. Menie Grégoire in *Cross Currents Symposium*, p. 261.

the way to speaking and hearing. This is why verbal behaviour is so closely linked with the emotional dynamics of the self and especially with sexuality.

Sexual behaviour, response, and creativity can be a means of communication from self to self. This is its first and greatest service to love. Paul Ricoeur, in the perceptive essay we have already quoted, seems to be denying what we are saying here, or at least giving it a role of little importance when he says:

> The enigma of sexuality is that it remains irreducible to the trilogy which composes man: language, tool, institution. On the one hand, indeed, it belongs to a prelinguistic existence of man. Even when it makes itself expressive, it is an infra-, para-, super-linguistic expression. It mobilizes language, true, but it crosses it, jostles it, sublimates it, stupefies it, pulverizes it into a murmur, an invocation. Sexuality de-mediatizes language, it is Eros and not Logos.[12]

We can recognize what Ricoeur is saying, but put it in a different context. Ricoeur is thinking of language in 'verbal' terms. Non-verbal communication uses all sorts of language; gestures, symbols, overt acts, silences and attitudes. One may not want to ascribe the term 'language' to all of this, but it certainly has a *Logos*, that is, an intelligible order. It is the Logos of immediate personal communication. Rather than say sex 'demediatizes' language, we come closer if we say that it may be the most immediate of all languages. We say 'may be' for *what is communicated through sexual behaviour is never fully determined by sexuality or the sexual act in itself.* Every personalistic doctrine must stress this. Man is the peculiar creature who lives both a biological and psychic existence. He shares sex with the animals, but for man the organic urges and acts are never detached from the search for meaning. That search may be successful or destructive, wholesome or corrupted. It is always the self's search for belonging through communication with another. This is why sexual attraction by itself is such a fleeting, superficial, and un-dependable indicator of what sexuality really is. There is an implicit question in all human sexual attraction: 'What use will you make of me?' 'What do you want and expect of me, and are you exploiting me or loving me?'

This understanding of the search for communication requires analysis of the general function of symbolization. Language is a special case of symbolic expression, and the dynamics of symbol formation in the life of the self are of especial importance in the sexual life.

12. Paul Ricoeur, *loc. cit.*, p. 141.

In our attempt to speak and to hear, to express our feeling and find communicative response in another, anything in existence or imagination can become a significant symbol. Depth psychology has shown that every act has to be understood through its internal linkage with other acts and experiences. This present rage has some relation to experience with that parent or brother or other person. This release from fear and discovery of courage has its dynamic connection with past moments of doubt, distrust, and anxiety. The objective symbols of human culture are the spirit's means of identifying its feelings and expressing their linkage with the self's ultimate cravings.[13] Hence the human body with its gestures and expression, its beauty or ugliness, its reflection of spirit in the human face, its postures of tenderness or hostility, its acts of intimacy and separation, articulates the language of the self. Alfred North Whitehead brilliantly defines the human body as the primary field of human expression.[14] So every bodily action becomes symbolically the incarnation of a human attitude in the whole gamut from ecstatic fulfilment to boredom and despair.

One implication for a sexual ethic we see at once. It is always false to judge a sexual act as something completed in itself. Its meaning is what it expresses. What kind of personal communication does it serve? Is it merely the using of one person by another? The injunction to 'watch your language' might be one way in which moral cautions about sexuality could be given. Sexual play without the deepening of personal understanding is a violation of the search for reality. It becomes the language of brutality or exploitation. It is often said that women know this communicative dimension in sex more intuitively and deeply than men, and this is one reason for the male's relative freedom from psychic scars in casual sexual experience. But when we consider sex as language it appears that men cannot employ the language of sex without consequences any more than women can. An exploitive sexual relationship stupefies the spirit. Its result is insensitivity to the depth and glory of personal communication.

The doctrine that sexuality is a primary means of communication bears upon our appraisal of the new freedom of sexual language and imagery in the literature and art of our century. This freedom is often pointed to as a sign of disease and moral decay. Certainly it has its pathological aspects. Anything which evokes a sexual response

13. I have developed this doctrine of 'linkage' briefly in *The Minister and the Care of Souls* (New York: Harper & Row, 1961).
14. A. N. Whitehead, *Modes of Thought* (New York: Macmillan, 1938, p. 30; Cambridge University Press, 1938).

can be exploited for profit and the commercial exploitation of sexual curiosity is a demonic feature of our culture.

We should however be clear about where the evil is. It is not in the overt expression of sexual ideas, language and imagery. We can judge freedom of expression only in the light of what is being expressed. What is happening is that deeper levels of human experience and new styles of personal life are given public expression. Any society must ask what the legitimate limits of such communication are, and how to protect immature life from too early exposure to some experiences. But we should hear what honest and sensitive searchers are saying, even if we reject the ways of life they may defend. Merely to censor or turn away is to refuse what may be a cry for help, or a creative new truth, or the furnishing of a new symbol in the search for authentic love.

The incarnation of the Word of God means God's self-communication in Jesus Christ. There is a reflection of the incarnation of the 'Word' in all human living. Every act and gesture is a word spoken. We are not platonizing or over-spiritualizing our view of sex when we say that every sexual act, feeling, or emotion has the power to become a disclosure of spirit to spirit. Sexuality is never something 'by itself'. It is always a meaning incarnate.

The third aspect of sex is its relation to the creative self-expression of play. By 'play' I do not mean just idle enjoyment, and certainly do not mean the cynical exploitation of sex which constitutes much of what passes for humour about it. The real significance of play has never been adequately assessed. Life is far too serious to be bearable without the delight of play, laughter, and celebration for sheer joy. Sex has an energy and quality of play.[15]

The practice of religion has usually shown an element of free creativity which is akin to play. Music, poetry, ritual celebration, the festival, and aesthetic creativity have all been woven into the texture of religion. In this the sexual emotions certainly have had a part. The language of the mystics is filled with sexual imagery. The experience of God is more than the sublimation of sexuality, but the power and tonality of sexual emotion certainly enters into the celebration of life and the enjoyment of God.

If the chief end of man is to glorify God and enjoy him forever, this includes the sexual life. One of the symptoms of sickness in the treatment of sexuality in much modern literature is that there is so little gratitude for it. Sex is treated as torment, or possession, or weapon against the world; but the note of gratitude for sexuality as enrichment of life, for ecstatic joy and the serenity of faithful

15. Johann Huizinga, *Homo Ludens* (Boston: Beacon Press, 1950).

companionship, all this gets left out of the meaning of sex. Albert Camus points out that the orgy is drearily ascetic and monotonously cheerless.[16] This throws considerable light not only upon the meaning of sexuality, but also upon what our culture has done to it.

The traditional Roman Catholic doctrine that the only legitimate function of sex is procreation has contributed to this repressive attitude. The enrichment and joy of human relationships in sex has been denied its importance. It is noteworthy that more recent Roman Catholic discussion has sharply criticized the tradition on this point.[17]

One aspect of biblical faith helps to explain why the tradition has been wary of giving sexuality an important place in religious life. The old Testament affirms the goodness of life and sexuality, and sexual language is freely used to describe the relationship between God and his people, but the prophetic tradition is consistently and radically opposed to the kind of sexual worship found in Baalism. We need not assume that even the greatest prophets were infallible in their judgments about other religions, but here obviously they saw an issue.

Two elements in the sexual practices of Baal worship drew the prophetic criticism: idolatry and prostitution. Both violated the covenant relationship between God and Israel. Martin Buber states the decisive point in the Hebraic view of sex:

> Sex is hallowed by the sacrament of the circumcision covenant which survives in its original purity and not only confirms the act of begetting but converts it into a holy vocation. . . . Hallowing transforms the urges by confronting them with holiness, and making them *responsible* toward what is holy.[18]

The religious sensibility we have inherited respects this hallowing of human emotion, but has lost the delight in its expression. Sex can temper solemnity with laughter and refreshment. Anxieties about sex rob us of one dimension of the celebration of life and of gratitude to God. God, not Satan, created sex.

The fourth aspect of sex arises from the self's freedom. Every human expression implies a decision about how we accept, interpret and fulfil it. The meaning of an impulse is never given in the impulse itself. It involves the person. We have no choice about being sexual, but we have a margin of freedom about how we live sexually. One

16. Albert Camus, *The Rebel*, pp. 42–4.
17. Cf. Vatican II, *Constitution on the Church and the Modern World*, Pt. II, Chap. 1, on marriage and family.
18. Martin Buber, *Israel and the World* (New York: Schocken Books, 1948), p. 181.

of the extraordinary things about human sexuality is the variety of disciplines, restrictions, commitments, and styles of life which it achieves.

The context of decisions about sexual activity is the web of relationships in which we live. Sexual intercourse is the way of procreation, and even where for reasons of natural circumstances or human intervention new life is not begotten, the act is never wholly separated from this meaning. The responsibilities of parenthood are implied in most sexual expression either indirectly or directly. But this interconnectedness of sex and new life involves more than procreation. Every sexual feeling and expression is an event in the self's becoming, its commitments, its pilgrimage. As Whitehead says, 'the greater part of morality hinges on the determination of relevance in the future'.[19] The total life pattern is present in the most transitory and intimate of human experiences. Here the theme of sex as play receives its counterweight in the theme of sex as responsibility for oneself, for other selves, and for the full consequences of every act.

Christianity has always asserted a spiritual basis for the renunciation in a celibate way of life. The rationale of celibacy in the Christian faith is never renunciation for its own sake, but always that love for God and the neighbour may be fulfilled this way. A Protestant theologian, Max Thurian, speaks of the Christian's voluntary celibacy as 'a parable for a world without God . . . the Christian can renounce everything for the sake of Christ and the Gospel'. Jesus commends those who have made themselves eunuchs for the sake of the Kingdom of heaven (Matthew 19: 12).[20] Christian celibacy is dedication to a pattern of life in which one fruitful and natural kind of experience is renounced for the sake of service to God and neighbour. It should be noticed, and we are clearer about this in the light of modern psychology, that it is not sexual feeling or emotion which are renounced, but the fulfilment of the sexual relationship. No one can discard his sexuality, but it can be sublimated, and its involvements renounced for the sake of one's vocation.

Every pattern of sexual life involves vocational decision in the Christian view. It is not a question of one way being higher than another. Luther and Calvin made this clear in their doctrine of vocation. The way of love can be lived in this world in all its forms and orders. But there is in every vocation a place for the freedom of the spirit and responsible decision in the light of the possibilities, demands, and personal commitments required for the service of God.

19. A. N. Whitehead, *Process and Reality*, p. 41.
20. Max Thurian, *Marriage and Celibacy* (London: S.C.M. Press, 1959), p. 16.

So also the Christian faith should lead to understanding for those to whom life brings unwanted and difficult circumstances, such as those who want the companionship of marriage and are denied it, those for whom physical or psychological illness makes sexual experience impossible, those who have had tragic and wounding experiences and must find their way through them. These problems cannot be solved by rule alone. They call for decisions taken in courage and judged with compassion.

There is a large element of fate and accidental circumstance in the realm of sex. The importance of physical attractiveness, the fatefulness of sexuality—being a man or a woman, the accidents of childhood experience, the uniqueness of each personal relationship. Yet fatalism should be rejected here as it is elsewhere in the Christian faith. Fate becomes destiny when we freely take the measure of circumstances and make a personal response to them. Just here, the Christian doctrine that love is mercy is often forgotten at a point where it is sorely needed. The sexual life participates in the realm of freedom, in both sin and grace. The *agape* which redeems and reconciles does one of its greatest works in the infusing of the sexual life with the spirit of humility and charity.

There is an enormous amount of silent suffering which people bear in relation to sex. I write here out of experience as pastor and counsellor, the burden of guilt, the mismanaged lives, the hurts given and received, the tragedies of broken families, the search for integrity in the midst of violent passion. All this bears the added burden of the consistent distortion and exploitation of sexuality in our culture. Between sentimental kinds of romanticism at one pole, and the cynical despair of much literature and art at the other, sexuality is seen only in a half-light of distortion, violence, prettiness and ugliness. It is not easy to grasp its potential for wholeness and creativity amid this distortion, but we must try.

(3)

Sex, Love and Faithfulness

These first four aspects of sex—its pervasiveness, its power of communication, its relation to play and creativity, and to human decision—can be discussed at least in a preliminary way without specific reference to love. Sexuality is not love, and much sexual experience may be independent of that mutual affection, commitment, and union of two personal histories which we call human love.

Jean-Paul Sartre says that desire for being is more fundamental than sexuality in the relationships of men and women.[21]

Sex must transcend itself to become love. The physical and emotional attraction of another person laden with the possibilities of sexual fulfilment may lead to the will to unite one life with another, and to an acceptance of the needs of the other as redirecting the course of life. Then it has become love.[22] This is not to say that love in itself requires even implicitly a total commitment for life. People fall in and out of love in many circumstances and at many levels of personal commitment. Sexual attraction can be incorporated into the love relationship, and normally in the love of men and women it is, but it never by itself determines the presence or fulfilment of love.

Love, we have said, has a history, and it has a history in each individual love. The beginning is only the invitation to a shared life. Hence in its initiation the experience of sexual love becomes one illustration of the truth that all human loves mean a call to acceptance of another, and the willingness to be transformed for the sake of the other. It is precisely this will which marks the difference between loving affection and sexual exploitation. Sexual relationship without love, therefore, tempts the self to violate its essence. Certainly the elements of play, self-expression and self-discovery, the wary search for the other person which accompany sexuality in every culture, are the foreplay of love. Art, literature, music, the dance, social recreation are filled with parables and evocations of sexual feeling. But the inner destiny of the sexual experience is toward the intimate and transforming discovery of love. This is why the sexual life becomes burdened with the issue of personal commitment in the midst of the colourful panorama of sexual symbols and play. The point is that the moral issue in sexual life is not the consequence of an externally imposed law, but the nature of personal existence. What sexual behaviour will serve rather than destroy the growth of authentic love? It is a reflection of cultural superficiality that in the present discussion about sexual freedom on college campuses, there is so much attention to sexual intercourse and so little to the question of what love for another person means.

The love of men and women takes innumerable forms, and

21. Jean-Paul Sartre, *Being and Nothingness* (London: Methuen & Co., 1957; New York: Washington Square Press, 1966), Pt. IV, chap. 2.

22. In the discussion which follows I am dealing primarily with the love which leads to the union of man and woman. Of course there are innumerable inter-personal relationships. In every case, however, love means more than sexual attraction and satisfaction. An infant's love of the mother is the beginning of the recognition of the mother as person.

involves the uniqueness of each person. Human culture is filled with stories of loves, of gods and goddesses, of strong and weak persons, of love which breaks the lines of caste and convention, of what Lesley Branch has called the 'Wilder Shores of Love' in her account of some remarkable women.[23] We can discount the significance of the so-called 'great lovers', the Don Juans—a rather sorry lot—who are for the most part incapable of real love, and have little to tell us about it. But the rise and disappearance of the romantic tradition of love seems a critical aspect of our history and we must give some attention to it.

There has undoubtedly been a break in the twentieth century with the tradition of romantic love which arose in the later phase of medieval culture, flourished in the 'courts of love' in the fifteenth century, gave birth to the literature of the romantic movement, reached conventional respectability and domestication in the nineteenth century, and now seems out of date. Tibor Koeves has written that 'romantic love was born in the fifteenth century and died in the twentieth'.[24]

One of the most important studies is Denis de Rougemont's *Love in the Western World*, which makes a brilliant attempt to prove that romantic love was born of a Christian heresy, the *catharism* of the Middle Ages.[25] This quasi-secret religion used conventional religious language to mask its own inner intent which was the celebration and mystical idolatry of sexual union. De Rougemont argues that the real spirit of this romanticism was the longing of the lovers for union in death. The legend of Tristan and Isolde furnishes the classical pattern for this thesis. The lovers are absorbed in a passion which can only lead to their destruction, but this is what they secretly want. The ecstasy of love is the leap into eternity through death.

De Rougemont has detected and described one strand in the development of romantic love. If one wishes to define romantic love as synonymous with this historical form, then he is free to do so. But De Rougemont's determination to identify romantic love as heretical religion has, I think, obscured from him some considerations which are no less theological and ethical, but are of first importance.

23. Lesley Branch, *The Wilder Shores of Love* (New York: The Viking Press, 1954).

24. Tibor Koeves, 'The Death of Romantic Love', *The United Nations World*, Vol. IV, July 7, 1950.

25. Denis de Rougemont, *Love in the Western World*, rev. ed. (New York: Pantheon, 1956).

De Rougemont pays little attention to the social arrangements in feudal society which brutalized human marriage by founding it on political and economic convenience. In royal families five-year-old girls were betrothed to six-year-old boys as a matter of political expediency.[26] Wives were property first and only secondarily persons with freedom to love. A culture grown sick with its own rigidities is bound to produce a rebellion, and romantic love was that rebellion. It is a stage in the history of the search of men and women for freedom of the spirit in love and marriage.

It must be further pointed out that De Rougemont takes the most elaborately dramatized and perverse examples of romanticism such as the Tristan legend with its turgid morbidities, its pathos, and its obsession with adultery, and treats this as the essence of romantic love. Interestingly he has nothing to say about the Shakespeare of the Sonnets, or even of Romeo and Juliet. Why should the tradition of romanticism not be judged also as in the sonnets of Elizabeth Barrett Browning:

> The face of all the world is changed, I think
> Since first I heard the footsteps of thy soul.

I deliberately choose this Victorian example, not to argue that what may seem quaint in the twentieth century can be reinstated, but to point to the modern search for a sexual love which expresses the uniqueness and freedom of two human beings who find one another and commit their lives to one another.[27]

When De Rougemont suggests his theological alternative to romanticism he has nothing to put in the place of human love but the carnal *eros* conjoined with the absolute love which is the *agape* of the Gospel. He finds little worthy even of comment in the many-sided life of the self, its freedom, its rationality, its creativity. Father D'Arcy has detected this 'reductionism' in De Rougemont's view of man.[28]

If there be a 'romantic passion' which is creative in the sexual life, how and where does it become a genuine personal love? The answer to this question leads to the meaning of faithfulness in human love. The real test of love as seen in the deeper moral traditions of man-

26. Amy Kelly, *Eleanor of Aquitaine and the Four Kings* (Harvard University Press, 1950; London: Cassell & Son, 1952).

27. As Charles Williams profoundly understood. *The Figure of Beatrice: A Study in Dante* (London: Faber & Faber Ltd., 1943) and the admirable book on Williams by Mary McDermott Shideler, *The Theology of Romantic Love* (New York: Harper & Row, 1962).

28. M. C. D'Arcy, *The Mind and Heart of Love*, pp. 40-1 (London: Collins Fontana, 1963).

kind, and in the Christian faith, is the willingness of persons to commit their lives and sexual being faithfully to one another 'till death do us part'.[29]

Such commitment is never fulfilled in sexual relationship alone. The family enlists all the powers of human understanding, identification, and suffering with the other, and the learning of mercy and forgiveness. Thus the need for *agape* appears in the very inception of sexual love. *Agape* does not come to human love merely as a rescue operation when fidelity fails and reconciliation is needed. The need for the love which gives faithfulness to the other, suffers with and for the other, and accepts the other, pervades the whole sexual experience. We say the need for *agape* because we are often far from realizing or accepting its presence. It can make itself known as need long before we know its creative and healing power. The Christian affirmation that the love of God and neighbour is the foundation of life can be discerned in the mystery of sexual love when it leads persons out of themselves into a new dimension of love.

The mystery of love in God's creation is nowhere more powerfully revealed than in this: the sexual attraction which man shares with the animals is immediate, self-centred, and gratifying, yet it leads to the possibility of a love which requires commitment and loyalty and in which physical and emotional gratification become sacraments of the spirit. What faithfulness means is in essence clear enough. It means that each can count upon the other in devotion and support whatever happens. Faithfulness and integrity are partners, for to be faithful means to give the whole of one's loyalty without reservation to the one who counts upon us and upon whom we count.

Monogamous marriage is a form of cultural institution for the ordering and guidance of the sexual life. Its justification from the point of view of the human spirit includes but transcends pragmatic social values. Its basis is the need of the human spirit for the fulfilment of loyalty in the one intimate, lifelong, mutually supporting community we can know. There are of course alternative ways of ordering family life. There is however a remarkable persistence of the ideal of restriction of sexual intercourse within the commitment of husband and wife. Every society has some restrictions. In the polygamous family there are restrictions and obligations for its protection. The Koran forbids more than four wives.

Provision for a stable family structure usually has in view the protection of children. Here again one obvious justification of the

29. The Form of the Solemnization of Matrimony in *The Book of Common Prayer*.

monogamous family is that it offers the healthiest community for the growth of children.

Christianity can appeal to such arguments for the monogamous family, but the Christian faith sees an even more fundamental reason. It is the protection, guidance, and release of the power to love in all the human ways, and the power to give love to God and the neighbour, which justifies the restraints, disciplines and prohibitions in the Christian ideal of the union of man and woman. This is the teaching of the Scripture and the implication of the doctrine of the good creation. Man bears the image of God as his power to enter an enduring, mutually supportive community which incorporates suffering constructively since self-giving always involves suffering. Love disciplines itself for love's sake.

Certainly faithfulness means spiritual loyalty, not simply objective obedience to a law, and there are issues concerning the ideal of faithfulness amidst all the disorder and exigencies of actual life. But the Christian conception of the life commitment of one person to another in a sexual union is justified fundamentally as a recognition of the highest possibilities of human love, not as a concession to human weakness or a search for a convenient way to preserve social order.

Where the church has failed is not in its high standard of fidelity, but in its tendency to treat sex as incidental to the fulfilment of marriage, or as at best a minor element in fulfilment. Hence it has failed to provide a climate and an ethic which releases the full power of sexual love to serve human life. And it has left the whole area of man's growth in sexuality, 'pre-marital experience', the meaning of sexual self-discovery, in a limbo of silence or prohibition, as if nothing needed to be done except to wait until marriage, sex will be domesticated, and all problems will be solved.

Here is the serious point, I believe, of the present revolt against Christian standards. It is not always an irresponsbile rejection of the faithfulness of monogamy, but an assertion of the positive power of sexuality to express, communicate, and release the self. This revolt has spawned a popular modern heresy, but a heresy, from which the church may learn. The heresy in its crudest form is that sexual satisfaction constitutes the good life. One can find innumerable variants in popular literature. In Louis Malle's motion picture, *The Lovers*, the message is, as a discerning critic has commented, that 'sex in its most instinctive form, most carefully freed of any spiritual contact, has become the way of salvation'.[30]

D. H. Lawrence was the great modern prophet of the faith that

30. Menie Grégoire, *Cross Currents Symposium*, p. 259.

sexuality is the key to existence. His view has been examined in an able book by Dorothea Krook, *Three Traditions of Moral Thought*. She discusses Lawrence's belief that there is the intrinsically redemptive power of sexual love when it springs from tenderness, and is sustained by the true union of hearts and minds.[31] Miss Krook says the church denies what Lawrence is contending for. It grants redemptive power to sexual love only under certain conditions. It is the means of procreation, a remedy against concupiscence, and a source of mutual help and comfort. In short Christianity concedes certain uses of sex but accords it no special dignity in the life of the spirit. Krook believes with Lawrence that only a new Humanism can give to man's sexual life the meaning which rightfully belongs to it. She disagrees with Lawrence's view that Jesus suffered from the error of finding in love only that which gives and never receives. She says Lawrence was wrong about this. Jesus was vitally aware of the nature of the human loves. But with Lawrence she pleads for a new Humanism which will supersede Christianity, not by annihilating it, but by incorporating and transforming it; a messianic Humanism.[32]

This messianic element, it turns out, can be expressed in Christian terms. Miss Krook's view of the significance of sexuality for love supplies the element we have found missing in the Christian tradition. She criticizes the Anglican Lambeth conference statement for its 'vestigial Augustinianism' in the exaltation of sexual abstinence, and suggests that the bishops regard abstinence as an offering pleasing to God because it sacrifices a human pleasure. Against this she says:

Is not the mystery of the Incarnation that most fully and most powerfully illuminates, expresses, indeed *defines*, the mysterious and wonderful communion of spirit achieved by a husband and wife in the bodily consummation of their love; and is not therefore the act of sexual union in the profoundest sense a 'figure' of the incarnation—the Word, which is love, made flesh?

The development of this view is of such importance that I must give it at length:

The Incarnation (Christians sometimes seem to forget) is a very carnal affair. If therefore the analogy proposed is true to Christian experience, we may glance again for the last time at the beauty and strength of abstinence to ask, Would not, or ought not, the Christian to find it as unthinkable to abstain as a particular and special offering to God from

31. Dorothea Krook, *Three Traditions of Moral Thought* (Cambridge University Press, 1959), p. 277.
32. *Ibid.*, pp. 288–9.

worshipping *with his body*, expressing his passionate love of and joy in the woman with whom he is *one flesh*, as in the same circumstances to abstain from expressing his passionate love of and joy in Christ by the mystical eating of his Flesh and drinking of his Blood in the sacrament of the Eucharist? Indeed, with the Incarnation, the Crucifixion, and the Resurrection more intensely and vividly present to him, one imagines at these times than at others, it is not abstinence from sexual communion, but rather (one would suggest) the fullest, most joyful, most *grateful* expression of it that becomes at such times his just response to the costly redeeming love of God. The true virginity is not (as the Church has for so long held) the power to renounce bodily love. It is rather the power to rediscover and live, each time afresh, the peace, power, and joy of this most intimate of unions, to experience each time afresh, its inexhaustible wonder and mystery.

It is the man and the woman to whom the act remains, each time, as fresh and beautiful, as it was the first time, who are able to sustain and perpetuate their first sense of its glory in the midst of the sober or bleak or sordid realities of day to day life, and who can feel, afresh each time, a boundless gratitude for each other and for this blessed source of sweetness and strength—it is they who are the truly 'virgin', the truly pure and chaste; and (on the Humanist hypothesis) it is they who are the remnant selected by grace to be the true and spiritual seed of the risen Christ.[33]

Such a view of sexuality accords fully with the doctrine that the love of God incorporates and does not destroy the human loves. It is a New Testament theme which Miss Krook here rightly articulates, the love of man and woman is an image of the love of God. Thanksgiving for the holiness of life ought to arise in this love as in other natural loves. It is noteworthy that sexuality is rarely mentioned specifically in the public prayers of the church, though at least one of the Puritan fathers explicitly enjoined Christians to give thanks for sexual love.

With full appreciation for Miss Krook's exaltation of the meaning of sexual love her argument is incomplete. She neglects an important truth about love, that it must discover its own limitations, and undergo a transmutation for the sake of the creative purpose of God and his Kingdom. The discovery of self-giving can come in the sexual life as elsewhere. What both Krook and Lawrence forget is that the discovery of the meaning of love does not depend upon one kind of fulfilling experience, not even the sexual experience she so beautifully interprets. We must allow for human limitations and frustrations in the commitment 'in sickness and in health'. Like most

33. *Ibid.*, pp. 346–7.

humanists, Miss Krook exalts the perfection of man but forgets his dependence. The full understanding of sexuality includes both its contribution to the life of love, and the discovery that even the love of men and women does not require sexual fulfilment.

One mark of imbalance in the present discussion of sex is this 'all importance' which is assigned to sexual fulfilment. From a Christian point of view this is idolatry, just as the absolutizing of prestige, or status, or any other value is idolatry. The paradox here is that the most satisfying experience of sexuality comes when it is not made the centre of existence, but has its place as one dimension of personal being. The spirit learns a certain detachment while it gives thanks for all the blessings of this life.

(4)

Toward a Christian Sexual Ethic

The first principle of a Christian sexual ethic is that this side of life should be so ordered, disciplined, and released that sexual love becomes a creative aspect of the life of *agape*, the giving of each person in service to God and his neighbour. This principle holds whether the sexual life is fulfilled in overt expression, or within a vocation of celibacy and renunciation.

If God intends to create a community of persons who know the meaning of love, then sexuality belongs to the goodness of creation. It is a human analogue of the creativity of God, and a primary source of human creativity. This means sexual delight and joy, but at the same time nothing in human creativity is without pain, discipline, frustrations, and ambiguities. The sexual life exhibits these just as do other aspects of creativity. We are somewhat led astray by the tendency, even in the biblical tradition, to conceive the creation before sin as idyllic bliss. All human experience shows this is an over-simplification. Creative growth has aspects of suffering, of patient waiting, and the chaotic flow of energy. Certainly sin adds to the suffering and disorder; but there is something untameable about the creative urges of life. They exhibit the explosive power of God's creative life. Nature holds vast energies which man continually discovers in the world or in himself.

With all due reservations, we can (with Karl Barth) be glad that the *Song of Songs* is in the Scripture not as a cryptogram of theological meaning, but as the love song of man and woman. Human love can be transformed into the celebration of the ultimate love which embraces all things. It is not the case of the human sexual *eros* turning into *agape*. Nothing 'turns into' *agape*, but love experienced in depth within the context of faith in God's *agape* becomes an occasion for gratitude, humility and the celebration which expresses the life of God's people in his world.

The second principle for a sexual ethic is that we have to speak of sex, as of every aspect of human life, in a double way, from the standpoint of essential created goodness, and the distortion produced by sin. In all life and love we find both aspects. Rarely can we say that *this* act is essentially good and *that* act is the manifestation of sin; though we can see objectively the self-destruction resulting from sin and we can experience in part the fulfilment of created goodness. We must include in the ethical test of any action its consequences not only for one individual, but for the whole community. Sexuality turned into cruelty, cynical exploitation, and destruction of others is certainly evil, and sexual behaviour which leads to mutual regard and loving growth can so far be called good. But we know ourselves as mixtures of faith and fear, of capacity for love and the refusal of it, and in this uncertain light we have to move.

The basis, then, for Christian judgment about sexual practice in the network of questions concerning sexual adventure before marriage, pre-marital sexual intercourse, the obligations within the family, and the ethical issues involved in divorce is: what does the practice in question do to the creation of loving mutually supporting persons who can grow in love to God and the neighbour, who also have tendencies to exploit one another, and who must find disciplines of self-protection and self restraint for the sake of love?

What the sexual freedom now practised by many will contribute in answer to this question remains to be seen. Legalistic pronouncements are not going to alter sexual practice very much, even though there is danger in neglecting the wisdom of the centuries concerning sexual restraints for the sake of the full expression of love. What needs to be asked is how men and women can live in this culture filled with sexual symbols, sharing in the new freedom, and discover the creativity and satisfaction of authentic human love. Concentrated attention to that question will give a sounder basis for a sexual morality than the uncritical repetition of the formulas of the past. What in the past was enforced by society and the churches largely as social pressure, will increasingly have to depend upon the integrity of informed personal decision and responsibility. What is disheartening about much of the present sexual practice is not the freedom itself so much as the fact that no one seems clear as to what he is doing or why. Sexual obsession seems joined with a loss of true self-possession. The rules of monogamy, the proscription of sexual intercourse outside marriage, the traditional rules of sexual restraint, are important for the Christian style of life. They are the guide lines which have protected precious human relationships against wilful corruption. But the Church and the Christian conscience cannot rely upon law alone. It is the personal intent in the expression and discipline of sex which counts for the life of love. Instead of simply stating the law and reacting in panic when it is widely broken, those concerned for traditional moral wisdom would do much better to affirm the high possibility of the life of faithful love, and to understand with love what is happening to people in ghettoes, in college campuses, in the life of the family today. And we should remember that the Gospel of reconciliation bears also upon the life of sex. No one is without sinful self-centredness in thought and in act. All have to learn the meaning of faithfulness through the maturation and discipline of living within a commitment. Jesus' condemnation of self-righteousness, of thanking God that we are not as other men, brings judgment as surely in this area as in any other.

President Millicent Macintosh, in an address at Barnard College dealing with pre-marital sexual relationships, gives as the primary argument against it that the woman is likely to suffer permanent emotional damage. The act has a more lasting result in the woman's life than in the man's.[34] This may be so, but to put the case for sexual restraint primarily on this basis seems to me to let both men and women off too easily. Male callousness is as much a scar on the spirit as the damage to the sensitivities of women. What is happening to the possibility of growth in full and loving selfhood? That question is being answered in many different ways in this generation, but the final judgment on sexual action is what it means for the fulfilment of persons now and throughout life. This is a higher and more rigorous standard for self-discipline than any law of prohibition or permission.

The same rule applies to the obligations of marriage and the problems about divorce. The intent of Christian marriage is commitment of life between a man and woman until death. In the Christian view this is the way to the fulfilment of all the persons involved, husband, wife and children. In one sense, then, divorce or separation represents a failure of love. But when we bring the principle of growth of persons in loving relationship to the judgment of marriages where the partners discover that they have made a mistake and that two people are destroying the possibility of growth in freedom and love,

34. Millicent Macintosh, 'Out of Morals Revolution—a Moral Revolution', *Glamour*, January, 1963.

it is no violation of integrity to end the marriage so that each may seek a new life which is more responsible and genuinely productive. Love may require that this be done. Such decisions may be extremely difficult. Sinful self-interest can enter into them as well as into any other; but to fail to ask what this marriage is leading to, and whether it is destroying the possibility of loving relationship is also a failure of responsibility.

Those who prize the freedom of the spirit must also question the control of the marriage covenant by ecclesiastical authority, as in Israel today, and as in traditional Roman Catholic practice. Whenever the ecclesiastical establishment is given control of the possibility of legal marriage, the freedom of persons is violated. A religious profession or action is being required which persons may not be prepared to make. No society has a right to require a religious profession as the condition of establishing a family. A church or other religious body which cares about human love will offer its service, its wisdom, and its ritual to those who wish to have them; but it will not control the legal foundations of marriage according to its own prescriptions. The forms of legal coercion such as laws against bigamy, age limits for consent to marriage, the husband's moral economic obligations to support the wife, and so on are the province of the community as a whole. The religious bodies may have wisdom in those matters, but they should not control them. The present tangle of American divorce laws has resulted in part from the refusal of some religious groups to allow the general consensus of the community to be expressed.

The social ethical principles here arise out of love itself; which means the responsible relationship of people who commit their lives to one another. There are rules and principles which society must lay down. Many of the laws which surround marriage offer needed protection of some persons against others. The community cannot regulate love; but it can regulate aspects of human behaviour in which we can never depend solely on the wisdom of love, or what is thought to be love. But such rules are for protection at the boundaries of human love, where people hurt and exploit one another. They cannot enforce love, and they ought not to violate the freedom of those who are mature enough to take the consequences of their own acts.

Sexuality is a dimension of personal existence in which the meaning of love is to be learned and in which love between persons reaches a depth, intimacy and creativity of expression which is incomparable with most other loves. Love at its depth means the giving of faithful devotion to another person on terms which do not threaten or corrupt that devotion. Christianity in its essence does not look upon sex as something which belongs to the lowest part of human nature, but as a power which leads to one of the highest forms of communion.

(5)

EROS AND PHILIA: THE QUESTION OF JUSTICE

Discussion of sexual ethics usually centres on the sexual act, but we should not neglect the problems of justice which are just as difficult and important. Any love can become idolatrous. One ethical test is whether the obligations of justice are being honoured. We give much attention to the commandment against adultery, but it is no more vital to love than the injunction to seek justice. Family love easily becomes self-protective amidst the larger claims of justice. Difficult moral choices lie all about us. Consider the family which must decide about the placing of children in a State school. What constitutes legitimate protection of a child and what are the obligations of a family to protest against an injustice in school segregation, for example, and to open the way for better public education?

Generous and self-sacrificing impulses are exploited in the economic scramble. Many defend their economic privileges on the ground that they are providing for families. The ethical question is how far the self-protection of each family is justified against the claims of all families. In the world today, with its mass hunger, the question of how much of the world's goods, food, and land should belong to any family, becomes very acute. Space has become a spiritual and moral issue. The ethical obligation to limit the size of families arises from desperate human necessity. It is another case of seeing the human *eros* in its communal context and seeking to order life so that a humane and tolerable existence becomes possible for all.

The love which learns to protect its own, which is realized in the intimate communion of the family, should be the first school of the ethical obligation of love and the requirements of self-giving. Every marriage is a balance of power which needs a dynamic justice in its moral structure. Family love can be the soil for the growth of neighbour love. But unless the tensions between self-protection and obligation to the community are acknowledged, family love can become a self-centred existence, protected from learning the larger demands of love by its internal satisfactions. D. S. Bailey discusses the relations of *eros, philia,* and *agape* and remarks:

> Each has its contribution to make to the fullness of love. But balance and proportion between the different constituents of love is not automatic, and is usually attained only with that persistent effort which is one of the joys and responsibilities which lovers share.[35]

This surely is a classic understatement. Consider demands upon time and energy of individual members of the family for service in some larger cause. Fathers who leave families to make civil rights marches, politicians who sacrifice family life to the exigencies of political campaigns, wives who have to decide between a significant life in a public vocation and the demands of housekeeping, all should know the impossibility of any clear solution of this ethical problem.

Family love does not exempt us from the claims of the Kingdom of God. No person is ever fulfilled in the family alone and no romanticism about love should obscure that fact. The person is fulfilled in the world where God's work is being done. We have to find a union of love in its obligation to those with whom our lives are immediately bound; and love which calls upon each to become a creative member of the full society.

A modern novel, based upon a true story of persons who defied Hitler's tyranny, so perfectly expresses the fulfilment of eros in the love of justice that it has been vividly in my mind throughout this discussion of family love.

Alfred Neumann in *Six of Them* tells of a German professor of law who continued teaching in the early days of the Hitler regime, lecturing on justice with pointed reference to its subversion in the Nazi state.[36] When fired from his position, the professor, his wife, and a loyal band of students publish secretly copies of his lectures and other material attacking the injustices of the regime. Six of them are caught, and tried in a Nazi kangaroo court, itself a travesty of legal procedure. They are condemned to be executed. In the van in which they are being taken to their death the professor and his wife sit facing one another. They have had a lifetime of love and work together. They are old now, their energies exhausted by the struggle. Yet as they look at one another their love reaches its highest moment. It has been consummated in the service of a cause which transcends but does not negate personal *eros*. Sexual love has its fulfilment in personal existence when it is thus transmuted. Sexuality must be shattered in its self-centredness and redirected to something greater. That it can be so is a proof that this human love belongs with the creative action of *agape*.

35. D. S. Bailey, *The Mystery of Love and Marriage* (New York: Harper & Brothers, 1952), p. 28.
36. Alfred Neumann, *Six of Them* (New York: Macmillan, 1945).

(6)

JUSTICE BETWEEN MEN AND WOMEN

The issues of justice between men and women are so complex that a full discussion of them would require a shelf of books, and indeed a shelf has been appearing with Simone de Beauvoir's *The Second Sex*; Helen Deutsch's *Modern Woman, the Lost Sex*; and Betty Friedan's *The Feminine Mystique*, to mention some outstanding ones.

One obvious aspect of the moral issue is the overwhelming control of creative public life by men. This is an issue through the whole of culture, and certainly in the church where the ordination of women is in some areas still vigorously debated.[37] In the theological school, the writer has faced innumerable times the task of advising an able, educated and dedicated young woman concerning her professional life. She may be married to a prospective minister or teacher, and as capable intellectually and in other qualities as her husband. Not infrequently she is more capable. What pattern of life will serve the home, the husband's work, the coming family, and at the same time fulfil the deeply felt vocation to do significant work in the common life and the public world? It is an extremely difficult question to answer.

A just culture will provide for the equality, dignity, and companionship of men and women in the significant tasks of life, and yet take account of the enrichment which comes from the distinctive qualities, emotionality, and intellectuality of both men and women.

Movement toward this goal is doubly difficult because there is no way of completely disentangling the differences created by primal sexuality from those created by cultural conditioning and expectancy. Therefore a loving concern about this problem requires that men and women together try to learn what new possibilities of the organization of public life for both sexes there may be. It is an obvious case where the social forms in which love can be fulfilled have yet to be discovered. Changes such as new technological knowledge which alter the form of home life, the lifting of the burdens of manual labour, new patterns of family life which may give to the woman of forty the possibility of public service after children have left the home,

---

37. The Roman Catholic *aggiornamento* obviously raises questions about the male monopoly of the ministry. Cf. 'Women Clergy for Rome' by Rosemary Lauer, *The Christian Century*, Vol. 133, No. 37, Sept. 14, 1966. Most Christian communions have fundamental rethinking to do about the status of women in the church.

all are fraught with new possibilities. Perhaps the sins of 'male arrogance' and 'female aimlessness' will come into clearer light. *Agape* bids us seek justice here, not the stale justice of combat and compromise, but the justice of a search for a new economic, political, and ecclesiastical order in which sexuality can be fulfilling for each in a life which is a support and not a barrier to the love which binds all together.

CHAPTER XII

LOVE AND SOCIAL JUSTICE

Christians should get away from abstraction and confront the blood-stained face history has taken on today. (Albert Camus)

Christianity faces the world with terms, it does not merely suffuse it with a glow. (Peter Taylor Forsythe)

As love has a history, so there is a history of love in the cause of social justice. Love seems at best a whisper of the spirit in the clamour of history; yet our age of power is headed for catastrophe unless a new justice can be achieved. It is our aim in this chapter to see how the concern for justice leads the Christian ethic to some new forms of understanding love's work in the world.

Superficial views of Christian ethics see love and justice as entirely separate aspects of human relationships. Profounder moralists see that love must be concerned with justice, but some argue that justice is a quite different thing from love, and therefore love's work is different from direct action for justice. There are critical problems here for Christianity.

One position is that justice implies a different ethical criterion from love. Justice is impersonal where love is personal. Justice can be rationally defined as in Aristotle's ethics where it is distributive justice, giving to each his due, or commutative justice, establishing a collective order of freedom and mutuality. Love, it is argued, transcends these rational principles. It goes beyond justice through the spirit of brotherhood and reconciliation. A strong argument for this point of view is made by Emil Brunner who relates the difference between love and justice to the difference between the I and Thou relationship of persons and the abstractness of justice as impersonal principle.[1]

An even weightier argument for interpreting love and justice as diverse though related orders has been stated by Reinhold Niebuhr.[2] Niebuhr holds that the highest love is self-sacrificing whereas justice is always an accommodation of the interest of each in relation to the other. Niebuhr points out that every concrete system of justice

1. Emil Brunner, *Justice and the Social Order* (New York: Harper & Brothers, 1945).
2. Reinhold Niebuhr, *The Nature and Destiny of Man*, Vol. II, Chap. IX.

rests upon a balance of power. It is a compromise of interests, an uneasy truce between unresolved forces, ideologies, and powers. There are transcendant rational principles of justice which most ethics recognize, such as freedom, equality, order, and mutuality. But these transcendent principles are always applied in history by contending interests. The minds which conceive them have vested interests in their definition and application. Democracy means one thing to American capitalists and another to Russian communists. The 'just' wage looks too small to the worker who receives it and too large to the employer who pays it. Exclusion of Asians from immigration to the United States seems just to those who fear competition in the labour force, but it looks otherwise to those who need jobs and do not find them where they are. Such conflicts about what justice requires are omnipresent in life.

Reinhold Niebuhr has not only exposed the ideological bias in definitions of justice, but he reminds us that the settlement of conflicting claims always involves forces which operate above and beyond considerations of principle. Agreements as to the terms upon which issues will be settled are reached by compromises which may appeal to enlightenment and generosity, but also depend upon the power to make the settlement.

A clear example of this dependence of justice upon social power is the achievement of voting rights for such minority groups as Negroes. This has certainly come about in part through the sense of justice in the democratic tradition, and through constitutional guarantees. But the history of the voting privilege in the twentieth century shows that it takes the combined power of mass movements, economic pressures, and the Federal Government with its military force to give even a relative assurance that this requirement of justice will be realized.[3] It seems, therefore, that when we move from the perspective of love to concrete issues of social strategy and political power, justice is accomplished by a confluence of historical forces and humane considerations which indeed may be enforced by love, but which must have other sources.

Every Christian social ethic must take account of these facts about the search for justice. Love is not an alternative to involvement in the struggle for the rough justice of the world, but the love revealed in the Gospel leads to a distinctive view of the problem of justice. That view does not separate love and justice. It sees them as interrelated aspects of God's work of creating a community between himself and man and between man and man. The Bible never treats

3. A. Milton Konvitz and Theodore Leskes, *A Century of Civil Rights* (New York: Columbia University Press, 1961), especially pp. 83–9.

justice as a lesser order than that required by love, but as the objectification of the spirit of love in human and divine relationships. A Christian ethic must reconsider the biblical outlook on relation of love and justice. Some qualification of Brunner's and Niebuhr's doctrine is possible.[4]

(1)

LOVE AS THE FOUNDATION OF JUSTICE

As we examined the biblical foundations of the doctrine of love we saw that the Bible regards human life as a history in which God seeks to create a community of those who love him and one another, and who celebrate his love in a life of faithfulness and joy. The covenant with Israel is established as an act of God's love. Its structure is the human order which exhibits God's righteous purpose. God's righteousness is his justice, and his justice is manifest in his working to put down the unrighteous, expose idols, show mercy, and achieve reconciliation in a new order which expresses man's dignity as bearer of the divine image.

We have seen the apparent tension between God's righteous judgment which points to his rejection of a sinful people and his mercy through which he calls them back to himself. The word of Micah may seem to reflect a duality of mercy and justice:

> What doth the Lord require of thee but to do justly and to love mercy and to walk humbly with thy God (Micah 6:8).

But one of the clear notes in the ethic of the Bible is that the justice of God *includes* his concern for and mercy toward the hurt, the weak and the oppressed:

> Give the King thy judgments, O God, and thy righteousness unto the King's sons.
> He shall judge the poor of the people, and he shall save the children of the needy and shall break in pieces the oppressor (Psalms 72:1, 4).

God's righteousness is shown when he lifts the burdens of the weak and the hurt. This is echoed in Jesus' condemnation of those who 'lay heavy burdens on the poor'. Justice and mercy are both 'weightier matters of the law'. Jesus does not separate them.

It is true that the biblical writers on the whole do not interpret justice in the form of general principles, but as a universal personal

4. For a discussion of these two theologies on this point see Daniel D. Williams, *God's Grace and Man's Hope* (New York: Harper & Row, 1949), chap. 4.

concern for every man, for the strangers and alien as well as the elect people. Human obligations are grounded in the will of God and in the disclosure of his righteousness in history. Thus the prophets appeal for decent treatment of the stranger, 'because you were a slave in Egypt and the Lord your God redeemed you from there' (Deuteronomy 24: 18).

The New Testament keeps this historical concreteness in ethics. To serve God and the neighbour is to meet human needs. Indeed the New Testament may seem to take a further step away from the formulation of rational principles of justice. Love is the fulfilment of the law and therefore is the sole criterion of action. The eschatological expectation gave a certain freedom from responsibility for adjudicating every problem of social organization. Yet the state and its order is affirmed in Paul's thought and the acceptance of its authority is a Christian obligation (Romans 13).

We can summarize the biblical development in this way: the Bible sees the issues of human justice arising in the history of the Christian community as the people of God seek to bring peace and reconciliation to all men, and to show a special concern for the hurt, the needy, and the weak. Before God every Christian knows that he is the hurt, the needy, the weak person for whom there could be only condemnation, if there were no mercy in God's righteousness. Thus Paul asserts the foundation of all Christian consideration of the other, 'Have this mind among yourselves which you have in Christ Jesus, who . . . humbled himself and took the form of a servant and became obedient unto death, even death on a cross' (Philippians 2: 5–8).

Those who offer a contextual Christian ethic in our own day seem to be so far in accord with the biblical view that justice is to be sought as the expression of the life of the covenant community as it undertakes in the spirit of *agape* to bring reconciliation among men. Dr. Paul Lehmann has given a perceptive analysis of this conception in his *Ethics in a Christian Context*. He speaks of the 'politics of God' as the divine working toward the humanization of life. Men are being brought into a new community through reconciliation, and the Church is the initial and decisive expression of that community:

> . . . the empirical church points, despite its ambiguity, to the fact that there is in the world a *laboratory of the living word*, or to change the metaphor, a *bridgehead of maturity*, namely, the Christian *koinonia* [community].[5]

5. Paul Lehmann, *Ethics in a Christian Context* (New York: Harper & Row, 1963, p. 131; London: S.C.M. Press, 1963).

In this view, the question of what are we to do is answered from within in the action of the atonement. Christ has renewed the human community through re-establishing the ultimate loyalty which restores man to himself. This action of Christ is present, known or hidden, in every human history. The Christian seeks the kind of human relationship which follows from and embodies the reconciling deed. 'Every man is the brother for whom Christ died.'[6]

This conception of Christian ethics implies radical freedom and responsibility. The view of love taken in this book so far agrees with the contextualists that we must continually ask what love requires in each situation in the light of Christ's dying for us. History is the scene of Christ's conflict with everything that opposes or thwarts God's creative purpose. He reigns until he has put all his enemies under his feet, and the last enemy is death. We live in that embattled reign[7] (I Corinthians 15).

There are three implications of this view which form a prolegomenon to a Christian social ethic. By social ethic I do not mean something opposed to a personal ethic, but one which is concerned with the issues between groups and nations where the decisions taken alter the lives of multitudes of people and the direction of history.

The first implication of this Christological ethic is that decisions taken in the spirit of love express the search for communion, not simply obedience to law. This is the solid foundation of a contextual or situational ethic. We have still to discuss the nature of ethical principles; but so far as love is the ultimate criterion every Christian ethic is contextual. To love is to respond to what is present in history, with these specific people and their needs, their sin and their hope, and our sin and our hope.

We see however that the context of ethical decision is not the immediate situation alone. It is the history of God's reconciling work looking toward the new community. Action here and now has consequences for Christ's work everywhere. To say that the 'situation' determines what must be done is not, in its Christian sense, to give a purely 'practical' or relative rule. It means responsibility toward what is at hand, but it also means responsibility within God's atoning work as we, with all our limitations, understand that work.

The spirit of love leads to concern with the whole need of man in each concrete situation. It is participation in the movement toward

6. William Temple, 'Christians in a Secular World', *The Christian Century*, Vol. 61, March 1, 1944.

7. I have developed this doctrine of the 'reign of Christ' in *God's Grace and Man's Hope*, chapter 5.

the glory and fulfilment of all things. The suffering of love follows from this identification with everyman. It was said of Edith Hamilton, 'She felt as personal agony, the giant burden of mankind'. Capacities for feeling differ, but the meaning of *agape* is suggested in such a characterization.

The second implication of the Christological foundation of ethics is that we never identify what God is doing with wh at we are doing. The Christian is to seek the will of God and to do it, and express the love of God to every neighbour, but no one should claim that his acts are true and sufficient expressions of *agape*.

Since this point is critical for Christian ethics, let us consider it further. *Agape* forbids self-justification; for *agape* is God's love given for men whose deepest sin is their assertion of their righteousness before God, and their attempt to live independently of Him. God justifies us by beginning a new history; therefore every attempt at self-justification violates the meaning of love. But it may be protested, the coming of Christ and his forgiveness means that we are enabled to live the life of love. Surely Paul enjoins us to have the mind of Christ: 'Be transformed by the renewal of your mind.' 'As therefore you received Christ Jesus the Lord, so live in him' (Romans 12: 2; Colossians 2: 6).

Paul speaks here through injunctions. He addresses the consciences of those who have been called into the new life. He implies that the new life has begun but is not consummated. It is in the new life that we begin to see clearly why we should not claim to possess *agape*, or that any particular act of ours conforms to it. Self-sacrifice may be an aggressive act against others or a form of self-destruction. Psychological discoveries have reinforced our awareness of this truth. It is not only that we can never prove purity of motives; but we can never extract ourselves from the history of our life with its guilt, its weakness, and its limitations. Certainly, *agape* can qualify our actions, and perhaps there are pure acts of love in this human flesh, but they are such only by grace and not by clarity of our motivation or the strength of our will alone.

This knowledge of love as grace is the real meaning of I Corinthians 13, which ought to be studied more often for the ethics of social action. It is false to interpret Paul's hymn to *agape* as a recommendation to add something called 'love' to our actions so that we may know them to be true, and thus assure our justification. 'If I give my body to be burned and have not love it profiteth me nothing.' But Paul is not urging us to be sure to include love in our thoughts, speech and actions. He is not even demanding that we be certain it is love which guides our actions. He gives us not a recommendation, but the insight that where love is absent we do not do the will of God and do not fulfil our humanity. This is our real ethical situation, and we have to live, work and sacrifice within it, leaving the judgment to God about what love may do through us. In this light Paul's characterization of love becomes far more significant than any list of special virtues. 'Love is very patient, very kind, gives itself no airs, is always eager to believe the best.' This does not merely tell us what virtues to exercise in any situation. It recalls us to the spirit in which every virtue has its fulfilment. In the light of this interpretation Paul's final word that love 'beareth, believeth, hopeth, endureth all things' is not a rhetorical flourish by-passing logic, but a recognition that there are no bounds to love's participation in the world, its endurance of what has to be endured, its everlastingness.

Love is spirit, and such understanding as we have of it takes form from the spirit of the Servant and within our faithful response in our situation. But what love really requires of us, and what God does in, through and above us, is more than we ever fully grasp.

There is a third consequence of this approach to the problem of love and justice. Since love is the spirit at work in the community of reconciliation, the work which love prompts is to be done in actual history where the neighbour is met. This means that to love is to be involved in the issues of political justice. If each person were simply an individual unattached to any structure of social life, entirely independent of the orders, laws, and institutions which surround him, there would be no answer to those who say that to love is purely an individual and personal matter.[8]

If, however, the neighbour's life is bound up with the community, then he can be served only in relation to the social structure which shapes his life. Therefore the securing of a social order in which men can be neighbours to one another is a necessary expression of loving concern. We see that the development of strategies for social action through concern for a just political, economic and social order, is implied in what the New Testament explicitly enjoins. Loving the enemy, doing good to those who are persecuted, feeding the hungry, clothing the naked, binding up the wounds of the captive, treating the slave as brother, freeing him, honouring the wife as one who is to be loved as Christ loved the Church, all this is the clear consequence of the biblical conception of love leading to social action.

Concern for justice, then, is not something added to love, or a

8. For a statement of this view see Russell Clinchy, *Charity, Biblical and Political* (The Foundation for Economic Education, Inc., 1951), in a series entitled *In Brief*, Vol. 6, No. 2.

concession to the weakness of those who have not learned to love. *Justice is the order which love requires.* It forms the skeletal structure of love, the terms on which men may be brotherly toward one another and find reconciliation. We can formulate the Christian principle of justice in this way: the objective order of justice consists in the terms upon which men may so live together that the way is opened to reconciliation and communion. Henry Nelson Wieman puts this point in a brilliant chapter on justice:

> The constitution of a society prescribes the forms of justice only when it provides for that kind of interaction among individuals, and between individuals and the physical environment, which creates the human mind, and which sustains that scope of understanding, power of action and richness of appreciation which is distinctively human in contrast to the lower animals.

Wieman goes on to observe that

> . . . if this fluidity of the social order should lead men to derive the principles of justice increasingly from the demands of that kind of interchange which creates the appreciative mind with its meanings, we might be entering the age when for the first time a civilization can pass in safety the crisis of power which heretofore has brought every civilization into decline and finally to disintegration.[9]

Justice therefore cannot be identified with one type of social order which exemplifies certain principles, even the highest, because principles are abstractions. But justice involves principles, that is, structures of value and law which enter into the determination of human relationships. Here we reach the limit of contextualism as an ethical theory. On what terms can human life be tolerably and fruitfully organized? To seek an answer to that question is to search for principles which articulate the conditions of justice.

(2)

LOVE AND THE TERMS OF JUSTICE

We mean by justice an order of life which gives to each member of the community the fullest possible access to the sources of fulfilment. To seek justice is to be guided by the principles which must govern human conduct so that this concrete order of life can be realized. Love without regard for the terms of justice is sentimentality.

9. Henry Nelson Wieman, *The Directive in History* (Boston: Beacon Press, 1949), pp. 97, 100.

This point needs emphasis because in both traditional and contemporary Christian ethics there sometimes appears the suggestion that since love is personal it can dispense with principles. Love transcends law, it is said, therefore all law is merely a concession to human weakness. Luther says that so far as the real Christian is concerned no law is necessary.[10] But surely this would be true only if the 'real Christian' not only had a perfectly loving spirit but also knew fully all the conditions required for the growth of community among men. But we can never fully know those conditions. Hence we require a structure of moral and legal principles with the agencies of courts, legislatures, and political processes which establish laws in the light of the judgment of the people about their needs. For example, there is the question of punishment for crime. That there must be some penalty for violation of persons or their property is an accepted principle of every human society. The answer to the question 'what penalty' involves moral issues as well as legal fiat. The use of punishment as a deterrent, and the effect of the penal system upon persons and society as a whole, raise issues for moral judgment. In the discussion about the death penalty, there is the ultimate moral issue of the right to take life, and whether even the state has this right. There are the questions of the actual effectiveness for deterrence of the penalty and its effect upon moral sensitivity in the society. One of the strongest arguments in recent years for abolishing the death penalty has arisen, not from the moral prohibition against the taking of life, but from the fact that with rare exceptions those who are executed are people who lack the means to secure good legal assistance, or lack the educational background to make full use of such assistance, or lack the social status which brings the case to public attention.[11]

The search for justice is a many-sided task. Our present argument is that responsibility exercised in love leads to continual inquiry within the social and political processes where complex issues are decided. Certainly the question of what justice requires is not decided by abstract principle alone, nor does the answer arise spontaneously because love is present. The moral decision takes place in the context of human struggle with the realities of history. But the question of

10. Martin Luther, 'If all the world were composed of real Christians, that is, true believers, no prince, king, sword, or law would be needed'. *Secular Authority, To What Extent It Should Be Obeyed*, III.

11. The Society of Friends Committee on Social Order for the State of New Jersey observed that capital punishment 'is primarily applied to the poor, the friendless, the ignorant, the unfortunate without resources, and especially to Negroes'. Quoted in James A. Joyce, *Capital Punishment* (New York: Thomas Nelson & Sons, 1961), p. 157.

what is to be done involves the search for principles which can guide to the fuller realization of that concrete good which belongs to all.

For example, a child's right to privacy is a moral right, even against the will and good intentions of his parents. Loving concern should mean a respect for this principle, which can hardly be made a matter of law. It is a matter of the sensitivity of parents and an understanding of the worth of privacy for the growth of the person. By contrast, a child's right to protection from a parent's brutality is a matter of both moral principle and law which the courts will enforce. William Ernest Hocking points out in his *Man and the State* that the humanizing process requires the search for the principles which men can honour in their mutual relations.[12] The 'I-Thou relationship' which neglects this function of principles will degenerate into sentimentality or ruthlessness. If I love my neighbour I will seek and respect the principles which guide us toward common goals and which protect us from each other's whims and violence.

When we thus argue for involvement of love in the search for justice we are only transposing into a more general framework the Hebraic conception of the covenant. God offers his loyalty to his people with requirements. He declares the conditions which ought to govern human relationships. The prophets summon the nation to fulfil its obligations under the divine justice.

Our doctrine of love therefore leads to a qualification of a contextual or situational ethic. While abstract principles in themselves may give no absolute guidance in the concrete situation, responsible and loving action will seek the principles of equity and order which ought to govern human life. Ethics always has a future as well as a present reference. We can never know the full consequences of present action. Therefore we have to respect those principles which point beyond present decision to an order of life which we can specify only in general and revisable terms. The right of petition of a people for redress of grievances must be affirmed as a right precisely because we do not know what grievances will occur, whether they will be real grievances, or what the future government can do about them. The affirmation of human rights is the demand upon present action for respect of guiding principles as we move toward an undefined future. Love needs law.

In some contemporary Christian theories of law the need for principles is recognized, but it is held that in a Christian ethic all principles must have an exclusively Christological derivation. The Christian moralist, it is argued, does not need a secular approach to

12. William Ernest Hocking, *Man and the State* (New Haven: Yale University Press, 1926), p. 13.

jurisprudence since he derives his principles exclusively from the final revelation.

Dietrich Bonhoeffer wrote in his *Ethics*:

> What the church has to say about the secular institutions follows solely from the preaching of Christ, and the Church possesses no doctrine of her own which is valid in itself with regard to eternal institutions and natural or human rights such as might command acknowledgement even independently of faith in Christ. The only human and natural rights are those which derive from Christ, that is to say, from faith.[13]

In the first part of this statement Bonhoeffer might be saying only that the Church cannot impose some tradition of its own upon the human search for justice, as if it could dictate those terms; but the last sentence seems to say there can be no basis at all for human rights except within the Christian faith.

This would mean that Christians would have to ask all men to accept the Christian faith before discussing human rights. With all respect to Bonhoeffer's position, this surely will not do. Men have always discussed justice on the basis of reason, experience, tradition, and sometimes arbitrary dogmatism. To say that nothing whatever has come out of that discussion is to make nonsense out of all the great moral traditions—Stoic, Buddhist, humanistic, or democratic, as well as Christian.

One of the profoundest interpretations of the law in our time is that of Edmond Cahn. His book, *The Sense of Injustice*, shows how legal terms for human relationships have been won painfully and slowly out of long experience, guided by the religious tradition. Cahn gives full weight to the Old and New Testaments, but also to the secular growth of law in concrete cases.[14]

William Stringfellow has criticized Edmond Cahn's book, *The Moral Decision*, calling it blasphemous and immoral 'for the only affirmation Professor Cahn is really making is an affirmation of man as one who is justified by his own decisions founded in his own knowledge of good and evil. Professor Cahn is simply affirming Adam (Genesis 3: 5).' Stringfellow seems to want to establish a Christian approach to law on the basis that only from within the Christian faith can anything humane or significant be said. We may remark that his assumption that since a legal theorist does not invoke the name of Christ he knows nothing of sin or grace is certainly

13. Dietrich Bonhoeffer, *Ethics* (London: S.C.M. Press, 1955; New York: Macmillan, Paperback edition, 1965, pp. 360–1).

14. Edmond Cahn, *The Sense of Injustice:* An Anthropocentric View of Law (New York: New York University Press, 1949).

gratuitous. But Mr. Stringfellow leaves no basis for a meeting of people of different faiths in a search for principles of human justice. He says:

> Human justice is not a substitute for divine justification, nor is it even a corollary in preparation for the consummation of history. . . .
>
> The preservation of human life in society, though it is a tenet of natural law and the basic norm which informs positivism, is *not* a Gospel tenet. In fact, in the Gospel the preservation of human life in society has the fundamental meaning of death. . . .
>
> The tension between law and grace is such that there is no Christian jurisprudence. . . . The Christian sees that the striving of law is for justice, but knows that the justice men achieve has no saving power; it does not justify them, for justification of man is alone in Jesus Christ. The grace of God is the only true justice any man may ever receive.[15]

This is surely confused doctrine. It can lead to sheer opportunism without principles or terms, or to an ecclesiastically dominated society in which only those who share the religious orthodoxy control the pattern of the common life.

Reinhold Niebuhr recognizes this secular wisdom in the western legal tradition as he traces the development of democratic government. He shows how the weaknesses of traditional political ethics, both secular and religious, were exposed by hard experience. He traces the development of the fundamental democratic insights to a kind of 'common sense' which repudiated ecclesiastical control and the dogmas of individualism and collectivism.[16] The point is not that we should make an idol of the democratic tradition in any historical form. It is to see in history a process in which term-making achieves significant results through the struggle of men of different persuasions with the stubborn facts of human life guided by a developing 'sense of injustice'. Certainly that sense can be informed by the love of God and neighbour, but even the highest ethic of love must learn from history. Love requires participation in the historical process, always looking toward reconciliation and knowing that our sense of injustice needs reformation.

The question will be asked, 'If we admit secular knowledge and

15. William Stringfellow, review of Edmond Cahn, *The Moral Decision* in *The Christian Scholar*, Vol. XL, No. 3, September 1957, pp. 251–2. The quotation from Mr. Stringfellow is from his paper, *The Christian Lawyer as a Churchman*, *The Vanderbilt Law Review*, 'A Symposium on Law and Christianity', Vol. 10, No. 5, August, 1957.

16. Reinhold Niebuhr, *The Self and the Dramas of History* (New York: Charles Scribner's Sons, 1955; London: Faber & Faber, 1956).

experience into the term-making process, have we not brought something alien into the Christian ethic?' Have we left our Christological foundation? The answer is that we have not done so if we understand Christology in the authentic sense of the theological tradition. Christ is the *Logos* incarnate, and this gives a basis for the linking of common insight and experience with the truth which Christ fulfils. At the same time our final criterion is not in human reason and experience by themselves, but as illuminated by the Truth that has become acted out in love in the history of Jesus.

The *logos* tradition is complex. *Logos* as used in the New Testament means the Word of God. It includes logic and reason but points to their metaphysical ground.[17] *Logos* is the structure of being, the foundation of rationality and order, and of the interlocking character of all things in God's creation. The identification of Christ with the *logos* supports the search for rational coherence in the Christian faith. The inquiry for *logos* in ethics is the search for the principles which are required for human relationships. *Logos* implies the rights of reason as an open, inquiring, experimental, reflective, self-critical formation of mind. Without this man is less than human, and without this no ethic can light the way which the spirit of love should take.

The spirit of love requires participation in the 'dirty work' of history. The search today for some minimal order under law must go on in the threatening world of nations, some armed with nuclear weapons, and others preparing to be so armed. The politics of international power, the strategies of population control, the discriminating use of force to check destructive outbreaks of violence, the patient search for new terms of internal co-operation, are all part of the task. There is a tragic element here as the conflicts disfigure men in one another's eyes. We become enemies. We contend. We injure. There is killing. Yet love allows us no way through this dark reality except to live within it so as to find how men may so live together that they cease to be enemies and begin to become friends.

(3)

Love and Group Loyalty

Ex-president Nkrumah of Ghana had inscribed on his monument in the capital city: 'Seek ye first the political Kingdom and all else

17. C. H. Dodd, *The Interpretation of the Fourth Gospel* (Cambridge University Press, 1953), pp. 3–115, 263ff.

shall follow.'[18] Every historical order elicits and organizes group loyalties which are among the most powerful forces in human life. The achievement of justice is impossible without such loyalties. *Agape* as concerned with justice implies a positive appreciation of the loves of nation, of soil, of kindred and of tradition, just as it implies the created goodness of sexual love. Indeed, group loyalties always have elements of sexuality within them. At the same time, the spirit of *agape* is that of universal concern. It opposes the absolutizing of any loyalty other than the Kingdom of God. Therefore a Christian ethic must interpret the relationship between *agape* love and the group loves or be a pious irrelevance in history.

There is, of course, an important distinction between group loyalties which assert in principle the universal claim of all men to justice and brotherhood, and those which make an idol of one group. The great religions, Judaism, Christianity, Buddhism, Hinduism, and Islam, have embodied the loyalties of particular peoples within a universalistic ethic, and in principle reject the idols of clan or race. There are also universalistic political faiths such as Marxism and democracy which are rooted in the cultures of particular nations and civilizations, yet which hold the ideal of universal justice. There is an essential difference between a faith which recognizes responsibility for the universal human community but does not seek to dominate it, and master race theories such as Nazism, or the interesting new Japanese version of Nichiren Buddhism known as Sokka Gakkai (Value-Creating Society). In the following words we hear the ring of an imperious universalism which has been present in much religious history, and which has certainly had its parallels in some forms of Christianity:

> Born in the Land of the Rising Sun, We are the True Buddha, far more glorious than the moon. As the moon moves from west to east, so Sakkamuni's Buddhism, born in the 'Land of the Moon' was brought to Japan from India.

> As the Sun rises in the east and sets in the west, Nichiren Daishonin's Buddhism, born in the country of the Sun, is destined to go from Japan to India, and moreover, to all the world, from the East to the West.[19]

The complex relation between universalistic ideals and group loyalties requires careful analysis. Group loyalties are blends of many emotions, the sense of belonging, the will to power, the memory of

18. Quoted in *The New York Times*, January 1, 1967, magazine sec., p. 27.
19. Quoted from *The Sokka-Gakkai* (Tokyo: The Seikyo Press, 1962), p. 51. See also Richard H. Drummond, 'Japan's New Religions and the Christian Community', *The Christian Century*, December 9, 1964, pp. 1521ff.

past battles and sufferings, fear of others, the insecurities of life, gratitude for heritage and homeland. Universalistic ideals become fused with these emotional dynamics. Russian communism has drawn upon the spirit of Slavic nationalism. Chinese communism is empowered with national pride and historic resentment of the West. This blending of national and religious loyalties is a pervasive feature of most contemporary political ideologies.

U Ba Swe, whom Mr. Frank Trager, editor of a study of Marxism in Southeast Asia, calls one of the five most important political leaders in Burma, speaks of his comrades in the following terms:

> architects of revolution . . . building a Burmese Socialist structure . . . with Marxism (as) the guide to action . . . but only a revolutionary movement which is entirely Burmese, conforming to Burmese methods and principles can achieve any measure of success.

He further asserts:

> Marxist theory is not antagonistic to Buddhist philosophy.
> The two are, frankly speaking, not merely similar. In fact they are the same in concept.

Mr. Trager observes that Marxism in Southeast Asia has always come in ostensible support of nationalism.[20]

The democratic ideal in America carries a dynamic component of the ideals of the American heritage, 'a new nation conceived in liberty and dedicated to the proposition that all men are created equal'. Thus both democracy and Marxism have incorporated elements of national tradition, and both have tried to appreciate and encourage the nationalistic loyalties of the peoples they have been trying to win.

Leopold Dedar Senghor's address at Oxford University on the meaning of Negritude expresses succinctly the spirit of a particular loyalty and its relation to mankind. The President of Senegal said:

> Our revised Negritude is humanistic. I repeat, it welcomes the complementary values of Europe and the white man, and indeed of all other races and continents. But it welcomes them in order to fertilize and reinvigorate its own values, which it then offers for the construction of a civilization which shall embrace all mankind. The neo-humanism of the twentieth century stands at the point where the paths of all nations, races, and continents cross, 'where the four winds of the spirit blow'.[21]

---

20. Frank Trager, ed., *Marxism in Southeast Asia* (Stanford University Press, 1959), p. 11.

21. Quoted in Paul E. Sigmund, Jr., *The Ideologies of the Developing Nations* (New York: Praeger, 1963), p. 250.

An ethic of *agape* must incorporate the spirit revealed in such a statement, the integrity of group life within a universalistic and brotherly concern. The spirit of *agape* hovers over the group spirit as it does over authentic love between men and women, affirming the human loves while it holds before each of them the requirement of transformation by the Kingdom of God.

There is, however, a special difficulty in the group loyalties which Reinhold Niebuhr has exposed in an unforgettable way. This is their capacity to mask idolatrous or self-centred love under the form of universal benevolence. The temptation to this besets not only political loyalties, but also the highest religious aspiration. In fact, the universality of religion makes it peculiarly useful for the sanctification of imperious and parochial group interests.

We have come here to the heart of the problem of *agape* as a foundation for a visible social ethic. We say that the vital impulses manifest in love of homeland, of tradition and of the group must be affirmed. Even when corrupted by sin they retain the force of authentic humanity. But they all become at some point questionable in the light of the ultimate obedience in the spirit of *agape*. An ethic grounded in the love of God manifest in Christ must live in an ambiguous and difficult relationship to every concrete form of group loyalty. This most certainly includes the forms of life in the Church, the community founded on *agape*. No serious participant in the ecumenical movement can mistake the judging and purging power of *agape* as it moves within the centuries-old forms and symbols which have guided Christian devotion and have become infused with the very human loves of the familiar and the satisfying.[22]

In this clash of group loyalties the search for an ethical way which expresses *agape* has often taken either the way of humanitarianism or the way of protest. We need to examine both.

(4)

THE HUMANITARIAN WAY

'The fatherhood of God and the brotherhood of man' is a familiar phrase in modern Christian cultures. The brotherhood of man has often been affirmed as a humanistic ideal apart from a specifically Christian rootage. There is a concern for the needs of humanity,

22. At the Lund Conference on Faith and Order these elements of particularist group loyalties were identified, too simply I believe, as 'non-theological factors' which have to be taken into account in ecumenical understanding.

and a sentiment of benevolence toward every man just because we share a common human lot. This concern was given philosophic expression in the stoic sense of humanity as a universal community bound by the divine law to which the moral man can give his rational allegiance. It was recognized in the French revolutionary ideal of the 'fraternity' which binds 'liberty' and 'equality' together. It had another philosophic rationale in the idealist doctrine of the absolute truth and good reflected for every man in the community of value, as in Josiah Royce's thought. It has informed the American democratic ideal. The inalienable rights in the Declaration of Independence are held to be endowments from the Creator. Later democratic thought has sometimes found human idealism sufficient, as in John Dewey's philosophy.[23]

There are superficial and profound types of humanistic universalism. From a theological point of view we may see in every Western humanitarianism an element of ethical commitment which has been given substance to the universalistic attitude. We may regard that commitment as in part a deposit left by the biblical heritage in the humanistic philosophies; but we cannot deny that a form of universal human benevolence has appeared in both Western and Eastern traditions. It exhibits a concern for every man as a companion in the great community, and it leads to ethical sensitivity and self-sacrificing devotion.

Is such humanitarian love an authentic, though truncated version of Christian love? The identification of love of neighbour with humanitarianism has been vigorously criticized by some theologians. The Bible, it is said, does not call us to recognize a universal idealism as the basis of dealing with men. It finds the basis for a humane treatment of the neighbour in the historical revelation of God's love for a people. Only in this history do we discover who our neighbour really is, and therefore only here do we know the real meaning of the command to love.[24]

It is clear that every Christian ethic interprets the obligation to the neighbour within the action of God's creative power and mercy. But we may yet regard humanitarianism as a form of human love which, though it cannot be identified with *agape*, reflects human values which *agape* incorporates and fulfils It is true that the Bible does not speak of a general fraternity of humanity which we recog-

23. See John Dewey, *A Common Faith* (New Haven: Yale University Press, 1934). I am not certain that Dewey really rejects theism however. The book remains ambiguous in its statements about God.

24. Cf. W. W. Bryden, *The Christian's Knowledge of God* (Toronto: Thorn Press, 1940, pp. 139–44, 237; London: James Clarke & Co., 1960).

nize just because we are human. The Bible sees humanity in the concrete history of peoples and nations where the neighbour is present, sometimes as enemy, or as stranger, and always as one who bears the image of God. Yet the universalistic note in the Gospel is unmistakable. The Noachian laws, promulgated before the flood, have formed a basis for a Jewish version of natural law. The prophets assert the demand of God for just, humane behaviour toward all peoples, not just the Jews. There are obligations to the stranger, to the hurt and the oppressed, without regard to race or religion.

The parables of Jesus reiterate the demand to serve every man in need—the hurt, the hungry, and the enemy. These are not merely abstract commands, they are made in the name of God, not of any particular national tradition. God sends his rain on the just and unjust, so man ought to be merciful (Matthew 5: 45). Christ is present in 'the least of these' (Matthew 25). Paul interprets the history of Jesus as the fulfilment of the history of Adam who represents everyman. Jesus restores to all humanity the imaging of its divine origin.

If we cannot say that a disposition of benevolence toward other human beings, or a concern for humanity as a whole, is necessarily an expression of love as *agape*, neither can we say that *agape* is not present. The New Testament is quite explicit about this. Those who sit at the Lord's right hand at the last judgment had not known who he was when they fed the hungry, clothed the naked, and visited those in prison. That does not mean that every act of feeding the hungry is an adequate service of Christ. It might reflect a paternalistic, arrogant, self-centred spirit. But it is God's judgment and not man's as to when the love which redeems is present. Love which leads to human concern and mutuality is, so far as any objective test can go, that which expresses the mind of Christ.

What the Gospel does reject is the tendency to impersonality in humanitarianism. But humitarianism can have its own personalism of involvement in the neighbours' needs, and when this happens a Christian ethic can affirm that in this love for the other Christ is present *incognito*.

Humanitarian sentiment need not be abstract, impersonal, and unrealistic about what men need. Those who say that it is impossible to 'love' three billion human beings are certainly right if love means only person to person relationship. But they forget two important facts. First, there are elements of universal predicament and need in human life, and it is only through sin or a pathological condition that we forget this. The plea to remember that the other is a human being with feelings, hopes, pain, joy, may on occasion be ineffectual but it is never irrelevant, and it has its place in any ethic.

The second consideration is that in the twentieth century as never before there is one world and one common human plight. The interrelatedness of mankind is both a grim and a hopeful fact. Failure to control population, the possibility of the possession of atomic weapons by dozens of nations, the issues of race and colour which affect every society and every civilization, disclose the human condition shared by all. One of the authentic forms of humanitarian love appears in the response to this common plight. It is found in those who seek to deal objectively and dispassionately with the meeting of different cultures. It is expressed in the lives of a few persons, such as Albert Schweitzer or Jane Addams, who became spokesmen for mankind, not because they made this claim, but because they articulated a humane and universal spirit. Eugene V. Debs, one of the minor prophets of American democratic ethics, had this insight:

> So long as there is a lower class, I am in it;
> While there is a criminal element, I am of it;
> While there is a soul in jail, I am not free.[25]

There is a sense in which humanitarian love serves as a corrective to expressions of *agape* when we are tempted to claim superiority of ethical wisdom. In Taiwan in 1960, the following statement was made by some interpreters of Chinese culture:

> It is true that Westerners often have what Orientals do not have to such a degree: loyalty to ideals, a spirit of social service and enthusiasm and love toward others. But the highest feelings between human beings do not consist of enthusiasm and love only. Man's will to power and his possessive urge can pervade enthusiasm and love. . . . An ultimate solution can only come from removing the roots of the will power and of the possessive urge. To do this, love must be truly fused with respect. The most significant feature of this fusion of love and respect is the feeling that, since love towards others is based on God's boundless love, my respect for others is likewise boundless. It means that I must equal my respect toward others to my veneration of God. This is what is meant in China when it is said that the good man 'serves his parents like serving heaven', and 'governs the people like performing a great sacrifice'. There is no room here for any reflection on the fact that I myself believe in God and that I know His love, but that the other does not. Such an attitude places the other person on a lower level, and then my respect towards others remains unfulfilled. True respect must be unconditional and absolute. Then, human love, expressed in

---

25. Quoted in Wade Crawford Barclay, *Challenge and Power* (New York: Abingdon Press, 1936), p. 143.

the forms of etiquette, preserves its inner warmth and becomes mellow and mild. Thus the deepest human love is transformed into the feeling of commiseration and humanity.[26]

The danger of the prideful assumption of superior ethical knowledge is rightly exposed here. Identification with the other means respect for him and his truth, even when we believe ours is more profound.

Agape can incorporate humanitarianism, but it transcends humanitarianism. The reason lies in the history of sin and grace. *Agape* is identification with the neighbour and meeting his needs, but it is identification at the level of confession of our betrayal of the divine image, and hope for the possibility of renewal through the grace of suffering love. *Agape* is known in the history of the incarnation and the atonement. Therefore, while it recognizes human sympathy, fellow-feeling and identification, it has a new basis for identification with the other. This is participation in the history of the love which gives itself for sinners. To believe that 'everyman is the brother for whom Christ died', requires an identification with the neighbour which is deeper than any humanitarian sentiment, for now the neighbour is seen as one who is created to share in communion with God and his fellows in eternal life. It is the saddest of all commentaries on those who have glimpsed the meaning of redemption that they should take the knowledge of *agape* to give some kind of superiority over others, whereas *agape* implies confession that each stands in the same need of grace as every other.

In the confession of mutual need there is the meeting point of humanitarian ethics and Christian ethics. Certainly the love of God and neighbour may be recognized and practised by those who do not profess a biblical faith more adequately than by some who stand inside. Reinhold Niebuhr says in a classic sentence in his *Nature and Destiny of Man*:

> While Christians rightly believe that all truth necessary for such a spiritual experience is mediated only through the revelation in Christ, they must guard against the assumption that only those who know Christ 'after the flesh', that is, in the actual historical revelation, are capable of such a conversion. A 'hidden Christ' operates in history. And there is always the possibility that those who do not know the historical revelation may achieve a more genuine repentance and humility than those who do.[27]

---

26. Unpublished manuscript in my possession.
27. Reinhold Niebuhr, *The Nature and Destiny of Man*, Vol. II, pp. 109–10 footnote.

This does not make the historical revelation of no importance. It means that those who recognize the *agape* of God in the historical revelation can be thankful that it has come to them there, while they remember that it does not give them an exclusive possession of the truth.

In this discussion of humanitarian love we see again how *agape* uses the human loves, incorporating them into the human vitalities and the will to belong. The natural drives, longings and passions belong to the essential goodness of human nature. The love of home, of work, of soil, homeland, the tools of one's trade, the tradition, history, and language of a people, the comradeship of the community of work and celebration, the love of freedom, group spirit, indignation at injustice, and respect for common ideals are all affirmed within the ethic of *agape*. Every human community and nation lives from the vitalities of such loves. The Church itself draws upon them. Ecumenicity is, in its roots, the reality which unites the deep love of different traditions in new forms of community.

So far we must go with a theory of creative participation in the loves which inform human history. They are to be accepted with gratitude and honour and at the same time to be purged as they are brought into the service of the Kingdom. Yet because all the loves, even *agape*, work within the history of sin and idolatry, *agape* creates a double mindedness toward the human loves. They are affirmed yet they cannot be accepted as they are. Here the work of *agape* becomes protest.

(5)

LOVE AS PROTEST

Agape always has an aspect of protest. It may be overt or silent, but it will resist the tendency to absolutization in every group cause. The protest arises when we claim too much for our purity of intention and the adequacy of our goals. Pretensions of absolute righteousness are as offensive to love as positive unrighteousness. Even in fighting an enemy whom we believe to be wrong we may protest that in the enemy and that in ourselves which makes us enemies. As Paul Tillich says: 'Protest is a form of communion.'[28] *Agape* creates that freedom of spirit which transcends all self-justification. Thus the moral life receives from *agape* that which is essential to its integrity, the transcendant dimension in which the limits of our ethical justi-

28. Paul Tillich, *Systematic Theology*, Vol. I, p. 38.

fication can be confessed without our falling into nihilism and despair. *Agape* leads to the radical protest against the underlying sins of society and culture in which all share.

Protest involves the attempt to point unequivocally to what is demanded by love. It exposes the City of Wrong by pointing to the City of God. The work of Christ incarnates this ultimate dimension of protest. He is the protest of love against the unlove of mankind, and he will be in agony until the end of the world.

We have to ask then what this means for the ethical life of the Christian. Protest has to be enacted in history with the resources which human life provides. Every significant Christian ethic has sought a strategy for protest.

Augustine saw the City of God moving in history within the Church which preserves the truth in love, and represents the absolute sacrifice of Christ through the sacraments. The Church is the protest against the Kingdoms of this world. But how can there be a protest against the Church as it is? As we have seen, the Church protected itself against St. Francis's protest by enfolding his witness within the larger structure.

The Franciscan way of protest seems the most direct and sacrificial. It renounces many worldly involvements for the sake of pointing to the way of love. But we have also seen that this is done at the cost of losing direct effectiveness in the guidance, restraint, and judgment of the structures of power which shape the social order. Albert Schweitzer consistently refused political involvements and judgments, though he did join in protest against the use of nuclear weapons. Another example is the pacifist protest against war, which has been a form of Christian witness from the early days of the church. To some this has always seemed a clear case of where love requires an absolute stand against the killing and destruction of warfare. Some Christian pacifism has made its radical protest on that point alone, the refusal of military service, but more often it has appeared as the declaration of a way of life intended to express love directly, as in the Society of Friends.

Sectarian and confessional forms of protest can both be found in Protestantism. The sectarians created religious communities which at first sought detachment from worldly involvements, and tried to express the spirit of love in intimate personal communities. Sometimes they withdrew from participation in the wider communities, but they could also take the form of radical political movements as in the Diggers and Levellers in England. Most Protestant churches have made an adjustment to the structures of the general community while claiming and fighting for the freedom to witness to the Word of God, and to protest against the absolutizing of any form of power. In the Calvinist tradition this was first coupled with the attempt to create a form of theocratic society in Geneva, and then broadened out into the reformist temper of modern Christian liberalism with its effort to bring a wider democratic justice into all social relationships.

The sects and the churches both tend to become involved in the secular order, however radical and pure their initial dedication to the way of the Kingdom. Existence in history means involvement in established powers and orders. Even the most radical forms of individual protest are in some way dependent upon the existing society, for no individual exists without the structures of communal life. The revolutionary joins with a group or party which has its own structures of power with their ethical ambiguities.

While thus recognizing the pragmatic element in all protest, we must say that the witness to God's love as protest even when it is not given in absolute purity, and when its consequences may not be visible, is still an indispensable work of love in history. Socrates' protest against compromise with the truth remains a point of light in the human pilgrimage just because the same issues persist in every age. Albert Camus's interpretation of the call to the contemporary artist to 'create dangerously' is founded upon the spirit of protest made all the more convincing by Camus's recognition of the involvement of the protester in the evils which he fights:

We writers of the twentieth century shall never again be alone. Rather, we must know that we can never escape the common misery, and that our only justification, if indeed there is justification, is to speak up, insofar as we can, for those who cannot do so. But we must do so for all those who are suffering at this moment, whatever may be the glories, past or future, of the States and parties oppressing them; for the artist there are no privileged torturers.[29]

There is, finally, the work of love in the inwardness of the spirit. Protest appears in prayer, and in inner resistance when no outward remedy appears. Jesus' word, 'render unto Caesar the things that are Caesar's and unto God the things that are God's' does not give a guide to social action. As protest against all false claims upon the conscience it offers the ultimate basis for Christian ethics, and it leads to action against concrete evils.

---

29. Albert Camus, 'Create Dangerously', the Uppsala Lectures included in *Resistance, Rebellion, and Death* (New York: The Modern Library, 1960), p. 204.

(6)

LOVE AND CONFLICT; THE STRATEGY OF NON-VIOLENCE

All human life involves conflict of person with person, life with life, and will with will. If love means renunciation of conflict then it must be the 'impossible possibility' without direct political relevance. André Beaufré's study of international conflict, *An Introduction to Strategy*, is an admirable introduction to the discussion of ethics and love; for he sees strategy in politics as the means of conducting conflict. He defines strategy as 'the art of the dialectic of force, or, more precisely, the art of the dialectic of two opposing wills using force to resolve their dispute'. Force does not always mean overt violence. It includes direct threat, indirect pressure, actions combining threat and pressure, protracted conflict when resources are thin, and, finally, violent conflict aiming at military victory. Beaufré also adds logistic strategy, that is the production of new weapons to render an opponent's obsolete.[30]

Here the spirit of love meets the ultimate ethical dilemmas which have reached their most terrible form in the nuclear weapons whose destructive capacity approaches totality. The conscience informed by love must seek strategies which offer an alternative to wholesale destruction and lead to reconciliation. We have then to consider the relation of non-violent strategies to the ethical claims which arise from the love manifest in Christ.

The experiment with strategies of social change through non-violent action is an important movement in the modern history of love. Non-violent action can, of course, be undertaken without reference to love, but one characteristic of most of the non-violent ethical movements has been the conviction that this strategy is required by love and provides a way of giving love a direct expression in social conflict. Gandhi's conception of the strategy of non-violence was coupled with the doctrine of *Satyagraha*, soul force as a spiritual power, which is exercised in love against all material power.

Belief in non-violence is based on the assumption that human nature in the essence is one, and therefore unfailingly responds to the advances of love. . . .[31]

30. André Beaufré, *Introduction à la Stratégie* (Librairie Armand Colin, 1963, p. 16; American ed., Praeger, 1965).
31. This and the following quotations are from Gandhi's writings and are conveniently gathered together in an anthology edited by Louis Fischer, *The*

The word 'unfailingly' here is usually interpreted by Gandhi to mean 'ultimately'. When he recommended non-violent resistance against an invading army he said:

> The unexpected spectacle of endless rows upon rows of men and women simply dying rather than surrender to the will of an aggressor must *ultimately* melt him and his soldiery.[32]

And again:

> In the case of non-violence, everybody seems to start with the assumption that the non-violent method must be set down as a failure unless he himself at least lives to enjoy the success thereof. This is both illogical and invidious. In Satyagraha (Soul-Force) more than in armed warfare, it may be said that we find life by losing it.

And Gandhi was not dissuaded but reinforced in his position by the atomic bomb:

> The moral to be legitimately drawn from the supreme tragedy of the bomb is that it will not be destroyed by counter bombs even as violence cannot be by counter-violence. Hatred can be overcome only by love. Counter hatred only increases the surface as well as the depth of hatred.[33]

Here, then, the non-violent strategy for conflict is recommended, not only for individuals, but also for groups and nations as a direct expression of love. This strategy is a use of power which has its own tactics and leads to consequences which no other way can accomplish.

Gandhi's doctrine of non-violence was a blend of Hindu, Christian, and rational ethics. In part it was based upon the Hindu doctrine of Ahimsa, the non-injury of any living thing; but this was usually coupled with Christian motifs. The non-violent action in the salt boycott, and the lying down in front of trains in India constituted passive resistance. Gandhi sometimes made non-violence synonymous with the kind of civil disobedience he found dictated by Soul-Force. At other times he would distinguish Soul-Force from passive resistance in so far as passive resistance may be undertaken from many motives, whether it is passive or not. It could involve the will to injure the opponent which Soul-Force forbids.

The influence of Gandhi on American pacifism and the development of non-violent strategies in the civil rights movements deserves careful study. The American pacifist minister and ethical leader,

---

Essential Gandhi (New York: Vintage Books, 1963, pp. 331, 333; London: Allen & Unwin, 1963).

32. My italics. 33. *Ibid.*, p. 336.

John Haynes Holmes, preached a sermon in 1921 entitled 'Who is the Greatest Man in the World'.

> When I think of Mahatma Gandhi, I think of Jesus Christ. This Indian is a saint in personal life; he teaches the law of love and soul force as its practice; and he seeks the establishment of a new social order, which shall be a Kingdom of the Spirit.[34]

The historian of non-violence, William Robert Miller, says that the first explicit reference to non-violence in the Montgomery, Alabama, bus boycott came from a white librarian, Juliette Morgan, who compared the boycott to Gandhi's salt march in a letter to the *Montgomery Advertiser* on December 12, 1955.[35] The development of non-violent strategies in the civil rights movement of the 1950's and 60's arose partly from belief in pacifism as an expression of love in the Fellowship of Reconciliation and Society of Friends from whom many leaders of the movement for racial justice came. The strategy also developed in spontaneous reaction to a situation in some ways analogous to that of the Indian masses confronted by the British rule. There are undoubtedly influences of Gandhi's example, but these have been fused with elements derived from a wide range of American experience and from Jewish and Christian religious attitudes.

Whatever its sources, the civil rights movement has exhibited to an extraordinary degree both leadership and mass support which have been willing to seek a non-destructive strategy in which love and reconciliation are affirmed, and the suffering involved is accepted. This is not to say that love is the only spirit at work in this movement. Revolutions are never tidy. The drive for justice always has many types of emotional charge.

The development in the civil rights movement of doubts about the full effectiveness of non-violence may represent in part a yielding to emotions less disciplined by ethical considerations; but it also reflects the discovery of some complexities of effective social action. The question of the rights of self-defence for example have come to be asked more insistently.

It remains true however that the civil rights movement has written a new chapter in the possibilities of a social and political strategy which involves a commitment to a love which has elements both of humanitarian universalism and the will to reconciliation

34. I am indebted for this quotation to Dr. Carl Hermann Voss in his *Rabbi and Minister: The Friendship of Stephen S. Wise and John Haynes Holmes* (New York: World Publishing Company, 1964), p. 198.

35. William Robert Miller, *Non-Violence: A Christian Interpretation* (New York: Association Press, 1964), p. 301.

found in the biblical faith. This becomes all the more obvious when, as must happen, emotions become polarized and the depths of hatred and resentment in many quarters are disclosed as the background against which the will of love must take its stand. An account by a Protestant minister, the Reverend Andrew Juvinall, of the memorial service in Selma, Alabama held after the killing of the Reverend James Reeb is an authentic document in the history of love:

> ... this movement to procure civil rights is distinctly a religious movement, rooted in the conviction that God has 'made of one blood all the nations of mankind' and it is His will that all should stand erect in their full manhood. The movement of the Southern Christian Leadership Conference has political and economic aspects but it is most of all a profound spiritual movement. Its leaders, Martin Luther King, Ralph Abernathey, Dr. Bell, Andy Young and the others are men of Christian conviction, unquestioned integrity, courage, intelligence and a sense of responsibility. The rank and file of the people who follow them are devout Christians who know more than any other Americans what it means to be persecuted for righteousness' sake and to be imprisoned and reviled.

> In our Bible we often read such beautiful phrases as: 'Love your enemies, bless them that curse you, do good to them that hate you and pray for them that despitefully use you'. To us this may be pious poetry but to these people it is reality.

> ... these people were able to sing: 'I love everybody in my heart. . . . I love George Wallace in my heart. . . . I love Jim Clark in my heart. . . . I love the State troopers in my heart. . . .' And their leaders again and again repeat their guiding philosophy of non-violence.[36]

The justification of non-violence as a strategy usually combines the appeal to love with arguments for the effectiveness of non-violent strategies for overcoming the opponent and for opening the way to reconciliation. Non-violence means the refusal to inflict injury on an opponent, or at least to keep injury to a minimum. The problem of the boycott which may bring suffering even on the innocent must, of course, be faced, where that is recognized as a legitimate non-violent strategy. Non-violence in principle means that the opponent will not have the memory of violence done to him. It includes the possibility of direct expression of love for the enemy in personal address and in prayer. This has been a conspicuous feature of some civil rights demonstrations. The non-violent way involves the acceptance of suffering. The protester accepts the con-

36. Quoted in the *San Francisco Sunday Chronicle*, March 21, 1965.

sequences of his actions and receives injury without retaliation in kind. This means refusal to inflict injury upon the other, and submitting to the power of the state to jail and fine. Since this is undertaken willingly the suffering becomes a witness to the will for reconciliation in the midst of conflict. We should not forget the pragmatic consideration that the non-violent resistance of an unarmed populace against armed police or military authority may be the only feasible kind of protest. It is a strategy for the masses against guns which may offer the most hope of avoiding disastrous retaliation. These practical advantages should not obscure the way in which the spirit of love may inform non-violent strategies.

Agape takes many forms in history, and although we cannot infallibly judge any human action or intention as the expression of *agape*, the Gospel love of neighbour and concern for the neighbour is surely present here. Purely sociological or political interpretations of this movement will misunderstand it.

At the same time, as we examine the ethics of non-violence in the search for the work of God's love in history, we find some difficult issues concerning the place of coercion and physical force in society and politics.

We observe first that the strategies of non-violence presuppose that a certain minimal order has been achieved in society, else there may be no possibility of an effective expression of any ethical purpose. Minimal order is necessary not only to life but to love itself. Political chaos may be an impossible environment for direct strategies of love. This has been shown in the civil rights struggle. There are many forces at work, including the force of the Federal law, backed by Federal troops. The March from Selma to Montgomery had the United States Army alongside, a protection many members would have been willing to forgo, but which may have prevented violence.

It is true that law enforcement officers may be part of the structure of injustice. Policemen and sheriffs have been indicted for conspiring to deny civil rights. But society cannot exist without elements of coercive restraint which protect some from what others would do to them. That this is so may be regarded as a tragic aspect of love in this world. But if it is so, then the real difficulty in ethical doctrines based exclusively on non-violence is that they isolate love as spirit and as strategy from the full context of the situation in which it must work. If love is concern for the neighbour, it requires responsible attention to those things which are necessary for a common life in which the neighbour can be met, can live, and be restrained from violating the rights of other neighbours. This is the truth in

St. Paul's dictum, which indeed must not be interpreted too simply, that the state serves God when it wields the power of the sword (Romans 13).

A second point is that every social conflict is a contest in which each seeks to change the order of life for the other, no matter how purely the good of the other is intended. There is no political movement in which innocent people do not suffer injustice. So far Hans Morgenthau is right, that the art of politics is that of doing the least evil.[37]

This is a hard but necessary truth. There are well-intentioned people who resist all social change on the ground that some innocent people will be hurt. When the *bracero* programme for Mexican farm workers in the United States was eliminated a hardship was created for some Mexican families. Some who profited from the exploitation of farm workers expressed deep concern for those who would be put out of work. The real question, however, was clearly a humane and decent pattern of wages which will cause higher prices for food. This will make life more difficult for families living on tight food budgets. There is no way to justice except through the re-ordering of human affairs, and this is never without its cost.[38]

Third, the adoption in a loving spirit of a well-intentioned ethical strategy does not guarantee that its specific goal is righteous. When Gandhi fasted on one side of issues dividing religious groups in India, others were fasting on the opposite side. Soul force can come into conflict with soul force. The judgment of God t anscends our judgments in history.

An ethic of love has now to confront the use of atomic weapons. It is possible that the present issues for conscience over the use of nuclear weapons have no precedent in human history. The weapons seem to be those of maximum imprecision, and their use in the present state of armament practically guarantees mass destruction, and the possibility of total destruction of human life on this planet. Can there be any answer of an ethic of love to this situation other than to press for the total renunciation, unilaterally if necessary, of the use of such weapons?

We must distinguish between what love would lead us to choose in the realm of abstract possibility and what love may require us to do in the actualities of history. The absolute directive in love is to do what needs to be done to serve the growth of communion

37. Hans Morgenthau, 'The Evil of Politics and the Ethics of Evil', *Ethics*, Vol. LVI, No. 1, October 1945, p. 17.

38. Cf. Ernesto Galarza, *Merchants of Labor: The Mexican Bracero Story* (San Jose, Rosicrucian Press, 1964).

between man and man and between man and God. Even if unilateral disarmament by one nation were a genuine possibility, which is doubtful, we have to ask what its consequences would be. We cannot know it would prevent atomic destruction, so long as any nation possesses the weapons.

There is not a final contradiction here between what love requires and what we accept as political necessities so long as we recognize that the threat of nuclear destruction may help to restrain nations from all out war long enough to allow the growth of a minimal world order under law which can bring the weaponry under control.

This position does not require us to show that a nuclear stalemate can be permanently held, though we seem to have something like it at mid-century. We can see that the course of world history might have been far more terrible and destructive in the twenty years after World War II had the bomb not been in existence. There is sufficient threat of total destruction that no one can have any assurance of surviving a nuclear war.

An ethic of love will always allow for alternative political decisions. Love does not tell us what to do. It is the spirit which calls us to a responsible concern for all of life and the search for a wider, more adequate human community. Some will hold that violent resistance cannot serve that end, but that, too, is a judgment about conditions and consequences; it is not one which follows automatically from the nature of love. The spirit of love seeks communion with every other life. We are called to discover what will serve that end. Love alone does not tell us what that may be, and it does not give us freedom from the dialectic of force in human affairs.

This assessment of the ethical problem requires the imaginative search for possible new strategies. How can the love which gives loyalty to the Kingdom of God find rootage and power in this world?

(8)

LOVE AND NURTURE

Because the spirit of *agape* transcends group loyalties without renouncing them, the question of the nurture of the personal life and its love becomes a critical one for Christian ethics. There is no educational technique for producing loving concern, yet the forms of group life are the vital context of the nurture which is necessary to love.

There are two primary candidates for the role of providing the group life in which love may grow. One is the family and other intimate personal friendships where we have the depth of direct personal relationship. These are communities in which the I-Thou relationship is a possibility. The other is the community which has God's *agape* as its own ground, the Church.

Every Christian ethic will show especial concern for the freedom of the churches to worship and witness to the faith. These are the nurturing groups in which man can realize freedom to know God and his neighbour in the spirit of love. But we must make two qualifications of this high estimate of the place of family and church in the history of love.

The first is that the quality of life in families and churches is in part a function of the public order in which they exist. Love in family and church is in part shaped by the social structure. Family love and fellowship in the church are conditioned by the attitudes, privileges, and spirit of a society and its classes. For example, attitudes of racial exclusiveness can be fostered both in family and by segregation in the church. Thus *agape* is twisted into a sentimentality or an illusion. A minister who has preached on Christian love for twenty years in a white congregation and then finds resistance even to the admission to the church of a member of another race experiences this hard fact.

Second, there is the possibility that the primary groups will become merely self-protective and exclusively self-centred. This can happen in the exclusiveness of one form of Christianity and in the absolutizing of one form of religion. The security of belonging within a familiar community is so great that it can create anxiety about anything which calls for assuming the risks of a larger experience. As Kenneth Boulding says, 'One of the great obstacles towards the realization of the human identity is the fear that taking on the human identity will destroy our other identities'.[39]

Distortions of *agape* are often reinforced by appeals to love which exploit the group spirit. The Nazis used the word from John's Gospel, 'Greater love hath no man than this, that he lay down his life for his friends'. It is a tragic fact that love's counterfeits, caricatures, and even its authentic symbols may become the tools of unlove. Every doctrine of the church must recognize that the community founded on *agape* may betray it.

In a study of anti-Semitism in Christian tradition Father Edward J. Flannery has traced a sorry history:

39. Kenneth Boulding and Henry Clark, *Human Values on the Space-ship Earth*, National Council of the Churches of Christ, U.S.A. (1966), p. 19.

The chronicler of anti-Semitism is beset at every turn with the problem of superlatives. Long before reaching the contemporary scene he has exhausted his supply . . . the problem is not only verbal but real. From the first literary strictures against Judaism in ancient and early Christian times to almost any major manifestation of anti-Jewish animus in a later epoch, a crescendo in violence has unfolded, each grade of which has promised to be the upper limit but which unfailingly paled before what followed.

He makes clear that the incredible rationalizations and justifications of anti-Semitism which have been offered have been perversions of the very *agape* which Christ incarnates:

The sin . . . is many things . . . in the end it is a denial of the Christian faith, a failure of Christian hope, and a malady of Christian love.[40]

Since there are no certain remedies for the maladies of love, every doctrine must include the theme of repentance in the knowledge of *agape*. One of the marks of the presence of the Holy Spirit is the acknowledgement by fallible men that the pure love of God cannot be claimed for any human community, even the Church.

At the same time the Church is that community which believes that its life can be renewed by a fresh grasp of the meaning of love. The present ecumenical movement, and here we include the meeting of Christians and Jews, and the meeting of the Christian community with other religious communities, has an authentic element of charity within it. The history of the ecumenical movement is unintelligible without the recognition of love moving among the divisions of Christendom, and sustaining men in working through centuries old divisions. A commentator on the Pontificate of John XXIII says, 'The warm love of his spirit melted and broke through this hardness, this crust, revealed tenderly the substance of our inheritance in the saints of God'. The author of this statement says that both Roncalli and Montini followed Cardinal Bea in adopting this theme of truth in love as the foundation of a new ecclesiastical attitude. Truth in love means:

'Truth is one, but men seek it in different ways depending upon their background, education and environment; the only reasonable way for any modern man to act when faced with this pluralism of ethical and moral thinking is to seek to know the truth held by the other person, but with love and respect and openness.'[41]

---

40. Edward J. Flannery, *The Anguish of the Jews:* Twenty-three centuries of anti-semitism (New York: Macmillan, 1965), pp. 205–7.

41. Michael Serafian, *The Pilgrim* (New York: Farrar & Strauss, 1964, pp. 104–5, 95; London: Michael Joseph, 1964).

The struggle for justice in a blood-stained history is one of the ways in which love does its work. The Church is not the only group in which man is moved by *agape* and seeks its leading; but it is the one community which in accepting *agape* as the meaning of its existence places itself squarely under the judgment of the love which seeks one redeemed humanity in the Kingdom of God.

CHAPTER XIII

LOVE AND THE INTELLECT

The intellect is a cleaver; it discerns and rifts its way into the secret of things.
—Henry David Thoreau.

The greater our knowledge of anything, the more we love it.
—Leonardo Da Vinci.

We come at the close of our inquiry to an ancient and persistent question in Christian theology and in philosophy—the relation of love to the intellect. We have been seeking an interpretation of the meaning of love in the Christian faith. We have reflected on the biblical witness, the traditions of Christian thought, and the philosophical search for categories with which to talk about the world we experience. When we talk about love we feel a certain restlessness about formal concepts and logical analysis. If love can only be known through love itself, is not all intellectual analysis bound to fail? There are two sources of tension about this problem; the first comes from within theology, because faith transcends in some way the rational categories. The other arises in our culture, with its split between the drive toward scientific rationality and its existential sense of the meaning in experience expressed in myth and symbol. We need to examine these two aspects of the relation of intellect to love.

The Christian interpretation of the intellectual life has always shown a profound inner tension between two aspects of the truth which God has given in Jesus Christ. On one side there is the mystery of God himself and the supreme mystery of his self-revelation. God is known through his acts in which he discloses his power, his purpose, and his gracious intent. He is not reached at the end of an intellectual exploration. The truth of his mercy, in which he takes our sin upon himself, is not only beyond all rational expectation but beyond all human understanding. The Gospel is foolishness or scandal to all who approach it with anything other than the categories which the Gospel itself provides. Therefore the view that the Gospel is above reason has been one of the persistent assertions of Christian thought. In our day Karl Barth's theology represents in the extreme form the position that the interpretation of the faith must arise within the revelation which God himself has given. It is not against reason, but it does not arise from reason, nor can it be subjected to the canons of human tests of truth. On this theme that the Christian faith is not another philosophy which can be grasped from within the general criteria of rational understanding there has been a consistent if not complete agreement in theology.

There is, however, another side to the Christian view of the claim of reason. The Christian faith has been able to cope with the development of human thought through the centuries because it has held that the mind belongs to the image of God in man, and has its rightful place in the interpretation of the truth of the faith. The first great commandment includes the injunction to love God with the whole mind (Luke 10: 27). Every Greek who heard the word *Logos* which the author of the Fourth Gospel used when he spoke of Christ as the *Logos* who became flesh, would understand this word, whatever its other connotations, to mean the eternal and intelligible order of things. The *Logos* is the truth which the mind seeks when it tries to understand the principles which govern the life of the world. One important implication of faith in the trustworthiness of God is this ultimate unity of truth. The Christians affirmed that this unity is manifest in Christ. 'In him all things cohere', says the letter to the Colossians (1: 17). The apostle Paul has a profound sense of the mystery of the Gospel beyond all human reason, yet he protests against obscurantism. 'Whatsoever things are true, lovely, and of good report, think on these things' (Philippians 4: 8). Karl Barth says that Christianity should not associate itself with the irrationalist tendencies which characterize some forms of modern culture.[1] We see within Christian theology an internal restlessness which allows neither total rejection nor total acceptance of a purely rationalistic approach to truth. What is the relation of the love disclosed in the Gospel which has its reflection in all human love to the life of the intellect? Every interpretation of love brings us back to this question.

A discussion in secular terms of the relation of love and mind pervades contemporary culture in this 'age of analysis', as Morton White has called it. The intellect has triumphed in the form of scientific knowledge and technological skill. It has not only transformed man's relationship to nature and his understanding of the world, but also it has altered man's self-understanding. He conceives nature itself and his relationship to nature in new ways through the power which is now in his hands.

It is a paradox that our time which has seen such scientific conquests as mathematical logic penetrates the structure of the atom and the cosmos, at the same time seeks reality through the absurd,

1. Karl Barth, *Church Dogmatics*, I/1 Sec. 1, 3; Sec. 7, 2.

the irrational, and the form-breaking capacities of symbolic expression. The visual and dramatic arts have plumbed the realm of the Absurd, the Paradoxical, and the Creativity of Dissonance.[2]

While this juxtaposition of logic and the irrational is indeed a paradox, the two movements are connected. Man, the microcosm, unites diverse aspects of being. When the rational side of his nature grows strong and tends to rule, something within him moves in the contrary direction. Thus our age produces the rationalistic evolutionary philosophy of a Teilhard de Chardin, who interprets the course of the universe as a steady movement toward perfection. It also produces the despairing stoicism of Bertrand Russell's *A Free Man's Worship*, in which man defies without ultimate hope the trampling march of unconscious power.[3] George Orwell's prediction of the devastation of a rationalized society in which man succumbs to an inhuman tyranny is countered by the contented, unheroic, and satisfied human existence of B. F. Skinner's *Walden II*.[4]

Thus the issue concerning the relation of intellectual understanding to the guidance of human life is posed at the centre of twentieth-century culture. Science has increased immeasurably man's knowledge of his environment, and of the incredible capacities and pathologies of the human organism. The question is whether man needs and has another mode of self-knowledge. The existentialist movement has tried to point to the limitations of scientific and rational understanding. The revolt of the existentialists has not been anti-intellectual, nor anti-scientific. It has sought to transcend science through reflecting upon the concreteness of experience. This concreteness includes the freedom, decisions, emotional tonality and all the distinctive structures of human consciousness including the irrational elements which may be expressible only in symbols which defy purely rational explication. John Wild has contrasted this way of understanding with that of objective reason in his analysis of the 'life-world' (*Lebenswelt*) disclosed in man's subjectivity.[5]

2. Edward F. Rothschild, *The Meaning of Unintelligibility in Modern Art* (Chicago: University of Chicago Press, 1934).

3. Teilhard de Chardin, *The Phenomenon of Man* (New York: Harper & Row, 1959; London: William Collins Sons & Co. Ltd., 1961). Bertrand Russell, 'A Free Man's Worship', in *Mysticism and Logic* (London: Allen & Unwin, 1917; New York: W. W. Norton, 1929).

4. George Orwell, *1984* (London: Martin Secker & Warburg Ltd., 1949; New York: Harcourt Brace, 1949). B. F. Skinner, *Walden II* (New York: Macmillan, 1948).

5. John Wild, 'Devotion and Fanaticism', in *Process and Divinity*, edited by Reese and Freeman (Open Court: La Salle, Illinois, 1964).

When the relation of love to the intellect is an issue of such perplexity, the vocation of the intellectual becomes a question which gives rise to much dispute. Intellectuals have sometimes accused themselves of treason to humanity for failing to recognize and oppose the dehumanization of modern political and technological life.[6] Anti-intellectualistic tendencies lurk within most contemporary life and they have especially deep roots in some phases of American culture.[7] At the same time we are putting the greatest pressure ever known in human history upon the new generation to demonstrate intellectual capacity, master the technologies, and compete in a world where knowledge has become power in a frighteningly obvious way.

One thesis is that the intellect needs love and that love needs intellectual understanding. Without a right appraisal of this relationship love loses its integrity of aim and its balance, and intellectuality becomes self-destructive.

(1)

Faith, Love, and Reason in the Christian Perspective

Each of the types of interpretation of Christian love has a theory of the role of intellectual powers in the life of faith and love. Augustinian, Franciscan, and Reformation theologies all come to a settlement with the place of the intellect, and they all leave many issues for Christian culture. A contemporary interpretation will owe something to each of these traditions. The view taken here is fundamentally Augustinian, but it qualifies St. Augustine because he fails to do justice to the power, openness and tentativeness of empirical reason. To that insight both Franciscan and Reformation theologies have contributed, but I shall argue that there are decisive aspects of man's rationality which we owe especially to modern science. Theology must incorporate into its doctrine of reason the truth which God has made known through the scientific movement, sometimes against the opposition of church and theologians. The 'History of the Warfare of Science with Theology' is not simply a matter of the exposure of antiquated religious notions.[8] The more important point is that

6. Archibald Macleish, *A Time to Speak* (Boston: Houghton Mifflin, 1941).
7. Richard Hofstadter, *Anti-intellectualism in American Life* (New York: Knopf, 1963; London: Jonathan Cape, 1964).
8. The phrase is taken of course from Andrew D. White's classic *The History of the Warfare of Science with Theology* (New York: Appleton, 1914; London: Dover: Constable).

the scientific movement, which arose partly through biblical and theological insights, has had to oppose theology for the sake of a sounder view of reason and more adequate methods of getting truth.[9] In order to justify this view we need to consider again where Augustine leaves the relation of reason and love.

The essence of St. Augustine's understanding of the relation of love to the intellect is that the intellect seeks the same object as love, that is, God's being and his truth, but that the intellect can do its proper work only when it is oriented within the life of love. For St. Augustine this means that it is through *agape* with its consequent repentance, humility, and understanding of human limits that the intellect receives its foundation, direction, and fulfilment.

Augustine has a profound respect for the values of intellect in the sciences, in logic, and in philosophy. He continually appeals to the elements of rational structure in the mind and in the world to refute the sceptics. But he holds that the mind can recognize the reality of God only when it is oriented in the right direction, and this means that disoriented man with his misdirected love must be turned about. It is grace, the infusion of the divine spirit given through Jesus Christ, which accomplishes this. Augustine agrees with the platonists that knowledge of the truth requires a re-orientation of the intellect through the discipline of the self, and a transformation of the spirit guided by love. Where he differs with them is that he takes his understanding of love from the Gospel of the incarnation, the grace of God given in Christ, rather than from the *eros* of aspiration toward the good, the true, and the beautiful, though he regards that *eros* as itself a reflection of man's origin in love.

Augustine gives us his great formula: 'Faith seeking understanding.'[10] Faith means not primarily belief in dogma, though it includes such belief, but it is the self's acceptance of the grace of God, its trust and self-giving in dependence upon God. Augustine estimates highly the rational understanding of which faithful reason is capable. He finds in the mind and its ways of knowing, analogies of the Holy Trinity, the very being of God. God is being itself. He is truth, goodness, and beauty. The mind, therefore, moves toward Him as it grasps the structures of the world. Thus the sciences and other intellectual disciplines can glorify God and articulate the pattern of his handiwork. For Augustine confidence in reason is not misplaced when it is faithful reason. The ontological argument which finds the

9. Alfred North Whitehead, *Science and the Modern World*, chapter 1.

10. Augustine, Sermo (de Script. Nov. Test) CXXVI, i, i, ii, 3. On Augustine's anticipation of the ontological argument see De. lib. Arb. II, xv.

truth of God's existence in the very structure of the rational concept of God expresses the Augustinian confidence in the mind's participation in the divine truth. It is in Augustine's thought that the ontological argument to which St. Anselm later gave logical expression has its source.

Augustine is acutely aware of the limits to the mind's power to understand God. 'That which thou understandest is not God.'[11] The mind must acknowledge its finitude, and there is always more to be known. Charles N. Cochrane has said that Christianity's greatest contribution to classical culture was its sense of the depths of personal experience which cannot be reduced to the general definitions of truth and justice by which classical culture tried to live.[12]

Christianity contributed its faith in the rational but inexhaustible logos, the source of a creative and dependable order, to western civilization. Whitehead regards this Christian foundation as an indispensable element in the rise of scientific method. Yet the Christian interpretation of the work of reason fell short and had to undergo a drastic purging in the course of modern thought. The reasons why this is so should not be over-simplified, but a major failure was the inability to see the significance of the method of empirical inquiry. There were other factors at work. Faith was closely identified with belief in dogma, and the metaphysical framework of dogma had incorporated a prescientific world view. Moreover, there were inadequacies in all ancient conceptions of the relation of experience to knowledge. There are problems in the nature of scientific theory and in the relation of fact and theory in which St. Augustine is not interested, and for which Aristotle himself had inadequate tools of understanding. It took centuries for the logic of scientific discovery to display its full complexity, and the interpretation of scientific theoretical development still goes on as Thomas Kuhn has shown in his *The Structure of Scientific Revolutions*.[13]

What our time can learn from the Augustinian tradition is that the intellect in all its operations belongs in the service of love, and that intellectuality without *agape* loses its source of hope and its full power to learn about the world. The intellect has its own *eros*, the drive to know. St. Augustine recognizes and accepts this *eros*,

11. Augustine, Serm. (de Script. N. T.), LII, vi, 16.
12. C. N. Cochrane, *Christianity and Classical Culture* (New York: Oxford University Press, 1944).
13. Thomas S. Kuhn, *The Structure of Scientific Revolutions* (Chicago: University of Chicago Press, 1962).

but like all other *eros*, it falls into either despair or self-worship without the illumination and redirection of *agape*. We need, then, an Augustinian interpretation of the intellectual life, but one which has undergone the discipline of the scientific way of relating fact and theory in a continuing responsible inquiry. Let us see where such a revised Augustinianism would lead.

(2)

THE NATURE OF MIND

Love has a history and so also does intellectuality. Many treatments of the nature of mind are vitiated by the assumption that the intellectual function remains identical in every culture. Intellectuality in religion is often identified with its Greek expression. Since Greek philosophers thought of God as the pure idea which is the goal of intellectual reflection, this, it is concluded, must be the goal of every rational attempt to understand God. I have put the point crudely, but it is astonishing how many modern theologians have accepted some such argument as final.

Two familiar arguments put intellect in opposition to love. While these rarely lead to an outright rejection of reason in religion, they give it a precarious and suspect place.

The first is that the intellect destroys, or at least depersonalizes, by analysis. 'We murder to dissect' (Wordsworth). Analysis is appropriate in the search for scientific knowledge, but it misses the concrete reality of personal experience. The intellect makes impersonal concepts out of everything it touches. Hence reason must be sharply curbed as a way to personal meaning and in the expression of faith. Emil Brunner, for example, based his entire theological construction on the premise that reason always seeks impersonal structures.[14]

The second argument is that the intellect is essentially self-centred and power-hungry. Reason tries to bring the whole of things into its own sphere and to master it. Hegel's grandiose system with its claim to exhibit the absolute philosophy as the truth of Christianity is often adduced to show this self-worshipping tendency in rational thought.[15]

A qualified but similar view of mind is found in Father M. C.

14. Cf. D. D. Williams, 'Brunner and Barth on Philosophy', *The Journal of Religion*, Vol. XXVII, No. 4, October 1947.
15. Reinhold Niebuhr, *The Nature and Destiny of Man*, Vol. I, pp. 116–18.

D'Arcy's *The Mind and Heart of Love*, which we have already discussed.[16] We can recall its main points. D'Arcy distinguishes between two 'loves', power-minded, grasping, self-assertive love and sacrificial, self-giving, heedless love. The first is identified as masculine and intellectual. It is the human analogue of *eros*. The second is feminine and intuitive, the analogue of *agape*. D'Arcy wants to keep the constructive aspects of both loves together in the Christian person. Neither can nor should be abandoned. Reason must be united with self-giving. '*Eros* and *Agape* are friends.' This doctrine thus puts reason in a certain ineluctable tension with *agape*. Reason is essentially self-centred, self-fulfilling, and in tension with the sacrificial spirit of *agape*.

The view that love transcends reason and that therefore faith must go beyond reason is indeed characteristic of Christian thought. D'Arcy's theory gives one version of this final judgment upon reason, its limitation in trying to grasp the full truth of love.

I suggest, however, that there is an important issue raised in this doctrine that reason is *essentially* grasping, imperious and self-assertive. For if this be so, love as *agape* must not only transcend reason but also in some sense contradict it, for the spirit of *agape* is never imperious and self-assertive. If D'Arcy's view is correct there is nothing in reason which prepares the way for *agape*, or in any way leads the person toward it. This is a plausible position, and D'Arcy gives it a penetrating anthropological and psychological foundation. But attractive as it is, it leads to that anti-intellectualism which has supported the obscurantist elements in theology and religion, an outcome which D'Arcy certainly does not want. It leaves human culture hopelessly split between authentic understanding and faith informed by love.

I propose as an alternative to D'Arcy's view the doctrine that reason in man is something other than the imperious will to control. It should be noticed that we are seeking the essential structure of reason in the midst of its distortions. There is no doubt that reason, under the conditions of man's finitude and estrangement, is subject to every corruption with which it has been charged. It is quite possible that there is a pride of intellect which has a peculiarly strong hold upon anxious man and that the philosophical tradition may give some flagrant examples of it. One thinks of Immanuel Kant's title of his book: *A Prolegomenon to Every Future Metaphysic*. Here the reasoner claims to shape the entire future thought of mankind.

But it is men who are prideful, not reason. The question is whether

16. Supra, chapter 4.

reason, man's intellectual capacity, necessarily and essentially betrays the spirit of love. Here a reflection upon modern philosophy and science can help us, for at the heart of science there has been reason's discovery of its context and its limitations. In following this clue to the nature of reason we owe most to Albert North Whitehead and process philosophy. Our view differs sharply from many traditional interpretations. It is not a deification of reason, quite the contrary; but it interprets the nature of intellect by considering the self-criticism which has been the essence of the scientific spirit.

First, we must specify what we mean by reason and intellect. We are talking about a specific function of the human psycho-physical organism. It is the function which conceives, analyses and relates the structures of anything in existence or in imagination. We may use the term 'intellect' in a somewhat narrower sense than reason. Intellection specifies the abstraction and conceptualizing function considered in relative independence of emotion or intuition, whereas reason may be used more generally for the entire concrete process of reflection, imagination, and interpretation. There are subconscious processes, intuitive perceptions, flashes of insight, all of which belong to the reason; whereas intellection is the recognition and construction of concepts.

We shall use reason as the more inclusive term, recognizing that it always has an aspect of intellection. All reasoning takes place in personal histories which involve drives, impulses, emotions, and other factors which are more than 'rational', however rationally they may be conceived and criticized. This doctrine of the unity of the person in which reason is a function within the total organism and its goal and needs is a characteristic theme of much modern philosophy. Pragmatism, existentialism and modern idealism have all tried to understand reason in its fully personal context. The process philosophers such as Bergson and Whitehead have given special attention to the implications of this view for understanding man and his philosophies. The reasoner has valuations, desires, purposes and emotions. The injunction to 'listen to reason' must reckon with the fact that reason is never effective by itself. We become reasonable by exercising personal restraint, refusing to jump to conclusions, confessing and re-examining our prejudices, and getting over our defensiveness. Thus the reason will be informed by the loves of the reasoner, and distorted by the corruption of his loves. The ideological taint is the distortion of reason through a deficiency in the courage and valuations of the person. James Luther Adams has put the matter poetically and concisely:

CURIOUSLY ENOUGH

The world has many educated people
who know how to reason,
and they reason very well;
but, curiously enough,
many of them fail
to examine the pre-established premises
from which they reason,
premises that turn out to be
anti-social,
protective camouflages
of power.
Where a man's treasure is,
there will his heart be also.
And where his heart is,
there will be his reason
and his premises.[17]

A second important doctrine concerning reason concerns the use of symbols in grasping abstract aspects of meaning. The topic of symbolism is a large one, and the relation of reason and language has complexities which need not detain us here. But it is necessary to analyse the abstracting process, for it is here that much of the trouble lies in the traditional conception of reason.

In Whitehead's doctrine all realities from God to atoms have abstract aspects, but they are more than abstractions. Actuality exhibits the creative movement of entities which synthesize past concreteness and future possibilities in new events of realization. Abstract patterns are exhibited in all events. If this were not so there would be no rational intelligibility. The primordial nature of God is the abstract order of all possibilities and values. But God is not abstract order alone. He is concrete personal activity. Every creature participates in the formal structure of things, but no creature is only a form.

Clearly reason must deal with the abstract aspects of things as it seeks comprehension of relations and structures. To reason is to try to see what things are and how they go together, and this means that nothing can be experienced in its full concreteness by intellect alone. If I try to understand the beauty and meaning of Webern's music, I cannot succeed merely by listening to it over and over. Understanding requires reflection upon what I have heard, and that means attention to structural aspects of what is there. That means to derive abstractions from the full concreteness. To be sure, I

17. *The Protestant*, October, 1943.

experience the aesthetic concreteness as I reason about it, and reason itself can show that the abstract patterns are less than the full reality.

Whitehead's view of reason thus inverts the platonic tradition. Plato saw that reason seeks pure structure, abstracted from the flux of things; but Plato identifies that pure structure with being itself. Consequently, for Plato, reason gets nearer the truth the further it gets from time, change, and passage. But Whitehead denies that the structure itself is pure being; the structure is the abstract aspect of pure being. Real being is concrete feeling-events.

This doctrine that the structures which reason abstracts are set in the concreteness of process is a discovery which reasoning has helped to make, and to which modern science and philosophy have contributed. The movement of modern thought has been toward recognition of the tentativeness of all formulations of reason, and the incompleteness and revisability of all scientific theory. The equating of reality with rationally intelligible pattern can, of course, still be done but it goes against the evidence. We conclude then that one common criticism of intellectuality is based on a misunderstanding. This is the criticism that the intellect 'abstracts' from reality and therefore falsifies it. Certainly the intellect abstracts, that is its business. The error lies not in abstracting, but in mistaking the abstractions for the concreteness of reality.

The implication of this discussion for the meaning of love is clear. When the intellect motivated by love seeks concrete knowledge and relationship to the other, this does not exclude abstraction, but it holds abstractions in the service of love and sees them in relation to the reality in which they are embedded.[18]

A further consequence of these first two characterizations of reason is that reason does its proper work not when it is self-assertive and domineering, but when it submits its judgments to the continuing revision of experience, and the continuing criticism of further reflection. True rationality recognizes its limits. Reason achieves dependable knowledge of the structure of things when it is held subordinate to the view that the structure is not the whole reality but an abstracted aspect of reality. We recognize through the work of reason that there is nothing, not even the pure structures

18. The difference between Whitehead's view and Bergson's is important here. Bergson holds that the intellect falsifies, but he never integrated this doctrine with his attempt to construct a metaphysics based on 'new and fluid concepts'. Whitehead avoids Bergson's dilemma of trying to conceive the inconceivable by affirming the primordial structure in God without denying the concrete process which exhibits the structure. See Henri Bergson, *Introduction to Metaphysics* (New York: G. P. Putnam's Sons, 1912; London: H. Jonas & Co.), and A. N. Whitehead, *Process and Reality*, p. 319.

of logic, which can be fully understood through reason alone. Gödel's theorem seems to have at least this consequence for all attempts to complete the rational foundations of logic.[19] If this be true for the abstract and formal structures of logic, then it is clearly true for the understanding of the richness and complexity of concrete experience.

There is a further implication. Reason is likely to be most competent when the reasoner is most deeply aware of his bias and his temptation to rationalization. The discovery of bias is both a personal and a rational discovery and its confession is one of the marks of a disciplined intellect.

These assertions about the nature and function of reason do not rest upon purely rational discoveries. Neither are they the discoveries of pure love. Most of them have been forced upon us by tragic experience, the stubborn insistence of facts, and the determination of inquirers to look at the facts. They have come in part through the freeing of the mind from institutional dogmatisms, so that the depths and antinomies of reason can be explored, and we discover in how many different ways we can think about the world when the mind is free. As Henry Nelson Wieman has continually insisted, it is the work of God and not of men which opens up new possibilities, reveals new structures, and discloses riches of reality beyond our present knowledge.[20] This discovery of the place of reason in personal existence means a new situation in man's search for knowledge of himself, and for the meaning of love in human experience. A new assessment of the nature of personal knowledge is possible as we come to the relation of loving and knowing.

(3)

LOVING AND KNOWING

Whatever opens the person to the richness of the world beyond himself, whatever encourages the mind to give itself to the search for what is there to be known, whatever releases the person from defensiveness about his present structure of thought, and whatever

19. Cf. Ernest Nagel and James R. Newman, *Gödel's Proof*, in *The World of Mathematics*, ed. by James R. Newman (New York: Simon & Schuster, 1956, pp. 1668–95; London: Allen & Unwin, 1960. *Gödel's Proof* publ. sep. London, 1959, Routledge & Kegan Paul).

20. Henry Nelson Wieman, *The Source of Human Good* (Chicago: University of Chicago Press, 1946).

overcomes distraction and triviality in the search for truth, contributes to the work of reason. And here surely we are not far from a definition of love. It will be recalled that the categorial analysis of love stresses the freedom to enter into relation with the other, and to set the other free to be himself. Love means willingness to participate in the being of the other at the cost of suffering, and with the expectation of mutual enrichment, criticism and growth. Love gives to the search for knowledge the indispensable personal context and spirit in which reason can work successfully and bring knowledge into the service of the fulfilment of personal being. Reason needs the spirit and impetus of love to realize itself and to become the servant of the Kingdom of God.

Whatever gives the person a motive for searching, for continuing the struggle for knowledge, for enduring the pain of creativity in the realm of ideas will be a service to reason. It is love, human and divine, which is the source of valuation. It is love which restrains present desire in the service of ultimate realization and the will to serve the other in his need. The ills of intellectuality, I am arguing, are not traceable to the function of conceptualizing in itself. That function is as natural, necessary, and constructive as any other human function. The ills of the intellect are in its triviality, its detachment from vital concern, the obfuscation of reality behind the symbols and the concepts, and its turning away from significant issues to meaningless dispute. And they are also in fanaticism, the refusal to yield a point in the face of evidence, the deification of the system against the reality, the rationalizations of idolatry. But these all have their roots in the self—not in intellect alone.

Disorder in the self and its loves is reflected in the disorder in reason. That disorder may take many forms, and it may not be apparent in much of the work of reason what sort of personal life it reflects. But the life of mind is not detached from the self and its loves, and it needs the power of ordered love.

We must not overstate the case here. Like other parts of man's natural equipment, intellectuality is unpredictable in its appearance, and often eccentric in its expression. The best reasoners are rarely models of integrated personality. Often intellectual brilliance seems to involve considerable personal struggle and even disorder. Like artistic creativity, it may feed on the sensitivity derived from suffering, and whatever love is present may appear more chaotic than orderly. Love does not depend upon the full integration of the personality. Since love is learned in part through suffering, there are those who are torn by inward struggle or crushed by the weight of concern for others who know the hunger for love and its compassion more deeply than some well balanced and conventionally reasonable souls.

Our argument so far is that reason has its fulfilment when it is set within a non-defensive search for truth. The self learns that it can have the truth only through being open to self-corruption, and allowing the object of knowledge to 'be itself'. The reasoning person wants to grasp reality. The mind wants to understand, to see, and to order its knowledge. It may even desire to achieve 'the world as Idea', to use Schopenhauer's phrase. But the description of this as the imperious will to dominate misses the essential character of successful mind. The claim to absolute possession of truth, to reduce the world to idea and pure form, obscures the mind's real destiny. It is the essence of rationality that mind respects the givens of experience, and does not permit the self to dictate reason's results for the self's gratification. To take the results of reason's distortion through sin, and to identify this with the nature of reason, is an error similar to identifying the essence of man with his distorted loves.

It may be said that the qualities of respect for the object and willingness to undergo self-correction are not the same thing as love, so that we have yet to establish a relationship between love and reason. It would certainly be too much to claim that these qualities are identical with love. But they are inseparable from it. They are among the qualities which we have found in the categorial structure of love. We can put the matter this way: the elements which contribute to the successful functioning of reason are those which are nourished by the growth of the power to love. We are dealing, of course, with the growth of the person, and with love's ultimate contribution to reason. The significance of the context in which man reasons is never disclosed all at once.

Our general characterization of reason has been based upon the function of reason in science, in common sense, and in any systematic reflection which involves concepts and symbols. We have so far made no special appeal to the function of reason in knowledge of other persons. This has been deliberate. There is a considerable body of theological and religious thought which has sought to establish the uniqueness of personal knowledge in the I-Thou relationship, and which treats this kind of knowledge as if it obeyed a quite different set of rules from the knowledge of objects. Those who hold this view usually see the relation of reason and love exclusively in the special realm of knowledge of persons.

I believe this doctrine of the 'I-Thou' school to be a misleading exaggeration of a truth. It distorts the way we come to know other persons. In the categoreal analysis of love we have shown that knowledge of other persons involves the capacity to see the other objectively, and that means to recognize the structured relationships in which the person lives. Reason is not set aside in the knowledge of the loved person. It is released, motivated and disciplined to become a more objective, courageous and creative reason. It should not lose its concern with clear concepts derived from the objective order of things, but it needs to bring this into the service of the personal relationship. It recognizes structures of thought for the abstractions they are. It does not allow the other person to become only an object or a type; but it continues to seek that costly objectivity which requires transformation of the self for the sake of the relationship to the other in the truth.

The so-called 'I-Thou' knowledge is therefore not absolutely different from 'I-It' knowledge. Both have their place in the process of knowing other persons, and both are necessary to serve the purpose of love, that is the opening of the way to communion. It is curious how the analysts of the I-Thou experience forget how much of human growth in mutual understanding comes not from attention solely to the other, but from sharing a mutual quest for objective knowledge or participation in a common interest. A friendship which was nothing but an I-Thou confrontation could be a very dull affair.[21]

Yet with this necessary qualification we can still agree with the personalism of the dialogical philosophy that there is something in knowledge of other persons which differs from other knowledge, and that in this knowledge love plays a special role.

Notice first, that all the requirements which have been stressed for any kind of knowledge are present and heightened in knowing other persons. There is the requirement of openness to the other's being in his freedom, and the refusal to dominate or control the other to satisfy some preconceived plan in our own imagination. There is the requirement of the break with self-centredness which is a precondition of a genuine knowledge of the other.

Love for another person opens the way to a kind of knowledge which can never be given without it. This is true because love becomes a new discernment of the other in which there occurs insight

21. The classic statement of the dialogical philosophy is of course Martin Buber's *I and Thou*, 2nd edition (New York: Charles Scribner's Sons, 1958; Edinburgh: T. & T. Clark). In my criticism I am agreeing with Ronald Hepburn in his *Christianity and Paradox* (London: Watts, 1958), chaps. 3–4, that the case for knowledge of God is weak if it is founded on unique claims to knowledge in the I-Thou relationship.

and communication otherwise lacking. The familiar saying, 'love is blind', is a half truth stressing one side of love's knowledge. But it really means, or ought to mean, that love sees *more* clearly. Love is light, insight, and understanding. It reaches the other's being and yields an awareness otherwise impossible.

It is equally important that to love another is to discover oneself. The experience of teaching offers continued confirmation of this. The student who discovers that he loves mathematics, abstract painting, or the study of history discovers something about himself. He comes to know who he is through the loves which grow within him.

Certainly the emotions of hatred, dislike, and offence may also contribute to self-discovery. Personal growth involves every kind of experience. But love is not one emotion among others. It is the whole person's growth in power to enter into community. It is his will to belong. Without love any emotion becomes self-destructive, and leads the intellect to a dead end. Love does not solve every problem; but without growth in love and in the capacity to receive love, the kind of knowledge of the world and of other persons which requires objectivity, dependability, and insight does not come. The evidence for the contribution of love to understanding from the realms of psychotherapy, education, aesthetic creativity, and the social sciences is overwhelming and need not be detailed here. Martin Buber is quite right that it is a sign of sin when we make other persons into objects to be used, and use reason to turn personal reality into impersonal structures which we absolutize as the truth. Without love the mind becomes the weapon of sophisticated violence. The love of wisdom becomes self-serving pride. Tradition becomes frozen dogma and descends into triviality and dishonesty. Scientific research into human problems becomes a wasteland of abstractions which never reach the human, or science may serve a demonic and inhuman evil as in the Nazi medical experiments. The intellect can serve love only when it is given its power and direction by love. This truth rests on no theological special-pleading, but on the evidence of human experience.

Much is rightly made in some philosophies of knowledge of the role of dramatic imagination in presenting the truth which relates subject to subject. It is entirely in accord with the theory of reason here presented to stress the creative synthesis of imaginative vision as the supreme way in which understanding of personal existence can be expressed. It is significant that two of the greatest philosophers of the twentieth century who approached the problem of knowledge from very different perspectives, Heidegger and Whitehead, both came to the conclusion that it is in poetry rather than in the formal concepts of philosophy that the truth of existence is ultimately articulated. Heidegger sees the philosopher in his search for being arriving at the point where he must stand and wait for the revelatory word to be spoken by the poet, a word which philosophy itself cannot wholly achieve.[22] Whitehead gives the poets the highest place in recalling man to the concrete experience of nature and beauty, and in synthesizing the ultimate intuitions which become the fruitful sources of rational reflection.[23] This point bears upon humanity's present need. Lillian Smith, who expressed so profoundly the case for human communion against racial separation said in one of her last public addresses:

> Once we begin to realize by an act of imagination and heart the meaning of what is happening to us, then things will fall into line, chaos will resolve into new forms.
> And it is the poets' job to show us. For only the poet can look beyond the details at the total picture; only the poet can feel the courage beyond fear. It is his job to think in spans of 10,000 years; his job to feel the slow, slow movement of the human spirit evolving; to see that the moment is close for mankind to make another big leap forward.[24]

We now take a further step into the meaning of love for reason, because we are concerned with the love of God and the knowledge of his love which transcends while it fulfils all human loves. Can *agape* be known by reason?

(4)

FAITH, KNOWLEDGE AND LOVE

We have now to consider the view that the love of which the Gospel speaks transcends all human understanding. That faith goes deeper than reason is one of the persistent themes of Christian theology. It is rooted in the biblical affirmation that the truth disclosed in God's self-revelation is not attainable by human reflection. The wisdom of God made known in the cross sets at naught the wisdom of this world (I Corinthians 1: 18–25).

This appeal to a knowledge which is accessible only to faith seems

22. Martin Heidegger, 'What is Metaphysics' in *Existence and Being*, trans. by Werner Brock (Chicago: Henry Regnery Co., 1949, pp. 391–2; London: Vision Press, 1959). Cf. the essays on Hölderlin and poetry in the same volume.
23. Alfred North Whitehead, *Adventures of Ideas*, pp. 291, 319, chapter xviii.
24. Lillian Smith, address to the Women's Division of the American Jewish Congress, quoted in the *New York Times*, March 20, 1965, p. 44.

confirmed by Christian experience. Untutored minds uncomplicated by intellectual analysis surely grasp the meaning of the love which is patient and kind, and endures in all things. Certainly such knowledge does not appear only among those with highly reflective intellects. There is even a perennial suspicion that the work of intellectual analysis may draw the soul away from its clear perception of the saving truth which God offers to all. When the intellectual task of theology is carried to its most intense and complex expression we surely find that we are on the threshold of unfathomable mystery. The being of God, the cosmic creativity, the expression of the divine love in the trinitarian symbols, the wonder of the incarnation, the experience of dying and rising with Christ and being ingrafted into his body, the hope of eternal life, all this takes us beyond rational grasp and justification. Theological work appears to take on the character of confession rather than rationally intelligible discussion. We know that the language of theology includes symbols and modes of expression which are poetic rather than scientific. Faith seeks understanding, but something happens to the mode of understanding when it moves toward the ultimate matters in which the meaning of love is disclosed. Faith involves a re-orientation of the mind which cannot be accomplished by the mind's own resources, but which requires the illumination of grace. Hence the canons of reason seem to be broken, or at least subjected to a higher requirement, in the Christian view. So runs a very powerful argument in the Christian tradition.

Whatever our conclusion about the relation of faith and reason, and there have been a variety of positions in theology, we need to recognize that along with the insistence on the limits of reason the search for as much rationality as we can get has usually been affirmed. Faith has an inner tendency to seek understanding precisely because God is the truth, and in Christ the Truth all things cohere. The theme of believing 'because it is absurd' associated (although perhaps not correctly) with the name of Tertullian, represents a position eccentric to the main line of Christian reflection through the centuries. Kierkegaard's attack on 'objective reason' has reshaped much of the discussion of the problem in modern theology; but Kierkegaard uses a highly rational dialectic in opening the way for the 'leap of faith'. The existentialist philosophies which follow him, while seeking the distinctive nature of personal knowledge, are usually not obscurantist or anti-rational.[25]

It is noteworthy that much of Karl Barth's theological system

25. See Paul Tillich, 'Existential Philosophy: Its Historical Meaning' in *Theology of Culture* (New York: Oxford University Press, 1959).

tries to correct the tendency toward a kind of irrationalism which was present in his *Commentary on Romans*, so strongly influenced by Kierkegaard. Barth, we recall, has written explicitly about the dangers of irrationalism. And Emil Brunner, who wrestled courageously with the issue of faith and reason in all his theological pilgrimage, says that 'faith itself is truly rational thought about God and about life as a whole'.[26]

When we raise this question of the place of the intellect in the life of the spirit and our knowledge of God, we are at the heart of a critical issue for our scientific culture. It is an issue which has a special bearing upon the vocation of the intellectual in the Christian church. It would be absurd to propose at the end of this study of the meaning of love that this perennial discussion of faith and understanding can be neatly settled, but we can show that reflection on the forms of love in Christian history opens up some new aspects of the life of the mind. If love is the key to life, then it ought to guide us toward a right appraisal of the work of intellect. I propose that we have at hand one important clue in the search for a fruitful tension between love and intellect and their ultimate reconciliation. The clue is this: just as we have seen love 'take form in history', so also reason 'takes form in history'. The relations of faith, love, and reason have been shaped by a series of historical circumstances in Christian history which cry out for reassessment in our century.

There are three main aspects of this history which concern us: First, there is the use of reason in the formation of Christian dogma in the first centuries of the church's life when the concept of reason was determined by Greek and Hellenistic philosophy. Second, the early development of the view that not only the truth of the Gospel as the saving word of God, but also the dogmatic formulae in which this truth was expressed were divinely and infallibly given. Third, the shaping of the biblical witness and original structure of Christian theology within a prescientific world-view, and without the methods of inquiry which the development of science and modern philosophy have made possible. In what follows I am not arguing that our insight or knowledge is superior to that of earlier centuries, or that we should disparage what the fathers of the church achieved in the formulation of Christian doctrine. But I believe that the terms upon which the relations of faith and reason were once stated are outmoded, and should no longer define our analysis of the problem or determine our methods of stating the truth we know in Jesus Christ.

Our first point is that the formulation of the relation of faith and

26. Emil Brunner, *Revelation and Reason* (Philadelphia: The Westminster Press, 1946), p. 429.

reason was historically shaped by the fact that it was Greek reason which the biblical message first encountered. It was Neo-Platonic philosophy, and to an important extent Stoic philosophy, which offered the terms on which the intelligibility of faith was sought. Some theologians like Adolph Harnack regarded the development of the dogmas of the church under these influences as beclouding the Gospel message for centuries.[27] Others, and they represent the larger group in Christian theology, see the development as the natural fulfilment of the expression of the Gospel message in terms which could meet the questions and criticism of philosophy in that time and maintain the essential truth of the Gospel.[28] A third view has been growing in the modern period. It is that the synthesis of the biblical message and Greek philosophy was a viable and necessary result in the first centuries, that its consequences should be regarded neither as disastrous nor as the achievement of pure and final solutions, but rather as ambiguous and not beyond criticism. For example, the dogma of the incarnation, the two natures in the one person is a formula which preserved the essential Christian witness to the meaning of the incarnation, but with the use of categories of 'nature' and 'person' as defined within the philosophies of the first centuries, and which leave us with the necessity of re-examining the meaning of nature, of person, and of the action of God in the incarnation.

The important insight to come out of this new perspective on theology in the first centuries is that the meaning of 'reason' in the Christian tradition received a certain stamp in what happened in the first five centuries of the church's life. Modern theology and modern philosophy are still struggling to get free from that neo-Platonic view of reason which, with all its profundity, leaves us with critical perplexities in a scientific age. Greek platonism, and one strand of Greek religious aspiration, sought to mount through rational structures to 'being-itself' as the ground of all things and all truth. Pure reason was identified with an absolutely transcendent reality above all the limitations of finite structure, time, becoming, and suffering. As reason soared into this unconditioned realm, it displayed its truth in the form of eternal principles which were identified with the particular scientific concepts and world view of the culture.

27. Adolph von Harnack, *History of Dogma* (Boston: Little Brown, 1901), Vol. IV, chap. 3, pp. 180, 223.
28. Paul Tillich, *Systematic Theology*, Vol. II, pp. 140–2. The Roman Catholic Leslie Dewart in his *The Future of Belief* (New York: Herder & Herder, 1966) takes a radically critical position against the 'hellenizing' of Christian doctrine, and makes a strong plea that the church recognize its dogmas are 'underdeveloped'.

The culmination of this process is not in St. Augustine, who was not especially interested in science, but in St. Thomas who took Aristotle's philosophy with its scientific doctrines about the nature of the physical, biological, and psychological orders, and brought them into a systematic relationship with Christian theology.

St. Thomas has less confidence than Augustine in the power of reason to reach directly into the being of God. Certainly reason points toward its divine origin. The arguments for God's existence are arguments which begin with experience and lead the mind to recognize the ultimate source and cause of all things, but St. Thomas significantly rejects the ontological argument. Only in eternal life can the mind directly know the truth of God's being. Hence faith for St. Thomas tends to become more identified with belief in revealed propositions than with the personal orientation of the self responding to God in love. Under the inspiration of Aristotle, St. Thomas tries not only to make theology the queen of sciences but also to bring all knowledge within the scope of a monumental dogmatic structure. We do not disparage the great synthesizers when we suggest that the problems they dealt with, while still our problems, must now be defined in the perspectives of a scientific age and its methods of knowing. Augustine seems closer to modern personalism because he thinks of the intellect as doing its proper work only when it is inspired and ordered by love.

A further aspect of the traditional synthesis is clearly seen in St. Thomas. This was the rationalizing of dogma, which reinforced the tendency just mentioned toward intellectualizing the meaning of faith. Ecclesiastical tradition from the beginning tended to equate faith with belief in certain propositions about God. St. Thomas defines faith as believing with assent. '*To believe* is an act of the intellect, in so far as the will moves it to assent.'[29] This uniting of faith with acceptance of truths in propositional form is the result of a long process. Ernst Troeltsch traced its origins in the first and second centuries not to the influence of Greek intellectualism, but to the need of the ecclesiastical community to preserve the authority of the church and the teaching function of the ministry.[30]

The elaborated structure of dogma became a rationalization of the claims of the church to the possession of grace, and to the interpretation of salvation as merited by the good works of men in response to God's prevenient grace. Luther's violent language against

29. Thomas Aquinas, *Summa Theologica* II—II Qu. 2, Art. 2; cf. I, Qu. 62, Art. 4.
30. Ernst Troeltsch, *The Social Teaching of the Christian Churches* (New York: Macmillan, 1931, pp. 94–6, 179; London: Allen & Unwin, 1931).

'Reason' must be understood in this context. He saw speculative reason as defence of the theology of merit and good works:

> Therefore they [the scholastics] attribute acceptation to good works; that is to say, that God doth accept our works, not of duty indeed, but of congruence. Contrariwise we, excluding all works, do go to the very head of this beast which is called Reason, which is the fountain and head spring of all mischiefs. For reason feareth not God, it loveth not God, it trusteth not in God, but proudly contemneth him. . . .

Luther goes on to declare that this pestilent beast, this harlot, should be 'killed by faith'.[31]

Of course there is a counter point in Luther to such extreme language about reason. He also regards reason as a gift of God which must be used for understanding his Word, and for the guidance of life.[32] Later Lutheran orthodoxy became more rationalistic than Luther had been, and produced a scholasticism of its own in which concern for 'purity of doctrine' emerged as the Protestant counterpart to the Catholic absolutism about dogma, the absolutism which reaches its limit and its absurdity in the dogma of infallibility.

It is interesting to see how the dogma of infallibility can be held so as to allow for freedom of reflection in the interpretation of faith. Cardinal Bea pointed out in the discussion of the Vatican Council that while the dogmas are not reformable their interpretations are. Even though they contain infallible truth the forms of dogma must be understood in relation to the historical circumstances in which they were promulgated.[33]

Our analysis shows that understanding of the relation of faith and love to reason has been conditioned by historical circumstances. In a creative history where God opens up new possibilities of understanding it is an error to confine the meaning of reason to the historical forms of certain cultural presuppositions and values. Reason is the creative function of men's self-understanding in response to God's action. It cannot be identified with a particular set of conclusions, or a particular type of method. This view of reason suggests that when reason's limitations are recognized and it is held within the context of humble, repentant and loving search for the truth, it may serve the knowledge of love, even the love of God, without pretending to encompass the love it is seeking to know.

We recognize two limitations on reason which keep it subordinate to human loves and to the love of God. The first is that love is

31. Martin Luther, *Commentary on Galatians*, Dillenberger, ed., p. 128.
32. Cf. Brian Gerrish, *Graceful Reason* (Oxford University Press, 1962).
33. Augustin, Cardinal Bea, *The Unity of Christians* (London: Geoffrey Chapman, 1963), pp. 97–101; 116–18, 139.

concrete action arising from personal devotion and concern, while reason is always an abstracting and guiding function, seeking the structured aspect of things and the relation of symbols to a reality which is more than symbol. Reason comes always 'after the fact' as reflection on what is given, however far in imagination it may anticipate new meanings in the facts. Thus reason depends always upon the creative presence and power of love to do its proper work.

Love is known within the creative mystery of life in which God works with inexhaustible spontaneity and freedom. The *Logos* of being is its meaningful order made known through the action of God. No objective exhibition of the elements of the structure of being exhausts its reality. What being is can only be experienced, felt, lived as we reflect upon it with our blurred vision and in our finitude. Reason is not a transcendent function which tells us about a reality entirely apart from our experience. It is a reflection and construction drawn out of experience and the life of the spirit as we seek communion with the source of our being.

As reason cannot produce the concreteness of being, or the love which works in that concreteness, so it cannot achieve the final definition of the obligations of love toward the other. These have to be discovered in love itself. We come here to the critical point of the meaning of *agape* as redemptive action. All love does more than any rational formula can prescribe. The gracious spirit of *agape* does not stop at purely rational boundaries. Yet we must state the position here with care, for reason does recognize elements of obligation and of consideration, and these should not be ignored or despised. A rational view of life has always led to some acceptance of obligation toward the other. Principles of equality, freedom, and justice can be derived from rational reflection on the nature of man, and they lead to the recognition of universal principles of order and balance among conflicting claims. A rational element is indispensable to any society which would avoid arbitrary authority and tyranny.

At the same time, we can recognize that the definition of human good and moral obligation is always more than a function of reason. It is men who reflect on justice, and the content of their reflections always contains more of their self-centredness and their love than the pure dictates of reason can encompass. Plato's vision of the just state has haunted and challenged, but also confused western ethics, because his pure ideal of justice seems bound up with a set of presuppositions about man and his nature. The 'rational' state is conceived as the completely rationalized state, whereas a truly reasonable order of life allows a large margin for freedom, spontaneity and that preliminary disorder out of which creativity can come.[34]

Perhaps F. J. E. Woodbridge is right when he says that Plato himself does not believe in the ideal state, and that in *The Republic* he demonstates through the socratic irony the limitations of all visions of ideal political order. If so, Plato too belonged to the company of those who say that rational definitions of the good and the right must be tested in history, and that wisdom in ethical judgments does not arise from pure reason alone, but from the spirit and its loves with all their deformity and greatness.[35]

This transcendence of *agape* over rational obligation has its analogue in the human loves. The view that human love as the search for mutuality always calculates the adequacy of the response of the other before giving of itself contradicts ordinary experience. Even forgiveness, humanly speaking, may be the reasonable action. 'Everyone has faults'; 'a man deserves another chance'. There are new possibilities which only forgiveness of the past can release. Edmond Cahn has given a superbly clear analysis of this rational avenue to forgiveness in his *The Predicament of Democratic Man*. A totally unforgiving person would be judged certainly irrational, if not insane.[36]

Yet the human loves meet frustrations and failures in the search for communion which leaves us asking whether any rational claim is left. We cannot decide our mutual obligations on the basis of rational justice alone. The spirit which forgives seventy times seven, which can accept any consequences for the sake of love, is justified only by a reason which is informed by love and therefore runs ahead of our purely intellectual comprehension. Reason does not create the spirit of love which most deeply informs it, but it can offer to love one dimension of responsibility toward the other. It can search for understanding of what really binds human life together. For example, in forgiveness we must ask what the other really needs, and what new situation is created by the act of forgiveness. Without this, forgiveness may degenerate into destructive sentimentality. Yet forgiveness cannot ever wait for full knowledge of its consequences.

We come to the final service of reason to human loves. Reason

34. William Ernest Hocking, *Freedom of the Press* (Chicago: University of Chicago Press, 1947), pp. 58, 99–104.

35. F. J. E. Woodbridge, *The Son of Apollo* (New York: Houghton Mifflin, 1929).

36. Edmond Cahn, *The Predicament of Democratic Man* (New York: Macmillan, 1961), pp. 150–4.

has its special vocation within the life of faith. We can love God with our minds. The intellectual love of God is possible because God's being is reflected in the finite forms which guide the search for truth. The integrity, courage, cleanness, and creative power of the intellect are resources for purging human loves of their sentimentalities and demonries. The present fashion of setting the intellect's power of objectivity in opposition to the understanding of faith is a sickness of our culture and of theology. We need to recover the reality of the intellect's integrity as an acknowledgement of responsibility toward God and toward man.

It is true that these qualities belong to the dignity of man and may be present without his acknowledgement of dependence upon God. Yet they suggest the movement of the mind toward God as the ultimate source of the unity of truth, the judge of all finite systems, and the fulfilment of the mind's search for what is real. To love God with the mind may be thought of as the culmination of the search for truth, the celebration of the knowledge God makes possible. Or it may be seen as the impulse of the spirit within the movement of the mind toward God. The intellectual virtues, like the other virtues, have their inner direction toward fulfilment in communion of life with life and mind with mind. Hence, to love God with the mind can infuse the spirit with hopefulness that sanity is possible, and that there is a truth which binds men together. It also can reflect the sense of dependence upon God and upon the community of human seekers which creates its own comradeship as we move deeper into the mystery.

We have seen that love is not only the impulse toward communion but the enjoyment of it. The intellect can delight in its powers and enjoy its reflection upon God. The so-called dryness of rational argument is often but the outward form or the tedious betrayal of what is really the riot of the mind's play with deity. To love God is to rejoice in the richness of truth, to enjoy the counterpoint of the absurd and the nonsensical, to engage in the conflict of ideas and the history of human argument. If science is a form of human joy, as a recent interpretation has beautifully described it, so also is thought of God a mode of human delight and a source of joy, whether it comes under the usually sober auspices of theology, or the expressiveness of poetry, or the plain delight of minds finding their way to one another through mutual reflection on the inexhaustible theme of the being of God.

Certainly the intellectual love of God is subject to the corruption of sin and self-centredness, just as are all the other loves, whether religious or secular. But the search for the vision of God, the *eros* for truth, is one manifestation of that will to belong which, we have seen, is the image of God in man. We need intellectuality informed by love. Knowledge is not love, but knowledge which serves the communion of spirit with spirit, and which recognizes our human limitations in that search, comes into the service of love. The real adventures of ideas, to use Whitehead's phrase, are those which lead spirit to share its discoveries with spirit. The truth makes us free, and freedom is an indispensable condition of love.

Man's intellectual exploration of his world has given him power beyond the imagination of previous centuries; but that power will lead to self-destruction unless man can live in understanding with man. If in the vast universe there are other spiritual beings and intelligences to be known, the impetus to discover them and be discovered is surely not for curiosity's sake alone, but the craving of mind seeking mind and spirit seeking spirit.

The search for communion makes the adventure of the mind worth its cost. The sane mind is not in love with itself, but with God and his world, and with every other mind which seeks to know. The intellect itself can put on the form of the servant in this strange history of man's search for loving communion with God and his fellows.

INDEX